Effective Written Advocacy

A Guide for Practitioners

Second Edition

Effective Written Advocacy

A Guide for Practitioners

Second Edition

Andrew Goodman

LL.B., MBA, FCI.Arb., FInstCPD, FRSA

Of the Inner Temple, a Master of the Bench
Professor of Conflict Management and Dispute Resolution Studies, Rushmore University
Visiting Lecturer in Dispute Resolution, UCL and SOAS, University of London and BPP University College
Convenor, Standing Conference of Mediation Advocates

Wildy, Simmonds & Hill Publishing

Effective Written Advocacy: A Guide for Practitioners, 2nd edition

British Library Cataloguing in Publication Data
A catalogue record for this book is available from the British Library

ISBN 978-0854900-954

Typeset in Palatino Linotype and Optima LT Std by Cornubia Press Ltd
Printed and bound in the United Kingdom by CPI Group (UK) Ltd,
Croydon, CR0 4YY

First published in 2012 by
Wildy, Simmonds & Hill Publishing
58 Carey Street
London WC2A 2JF
England

Foreword and Acknowledgements

In 2005 I began this work as something of a journey to find what makes a really persuasive written argument. Then, the technique of written advocacy was still very much in its infancy, even though the requirement to produce skeleton argument had been with us for a while. In the intervening years practitioners have developed a greater sophistication in both technique and applied content. New entrants to the legal profession are given much more of a feel for the importance of written argument, although tuition is still rather cursory. Judicial acceptance of written argument as normative has grown, even to an extent in both criminal and family jurisdictions, and pronouncements on the importance of compliance with practice directions on skeleton arguments have been made. This work therefore has been extended to include the impact of The Consolidated Criminal Practice Direction Part II: Further Practice Directions Applying in The Court of Appeal (Criminal Division) and PD 30A of the Family Procedure Rules 2010.

For this edition I have had the good fortune again to persuade many of the leading practitioners at the Bar to kindly donate material for use here as worked examples. I am extremely grateful to the following for having exposed samples of their written advocacy to my scrutiny and kindly granted me permission to select from among them: Lord Faulks QC (with Andrew Warnock, Charles Brown, Sarah Paneth and David Thomson), Simeon Maskrey QC, John Norman, Lord Pannick QC (with Dinah Rose QC, Louise Mably and James Segan), Spike Charlwood, Lord Sumption QC (with Guy Philipps QC, David Anderson QC, Rodri Williams QC, Jemima Stratford and Martin Chamberlain), Richard Lissack QC (with Keith Morton, Clare Baker and Oliver Assersohn), Ronald Walker QC (with Catherine Foster, William Evans and Nigel Lewers), Sue Carr QC (with Jonathan Hough), Andrew Hochhauser QC (with David Craig and Andrew Mitchell), Dr Michael Powers QC, Simon O'Toole and Thomas Crockett.

I am keen to promote a debate in this area, and to have much more time devoted to train in this skill at the earliest opportunity for law students and intending practitioners. I hope this book fosters such efforts.

Andrew Goodman
1 Chancery Lane
October, 2011

Foreword to the First Edition

During the course of 2003 and 2004 I had the pleasure of interviewing a number of judges and practitioners in preparation for my book on deconstructing civil judgments. This was published under the modest but utilitarian title, *How Judges Decide Cases – Reading, Writing and Analysing Judgments*. I was persuaded by a reader that what actually influenced the judicial decision making process, effective advocacy, was worthy of greater attention. Many works have been written on advocacy, but despite the filing of skeleton submissions having been made a requirement some ten years ago, I had yet to see a work devoted entirely to written argument. We still fondly believe that our great oral tradition is what sways the court. Not a bit of it. Increasingly judges form pre-trial opinions of the likely outcome, and these they derive from written material. The application, or trial or appeal then becomes a process to measure the judge's pre-formed view, however strong that may be.

In order to find what makes a persuasive written argument I went in search of the best examples, composed by the most successful practitioners. I asked the judges exactly what they wanted from written advocacy, rather than what the Civil Procedure Rules formally require. And I wanted to consider the most common form of all written advocacy – the pre-action letter of claim and its reply, followed by Part 36 correspondence. The results of my quest are in these pages, together with an analysis of the best of advice from jurisdictions which have a much longer history of written argument by lawyers.

The advice given is entirely practical. And it works.

Any polemic which has strayed into these pages is entirely my own.

It goes without saying that I have a substantial number of people to thank for their kind assistance. For busy practitioners and judges to spare their time for my inane questions is most generous. And the willingness of senior and well known members of the Bar to give me permission not just to use their work (anonymised where requested) but, in effect, to analyse their professional skills in writing, was a little overwhelming (not that I was prepared to take 'no' for an answer).

I also wish to thank a number of solicitors for permission to reproduce correspondence drawn from actual files, although edited to remove identification.

I would therefore like to express my warm gratitude to the following.

David Anderson QC, Roger Bartlett, Her Honour Judge Bevington, David Bigmore, Edward Bishop, Zachary Bredemear, Charles Brown, Dr. Guiseppe Cala, Sue Carr QC, James Carter, Emma Chadwick, the Rt. Hon. Lord Justice Chadwick, Henry Charles, Spike Charlwood, Nicholas Davidson QC, Robin de Wilde QC, Edward Faulks QC, Robert Francis QC, Kate Gallavent, Toby Hooper QC, His Honour Judge Iain Hughes QC, The Hon. Mr Justice Jackson, Michel Kallipetis QC, Simeon Maskrey QC, Philip Naughton QC, The Rt. Hon.Lord Justice Neuberger, John Norman, Diana Oxford, Sarah Paneth, David Pannick QC, Guy Philipps QC, Michael Pooles QC, Simon Reedhead, Dinah Rose, John Ross QC, David Schmitz, Andrew Spencer, Roger Stewart QC, Jemima Stratford, Jonathan Sumption QC, Dr David Thomson, Andrew Warnock, His Honour Judge Welchman, Master Whittaker, John Zucker.

I also wish to pay tribute to Andrew Griffin and the staff of xpl publishing for turning this project into fruition so successfully.

Andrew Goodman
1 Serjeants Inn
October, 2005

Contents

Table of Cases

References are to page number

Introduction: The Trend Towards Written Advocacy in Practice

Many judges, whatever they may say for public consumption, read skeleton arguments or written submissions and make up their mind about who should win before hearing oral argument. The hearing then becomes a test of their first inclination. Even if they can resist that temptation, it is not possible to be immune to written legal argument read in advance of a case which is concise, accessible in its language, well structured, persuasive, restrained and tactically astute.[1] Whether it stands alone or is a vehicle to introduce and then channel the strands of oral argument, the effective written submission is now a vital tool that attracts judicial favour to the advocate's claim. Yet the requirement to produce skeleton arguments has been with us for two decades. The hurried, ill thought-out and unstructured skeleton can do as much to damage the client's case as an unprepared oral presentation. Thus the advocate who pays lip service to the construction of a proper paper skeleton runs a considerable risk should his oral hearing not go well.

The truth is that skeleton arguments are now of essential importance in modern civil procedure. In his January 2004 lecture to the Chancery Bar Association Conference entitled 'Advocacy – A Dying Art?' Mr Justice Lightman described skeletons as "the first (and often enduring) opportunity to present the party's case without interruption in a clear and considered way. They may properly enable the judge to form a provisional view of the case as a whole and the merits of some or all of the issues, and it is perfectly legitimate for the judge to do so and so inform the parties, putting them on notice of the hurdles to be surmounted: see *Costello v Chief Constable of Derbyshire* [2001].[2] In a word cases can be won and lost on skeleton arguments."

This is an entirely modern practice. The development of required written argument in this jurisdiction is a product of case management. Only fifty or so years ago the Court of Appeal expressed strong disapproval at the presentation to it, by a litigant in person, of an American style written

---

1 *Inner Temple Advocacy Handbook* 7th edn 2004–5 ed. Toby Hooper QC p.55.

2 [2001] EWCA Civ 381; [2001] 1 WLR 1437 at 1440 para.[9].

appellate brief[3] Lord Justice Dankwerts described it as "wholly irregular and contrary to the practice of the court" and said, "in my opinion (it) should not be allowed as a precedent for future proceedings. It appears that counsel was in fact available to appear … without a fee, and the course mentioned …was deliberately adopted."[4]

Until the late 1970s the higher courts regarded the idea that a party could put before the court a written skeleton argument setting out his case with abhorrence. The suggestion that it should be mandatory in most cases would have been risible. Gradually through the 1980s the concept of the written submission became at first permissible and then an expected feature of any case of substance. From then on the primacy of oral advocacy in the traditional English adversarial system became substantially diluted.

A series of directions to regularise practice was given by the heads of division from 1982 onwards. In that year the Scarman Committee on the practice of civil appeals recommended that better use must be made of time: the court's time, counsel's and solicitors' time and the parties' time. Amongst four main sources of wasted time, the committee identified the length of oral hearing as the most important because of the number of people involved. This led to the new RSC Order 59 and the creation of the office of Registrar of Civil Appeals. In trying to tackle the problem Lord Donaldson MR, in a Practice Note of 4th October 1982 on new practice and procedure in the Court of Appeal, Civil Division, said:[5]

> "This brings me to the question of whether it may not be possible to make more economical use of time spent in court. Such time, it must be remembered, is relatively very expensive because it involves the attendance not only of the judges but also of counsel, solicitors and often the parties. The Scarman Committee considered and rejected a change to the system of written briefs and limitations on the time allowed for argument which is the practice in some other jurisdictions. They did so on the ground that, although such an approach has advantages, it is alien to the British tradition of oral presentation and argument and is not necessarily less expensive because of the time which has to be devoted to preparing highly complex briefs.
>
> However, the Scarman Committee suggested that substantial savings in this expensive time could be achieved if, before the oral hearing began, the judges were able to inform themselves of the general background to the dispute, the decision of the court below and the effective grounds of appeal. With this in mind it recommended an adaptation of the system of perfected grounds of appeal which is in use in the Criminal Division. The judges would come to court having read the judgment under appeal together with the perfected

---

3 See *Rondel v Worsley* [1967] 1 QB 443. Admittedly the document was a typescript of 116 pages, closely argued, concerning the immunity of counsel from suit.

4 At p.509C.

5 [1982] 3 All ER 376 at 377g et seq.

grounds of appeal or some analogous guide to the issues in the appeal and counsel would be able to dispense with any lengthy opening as well as being able to display greater brevity in the argument itself. We, for our part, fully accept the committee's approach. It is in everyone's interest that the cost of litigation should be reduced by a better use of time. Under the revised Ord 59 the registrar can give directions as to the documentation to be made available to the court before the hearing and appeals can be listed in such a way as to give the judge time to read appropriate parts of the documentation before the oral hearing begins. What can and cannot profitably be pre-read by the judges will vary from appeal to appeal, as will the best method of informing the judges of the issues in the appeal. In some cases it may well be that the original notice of appeal and the judgment appealed from may suffice. In others it may be desirable to ask for a perfected notice of appeal or even a skeleton of the argument for both parties. This is an area where there is really immense scope for innovation, experiment, trial and, let me stress quite inevitably also, error. But, with the assistance of counsel and solicitors engaged in particular appeals and that of both sides of the profession on a more general basis, there can be no doubt that very worthwhile improvements can be made."

In 1995 Lord Taylor CJ issued a Practice Note of 24th January on Case Management in Civil Litigation[6] for use in the Queen's Bench and Chancery Divisions of the High Court except where other directions specifically applied. For the first time this created an obligation for parties to provide a written skeleton argument prior to the hearing of every action, and provided for closing written submissions where necessary:

"8. Not less than three clear days before the hearing of an action or application each party should lodge with the court (with copies to other parties) a skeleton argument concisely summarising that party's submissions in relation to each of the issues, and citing the main authorities relied upon, which may be attached. Skeleton arguments should be as brief as the nature of the issues allows, and should not without leave of the court exceed 20 pages of double-spaced A4 paper.

9. The opening speech should be succinct. At its conclusion other parties may be invited briefly to amplify their skeleton arguments. In a heavy case the court may in conjunction with final speeches require written submissions, including the findings of fact for which each party contends."

On 31 January 1995 Sir Stephen Brown P. issued a Practice Direction[7] for use in the Family Division which followed, in modified form, that for the other Divisions. In paragraph 7 he added the qualification, 'It is important that

---

6 [1995] 1 All ER 385.

7 [1995] 1 FLR 456; [1995] 1 WLR 332; [1985] 1 All ER 586.

skeleton arguments should be brief.' By 2000 in many cases skeleton arguments were to be included as part of the court bundle.[8]

With the coming into force of the Civil Procedure Rules 1998, and ever since, the obligatory contents and detail of written arguments were set out separately in the practice guides issued from time to time for the Queen's Bench and Chancery Divisions, the Commercial Court, the Technology and Construction Court, the Patent Court, arbitration proceedings within the CPR, the Court of Appeal, the Administrative Court and, in the Practice Directions 5 and 6 to the Supreme Court Rules 2009, the Supreme Court of the United Kingdom and the Privy Council. In addition Practice Direction 5.8(c), 5.9(f) and 5.13–5.22 to the Family Procedure Rules 2010, for the Family Division, and Part II: 17 of the Consolidated Criminal Practice Direction of the Criminal Procedure Rules 2010, together with further Practice Directions applying in The Court of Appeal (Criminal Division)[9] governs the preparation of skeleton argument in the criminal courts. These are all dealt with in Chapter 1, 'What the Court Requires'.

We have now moved so far in the direction of core arguments always being in written form that in 2004 Mr Justice Lightman was able to say:[10]

> "advocacy...today...transcends its traditional form of oral presentation in court and includes and finds critical expression in written forms in which expertise is called for of the advocate and which can have a decisive effect on the outcome of a case."
>
> "Skeletons can have a substantial if not decisive effect on the course and indeed the outcome of proceedings. Counsel now requires expertise at least as much in preparing skeletons as in making oral submissions...The judge generally comes to a case blind. On occasion he leaves the case in the same condition. He is in need of illumination of the task before him in concise form. The essential minimum requirements are: (1) a chronological account of relevant facts; (2) a statement of the issues of law and fact; and (3) a statement and evaluation of the rival answers to those issues. There is like importance to be attached to final written skeletons at the end of trials containing all relevant page and other references to the evidence adduced."
>
> "The advocate remembers that the judge is looking to counsel for assistance in reaching and reasoning his judgment. For many (if not most) judges the recourse to a written skeleton is the first resort in writing his judgment. The tedium in preparing a skeleton pays off."

---

8 Practice Direction (Family Proceedings: Court Bundles) [2000] 1 WLR 737; [2000] 1 FLR 536; [2000] 2 All ER 287 per Dame Butler-Sloss P.

9 Practice Direction (Criminal Appeals: Skeleton Arguments) [1999] 1 WLR 146; [1999] 1 All ER 669, CA; 15/12/98; Practice Direction (Judgments: Form and Citation) [2001] 1 WLR 194; [2001] 1 All ER 19; [2001] 1 CrAppR 426; 11/01/01.

10 Address to the Chancery Bar Association Conference, 26th January 2004.

For a long time experience in the American appellate courts has been that written arguments almost always decide the case. Here some Court of Appeal judges will freely admit that cases are decided before oral argument on the strength of written skeleton arguments, and this must be so since, statistically, in about 40% of appeals heard between 2009–2010, either one side or the other was not called upon to make an oral presentation. That figure is rising, although more recent statistics are hard to find. Cases turn on the persuasiveness of skeleton arguments now more than ever before. Oral argument is much shorter than in the past.

Conversely, judges are now delivering more and more reserved judgments at every level. Whether for trial or on appeal, your written submissions are available for members of the court to use long after the oral hearing finishes. For that reason alone it is the written argument that must be the keystone of your advocacy. And if in a large number of cases judges reach a firm inclination in advance of the hearing just from reading a well prepared and argued skeleton, where oral argument fails to dissuade, the winning piece of advocacy is written, not oral. If the judge has formed a view on the merits, having read the skeleton at an early stage, the chances of persuading him to abandon an adverse inclination are not high.

What is also indicative of the overwhelming importance of written advocacy is the decline of skeleton arguments being, in fact, skeletal. When established, the Supreme Court recognised that it should not impose very detailed requirements as to the manner in which documents were to be prepared for appeal hearings.[11] Although it favours brevity in the written case, in contrast with the former Blue Book requirement of a maximum length of 20 pages for a case argued in the House of Lords, the Supreme Court does not prescribe any maximum length for the concise summary of argument to be developed.[12]

Having said that, the stated purpose of a skeleton argument 'is to identify and summarise in writing the relevant issues of fact and law. It is not to argue to them fully in writing'.[13] Received wisdom believes a skeleton is intended as a vehicle for putting your best points shortly and in the most attractive light – a clear, logical and precise exposition of your case, but most importantly, concise. In 2008 Mummery LJ said[14] (admittedly in a case where one side had put in a skeleton running to 110 pages):

> "Practitioners who ignore practice directions on skeleton arguments...and do so without the imposition of any formal penalty are well advised to note the risk of the court's negative reaction to unnecessarily long written

---

11 See para.6.1.1 General Note to PD 6 Supreme Court Rules 2009.

12 Para 6.3.1 ibid.

13 *Inner Temple Advocacy Handbook* 7th edn 2004–5 ed. Toby Hooper QC p.55.

14 *Raja v Van Hoogstraten (No.9)* [2008] EWCA Civ 1444; [2009] 1 WLR 1143 at para.125.

> submissions. The skeleton argument procedure was introduced to assist the court, as well as the parties, by improving preparations for, and the efficiency of, adversarial oral hearings, which remain central to this court's public role."

Increasingly however, the courts are unconcerned with length where the material being provided is necessary, persuasive and assists the court to solve the problem before it. If you receive a written submission from your opponent running to 25, 30 or 40 pages, you may well wait in vain anticipation for the judge to tear into him or her for its size. If the arguments are sound, unambiguous and logical, and if the judge is enlightened by the proposed answer, he will not criticise a document unreasonably for being overlong.

In reality though, the written submissions of the finest advocates are, in fact, quite short. A particular skill of the really successful practitioner is to précis both the facts and the law, and to create a well-signposted, logical and irresistible path for the judge to follow to the desired conclusion over as few pages as are really necessary, whether they be 10, 20 or 30.

The winning advocate persuades the court to accept his skeleton as the most accurate and complete statement of the case; and this book is intended:

- to tell you how to do the same;
- to show you the means to create a written submission so powerful in its argument that you should not be called upon except to respond to your opponent;
- to persuade you that presentation matters enormously; and to make you understand that whatever attracts judicial favour to the advocate's claim is useful; whatever repels it is useless or worse;
- to have you take written advocacy seriously – it is an essential tool which enables you to damage your opponent without even opening your mouth, and a unique opportunity, not to be wasted.

Part 1
Skeleton Arguments and Written Submissions

1 What the Court Requires

Advocates are obliged to provide skeleton arguments to the court under the direction of the Civil Procedure Rules 1998, the Queen's Bench and Chancery Guides, and the practice notes for the Specialist Proceedings of the civil court set out in volume 2 of *Civil Procedure* (the "White Book"). Although separate directions are set out for the various divisions of the High Court, the Administrative Court and the Court of Appeal, the structure and contents of what is required for the different courts are broadly consistent with each other, as are they in appeals to the Court of Appeal (Criminal Division) and appeals under the Family Procedure Rules 2010.

In practice the individual and personal style of advocates means that whatever the Rules Committee envisages as most helpful to the courts, judges are beginning to form strong views of what they want, and more particularly, what they do not want. By the same token successful advocates are discovering whether what they provide works or not.

In this section I set out the technical requirements of the CPR, FPR, SCR and other relevant directions, and for criminal advocates the requirements of the Registrar of Criminal Appeals, and compare them with what those members of the judiciary, who have been kind enough to assist me in this study, have indicated is most helpful to them. The master or district judge dealing with a contested application, the first-instance judge, and the appellate judge each have different concerns and different needs which are not always reflected in the rules of practice. You will want to address them. Equally those advocates who achieve great success, part of which they attribute to their written advocacy, are less concerned about complying with the strict requirements of the relevant directions than supplying the court with a document which helps both their cause and eases the task of the judge. In the third part I look at what it is that successful advocates provide built around the analysis of 17 examples drawn from actual contested cases.

Since it is fundamental that you, as an advocate, are familiar with the current Rules of the Court in which you practice in order to comply with them, let us start by considering what you are expected to provide to the court.

Queen's Bench Division

Directions for Queen's Bench actions are contained in the *Queen's Bench Guide*.[1] The rationale for giving directions concerning preparation for

---

1 *Civil Procedure* 2011 Vol.2 QB Contents 1B-51 (7.11.12).

hearings is to ensure that court time is used efficiently.[2] This includes the writing and exchange of skeleton arguments, the compilation of bundles of documents and giving realistic time estimates. Active case management means that the parties should use their best endeavours to agree beforehand the issues, or main issues between them, and must cooperate with the court and each other to enable the court to deal with claims justly; parties may expect to be penalised for failing to do so.[3]

In addition to lodging a bundle of documents in an approved form for use at the hearing, for trial and most appearances before a judge, and substantial hearings before a master, a chronology, a list of the persons involved and a list of the issues should be prepared and filed with the skeleton argument.[4] A chronology should be non-contentious and agreed with the other parties, if possible. If there is a material dispute about any event stated in the chronology, this should be stated.

Under paragraph 7.11.12 of the QB Guide a skeleton argument should:

- concisely summarise the party's submissions in relation to each of the issues;
- cite the main authorities relied on, which may be attached;
- contain a reading list and an estimate of the time it will take the judge to read;
- be as brief as the issues allow and not normally be longer than 20 pages of double-spaced A4 paper;
- be divided into numbered paragraphs and paged consecutively;
- avoid formality and use understandable abbreviations; and
- identify any core documents which it would be helpful to read beforehand.

Chancery Division

The general rule contained in the *Chancery Guide*[5] is that for the purpose of all hearings before a judge skeleton arguments should be prepared. The

---

2 7.11.5.

3 7.11.6.

4 7.11.10.

5 *Chancery Guide Civil Procedure* 2011 Vol.2 1A-43, 5–52; 1A-62, 1A-68-73 7.18–7.30 and Appendix 7.

exceptions to this are where the application does not warrant one, for example because it is likely to be short, or where the application is so urgent that preparation of a skeleton argument is impracticable or where an application is ineffective and the order is agreed by all parties. Skeleton arguments should be prepared in respect of any application before the master or district judge of one or more hour's duration and certainly for any trial or similar hearing.[6] In most cases before a judge, a list of the persons involved in the facts of the case, a chronology and a list of issues will also be required. The chronology and list of issues should be agreed where possible. Where a skeleton argument is required, photocopies of any authorities to be relied upon should be attached to the skeleton argument.[7]

The court suggests that advocates should consider preparing their skeleton arguments as soon as the case is placed in the Warned List, so that they are ready to be delivered to the court on time. Preparation of skeleton arguments should not be left until notice is given that the case is to be heard since it is possible that a notice may be given that the case is to be heard the next day.[8]

In the more substantial matters (e.g. trials and applications by order) skeleton arguments must be delivered not less than two clear days before the date or first date on which the application or trial is due to come on for hearing.[9] On applications without notice to a judge the skeleton may be placed with the papers which the judge is asked to read on the application.[10] On all other applications to a judge, including interim applications, the skeleton should be filed as soon as possible and not later than 10 a.m. on the day preceding the hearing. If the name of the judge (other than a deputy judge) is known, skeleton arguments should be delivered to the judge's clerk, otherwise where the name of the judge is not known, or the judge is a deputy judge, skeleton arguments should be delivered to the Listing Office.[11]

Unless the court gives any other direction, the parties arrange between themselves for the delivery, exchange, or sequential service of skeleton arguments and any accompanying documents or authorities. Such an exchange should be made in sufficient time before the hearing to enable them to be properly considered.[12]

---

6 7.20–22.

7 7.33.

8 7.24.

9 7.21.

10 7.22.

11 7.25, 7.26.

12 7.43.

Appendix 7 to the *Chancery Guide*[13] sets out specific guidelines on the contents of skeleton arguments, chronologies, indices and reading lists. The contents of skeletons should be as follows:

> "Skeleton arguments
>
> 1. A skeleton argument is intended to identify both for the parties and the court those points which are, and those that are not, in issue, and the nature of the argument in relation to those points which are in issue. It is not a substitute for oral argument.
>
> 2. Every skeleton argument should therefore:
>
> (1) identify concisely:
>
> (a) the nature of the case generally, and the background facts insofar as they are relevant to the matter before the court;
>
> (b) the propositions of law relied on with references to the relevant authorities;
>
> (c) the submissions of fact to be made with reference to the evidence;
>
> (2) be as brief as the nature of the issues allows – it should not normally exceed 20 pages of double-spaced A4 paper and in many cases it should be much shorter than this;
>
> (3) be in numbered paragraphs and state the name (and contact details) of the advocate(s) who prepared it;
>
> (4) avoid arguing the case at length;
>
> (5) avoid formality and make use of abbreviations, e.g. C for Claimant, A/345 for bundle A page 345, 1.1.95 for 1st January 1995 etc."

The judge may also direct that the parties submit written summaries of their final speeches before they begin to set out the principal findings of fact for which the party contends and grant an adjournment for this purpose. The guidelines in Appendix 7 are intended to apply to written summaries of opening and final speeches. Even though in a large case these may necessarily be longer, they should still be as brief as the case allows.[14]

Note that under PD r.7-23 in the Royal Courts of Justice, a log will be maintained of all late skeletons and bundles. The log will regularly be inspected by the Chancellor who will consider such further action as

---

13 Vol. 2 *White Book* 1A-216.

14 1A-216.3 Appendix 7 to the Chancery Guide.

appropriate in relation to any recurrent failure by any chambers, barrister, or solicitors firm to comply with the requirements of the CPR and the Guide.

Admiralty, Commercial and Mercantile Courts

The practice directions for the Admiralty Court and Commercial Court are set out in section 2 of the Specialist Proceedings under Part 49 of the Civil Procedure Rules and Part 58 dealing with the Commercial Court. The current Guide[15] incorporates the recent Practice Directions on Arbitration Appeals, E-disclosure and the Electronic Working Scheme. It also reflects the recommendations made in the Jackson Report. For present purposes practitioners need to familiarise themselves with the provisions relating to lists of issues (D6.1), skeleton arguments (Appendix 9.1 and 9.2(d)), core bundles (Appendix 10.4) and bundles of authorities (F13.4). Guidelines on the preparation of skeleton arguments are set out in Part 1 of Appendix 9.[16]

This specialist jurisdiction provides parties with two additional opportunities to engage in written advocacy: the preparation of the case memorandum, and the list of issues.

In order that the judge conducting the case management conference may be informed of the general nature of the case and the issues which are expected to arise, after service of the defence and any reply the solicitors and counsel for each party shall draft an agreed case memorandum. The case memorandum should contain (i) a short and uncontroversial description of what the case is about; and (ii) a very short and uncontroversial summary of the material procedural history of the case.[17] The only purpose of the case memorandum is to help the judge understand broadly what the case is about. The case memorandum does not play any part in the trial. It is unnecessary, therefore, for parties to be unduly concerned about the precise terms in which it is drafted, provided it contains a reasonably fair and balanced description of the case. Above all the parties must do their best to spend as little time as practicable in drafting and negotiating the wording of the memorandum and keep clearly in mind the need to limit costs.

After service of the defence (and any reply), the solicitors and counsel for each party must produce a list of the key issues in the case. The list should include the main issues of both fact and law. The list should identify the principal issues in a structured manner, such as by reference to headings or chapters. Long lists of detailed issues should be avoided, and sub-issues should be identified only when there is a specific purpose in doing so. A separate section of the document should list what is common ground

---

15 Vol.2 White Book 1A-39.

16 Vol.2 White Book 1A-220.

17 D5.1–5.2.

between the parties (or any of them, specifying which).[18] The list of issues is intended to be a neutral document for use as a case management tool at all stages of the case by the parties and the court. Neither party should attempt to draft the list in terms which advance one party's case over that of another.[19] In most cases it should be possible for the parties to draft an agreed list of issues. However, if it proves impossible to do so, the claimant must draft the list and send a copy to the defendant. The defendant may provide its comments or alternative suggested list to the court (with a copy to the claimant) separately.

At the first case management conference and any subsequent case management conferences which take place, the court will review and settle the draft list of issues with a view to refining it and identifying important sub-issues as appropriate and as required in order to manage the case. It will be used by the court and the parties as a case management tool as the case progresses to determine such matters as the scope of disclosure and of factual and expert evidence and to consider whether issues should be determined summarily or preliminary issues should be determined.

Unlike the other guides the Commercial Court provides for the sequential service of pre-trial skeletons. Each party should prepare written arguments and unless otherwise ordered, these should be served on all other parties and lodged with the court as follows:

(i) by the claimant, not later than 1 p.m. two days (i.e. two clear days) before the start of the trial;

(ii) by each of the defendants, not later than 1 p.m. one day (i.e. one clear day) before the start of the trial.[20]

In heavier cases it will often be appropriate for skeleton arguments to be served and lodged earlier, in which case the timetable should be discussed between the advocates and may be the subject of a direction in the pre-trial timetable or at any pre-trial review. The claimant should provide a chronology with his skeleton argument. Indices (i.e. documents that collate key references on particular points, or a substantive list of the contents of a particular bundle or bundles) and dramatis personae should also be provided where these are likely to be useful. Guidelines on the preparation of chronologies and indices are set out in Part 2 of Appendix 9.

Appendix 9[21] of the Admiralty Court and Commercial Court direction follows almost exactly the wording of Appendix 7 of the Chancery Guide

---

18 D6.1.

19 D6.2. However it is possible to do so: see Chapter 6, pp.57–59.

20 2A-89 F5.5.

21 Vol.2 White Book 1A-220.

with regard to the nature and contents of skeleton arguments. Although it contains the stricture that parties should avoid arguing the case at length, it does not state that the written summation be as brief as the nature of the issues allows, or that it should not normally exceed 20 pages of double-spaced A4 paper.

As far as possible, chronologies and indices should not be prepared in a tendentious form.[22] The ideal is that the court and the parties should have a single point of reference that all find useful and are happy to work with. Where there is disagreement about a particular event or description, it is useful if that fact is indicated in neutral terms and the competing versions shortly stated. If time and circumstances allow its preparation, a chronology or index to which all parties have contributed and agreed can be invaluable. Chronologies and indices once prepared can be easily updated and are of continuing usefulness throughout the life of the case.

The directions of the Admiralty and Commercial Courts are not confined to pre-trial skeletons. Unless the judge directs otherwise the parties should prepare skeleton arguments for the hearing of applications in the course of trial;[23] and in a more substantial trial, the court will normally also require closing submissions in writing before oral closing submissions.[24] In such a case the court will normally allow an appropriate period of time after the conclusion of the evidence to allow the preparation of these submissions. Even in a less substantial trial the court will normally require a written skeleton argument on matters of law. Express provision is made that if the authenticity of any document or entry in any document is challenged, such challenge must be contained in the skeleton argument.[25] In collision claims the skeleton argument of each party must be accompanied by a plot or plots of that party's case or alternative cases as to the navigation of vessels during and leading to the collision. All plots must contain a sufficient indication of the assumptions used in the preparation of the plot.[26]

As with the Commercial Court, Mercantile Courts function as specialist lists within the Queen's Bench Division of the High Court. The functions and procedures of the Mercantile Courts are governed by CPR Part 59 and its accompanying Practice Direction. Under the Jackson reforms the Mercantile Courts will have their own guide to be published during the lifetime of this edition. Presently the directions template for the Mercantile Courts is at 2B-14.1 of the White Book, though it is the responsibility of each court to determine the appropriate directions for each case. Specimen directions for each Mercantile Court can be found in the template in the Forms section of

---

22 Appendix 9.

23 J9.2.

24 N9.3.

25 J.11.1.

26 2A-136 N9.2.

the website: http://www.justice.gov.uk/guidance/courts-and-tribunals/courts /mercantile-court/our-work.htm (click on 'Forms' in the right-hand box).

The Technology and Construction Court

Proceedings in the TCC are governed by CPR Part 60 and its practice direction. The TCC Guide is at 2C to volume 2 of the White Book. In the case of all but the simplest applications, the court[27] expects both parties to lodge with the judge's clerk skeleton arguments and a list of any authorities to be relied on no later than 4 p.m. on the day before the date fixed for the hearing.[28] Directions concerning the exchange and filing of trial skeletons or opening written submissions will be given at the pre-trial review.

In TCC proceedings to enforce an adjudication award[29] subject to any more specific directions given by the court, the parties should lodge, by 4.00 p.m. one clear working day before the hearing, a bundle containing the documents that will be required at the hearing. The parties should also file and serve short skeleton arguments and copies of any authorities which are to be relied on (preferably as an agreed joint bundle), summarising their respective contentions as to why the adjudicator's decision is or is not enforceable or as to any other relief being sought. For a hearing that is expected to last half a day or less, the skeletons should be provided no later than 1 p.m. on the last working day before the hearing. For a hearing that is estimated to last more than half a day, the skeletons should be provided no later than 4 p.m. one clear working day before the hearing.

Arbitration

Where arbitrations are governed by section 2E of the Specialist Proceedings under Part 49 of the Civil Procedure Rules standard directions are provided for the filing and contents of skeleton arguments[30] to be used at the hearing:

> "Not later than 2 days before the hearing date the claimant must file and serve—
>
> (1) a chronology of the relevant events cross-referenced to the bundle of documents;
>
> (2) (where necessary) a list of the persons involved; and
>
> (3) a skeleton argument which lists succinctly—

---

27 Vol.2 White Book 2C-1 et seq.

28 7.5 PD to Part 60.

29 2C 98/9 9.3.2.

30 2E-44 (6.5–6.7).

(a) the issues which arise for decision;

(b) the grounds of relief (or opposing relief) to be relied upon;

(c) the submissions of fact to be made with the references to the evidence;

(d) the submissions of law with references to the relevant authorities.

Not later than the day before the hearing date the defendant must file and serve a skeleton argument which lists succinctly—

(1) the issues which arise for decision;

(2) the grounds of relief (or opposing relief) to be relied upon;

(3) the submissions of fact to be made with the references to the evidence; and

(4) the submissions of law with references to the relevant authorities."

The Patent Court

In the Patent Court,[31] in addition to the Reading Guide parties should lodge skeleton arguments in time for the judge to read them before trial. That should normally be at least two days before its commencement, but in substantial cases a longer period may be needed (to be discussed with the clerk to the judge concerned). It is desirable that each party should summarise what it contends to be the common general knowledge of the man skilled in the art. Following the evidence in a substantial trial a short adjournment may be granted to enable the parties to summarise their arguments in writing before oral argument.

The Administrative Court

In bringing claims for judicial review and other relief provided by the Administrative Court[32] issues concerned with application bundles and skeletons arguments are set out under CPR Part 54.16 and the Practice Direction at 54 PD 15. The claimant must file and serve a skeleton argument not less than 21 working days before the date of hearing. The defendant and any other party wishing to make representations at the hearing must file and serve skeletons not less than 14 working days before the hearing. The claimant must also file a paginated, indexed bundle of all relevant

---

31 Section 2F-124 of the Specialist Proceedings under Part 49 of the Civil Procedure Rules.

32 CPR 54.16.4; 54 PD 15.

documents. It must include those documents required by the claimant, the defendant and any other party wishing to make representations.

Skeleton arguments must contain:

(1) a time estimate for the complete hearing, including delivery of judgment;

(2) a list of issues;

(3) a list of the legal points to be taken (together with any relevant authorities with page references to the passages relied on);

(4) a chronology of events (with page references to the bundle of documents;

(5) a list of essential documents for the advance reading of the court (with page references to the passages relied on) (if different from that filed with the claim form) and a time estimate for that reading; and

(6) a list of persons referred to.

Family proceedings

The requirements for written skeleton arguments for use in appeals to the Family Division of the High Court and to the County Court from lower courts (as defined) are governed by Part 30 and Practice Direction 30A paragraphs 5.8(c), 5.9(f) and 5.13–5.22 to the Family Procedure Rules 2010.

By paragraphs 5.8 (c) and 5.9(f) of PD30A the appellant must file one copy of the appellant's skeleton argument for each copy of the appellant's notice that is filed. The criteria for such skeleton arguments are given at 5.13 onwards, and in particular:

> 5.16 A skeleton argument must contain a numbered list of the points which the party wishes to make. These should both define and confine the areas of controversy. Each point should be stated as concisely as the nature of the case allows.
>
> 5.17 A numbered point must be followed by a reference to any document on which the party wishes to rely.
>
> 5.18 A skeleton argument must state, in respect of each authority cited –
>
> (a) the proposition of law that the authority demonstrates; and
>
> (b) the parts of the authority (identified by page or paragraph references) that support the proposition.

5.19 If more than one authority is cited in support of a given proposition, the skeleton argument must briefly state the reason for taking that course.

5.20 The statement referred to in paragraph 5.19 should not materially add to the length of the skeleton argument but should be sufficient to demonstrate, in the context of the argument –

(a) the relevance of the authority or authorities to that argument; and

(b) that the citation is necessary for a proper presentation of that argument.

5.21 The cost of preparing a skeleton argument which –

(a) does not comply with the requirements set out in this paragraph; or

(b) was not filed within the time limits provided by this Practice Direction (or any further time granted by the court),

will not be allowed on assessment except to the extent that the court otherwise directs.

5.22 The appellant should consider what other information the appeal court will need. This may include a list of persons who feature in the case or glossaries of technical terms. A chronology of relevant events will be necessary in most appeals.

Criminal proceedings

The provision of written skeleton argument in criminal proceedings is governed by Part II of the Consolidated Criminal Practice Direction of the Criminal Procedure Rules 2010, Further Practice Directions Applying in the Court of Appeal (Criminal Division).[33] The specific requirements are dealt with at paragraph 17 onwards:

> (II.17.1) In all appeals against conviction a skeleton argument from the advocate for the appellant is to be lodged with the Registrar of Criminal Appeals and served on the prosecuting authority within 14 days of receipt by the advocate of the notification of the grant of leave to appeal against conviction or such longer period as the Registrar or the Court may direct. The skeleton may refer to an advice, which should be annexed with an indication of which parts of it are relied upon, and should include any additional arguments to be advanced.

---

33 Practice Direction (Criminal Appeals: Skeleton Arguments) [1999] 1 WLR 146; [1999] 1 All ER 669, CA; 15/12/98; Practice Direction (Judgments: Form and Citation) [2001] 1 WLR 194; [2001] 1 All ER 19; [2001] 1 CrAppR 426; 11/01/01.

(II.17.2) The advocate for the prosecuting authority should lodge with the Registrar and the advocate for the appellant his skeleton argument within 14 days of the receipt of the skeleton argument for the appellant or such longer (or, in exceptional cases, shorter) period as the Registrar or the Court may direct.

(II.17.3) Practitioners should ensure that, where reliance is placed upon unreported cases in skeleton arguments, short head notes are included.

(II.17.4) Advocates should ensure that the correct Criminal Appeal Office number appears at the beginning of their skeleton arguments and that their names are at the end.

(II.17.5) A skeleton argument should contain a numbered list of the points the advocate intends to argue, grouped under each ground of appeal, and stated in no more than one or two sentences. It should be as succinct as possible, the object being to identify each point, not to argue it or elaborate on it. Each listed point should be followed by full references to the material to which the advocate will refer in support of it, i.e. the relevant passages in the transcripts, authorities, etc. It should also contain anything the advocate would expect to be taken down by the Court during the hearing, such as propositions of law, chronologies, etc. If more convenient, these can be annexed to the skeleton rather than included in it. For points of law, the skeleton should state the point and cite the principal authority or authorities in support with reference to the passages where the principle is enunciated. Chronologies should, if possible, be agreed with the opposing advocate before the hearing. Respondents' skeletons should follow the same principles.

Paragraph 18 is concerned with the preparation of Criminal Appeal Office Summaries:

(II.18.1) To assist the Court the Criminal Appeal Office prepares summaries of the cases coming before it. These are entirely objective and do not contain any advice about how the Court should deal with the case or any view about its merits. They consist of two Parts.

(II.18.2) Part I, which is provided to all of the advocates in the case, generally contains (a) particulars of the proceedings in the Crown Court, including representation and details of any co-accused, (b) particulars of the proceedings in the Court of Appeal (Criminal Division), (c) the facts of the case, as drawn from the transcripts, advice of the advocates, witness statements and/or the exhibits, (d) the submissions and rulings, summing up and sentencing remarks. Should an advocate not want any factual material in his advice taken into account this should be stated in the advice.

(II.18.3) The contents of the summary are a matter for the professional judgment of the writer, but an advocate wishing to suggest any significant alteration to Part I should write to the Registrar of Criminal Appeals. If the Registrar does not agree, the summary and the letter will be put to the Court for decision. The Court will not generally be willing to hear oral argument about the content of the summary.

(II.18.4) Advocates may show Part I of the summary to their professional or lay clients (but to no one else) if they believe it would help to check facts or formulate arguments, but summaries are not to be copied or reproduced without the permission of the Criminal Appeal Office; permission for this will not normally be given in cases involving children or sexual offences or where the Crown Court has made an order restricting reporting.

(II.18.5) Unless a judge of the High Court or the Registrar of Criminal Appeals gives a direction to the contrary in any particular case involving material of an explicitly salacious or sadistic nature, Part I will also be supplied to appellants who seek to represent themselves before the Full Court or who renew to the full court their applications for leave to appeal against conviction or sentence.

(II.18.6) Part II, which is supplied to the Court alone, contains (a) a summary of the grounds of appeal and (b) in appeals against sentence (and applications for such leave), summaries of the antecedent histories of the parties and of any relevant pre-sentence, medical or other reports.

(II.18.7) All of the source material is provided to the Court and advocates are able to draw attention to anything in it which may be of particular relevance.

By paragraph 19 criminal practitioners are reminded that for the purpose of citing judgments in court reference should be made to paragraph 10.1 of Practice Direction (Court of Appeal (Civil Division)) [1999] 1 WLR 1027; [1999] 2 All ER 490. When a decision of the High Court given after January 13, 2002 is cited, the system of neutral citation must be used as set out in Practice Direction (Judgments: Neutral Citations) [2002] 1 WLR 346.

Under Part IV of the Consolidated Criminal Practice Direction: Further Practice Directions Applying in the Crown Court, provision is made for the preparation and delivery of skeleton arguments in abuse of process stay applications:

(IV.36.3) In relation to such applications, the following automatic directions shall apply:

(a) the advocate for the applicant(s) must lodge with the court and serve on all other parties a skeleton argument in support of the application at least five clear working days before the relevant date. If reference is to be made to any document not in the existing trial documents, a paginated and indexed bundle of such documents is to be provided with the skeleton argument;

(b) the advocate for the prosecution must lodge with the court and serve on all other parties a responsive skeleton argument at least two clear working days before the relevant date, together with a supplementary bundle if appropriate.

(IV.36.4) All skeleton arguments must specify any propositions of law to be advanced (together with the authorities relied upon in support, with page references to passages relied upon) and, where appropriate, include a chronology of events and a list of dramatis personae. In all instances where reference is made to a document, the reference in the trial documents or supplementary bundle is to be given.

(IV.36.5) The above time limits are minimum time limits. In appropriate cases the court will order longer lead times. To this end in all cases where defence advocates are, at the time of the plea and directions hearing, considering the possibility of an abuse of process application, this must be raised with the judge dealing with the matter, who will order a different timetable if appropriate, and may wish, in any event, to give additional directions about the conduct of the application.

The Court of Appeal

Skeleton arguments for and written submissions to the Court of Appeal are governed by CPR 52.4.5, 52.5.6, 52.12.1.4, and the associated Practice Direction at 52 PD paragraphs 5.9–5.11, 7.6–7.8, 11A–12.4, 19, 20, 36, 37 and 64. Every appellant who is represented is required (and appellants in person are encouraged) to prepare a skeleton argument, which, if short can be inserted into part 8 of the appellant's notice, or otherwise can be contained in an accompanying separate document. Alternatively the skeleton argument must be lodged and served within 14 days after filing the appellant's notice.[34]

The Court of Appeal regards the appellant's skeleton argument as a vital document: together with that of the respondent it assists in case management, allows the court to focus its attention on the true issues and proposed solution of the parties, and enables the members of the court to form a preliminary view, which is more often than not reflected in the judges' approach to counsel at the outset of the hearing. For the designated lead judgment writer, written submissions are a critical aid in the consideration and preparation of reserved judgments.

The content of skeleton arguments is dealt with in 52 PD 20 at paragraph 5.10 which states:

"(1) A skeleton argument must contain a numbered list of the points which the party wishes to make. These should both define and confine the areas of controversy. Each point should be stated as concisely as the nature of the case allows.

---

34 See 52 PD para.5.9.

(2) A numbered point must be followed by a reference to any document on which the party wishes to rely.

(3) A skeleton argument must state, in respect of each authority cited—

(a) the proposition of law that the authority demonstrates; and

(b) the parts of the authority (identified by page or paragraph references) that support the proposition.

(4) If more than one authority is cited in support of a given proposition, the skeleton argument must briefly state the reason for taking that course.

(5) The statement referred to in sub-paragraph (4) should not materially add to the length of the skeleton argument but should be sufficient to demonstrate, in the context of the argument—

(a) the relevance of the authority or authorities to that argument; and

(b) that the citation is necessary for a proper presentation of that argument.

(6) The cost of preparing a skeleton argument which—

(a) does not comply with the requirements set out in this paragraph; or

(b) was not filed within the time limits provided by this Practice Direction (or any further time granted by the court),will not be allowed on assessment except to the extent that the court otherwise directs."[35]

By paragraph 5.11 the appellant should also consider what other information the appeal court will need. This may include a list of persons who feature in the case or glossaries of technical terms. A chronology of relevant events will be necessary in most appeals.

Paragraph 7.6 of the Practice Direction obliges the respondent to provide a skeleton argument "in all cases where he proposes to address arguments to the court" and must either accompany the respondent's notice or else be lodged and served within 14 days after filing the notice. The content of a respondent's skeleton must conform to the directions at paragraphs 5.10 and 5.11 with any necessary modifications. It should, where appropriate, answer the arguments set out in the appellant's skeleton argument.

Where the appeal relates to a claim on the small claims track or the respondent is not represented, the respondent is not obliged to provide a

---

35 This paragraph incorporates the relevant requirements of the Practice Direction (Citation of Authorities) [2001] 1 WLR 1001. 31 Paragraph 5.10 is specific in its requirements and these are the costs consequences for non-compliance.

skeleton argument, but he is entitled to do so. In cases where there is no respondent's notice, the respondent need not serve his skeleton argument until 7 days before the appeal hearing.[36] However, if an appeal to the Court of Appeal is allocated to the short warned list, the respondent's skeleton argument may be required at short notice.[37]

Paragraph 15.11A of the Practice Direction permits the filing of supplementary skeleton arguments. The appellant's supplementary argument must be filed at least 14 days before the hearing and that of the respondent at least 7 days before. Any argument which is not contained in the original or supplementary skeleton arguments (timeously served) may be shut out by the court.[38]

Skeleton arguments and written submissions are not the only pieces of written advocacy which are received by the Court of Appeal. Where a refusal to give permission to appeal has been made on consideration of the papers alone, an appellant, who is represented, may make a request for a decision to be reconsidered at an oral permission hearing. By 52PD.11 paragraph 4.14A(2):

> "The appellant's advocate must, at least 4 days before the hearing, in a brief written statement—
>
> (a) inform the court and the respondent of the points which he proposes to raise at the hearing;
>
> (b) set out his reasons why permission should be granted notwithstanding the reasons given for the refusal of permission; and
>
> (c) confirm, where applicable, that the requirements of paragraph 4.17 have been complied with (appellant in receipt of services funded by the Legal Services Commission)."

Cases for the Supreme Court

The Supreme Court has its own Rules and Practice Directions which in 2009 replaced the Civil, Criminal and Taxation Practice Directions and Standing Orders of the Appellate Committee of the House of Lords previously known as 'the Blue Book'. The Supreme Court Rules 2009 are supplemented by Practice Directions issued by the President. These govern the presentation of written material for consideration by the Supreme Court and also the Judicial Committee of the Privy Council. The document which contains a

---

36 See 52 PD 20 para. 7.7 (2).

37 *Scribes West Ltd v Anstalt (No. 1)* [2004] EWCA Civ 835, [2004] All ER (D) 337 (Jun) at [24].

38 52 PD 20 para. 15.11A(4) and *Scribes West Ltd v Anstalt (No. 1)* op.cit. at [25]–[27].

party's written argument is known as a 'case'. This is separate from any statement of facts and issues.

The preparation and contents of the appellants' and respondents' cases are dealt with in Practice Direction 6. A separate direction at 5 concerns the preparation of statements of facts and issues which, essentially, are expected to be agreed between the parties and any passive or neutral stakeholders who may be participating in the proceedings.

Unlike the former Standing Orders of the Appellate Committee of the House of Lords there is no prescription that all the appellants must join in one case, and all the respondents must similarly join in one case unless it can be shown that the interests of one or more are distinct from those of the remainder. By paragraph 6.3.8 of PD6 15.9 parties whose interests in the appeal are passive (e.g. stakeholders, trustees, executors, etc.) are not required to lodge a separate case but need to ensure that their position is explained in one of the cases lodged.

The preparation and filing of cases is sequential, not an exchange. The appellants must lodge eight copies of their case in the Registry and serve it on the respondents no later than five weeks before the proposed date of the hearing. The respondents must lodge their case in response, as must any other party lodging a case no later than three weeks before the proposed date. Where there is a cross-appeal the cross-appellants' case for the cross-appeal is to be lodged three weeks before the hearing as part of their reply to the original appellants' case. Permission must be sought for the filing of supplemental cases (6.3.12).

By paragraph 6.3.1 the Court does not prescribe any maximum length but the Court favours brevity and a case should be a concise summary of the submissions to be developed.

Paragraph 6.3.2 directs that the case should be confined to the heads of argument that counsel propose to submit at the hearing and omit material contained in the statement of facts and issues (governed by paragraph 5.1.3 of Practice Direction 5).

If either party is abandoning any point taken in the courts below, this should be made plain in their case (6.3.3). If they intend to apply in the course of the hearing for permission to introduce a new point not taken below, this should also be indicated in their case and the Registrar informed. If such a point involves the introduction of fresh evidence, application for permission must be made either in the case or by filing an application for permission to adduce the fresh evidence (see paragraph 7.1 of Practice Direction 7 for applications).

By paragraph 6.3.4, if a party intends to invite the Court to depart from one of its own decisions or from a decision of the House of Lords, this intention must be clearly stated in a separate paragraph of their case, to which special attention must be drawn. A respondent who wishes to contend that a decision of the court below should be affirmed on grounds other than those relied on by that court must set out the grounds for that contention in their case. Transcripts of unreported judgments should only be cited when they contain an authoritative statement of a relevant principle of law not to be found in a reported case or when they are necessary for the understanding of some other authority. (6.3.5)

Paragraph 6.3.6 states that all cases must conclude with a numbered summary of the reasons upon which the argument is founded, and must bear the signature of at least one counsel for each party to the appeal who has appeared in the court below or who will be briefed for the hearing before the Court. The filing of a case carries the right to be heard by two counsel (6.3.7).

By paragraph 6.3.13 cases must be produced on A4 paper, securely bound on the left, using both sides of the paper with:

(a) numbered paragraphs; and

(b) signatures of counsel at the end, above their printed names.

Paragraph 6.4.1 then deals with the Court's requirements for the filing of core volumes.

2 What Judges Want

Although the Procedure Rules and practice guides set out what is required when providing the courts with skeleton arguments, and this is enforced by the penalty costs regime, in practice many of the successful advocates who have kindly contributed to this work pay only lip service to such technicalities as maximum length, form and subject matter. Curiously so do many judges. There are still some of an older disposition who disapprove of any form of written advocacy and will not even consider written submissions; however most members of the judiciary want as much assistance in writing as possible, believing that it will shorten the hearing. By far the majority appreciate and are genuinely assisted by written arguments which are clear, concise, coherent, structured intelligently, and formulated with a view to assisting the judge to solve the problem immediately to hand.

Immediate and future use

Judges rely on case summaries, skeleton arguments and written submissions to find the quickest way into the case. The pressure of business and the distribution of work, particularly in the superior courts, are such that applications and even trials will come before tribunals who do not have the time to absorb the papers. There are, of course, exceptions, such as the Technology and Construction Court where active case management in most cases by the eventual trial judge, means that he will know the case quite well. But where it happens that the judge comes to a contested matter entirely afresh, it is the well-presented and coherent skeleton that will be read before the statements of case and, if reliable, in place of them. In the Court of Appeal a dependable skeleton will subsume and deal with all of the live grounds of appeal: in an average appeal contesting the legal basis for the decision of the court below, unless skeleton submissions are unclear or extremely short, the lords justices of appeal need read only the two sides' respective skeleton arguments and the relevant part of the first instance judgment.

For a judge, the skeleton should tell him whether it is necessary to read anything else, and if so what, and in what order. This is particularly true for applications before the master and district judge. For these the case summary and skeleton are required to deal only with what arises at the instant hearing. That is not to say that judges do not differentiate between different forms of written advocacy. They do. The skeleton prepared for a two hour application before a master or a contested issue of case management will have a different structure and dissimilar contents from opening notes or closing submissions at trial; and between the style of written advocacy prepared for trial and that for appeal.

The impact of a well thought out and carefully crafted skeleton argument should not be underestimated. Written submissions do not cease to be useful to the court merely because the trial or appeal has commenced. In the Court of Appeal upwards of 60% of appeals now have reserved judgments: the written argument is not only used before the hearing to enable the judge to formulate a preliminary view, but also *afterwards* as an aide memoir to write his judgment. Much the same can be said of trial judges, and increasingly it is common for advocates to be asked to prepare closing submissions in writing, usually in lieu of closing argument, and to furnish the judge with a copy in electronic format.

What do judges want?

Judges want to get on with the job. They first want to be told what the case is about, succinctly and in the first two or three paragraphs of the skeleton. Then they want to know what is the problem, and what answer is proposed. Masters and judges dealing with applications need to know what you want them to do as quickly as possible, and will then test what is wanted against the submissions made.

In all but written advocacy prepared for trial, the salient facts, dates, features, issues and relevant law should be reduced to a pithy synopsis: the tribunal does not want to be overburdened, just receive well-focused information. Most judges wish to be guided into the case in a neutral way: they appreciate that the argument will, of course, be loaded, but the introduction which gives the reader the geography of the case is expected to be neutral.

The judges to whom I have spoken ask that advocates always bear in mind the following:

- If the judge or master has had no prior contact with the case the skeleton must tell him what, if anything, he needs to read next.

- In order for the judge to grasp points quickly, clarity of presentation is essential. For some this means that complex issues of fact or law should be broken down into small portions – the issues being identified, but not necessarily simplified. For all, this means well reasoned argument which, though skeletal, is thorough, internally coherent, has a logical progression and leads to clear conclusions.

- In form the skeleton will be more akin to the outline of a judgment, particularly where the document is a written closing submission at trial, or a written submission for the Court of Appeal. Coherence in any written document intended to assist the court is very important.

- If the judge has difficulty with a skeleton argument, because it is not easy to read, has no coherent structure, or is unreliable as to its contents, he is likely to abandon it and go to the statements of case. Should he do so there is a real risk for the advocate that he will not return to it.

The trial and appellate judge

There is a dichotomy between judges at first instance and those sitting on appeal, or hearing applications, as to what they want from a claimant's or appellant's skeleton argument. The trial judge wants the skeleton or opening note to set the scene, to enable him to master the facts and the law, and to understand the arguments. He does not want to form a view from one side's argument only. Experienced trial judges are progressively less willing to come to an early conclusion as provisional views are often wrong, and cases come alive when they are argued. They wish to see what the facts and arguments are and to go into the hearing with an open mind. That is what the parties expect.

Appellate judges view the skeleton submissions for an appellant slightly differently from those in a claimant's opening note for trial. Because of the pressure of time, the parties written submissions and the judgment given below are about as much as can be read in advance. The judge will want to begin the appellant's submissions before reading the judgment since it may well be unnecessary to read the whole judgment. The appellant should tell him what the case is about and what points he wants to argue – in effect, 'why he is where he is'. This skeleton will not set out the facts in any detail but show the court where the detail is to be found in the judgment if it is wanted. Generally the only facts that are wanted are those needed to address the points in the appeal since invariably many points will not be in issue. The appellate judge wishes to receive substantive points of law not points of procedure, and expects the submissions to build upon the grounds of appeal. Again, clarity and coherence are the watchwords, with perhaps each part of the written argument dealing with one ground of appeal.

Directions

It is rare for masters and judges to provide express directions as to the style, form and content of skeleton arguments since these are to be found in the Civil Procedure Rules and specialist practice guides. In some jurisdictions, slightly specialised directions may be given, for example that a case summary be directed at certain issues, that partnership accounts be drawn in a way that invites comment or argument, or that Scott schedules in the

Technology and Construction Court be expanded to enable parties to provide support or argument for any particular contention.

More usually there will be a direction that the issues between the parties be agreed, and perhaps formulated in a particular way. In asking for written closing submissions a trial judge may well invite the parties to frame agreed questions for him to decide.

Occasionally Queen's Bench Masters will issue a personal direction which modifies the operation of the relevant Civil Procedure Rules Practice Direction, and this is something you will have to watch out for and learn by experience. For example Master Eyre issued a direction dealing with the names of parties that:

"The parties must in any statement of case or other document prepared for use by the master, and notwithstanding anything in the Rules, be referred to as parties – "the Second Claimant", "the Fourth Defendant", "the First Third Party", &c. as the case may be – and not by names or initials, &c., save in those rare cases in which some other approach is required if the meaning is to be made clear."

To cater for the fact that a particulars of claim and probably a defence will already have been filed before the parties receive notice of this direction, it goes on to say:

> "Original documents that have been filed must not be altered. Instead, copies cleanly-corrected using 'Find-and-replace' must be provided for use at any hearing."

You may find these quirky local directions at County Court level as well.

Length

There is no consensus among judges as to the optimum length of a skeleton argument. It is broadly accepted that the length of opening and closing notes must be appropriate to the case and a distinction is drawn between these and skeleton arguments in interim applications.

Two schools of thought seem to have developed. There are many judges, including members of the Court of Appeal, who are unconcerned about length and like argument being developed. By contrast there are those who find excessive length irritating, and who feel that, while the element of spoon-feeding is sometimes an aid, it can be too long, except where unavoidable technicalities in the law require explanation. Only by discovering or gaining experience of any particular judge's views on this subject will you discover which your particular tribunal prefers.

An extreme view, taken in some parts of the Queen's Bench Masters' corridor, is that where a written argument is considered too long, the advocate should be put to an election whether the master should receive that document only and not hear oral argument, or whether the document be not read. I don't know how that squares with Article 6 European Convention on Human Rights. The masters with whom I have spoken were inclined to think that a document of between 2 and 3 pages in length was the maximum they required on most occasions.

Judges tend to advise that being succinct is far more convincing than being verbose – all they need is a sufficient understanding of what will lead to oral submissions.

Overall visual impression

Many of my interviewees instinctively said they were not concerned with the visual impression of the written submissions presented, as long as these skeletons were generally in accordance with the rules. However, when pressed, they agreed that readability, the setting out of the page, and ease on the eye did have an impact on them. Many made jottings in the margin or otherwise liked to write on the white space available. They do not, though, like line spacing set too wide: it is unnecessary and renders the document less succinct.

Comfortable readability for most judges means a decent sized margin, 12 point type using a font such as Times New Roman or Arial typefaces, and a line spacing of 1.5. Two other matters were frequently mentioned: that skeleton arguments be page numbered; and that the title should always say on whose behalf the document was being filed, particularly with supplemental skeletons and on any appendices.

Citation

Broadly speaking, the judges interviewed wished for a sparing use of authorities in skeleton arguments. The citation of obvious cases was unnecessary, as were authorities concerning procedure or first or general principles. Members of the court do not react well to the tendency of those advocates who put in authority for every proposition, whether it is contentious or not: the less contentious the proposition, the less authority is required.

Having said that, and subject to the Practice Direction on the citation of authorities,[1] most judges will accept patiently as many authorities as are felt necessary, particularly where the case is comparatively unusual. Advocates

1 Practice Direction (Citation of Authorities) [2001] 1 WLR 1001.

should not get carried away. If there is a recent Supreme Court or Court of Appeal decision on the point, or a case that reviews all predecessors in an area, it should be sufficient to refer only to that.

No universal rule is offered on the length or frequency of the quotation of judgments from authorities within written submissions; these must be appropriate to each case. However most judges want citation references only, since quotations merely extend the skeleton. Experienced counsel are expected to make sensible decisions about what and how much to cite. Judges prefer pithy, accurate quotes limited to a paragraph or two, which are very much on point. If anything longer is necessary the judge will go and read it himself.

It is sometimes helpful to provide a separate appendix dealing with the pertinent and recent law[2] that is the subject of the proceedings where the judge is, or is likely to be unfamiliar with it. It is useful to have key cases attached to the skeleton, especially Lawtel reports or short transcripts if the authority is new and not reported elsewhere.

Footnotes

It may come as a surprise but the use of footnotes in written submissions is still regarded by many judges as both a modern and unorthodox phenomenon. On balance the judges who have assisted with this project were marginally against their use, seeing them at best as a repository for citation references and at worst as a distraction, forcing the eyes of the reader to drop to the foot of the page. The only discussion by judges was whether or not the names and references to authority should be kept in the main body of text or removed to a footnote, but all agreed that substantive argument should not appear there.

Headings

Judges find that topical headings provide useful guidance in breaking up issues. Most prefer a heading to be neutral rather than argumentative, that is, an assertive, contentious statement of the party's position on the next issue being advanced. Nonetheless it is accepted that argumentative headings are useful in summarising passages of argument if used well and imaginatively.[3]

Judges tend to prefer the use of sub-headings to numbered sub-paragraphs; this helps a judge find his way around the skeleton more easily. All Judges are keen on marked signposts.

---

2 See the examples in Part 3 at C *Martindale* and J *Phelps*.

3 See pp.60–61.

Summaries

Summaries are generally thought to be useful, particularly at the beginning of the skeleton, and condensed into the first three paragraphs which tell the judge: what is the claim for; what is the central feature of the claimant's case; and what is the central feature of the defendant's case.

In skeletons produced for applications the court should be told immediately what it is being asked to decide. For closing submissions at trial or as appropriate in opening notes, the relief sought and the basis for granting it should be summarised.

Repetition

Almost all judges questioned do not like repetition in written submissions and find it irritating. They do not want any skeleton argument to be longer than is necessary. A short introduction or summary is acceptable. Tribunals wish to make sure they have every point, but the idea of repetition for emphasis is for juries not the judge. One circuit judge informed me that he would skip over anything he had read before, except material in a general introduction.

Abbreviations

Of all the various matters of style it is the use of abbreviations that gives rise to the most intense debate. You would imagine that judges find abbreviations quite helpful to keep things short, for example as specifically encouraged by paragraph 2(5) of Appendix 7 to the Chancery Guide.[4] Most prefer the use of C for Claimant, D for Defendant, A for Applicant, P for Petitioner and R for Respondent except where it is not practical, either because it is easier to use the actual names of parties who are, say, companies, or where there are multiple parties, or where parties either change or have different status during different parts of the claim (e.g. in a counterclaim, Part 20 Claim, or by reference to parallel proceedings, such as an arbitration). I denote a tension, however, between judges and the advocates who appear before them about the use of names that manifests itself in the argument concerning abbreviations. Judges want to know what people are, not who they are. In most cases it is better, not only for them but also for observers or readers of law reports, that abbreviations denote status rather than *persona*. Advocates, on the other hand, often want to *personalise* the case, hoping for example that a judge will be more reluctant to find Mr Bloggs or Mr Jones liable than Big Conglomerate Plc, perhaps referred to as BC Plc. They therefore want to avoid abbreviations and use real names. Even if the judge favours the use of status, abbreviations can be avoided by the

---

4 See p 10.

use of 'the architect' or 'the surveyor.' In certain cases it will be better for all to depersonalise.

Beyond the use of initials to abbreviate the names of parties or to denote their status, most judges dislike abbreviations. They do not help clarity. judges dislike having to keep referring back to the beginning of the document or to the *dramatis personae* or other key to find out about whom the writer is talking. Judges much prefer descriptive names to initials, and are usually only comfortable with abbreviated names where the name is obvious from its shortened form.

Old-fashioned courtesies should be observed. If you chose to abbreviate the parties to Smith and Jones, the judge will expect it to be Mr Smith and Mrs Jones. Personal titles are to be respected and are seen as important.

Statutes and authorities should be referred to in full when first cited, and afterwards may be abbreviated, for example, from the Inheritance (Provision for Family and Dependants) Act 1975 to "the 1975 Act", and say, *Metalloy Supplies Ltd (In Liquidation) v MA (UK) Ltd* to '*Metalloy*'.

Textual enhancement

The over liberal use of italics and bold type face can often be seen as a challenge to the judge's intellect. Therefore use textual enhancement sparingly. Italics should always be confined to the name of a case and those important few words that are cited as the key to or turning point in the argument. The use of bold should be even more restricted, and confined to the emphasis of small key parts of a document.

As with all kinds of enhancement, it is the sparing use of augmentation that makes it more effective and of greater worth as a visual aid.

Structure of the argument

Most tribunals say they want the skeleton argument to be just that – skeletal. The oral tradition forces them to maintain the view that the court operates most effectively with short introductory statements in writing that indicate each party's position, with oral argument used to develop, amplify and explain points, and to be a dialogue between the advocate and whatever the court is interested in or troubled by.

However short the skeleton, the argument must raise all live issues. The court and your opposing number should be aware of all points being taken, since judges strongly disapprove of surprises which arise because an advocate has either withheld a matter or has not dealt with his own client's position adequately. Apart from anything else, such a defect is likely to attract adverse costs consequences as being incompatible with the overriding objective under the Civil Procedure Rules.

Well-structured arguments are appreciated. They help the judge to focus, to concentrate and to reach a conclusion quickly. Muddle and ill thought out propositions irritate judges. They like a progression – logical consecutive arguments, broken down into a series of questions or stages. They welcome familiar signposts in the law, and, if by chance you come before the right judge, the development of the law on a point previously decided by him. But to score really well, find a hook to interest your tribunal – the great appellate advocates of our age, like Jonathan Sumption QC (now Lord Sumption) and Lord Pannick QC – succeed because they find something to say which the court has not thought of.

Having said that, Sumption himself says "at the end of the day the judge has got to have something to say, so you've got to work out what he is going to find appealing. Know your material backwards, spot your opportunities as they arise and know exactly what you have to prove. Reduce difficult argument to its simplest dimensions – ultimately law is just common sense with knobs on".[5] "In most cases, 99 per cent of the facts are irrelevant, either legally or factually or both," says Sumption. "The art of advocacy is to strip those away. When you're down to the last 1 per cent, the answer should be obvious."[6]

5 Interview with Matt Stadlen. *Five Minutes With: Jonathan Sumption QC* 31 July 2010 BBC News Programmes.

6 Interview for *The Lawyer* 18 December 2000.

Part 2
Developing Written Advocacy Skills

3 Skills for the Practitioner

The tradition of written argument is central to European systems of civil litigation, exemplified by those of France and Italy. There, as proceedings develop, advocates submit for filing on the court roll lengthy formal and technical documents which combine statements of case, argument, evidence and the procedural history of the claim. The court requires little oral argument. However for linguistic and cultural reasons, there is not much from these jurisdictions to assist us in developing a written style and design for our own. Rather let us turn for know-how to that common-law jurisdiction which has a mature and sophisticated procedure for drawing up formatted written argument in Federal and Supreme Court appeals, the United States.

The process of settling 'briefs' or written argument for the use of the American appellate courts is not only well developed, it has for decades attracted both judicial commentary and academic guidance. In 1961 Col. Frederick Bernays Wiener wrote his classic Briefing and Arguing Federal Appeals[1] and prior to this John W. Davis was producing material giving direction on drafting written argument to the New York Bar.[2] From then on American attorneys were given the benefit of regular advice on how to argue effectively in writing and how to write persuasively, a tradition which remains vital,[3] and which should be of practical help to us all.

Persuasive writing by lawyers is founded on the use of good and effective English. A body of literature has developed in this area as well, with two American practitioners being particularly prominent. Bryan A. Garner, who is to this generation of lawyers what Weiner was to his, has written *The Winning Brief: 100 Tips for Persuasive Briefing in Trial and Appellate Courts*[4] and *Legal Writing in Plain English: A Text With Exercises*[5] and Richard C. Wydick

---

1 Reprinted in 2001 by Lawbook Exchange, N.Jersey.

2 See *The Argument of an Appeal* (address to Association of the Bar of the City of New York 22.10.1940). 26 ABAJ 895.

3 See *Appellate Advocacy: Some Reflections from the Bench* (1993) 61 Ford L. Rev 829; *Writing to the Ear* James W. McElhaney Dec 1995 ABAJ 71; *Effective Appellate Advocacy* Hon. Paul R. Michel Litigation Summer 1998 19; *Winning on Appeal: Better Briefs and Oral Argument* Judge Ruggero J. Aldisert (1999); Effective Appellate Brief Writing Hon. Clyde H. Hamilton (1999) 50 SCL Review 581; *Appeals: The Classic Guide William Pannill Litigation* (Winter 1999) vol.25. no.2 p.6; *The Art of Appellate Brief Writing* Brian L. Porto 2003 29 Vermont Bar Journal and Law Digest 30.

4 2nd edn. OUP 2004.

5 Chicago 2001.

Plain English For Lawyers.[6] Although these texts are for American consumption, they travel across the Atlantic reasonably well and should be read by anyone who is serious about wishing to develop their skills in written argument.

As I noted in the introduction to this book, even after a decade of being a requirement in all civil actions, in terms of development and sophistication, written advocacy in England and Wales remains in its infancy. Only in recent years have the judicial proponents of good written argument been offering advice to practitioners. Among the forefront of these are the organisers of the respective Inns of Court advocacy training schemes who ensure that modules are available for training in writing skeleton argument; and the Bar Professional Training Courses now provide for some, albeit cursory, introduction to the subject. The Advocacy Training Council regulates training in advocacy.

Distilling the experience of over sixty years of American brief writing, and fusing it with judicial commentary from our own jurisdiction, let us consider how to develop a style of written advocacy, what literary techniques are available for the advocate to use, how to write persuasively, how to apply the lost art of précis, and what tasks you have to remember before lodging your finished document.

---

6 4th edn 1998.

4 Creating a Style for Written Advocacy

Let us start with the premise that, if nothing else, judges read skeleton arguments in advance of the hearing. It is worth ensuring at the commencement that they have done so, on pain of a short adjournment. In tribunals with more than one judge, the members of the court will confer with each other not solely after argument but also having at least made a cursory examination of the skeleton submissions beforehand. So, just as you would consider with care how to approach your audience – the hearer of your oral argument – so should you approach your reader. Your judge is intelligent and eager to get on with his job but knows nothing about your case or what you want the court to do. If you focus on telling him swiftly and precisely what he needs to know, in the order he needs to know it, pre-empting and anticipating questions where possible, you will assist both him and your client, and in the process you will develop a personal style of written advocacy.

Organising your thoughts

The impression received by the judge is of the utmost importance, and not merely the first reaction to the appearance of the document he is encouraged to read. The impression derived from a skeleton argument carries over into examination of the statements of case and trial documents. If you can arouse the interest of the judge and create a good impression at the outset of the hearing, that is something which is not easy for your opponent to dispel. Conversely, a poor impression can lead to a case being lost which should be won; or at the very least you will give yourself an unnecessarily hard time.

Without considerable planning you cannot hope to develop a successful technique that you can then replicate whenever you need it. You must learn to write with clarity, precision, confidence, forthrightness and lack of verbosity. This is the key to the rapid communication of ideas. But if you don't organise your thoughts before writing you are being inefficient with and wasteful of your time, and your document will ramble. A lack of organisation will give the impression that your writing has been dictated off the cuff and makes your argument difficult to follow, frequently repetitious, often internally inconsistent, and always unpersuasive.[1]

---

1 See Weiner op. cit. at 136–137 (note, all references are to the 2001 reprint edition).

Begin planning by considering the live issues – how many and what they are – and completing your basic research. Weiner suggested[2] things that most lawyers already do: "concentrate on your problem, turn it over in your mind, think about it in the bath or shower, try out your hypotheses on your associates, live with the case in every spare waking moment – but don't start to write until the sequence and direction of your points have fallen clearly into place in your mind." And before doing so ask yourself, 'do I understand this? Can I explain it to my reader?' Don't begin to write until you are satisfied the answer to both is 'yes'.

There are two principal techniques for preparing a working draft, the first of which lends itself to the lawyer who has a fixed idea of where he wants to take the court, and how he is going to get it there. This is to write a draft argument straight through without stopping to edit, using a form and language as near as possible to the way it would be expressed in speech. Revise it afterwards, in whatever detail is necessary, but only after letting it settle, or breathe for a while.

The second technique is for the more meticulous practitioner, the more conservative, the more pedestrian if you like, and I suspect it suits most of us better. This is for the note sifter, and follows this pattern of activity: make accurate notes prior to writing; set out every good point to be made; sift through, discarding some ideas.

What's left is the heart of your argument: sort out the order; prepare it as an outline and develop the argument from the outline.

The practical process

Write or type out your skeleton yourself. Do not dictate. That only produces wordy writing, and worse, the formal legal vernacular which can be so oblique in its meaning. If you cannot resist the temptation to dictate, because it is your standard working practice, at least never dictate an argument or any other kind of argumentative writing. As a process it undermines logical thought and the progression of ideas.

Suggestions for writing

Catch and seize the court's interest in the opening three paragraphs of your skeleton. The easiest way to do so is to provide a statement of purpose, one that controls the form, content, style and length of the rest of the document and gives by way of introduction a brief overview of your position. Within the space of a few lines tell the judge what the hearing is for; who you represent; what you want; something of the parties; the subject matter of the

---

2 Ibid.

case; the pertinent facts; as briefly as possible the recent procedural history, and if necessary describe previous argument accurately. If you state the nature of the case and outline its prior history it brings what is to follow into immediate focus for the judge. Carefully drafted headings and subheadings provide a good road map of the argument and in most cases make a summary unnecessary.

These suggestions work:

- *Deal with the facts before you write the argument*
  You should never forget the primacy of the facts – *ex facto jus oritur* – or that legal argument flows from the facts, and not vice versa. An analysis of the facts will receive and deserve primary attention because that is how the judge, more often than not, arrives at his decision on the merits of the case. Therefore, once you have compiled a summary of the facts it is easier to structure legal argument, and new arguments may suggest themselves.

- *State the facts chronologically*
  Do not analyse facts on a witness-by-witness basis.

- *Use relative time to add interest to the reader*
  In a narrative of chronological events, you can use time relatively but only after starting with a date (e.g. "On 12 April 2003 Mr Smith hired a car; he returned it two days later.") This enables you to avoid having a string of dates outside a formal chronology.

- *Write your argument consecutively*
  It is easier to write, read and, importantly, persuade if there is a natural progression to your argument. It does not matter whether you are following chronological steps, the elements of a cause of action, or a logical sequence. The pattern of development must be easy to follow. For the basic argument start with the opening point and follow through to the conclusion. Embellishment can come later. If you are able to do this you will avoid the strong temptation to deal with the easy points first and then tackle the difficult ones once your writing flows. To do this makes both the substance and form look lopsided.

- *Make the most of your affirmative case*
  Write in such a way as to accentuate the affirmative features of your own case. In sequential skeletons do not content yourself with a point-by-point reply to the other side, even if that is necessary, because to do so is to let the other side both put you on the defensive and shape your own document. Even if you must reply to all of them, do not follow the other side's outline of points. Put your own strongest point first. Never let the other side write or even shape your skeleton.

- *Write the summary last*
  If you are going to provide a summary of your argument, whether as a concluding or introductory paragraph, compose it only after all else is finished. You will thereby distil the virtue of what has been written, and not create some new tangent. It is difficult to summarise an argument that is incomplete and not fully understood and it may be dangerous to do so. Certainly you should never address in the summary subjects the argument does not address.

The Weiner essentials

In 1961 Col. Weiner suggested[3] there were nine really essential features necessary for effective written advocacy in U.S. federal court appeals. These can be viewed both generically and applied regardless of jurisdiction. I have modified them for our purposes and put them in the form of those questions you should ask yourself of your draft written submissions:

1. *Have I complied with the relevant rules of Court?*
   You must be familiar with the current rules and practice directions. Obsolescence is dangerous. Check the relevant specialist court guide, on line if possible, with regard to the layout and presentation, contents and length of what you are about to provide to the Court. Discover whether the inclusion of irrelevant or immaterial matter might actually offend the rule or direction and cause the document to be rejected. Remember that all rules are subject to change and to interpretation. If you are not a specialist in the particular area check with a colleague more familiar with the practice of that court. This goes back to the same adage, know your audience – the master or judge whom you are trying to persuade. Be aware of the jurisdiction and powers of the tribunal before which you are appearing.

2. *Have I provided an effective summary of the facts?*
   Judges are sensitive to the facts because they want to do substantive justice between the parties. The Court is concerned with the merits of a case at every level of jurisdiction, not merely at trial. You must therefore bring the facts to the judge's attention in such a way as to shape his decision. Write your summary in such a way that the Court will want to find in your favour before it even gets started on the legal argument.

3. *Do I use good, clear, forceful English?*
   Write your skeleton in such a way as you yourself would want to read it. Provide a clear, consecutive understandable picture of what the case is really about.

---

3 Op cit. pp.37–127. 4 See chapter 1.

4. *Do my headings assist the Court?*
Orient the reader from the outset. Tell him where you are going. If you provide signposts for the judge you relieve him of the need to engage in either physical or mental work. This can be in the form of headings, or within argument, argumentative propositions e.g. this appeal is without merit for the following three reasons...

5. *Have I presented the questions for the Court in an appealing way?*
Do not present the judge with a problem unless there is a solution to go with it. Provide a question that will make the judge think the answer, which favours your case, is self-evident.

6. *Is my legal analysis of the problem sound?*
Try to make the solution appear straightforward – the answer to the question posed by you together with what you want the court to do

7. *Is my presentation of the evidence in arguing the facts convincing?*
Properly written your analysis of the facts should be a complete story of vital events and, where relevant, the procedural history of your case. As you compile this you should identify to yourself the evidence available to prove all of those facts that you require in order for your argument to succeed. If you can do this you will be ready to cross-refer your argument to the evidence as you come to write it.

8. *Have I paid careful attention to all parts?*
It is essential to cover all live issues in adequate detail. If they are no longer live, an explanation of this must be given consistent with protecting your client's position on costs.

9. *Have I allayed the reader's doubts and satisfied his curiosity?*
Does the document do the job? If there are obvious deficiencies be candid. But above all 'be clear, concise, honest, balanced, buttressed, convincing and interesting'[4] Associate Justice Minton of the United States Supreme Court said,[5] 'Be concise, while at the same time elaborate in written form all the propositions laid out in your pleading.' If you can do this let the bench call upon your opponent with the awkward questions.

And some negative suggestions

- Never distort either the fact or the law: the discovery of this by the judge or the other side will be extremely painful.

---

4 Wiley B. Rutledge *The Appellate Brief* (1942) in *Advocacy and the King's English.*

5 Foreword 1961 edn. Weiner.

- Avoid hyperbole – overstatement leads to misrepresentation.

- Avoid personality attacks; the Court will discern how bad your opponent is without you having to say so.

- Avoid slang. Advocates are expected to have an adequate vocabulary without recourse to this.

- Avoid sarcasm. It demeans your profession.

- Do not repeat the adage for oral presentation – say what you're going to say, say it, then say what you've said – show some recognition of the Court's intelligence.

- Do not forget the Court's valuable time: don't waste it.

- Never be shy about seeking the criticism of a colleague.

In Part 3 we look at the techniques of some of today's most successful advocates. However you do not need to follow models slavishly. Use other people's work intelligently and eclectically and so develop what works for you.

5 Literary Techniques for the Advocate

English usage

Legal writing is stuffy, pompous, wordy, artificial, often ungrammatical, jargon-filled, and pretentious.[1] And bad writing makes the reader's job harder. So, since you are trying to get the judge to accept your client's case, why make your task more difficult by failing to use plain language? Avoid any word that does not command instant understanding – you need to let the reader see your ideas without struggling to grasp your meaning. Sentences should be constructed so the reader may read with understanding effortlessly. You are aiming to persuade the judge with good, lucid, forceful English that is grammatical, clearly written and reads naturally.

The writers to whom I have referred agree that the use of language is embedded in the way we perceive the world and that it is impossible for the lawyer or judge to focus exclusively on the merits of a case without being affected by the language used to express those merits. It follows that it is not enough to have a strong case. You must be able to convey that to the judge.

Poor English is not tolerated by judges, and when written down becomes an unnecessary distraction on the page. Advocates should know how to use English properly.

The creation of written submissions is as much a process of creative writing as any work of non-fiction. The purpose, however, is to persuade and not merely to inform or entertain. The best way to do so in literary form is to make your points as simply as possible. Master your thoughts so you can communicate them clearly. Simple arguments are winning arguments. Convoluted arguments will not persuade.[2]

Therefore:

- Use the active voice wherever possible to keep writing vivid: the passive voice leads to additional words and unnatural inflexion. We do not speak

---

1 *Legal Writing in Plain English: A Text With Exercises* Bryan A. Garner (Chicago 2001) Pt 1.

2 *The Winning Brief: 100 Tips for Persuasive Briefing in Trial and Appellate Courts* Bryan A. Garner (2nd edn. OUP 2004) Ch.15.

in the passive voice without seeming pompous and indirect – passivity fails to say who has done what and subverts the normal word order of English, making it harder for the reader to process and digest information. It should be used only sparingly, for example when the focus is the thing being acted upon and not the doer; when you wish to hide the doer; to avoid gender-specific language; or to generalise without using 'one' as the subject.

- Use short sentences, averaging no more than 20 words, with occasional variations up to 25 words. It is very effective, as any reader of Lord Denning's judgments will discover.[3] Reduce sentence lengths by stripping out the unnecessary and the verbose. This gives momentum to the material. It makes things seem simpler for the reader. It makes the argument appear more focussed, more confident and sharper. If you are not disciplined in this try the process mechanically – write and count – until it comes naturally.

- Break up the text with headings. Subject to the overall effect on the length of the document, show the judge often where you are going. Let him know what's coming next. Surprise him only with your efficiency, clarity, the extent of your knowledge, and the assurance shown in your problem solving.

- Use non-lawyerly language where possible: this demonstrates confidence in the simplicity of your argument. It follows the philosophy (unknown to most lawyers) that less is more and small is beautiful: small words; economical sentences; short documents; the exception being only the conclusion, where lawyers' custom is to write less than they should.[4]

- Use short paragraphs, on average less than 100 words or five sentences. If you vary the length while keeping them short you will have two or more paragraphs on the page. Visual variety is appealing to the reader. If you can begin each paragraph with an express or implied reference to the previous one you build a 'word bridge' to ensure that the narrative flows easily from one paragraph to the next.

- Do not 'argue by adverb':[5] 'clearly', 'obviously', 'undeniably', 'patently', 'undoubtedly' or use them in a different form e.g. 'it is plain that.' Let the judge formulate his own view based on substantive argument and reference to the evidence.

---

3 See for example *Hinz v Berry* [1970] 2 QB 40 at 42; *Lloyds Bank Plc v Bundy* [1975] QB 326 at 334.

4 Pannill. op.cit.

5 Garner *The Winning Brief* op.cit. Ch.79.

- De-clutter the text by moving citations into footnotes. Write in such a way that the reader will never have to look mid-sentence at what authorities you are relying upon.[6] He can focus on what you are saying, and then look for support for your propositions as a matter of choice after he has considered the argument.

- Use questions. They tend to arouse the curiosity of the judge and therefore command his attention more than, say, an incomplete sentence used as a heading.

- End sentences with an assertion. To write forcefully do not end a sentence with a name, a date, citation or a qualifying phrase.

Since you are writing creatively it wouldn't go amiss to adopt the advice of professional writers. For example, George Orwell promoted five basic rules for the use of language in his essay writing:[7]

1. Never use a metaphor, simile or other figure of speech which you are used to seeing in print.

2. Never use a long word where a short one will do.

3. If it is possible to cut out a word, always cut it out.

4. Never use the passive voice where you can use the active. It makes the writing easier to read and feel more vivid and lively.

5. Never use a foreign phrase, a scientific word, or a jargon word where there is an everyday English equivalent. Translate them into everyday English words or leave them out.

And if you want to develop a literary style that uses English at its best, even when idiomatic, study Francis Bacon, Winston Churchill and Ernest Hemingway or writers known to you for good English usage. For excellence in judicial writing look at the speeches of Lord Devlin in *McCutcheon v David McBrayne Ltd.*,[8] Lord Wilberforce in *Anns v Merton L.B.C.*[9] and in *Ansiminic v Foreign Compensation Commission*,[10] Lord Lloyd of Berwick in *Marc Rich & Co v Bishop Rock Ltd*[11] (dissenting), and compare the speech of Lord Goff in the

---

6 Ibid. Ch.22.

7 *Politics and the English Language* George Orwell 4 *Collected Essays*, Journalism, Letters of George Orwell (New York 1968).

8 [1964] 1 WLR 125at132.

9 [1978] AC 728 at 749.

10 [1969] 2 AC 147 at 206.

11 [1996] AC 211 at 218.

House of Lords in *White v Jones*[12] with the judgment of Sir Donald Nicholls V-C (as he then was) in that case in the Court of Appeal.[13]

Good legal writing, as exemplified here, actually reduces the number of legalisms. Such judges simplify jargon without affecting its meaning and do not take many words to do so. They use verbs that are strong and precise. They avoid double and multiple negatives, unnecessary Latin, legal formalisms (such as 'the said' 'hereinbefore' 'thereinafter'), and keep facts straightforward, unembellished and minimise the use of adjectives and adverbs.

Through vast experience in writing the judges point the way with certain other literary tips which they have recognised when honing careful reserved judgments: they tend to avoid tiresome repetitions including a party's status and name, authorities which have to be cited extensively and references to judges and jurisdiction. They are careful with acronyms. They use shorthand terms that assist understanding. Often they refer to people and companies by name rather than status to aid clarity and avoid confusion in a multi-party or secondary level matter. They avoid clichés, slang and contemporary idiom, which may pass out of everyday speech more quickly than we would imagine.

You can improve the clarity of your own writing with some basic guidance in English usage, and you may find much assistance in standard books on the subject.[14] From among many rules of style the following are particularly useful:

- Don't use *however* to start a sentence, use *but* instead. It quickens the prose and strengthens contrast.

- Change '*pursuant to*' to '*under*' or '*according to*'.

- Remove ambiguity in sentence structure by ensuring the words '*that*' or '*which*' immediately follow the noun they refer to. Use '*that*' to identify the object about which you are speaking. The word '*which*' provides further information about the object.

- Restrict the use of '*such*' '*said*' and '*same*' as pronouns or as demonstrative adjectives.

- Use dashes to highlight interruptive phrases – not parentheses – as they are far more useful for rhythm and emphasis.

---

12 [1995] 2 AC 207 at 252.

13 [1995] 2 AC 207 at 216.

14 See e.g. Garner op.cit.; *The Chicago Manual of Style* (16th edn Chicago Press 2010); *The Economist Style Guide 2010*.

- Avoid gratuitous quotation marks and typographical oddities.
- Don't irritate the judge with the incorrect use of apostrophes.
- The lead sentence of any block of writing is immensely important. Begin each paragraph with a topic sentence (but do not repeat the title, heading or subheading). This lets the reader know the focus of the paragraph. Do not end the preceding paragraph with what should be the first sentence of the next paragraph.

A literary style for lawyers

Having mastered a basic approach which suits your use of language, look for opportunities to grab the court's interest by using an engaging turn of phrase or unusual word to make a point, perhaps from outside the law – but one that is not clichéic or slang.[15]

It is important to remember that argumentative writing is not too concerned with beautiful English and does not have to be overly lyrical or discursive. Passages of argument should be forceful since advocates are not and should not be impartial. Look in particular at dissenting judgments as a source of good and forceful legal writing. Here the judge is justifying his opinion to his brethren who disagree, and as a minority he is doing so knowing he will not influence the immediate result. He hopes that his view may be accepted on appeal, or by specialist practitioners in the area under consideration, or at some point in the future, and his writing has to be all the better to give force to his argument. In doing so he must reign in any emotion both about the case, and about being put in the minority and therefore seeing the wrong side win. Emotive language is unnecessary. The facts and law should speak for themselves.

Davis recommended[16] that a safe stylistic structure is "chronology, candour and clarity". Chronology, because that is the natural way in which to tell a story; candour – telling the worst as well as the best, because the court has a right to hear it and any lack of candour, whether real or apparent, will destroy the most carefully laid argument. And clarity, which cannot be accomplished without clear thought and argument, because the heart of advocacy is persuasion. So make one point at a time. Edit systematically. Cut out and replace words as necessary. Polish the language. Check for misused words. And cut down sentence lengths wherever possible.

---

15 Pannill. op.cit.

16 Davis *The Argument of an Appeal* op.cit.

Document design

It is apparent from the comments of judges and practitioners in Chapters 2 and 3 that you must use a legible typeface and ample white space. But you can modify the text to make it more visually attractive. For example, highlight ideas with attention-getters such as indented bullets,

- which are particularly useful for presenting important ideas in lists.

Use charts, diagrams and visual aids when you can. Graphics break up text, add interest, and can be used to present information that is difficult or lengthy to describe in words. Use a table of contents for longer documents. This can itself be a persuasive document (see p. 61).

In terms of visual effect, where you are using white space put more above a heading than below it. According to research by Garner[17] white space above a heading informs readers to expect a change of subject; below suggests that the next writing functions as a unit.

Headings

For the design of a descending sequence of headings, the various manuals of style suggest: Roman boldface large; boldface; boldface italic; italic. These may be underlined as you consider appropriate. Headings should not be divided into two sentences. This weakens their assertiveness when introducing passages of argument. You should ensure that they are both consistent and will not generate judicial disbelief or resistance on a first reading.[18]

Cross-references

Your page design must accommodate cross-references to pagination in exhibits, the appropriate bundles and other documentary evidence. It is imperative for you to support all assertions of fact by reference to their appearance in the evidence. In appellate skeletons particular reference will be made to the judgment and findings of fact of the judge below. When arguing law in an appeal, it is effective and convenient to state "for the purposes of this appeal we accept the facts found by the trial judge at ..."

---

17 Garner *The Winning Brief* op.cit. Ch.65.

18 Weiner op.cit. p.71.

Footnotes

Do not use footnotes in skeletons merely as a show of erudition. Use them for citation references and qualifications to statements or secondary points that would otherwise interrupt thought if they remained in the text. Minimise the interruptions to the judge's progress through your submissions. Let him concentrate on the primary information. Never use them for substantive argument, e.g. parallel lines of argument – to do so detracts appreciably from the force of your contentions.[19] If a point is important it belongs in the text; if not, it does not belong in the skeleton.[20]

Textual enhancement

Try not to insult to the judicial reader's intelligence. To that end only use italics sparingly and preferably to cite names of authorities and for headings. It is perfectly possible to write a forceful skeleton without using a single word italicised for emphasis. Do not use capitals for emphasis. Resist the temptation to use bold in the text.

Citation

Put all citations in footnotes. Otherwise you hamper the coherency of your substantive argument and break the narrative flow. Taking citations out of the text increases readability and understanding dramatically. As it is, citations should be unobtrusive and used sparingly. Unless absolutely necessary you should refer only to leading and recent cases. Remember, when quoting passages of dicta, absolute and unswerving accuracy must be the goal. Inaccuracies of substance are particularly unforgivable and always dangerous. Courts particularly dislike a citation to fact A when all that citation establishes is fact B from which you proceed to draw an inference that fact A exists.[21] This must stem from a linguistic as much as a legal error.

---

19 Ibid. p.245. But cf. Example F at p.153 and Example G at p.170 *et seq* generally.

20 Ibid. p.246.

21 Ibid. p.222.

6 The Technique of Persuasion in Writing

Organisation

The mechanics of presenting your client's case in the most effective and cogent manner should be little different whether your argument is oral or written, but the written argument provides you with a significant benefit. The distinction to the recipient is that the listener hears, notes what he wants from the presentation, listens to something else and then returns later to consider what impression you made; the reader has something complete in tangible form to keep and scrutinise at length. If your work passes muster with the judge, and impresses him by the persuasiveness of your argument, he will carry it away as a reader to make use of, to your client's advantage. If it does not, he will discard it, and you will have failed your client.

In theory the task of writing persuasively should be straight forward: identify the points you wish to convey; state them cogently with adequate reasoning and support, and offer a workable solution to the judge which enables him to do substantive justice. The reality is that many lawyers fail through lack of organisation. There is an inadequate architectural structure to their writing. Lawyers act too quickly and think too little.[1] Writing involves thinking too, and revising, cutting back and simplifying the argument to perfect its flow.

You will have observed in chapter 5 not to commence writing your argument until you have carried out a sound analysis of the legal problem, researched your authorities, and you fully understand what you are to write about. Then try the following method:

- Start with a working statement of the issues.
- Draft these before writing anything else in order to keep your attention focussed.
- Break down each legal problem into its component parts.
- Determine which are principal and which subsidiary issues.

---

1 Garner *The Winning Brief* op.cit.Ch.2.

- Decide in what order to present the points, and how many you wish to advance without overwhelming the reader.

You may consider there should be one principal point of attack or defence only, together with two or three material subordinate points.

Remember that an argument is written to persuade. It should pull no punches, but it must be honest, and it must be accurate.[2]

Ensure that all matters required by the respective jurisdictional rules are there, whether the Civil Procedure Rules, Supreme Court Rules, Family Procedure Rules, Criminal Procedure Rules or particular tribunal practice notes or directions. Compliance with basic requirements is an imperative.

Using the facts to persuade

The facts are always the most important part of the skeleton. I shall say that again. The facts are always the most important part of the skeleton. If you can explain the facts clearly and completely, you will take a giant step towards persuading the court since generally there is no trouble over the law, not only because the law flows from the facts but so also does the equity of the case. If the equity of the case is with you, even if it takes a trip to the Supreme Court, you should win.

Tell a complete story arranging the facts in a logical, usually chronological order. Recite the facts fairly. Never misstate them. Highlight what is crucial. Let them be sufficient to enable the court to receive your narrative without having to supplement it by its own independent efforts,[3] but not in stultifying detail. Marshal the topics according to the development of the argument, dealing with evidence relating to each logical progression. Make sure the judge's interest does not flag and is carried forward in the direction you wish to take him.

Writing out the facts forces you to understand and organise the evidence in your own mind in a way that reading alone will not. It enables you to see logical connections, and to focus on using the facts alone to persuade without argument.[4]

Do not argue or editorialise, since it is better always to be straightforward. You want the court to feel it is getting the facts, not your opinion, comments or contentions. Indicate conflict where it exists. Strive to make the most favourable impression with the facts without actually arguing, by being

---

2 Weiner op.cit. 274.

3 Ibid. 45.

4 Ibid. 44.

honest, candid and accurate. And try to progress in a way that makes your conclusion irresistible – you want to analyse the facts so that they alone will make the court want to decide in your favour.[5]

Choosing the battle ground

Justice Frankfurter of the United States Supreme Court said 'In law the right answer usually depends on putting the right question.'[6] This is as true of our own courts and in particular the Court of Appeal. The phrasing of the question or issue to be decided is therefore of the utmost importance. If you can pose the question in a way which most effectively impels the reader to answer it as you want, you are choosing the battleground on which your litigation or application will be contested, with all the advantages of that choice.

Most courts expect the question or issue for decision to be formulated in a neutral way and agreed by the parties, invariably following a case management direction to that effect. Within such constraints you must select your own battleground wherever possible – do not permit opposing counsel to choose it for you. Never accept issues as framed by the other side. Wherever possible you should always re-work them to favour yourself. The aim is to frame issues as questions, to which the only reasonable response is, 'yes, of course'.[7] If you can do so, apply the technique of constructing the question or issue from salient facts or relevant citations which, while fairly stated, is strongly suggestive of an answer in your client's favour. The facts must be fairly stated – your opponent can have no objection to their inclusion as facts – and accurate, or this approach will backfire and prejudice you in the eyes of the court.

Not all situations are suitable for formulating the question presented by loading it with facts favourable to you. In particular where the factual merits are not with you it is not desirable to remind the court of this at the outset of the hearing. But even where the merits are not with you it should be possible for you to construct your case in the form of a question, usually using the word 'whether', in a way that is clearly and appealingly stated.

The position is even better defined on appeal. When seeking permission for an appellant to bring an appeal you must dress up questions invitingly in order to ensure the higher court will want to take the case. If acting for a respondent you want to preserve the status quo ante by adopting any premise in your client's favour found by the judge – you must minimise the

---

5 Pannill op.cit.

6 *Estate of Rogers v Comm'r* (1943) 320 US 410 at 413.

7 Ursula Bentele and Eve Cary *Appellate Advocacy: Principles and Practice* paperback edn 2004 333.

effect of questions raised by your adversary and make them appear unimportant or uninteresting to anyone other than parties involved or as turning on mere questions of fact.[8] Do so without belittling your opponent, and if the question is obviously of importance do not urge that it is unimportant: rather say the decision does not require further review.[9]

Conveying the issues

Since the court does not have luxury of time for detached contemplation never force the court to guess, even for a moment, the issues it will have to decide. They should be stated so simply and so clearly that the judge will grasp them at once. Give a sense of introduction to generate interest – do not miss the opportunity of capturing the judge's interest at the outset. It is part of your task to make a favourable first impression that will last.

To frame a good persuasive issue:

- Put it up front.
- Break it into separate sentences using a format based on asserting a fact, stating a premise that flows from the fact, then raising the legal issue to be decided by the court.
- Weave in enough facts so that the reader can truly understand the problem, but summarise – don't over particularise.
- Present each issue in a way that suggests that there is only one possible answer: the one you want.
- Phrase the issues in separate sentences.
- Use a maximum sentence length of no more than 15–20 words.
- Do not start with 'Whether'[10] or any other interrogative word ('Why', 'Where', 'How', or 'What'.
- Wherever possible use 'Can', 'Is', 'Should', 'Must', and 'Was' since these tend to push the reader towards the desired answer.

---

8 Weiner op.cit.80.

9 Ibid.

10 See Garner *Legal Writing in Plain English* op. cit. 58. *Quaere* unless you know the factual merits are not with you: contrast with p.57.

- Limit the total of the issues to a maximum of about 75 words, or five sentences. If you cannot do so you do not have a sufficient understanding to be able to convey the issues clearly to the reader.

The consistent theme of these suggestions is that issues raised before the court should not be merely informative, they should be influential too. You are writing them fairly but persuasively. The way issues are written will govern the court's first impression of the merits. Put each matter simply, concisely and accurately, without overstatement or being strident.[11]

If you provide the question, the judge will not have to; if you don't, the judge may formulate a question you do not want. It is therefore vital to give the judge the issue, to pose the question he must answer, and to pose the answer. Your skeleton will thus provide him with the justification for finding in your favour.

Advancing your argument

So we come to the nub of the matter – constructing your winning argument on paper. There seem to be two typical approaches, which I will call the logical development and the early knockout blow. Either way your goal is to write an argument your opponent cannot answer. For both if anything, err on the side of understatement. This forces you to build up your case by citing successive references to the evidence.

Whether logical development or knockout blow, find the strongest point in your case and lead with it. Be brief and to the point. Demonstrate fairness, justice, practicality and principle, but grab your opponent by the throat with the very first sentence of your argument and say something positive. Where you can, seize upon the central feature of the case and drive it home, shutting out anything for your adversary.

If you are creating an argument based on logical progression elaborate the legal premises and show how the facts fit. Imagine you are creating a flow chart. You proceed in a logical step-by-step progression where you must prevail on every point in order to win. If you come to a juncture in the argument where alternatives present themselves, place the most appealing one first, i.e. that which will meet the least judicial resistance to accepting the fact or the premise or the legal principle, being advanced.

Where one alternative involves requesting the court to overturn an unfavourable recently considered decision and the other has a clear path not so obstructed, always argue the latter first due to the effect on the court on the former. Occasionally a situation will call for grasping the nettle firmly

---

11 Garner *The Winning Brief* op.cit. Ch. 11.

and dealing with a really difficult point at the outset. Do not go back and forth. Stick to one course.[12]

If there is no logical sequence to adopt, you require the knockout blow strategy. Advance first the point that goes to the very heart of the matter. Build your argument around the court doing substantive justice by accepting your submissions on that point. If you have sufficient evidence to support your proposition, your opponent will have nowhere to go.

- Always remember that you are performing an exercise in persuasion.
- Do not fight the court on unessential propositions, either general or specific.
- Do not make your argument a crusade – it will diminish its effectiveness
- Keep your emotions to yourself

Using argumentative headings

This is a technique recommended by both Weiner[13] and Pannill[14] which is generally unfamiliar in this jurisdiction where judges have indicated that generally they prefer neutral headings. It is this: in passages of argument the headings and sub-headings should not be merely topical or even assertive, but must be argumentative. For example an argument concerning limitation gives you these options:

Topical heading (the label):

> 'Limitation'

Assertive heading (the statement):

> 'The Claim Is Barred By Limitation'

Argumentative heading (incorporating the contention):

> 'The claim is time barred having been issued after six years from the date of accrual of the cause of action pleaded.'

The argumentative heading is more wordy but effective. It tells the judge immediately and in a nutshell what your case is on the point. It goes straight to the heart of the issue. If used for each separate contentious matter, the

---

12 Weiner op.cit. 96.

13 Weiner op.cit. 67,68.

14 Pannill op.cit.

court will see instantly the progression and substance of your argument. If you learn to use this technique with flair, you should be able to create memorable headings that are single sentence summaries of your case which will become fixed in the mind of the judge. In that sense this is an opportunity that an advocate should not waste.

If you do adopt this style there are some basic rules to remember:

- Always set out your contentions affirmatively not negatively.
- The 'argumentative' element requires you to say why you make an assertion.
- The heading must be sufficiently detailed and specific so your reader knows the precise substance and scope of your argument, but at the same time, succinct.
- Never follow a main heading immediately with a single sub-heading. If you are unable to follow the argument without more than one sub-heading the main heading has not been correctly formulated and needs rewriting.
- If you are using an argumentative heading, the sub-headings should be argumentative as well.

Weiner suggested[15] that the absence of full and detailed argumentative headings detracts materially from the effectiveness of a skeleton argument, albeit that the text of the argument must be complete without the need for the court to refer back to the heading or to read footnotes. There are two other advantages. First, by carefully reviewing your headings and subheadings you will see the progression of your argument and can ensure completeness. This will also help strengthen any necessary revisions. Second, if you have a long document that warrants a list of contents, the court will glean the whole flow of the argument merely by looking at the contents page.

If you are uncomfortable with this idea and find it too alien, at least make the headings you use within your argument assertive. Avoid verbless headings e.g. 'Introduction', 'The Limitation Point', 'Damages' which are merely labels. Do not use blind sub-headings, i.e. those that give the reader no clue as to what the substance of the following argument will be. Do not use argumentative sub-headings when introducing the facts at the outset of the document. And do not repeat headings in the substantive text, particularly in the opening words of the next paragraph.

---

15 Op.cit. 69, 70.

Marshalling facts in argument

All cases turn on their facts. However frequently they turn not on the facts *simpliciter*, but on how they are arranged, and therefore how the judge views the factual matrix. Or, for your purpose, how the judge is guided to that matrix. Do not just line them up repeating, as it were, the introduction to your skeleton. Use facts as part of the argument by stating what you intend to show in three steps:

1. make an assertion;
2. present the facts to support that assertion;
3. submit what conclusion is to be derived from your presentation.

Marshal the evidence to make it thoroughly convincing to the judicial reader. Lay it out using quotations from documents stressing any inconsistencies in the case against you. Make sure the extracts you cite are accurate, being taken verbatim from the evidence. Highlight, in particular, any discrepancies or contradictions between your opponent's documents and his witness statements, or any damaging passages from contemporaneously made letters or notes. Whatever you can find, you must make the facts work for you. In an argument you will either rely upon such inferences as are to be drawn from undisputed facts or you will have to argue frankly a conclusion from disputed facts.[16]

Argument and reasoning

The supporting reasons for the conclusion you are urging are the key to success.[17] Do not fall into the trap of merely repeating your own opinion on the matter using different words, since that will not be enough. You have to make the judge agree with you, either by allowing him to form his own conclusions from the way the facts are presented[18] or by constructing some attractive reasoning that will connect with him. Merely asserting the rightness of your client's position is not a convincing argument: you have to establish in the judge's mind why your position is correct and what the implications of a decision in your client's favour will be.

More often than not it will be easier to negate the value of your opponent's position. To that end your reasoning can be wide enough to focus on whether what you want the court to do is both fair according to the merits,

---

16 Ibid. 115.

17 Garner *The Winning Brief* op. cit. Ch.13. 18.

18 Ibid.

and right under the circumstances and, where necessary, that it is good public policy.

Supporting your argument

It is clear from what judges want[19] that you should not crowd your argument with long quotations from the reports and offer multiple citations. It is better to cite a few leading and controlling decisions than assemble an encyclopaedic collection, although keeping them proportionate (I knew that wretched word would get in somewhere) to the case in hand.

A citation on all fours is likely to be weakened if accompanied by others only having a tangential bearing on the issue. You should go for the most recent decisions covering broad principle in the highest jurisdiction available, and avoid valueless authority i.e. cases that do not bind the court in question, or where the key question is evidential, or where the question is secondary or essentially illustrative.[20] You should keep the support for your argument vital.

You may have a strong temptation to show off your learning with what writers have called ornamental citation.[21] Occasionally this bit of vanity may give your submission an appealing overtone of erudition that a court may respect, if it does not interfere with or detract from the main stream of argument. Every once in a while the search for an ornamental citation pays off and compensates for what may also be seen as a vulgarly ostentatious display of learning.

There is a fairly basic approach you can use to support your argument:

- Get the citation right i.e. the approved designated reference: do not irritate the judge with mistaken citation references or misspelt names of well-known cases.

- Use accepted typographical conventions i.e. do not use personal abbreviations.

- Know and follow the Practice Directions on the citation of authorities and the order of citation.[22]

- Say something critical about the cases you cite – how and why they apply. Put them in context.

---

19 See chapter 2.

20 Weiner op.cit. 206, 208–9.

21 Ibid. 212.

22 Practice Direction (Citation of Authorities) [2001] 1 WLR 1001.

- Never quote elementary propositions.
- Never quote sentences out of context, unless you want to gift ammunition to the other side.
- Quote only when the quotation adds something to the proposition being asserted. This does not preclude you from using the language of a judge who has expressed something far better than you can.
- Use a quotation where:
    - the statement for which you seek support is insufficient to satisfy the curiosity of the reader;
    - you are relying on unfamiliar decisions – areas of the law untouched for some time;
    - your materials are obscure and not readily accessible to the court;
    - where the support for your point cannot fairly be summarised;
    - where it is necessary to go back to fundamentals in a situation where later authorities have developed and altered the original proposition of law to be advanced;[23]
    - where there is a clear diversity of opinion, or where the court below has apparently disregarded settled law.
- When abbreviating your repeat citation references use *supras* and *infras* sparingly. Judges do not like to have to go back and forth to find references.[24] Repeat the reference at least to the name of the case.
- Never cite an overruled case.

Irrespective of their source, the accuracy of your quotations is imperative. You must check carefully against the original to prevent significant words or even whole lines dropping out or becoming distorted. This is particularly the case where lawyers use dictation to prepare. Errors in transcription can be a significant problem for the judge, and the impact of a judge discovering that he cannot rely upon you may be disastrous.

Persuasive argument is the product of careful research, of unearthing authority, of dealing with trends – especially at appellate level – and of identifying whether the judge will extend an existing trend in a particular

---

23 Weiner op.cit. 211.

24 Ibid. 222.

direction and, if so, by how much, and whether he is likely to want to do so. Confine your law to the vital statute, or the strongest cases at the highest level. Identify the essential passages – as few as possible – and then apply the law to the facts, point by point. Where there is no obvious authority use analysis, reason, logic, credible analogy, legislative history, social history and invite the court to consider what the practical solution should be.

Remember that citing authority is not an end in itself. It is only the means by which your argument gains legal weight. Therefore ensure that your legal argument contains appropriate references to the facts as agreed or in contention or on appeal to the facts as found, the evidence paginated according to the trial bundles, and where appropriate the procedural history of the claim or appeal.

The value of candour

You must be candid with the Court to preserve its goodwill. Never intentionally misstate a position, either affirmatively or by omission. There is no such thing as a white lie. You must be fair, honest and accurate. This does not preclude you from using emphasis or nuance to advance facts in their most favourable light, as long as you don't exceed the limits of accuracy. Consider this – if you lose the trust of the Court on the facts it may not take the law from you: *falsus in uno, falsus in omnibus*.[25] The misstatement of facts by you will impeach your argument as much as a bad witness.

In spite of some of the survey results that I have referred to from experienced practitioners[26] the advice of Weiner,[27] Pannill[28] and Garner[29] is sound – grasp your nettles firmly: tell the Court about facts that hurt you, or your opponent will, and no matter how unfavourable they are, they will hurt you more if the Court finds out about the from your opponent or worse, by itself. Draw the sting and deal with all pertinent facts. Do not gloss over them but present them as best you can, indicating how you will deal with them.

Arguments in reply

You must deal with the counter-arguments and do so firmly, in keeping with the credo of dealing with your weaknesses and grasping nettles firmly. But do not reiterate them. The purpose of your argument is to persuade the court that your position is the correct one: restating the other side's

25 Weiner op.cit. 49.

26 See Chapter 3.

27 Op.cit. 104.

28 Op.cit.

29 *Legal Writing in Plain English* op.cit. 85.

contentions will not help you do that. There is also a real danger that you may re-state the other side's argument better than they have said it. If your opponent establishes that a point you have made is bad, concede it where it is possible to do so without fundamentally undermining your case.

If you are responding to an appeal always support the merits of the decision appealed against before dealing with any jurisdictional or legal argument. If an altogether new point is taken, reply to it directly. If the other side confuses an issue, make a short reply re-clarifying the situation. But if matters are accepted or issues are clear do not burden the court with more reading matter. To draw to the attention of the court a misstatement by the other side – not a minor error – it must be both material and significant since the Court dislikes point scoring. Do not give in to the impulse to get in the last word by putting in additional skeletons unless it is vital and you have the Court's permission to do so. You are justified only where you are meeting a request by the Court to deal with something missing.

Work out how to handle the authorities which are being used against you. Ignore precedent only when you can afford to, either because it is off the point or you can properly argue that the law, or indeed society, has moved on. Distinguish boldly, using broad grounds rather than finicky analysis.[30] Use dissenting opinion, particularly where it is expressed in strong terms. Avoid stirring up opposition on non-essential or collateral matters. Sometimes the answer is in a painstaking analysis of the controlling statute. Where that might be so, consider the setting and social context of the particular provision then check its legislative history and, where you have time, the parliamentary papers.

Matters to avoid

There are a number of common faults[31] that are bound to backfire in a costly way if you commit them. I have already touched on most of these but they are important enough to repeat for emphasis:

1. Avoid inexcusable inaccuracy. Know your case, and know the facts.

2. Don't exaggerate: if a lawyer exaggerates the facts he is simply asking for trouble.

3. Keep emotional content to yourself: it is unnecessary to involve the Court on an emotional level directly. Strong facts will speak for themselves, particularly if they are shocking. In particular, emotive language is frowned upon in appellate courts.

---

30 Weiner op.cit. 152–3.

31 Weiner op.cit. 61.

4. Avoid involving the Court in collateral inquiries as to the personality or conduct of lawyers on the opposing side. This will generally embarrass a judge. If the issue is there the Court will identify and raise it.

5. Do not waste time in emphasising elementary propositions. Allow the judge some intelligence.

6. Do not magnify trivia.

7. Abandon wherever possible weak propositions or questions in which you have no faith. The ability to discern weak points and the willingness to discard them constitutes the mark of a really able lawyer.[32] It requires real courage and self-confidence as an advocate to dispense with weaker points, particularly where your client wants you to press everything, or where you hope the Court will not spot the weakness. Their inclusion only serves to weaken the rest of your argument: to include a weak point is virtually certain to dilute every strong one.

8. Try not to evade difficult issues, either by not mentioning them at all or by relegating them to footnotes.[33] You cannot expect a central issue in a case to be glossed over. Do not ignore portions of opposing counsel's argument or his authorities on the basis that they are unfavourable to you. Deal with them. Grasp your nettles firmly.

9. Don't use arguments that appear to be those of last resort. They send a signal to the Court that your case is hopeless.

10. Avoid an out-and-out request to overrule an unhelpful precedent: ask for the case to be distinguished on one of many bases.[34] Courts are reluctant to say, in terms, that previous cases were wrongly decided, because continuity in the law or at least the appearance of continuity is important; judges are much more inclined to distinguish in order to do practical justice. This is one of the few occasions in which it profits you for your advocacy to be oblique.

11. Do not attack or criticise previous counsel. It does you no credit, and is a matter for the Court to raise if it wants to.

---

32 Ibid. 96.

33 Ibid. 104.

34 See Andrew Goodman *How Judges Decide Cases: Reading, Writing and Analysing Judgments* xpl 2005 pp.146–151.

Using a conclusion

Write a conclusion that is powerful and assertive. You need to close in a strong way, rather than formulaically, with a weak phrase such as 'for the above reasons.' It is tempting to do so and close the piece of work, but it wastes an opportunity to say something memorable by way of a summary of your case. If the Court is pressed for time it may be one of first things the judge reads; if you are unlucky it may be the only thing he has time to read. So don't be afraid to summarise and make it long enough to be effective. Use two or three sentences to remind the judge of your reasoning, and why it should prevail. Make it as appealing as possible, going beyond a mere assertion, although it should be a synopsis and not say anything new. For that reason you should compose it last of all.

Make sure that you end your document by telling the court precisely what relief you seek so the judge never has to ask. Be specific about it, so that the Court's order will be likewise.

7 The Art of Précis for Lawyers

Under the rules of case management argument today seems to be hedged about by strict limitations on time. At every level of jurisdiction judges feel the pressure of business and the desire for economy by advocates. The rapid pace of change in the law, and particularly procedural law, appears to limit what the judicial eye and ear is prepared to absorb. So there is a real need for the use of précis by lawyers – the method of preparing a salient summary of the points – at a time when that exercise in the use of written English is no longer taught in our schools.

The art of précis is not merely a method of shortening a piece of writing. It is a technique for improving clarity by condensing the amount of prose without losing its meaning.

You should plan to edit written submissions twice, once for substance and once for style. Good editing is very important. Sometimes you will find annoying errors even when reading through for a third time. If you are able to do so, leave some time between editing and your final read through. Come back to it with a fresh critical eye.

What to do if your document is too long

You should not shorten an essay by hacking out pieces in a way that destroys the meaning. Instead, see if you can improve the meaning by making the essay less verbose and more precise. This is entirely consistent with the message of chapter 6: try to replace clumsy or dull prose with shorter, snappier words to hold the reader's interest. Persuasive writing must grab the court's attention and hold it for the duration of the argument:

- *Be precise*
  Do you always know what you are saying, or are there places where you are just throwing words in? Replace vague passages that do not say anything important, and passages that ramble, with sentences that are to the point.

- *Focus*
  Try focusing your writing more on the title, headings or sub-headings of the document, and then check to see that the body of the text sticks to

what you focused on and does not wander all over the place. Remove material that is not relevant to what you say you are doing.

- *Understand what you write*
  As a general rule, do not write anything you do not understand. If you fully understand what you are writing, you should be able to control it. This should include being able both to expand it and make it more concise. If you write what you do not understand, in the hope that that is the right thing to say, you will have lost control of your writing. Some arguments are difficult to follow because authorities have been relied upon with no true understanding of their meaning. Passages cited are often too long as well, as the writer does not know what to cut out. If this is what you do, remember –you need to think the problem through and plan before putting pen to paper.

- *Use effective literary techniques*
  Omit surplus words.[1] Use the active not passive voice. Avoid compound constructions. Remove common word wasters – 'the fact that', 'the question as to whether' 'there is' or 'there are', 'it is', 'there have been,' 'I might add,' 'it is interesting to note,' 'it is important to bear in mind,' 'it should not be forgotten' – and hackneyed and unnecessary phrases, such as 'at this point in time' (now), 'take action' (act), 'make an assumption' (assume). Use short words as well as short sentences: e.g. 'use' not 'utilise'. You want to end up with clear, crisp, economical writing.

  - Avoid lawyerisms: 'hereinafter' 'heretofore' 'on point' 'on all fours' 'may I respectfully suggest'.

  - Remove double negatives.

  - If short, related sentences are kept to one main thought they may be combined. Minimise the use of adjectives and adverbs.

  - Use strong descriptive nouns and verbs. Avoid long conjunctions: 'nevertheless' 'notwithstanding' 'furthermore' 'inasmuch as' 'howsoever' 'consequently'. Garner says[2] is it really necessary to have four syllables? They are old fashioned, stilted and pompous.

  - Simplify wordy prepositions:[3] 'with respect to,' 'as to,' 'in order to,' 'in connection with,' 'as regards to,' 'in respect of,' 'according as to whether'.

---

1 "Unnecessary words waste space and the reader's time and they make strong writing weak" *The Elements of Technical Writing* 65 (1993) Gary Blake and Robert W. Bly.

2 *The Winning Brief* op.cit. Ch.45.

3 Ibid. Ch.46.

Using ways like this should improve the skeleton argument and shorten it at the same time.

The précis exercise

Précising and paraphrasing are good practice for any lawyer, and any piece of writing can be reduced by this exercise. Lawyers in fact do use précis often, since they almost always create a summary of the facts of the case and an abstract of their client's position or argument.

In the traditional précis students reduce a passage of writing to a third or a quarter of its original length by taking these steps:

1. Read through the whole passage to get an overall view;

2. Read it through again, underlining each point that needs to be included;

3. Write a summary of the passage with all the underlined points in the appropriate order, omitting all unnecessary matter;

4. Compare the summary with the original and add anything of importance that has been left out;

5. Check the approximate length to see how close to the length aimed at has been achieved;

6. Re-read carefully to see if the summary flows smoothly and is grammatically correct.

8 Tasks before Lodging

You have completed your document. You have printed it out. You have expended your effort. You are ready to send it off. But you have not finished.

Checking for accuracy

However mundane you feel the task to be, you must check meticulously all materials for accuracy and completeness:

- that the citation references are correct;
- that statutes have not been amended and provisions relied on are in force;
- that you have not misquoted dicta or legislation, or, for example, missed out a line;
- that you are not relying upon a case which was scrutinised on appeal, or was criticised or even overturned by a case in this morning's case alerter or *The Times*; and
- that references to exhibits and pagination in the trial, application or appeal bundle are correct.

A skeleton argument or written submissions in any form can not be proof read too often or too carefully, because nothing quite so destroys a court's confidence in a lawyer or in his argument as when it finds he has made inaccurate statements, either through carelessness or through design.[1] If at all possible find a willing (or not so willing) assistant, pupil or colleague to check citations, quotations and references for accuracy 'as your eye is likely to see what you intended, not what's on the page'.[2]

Filing

Regard the judge as a consumer. Offer him written submissions on a disc from which he can take parts of the key judgments or statutes you cite, and hopefully incorporate your submissions into his findings. Providing your

---

1 Garner *The Winning Brief* op.cit. Ch.7.

2 Weiner op.cit. at p.203.

document in electronic form is essential when producing closing submissions for a trial and for appeals where judgment is likely reserved. Remember, if the Court asks for electronic transmission of your skeleton it is for use, not for record keeping.

Taking a step back

There are two exercises that may help your final overview of the document you have produced.

- First, read it out aloud. You will get a better sense of how you want readers to hear what you have to say.

- Second, read the argument without reference to the authorities, examples, or evidence to see whether your discussion is convincing by itself.

The clarity test

Get others to help you assess the clarity of your argument. Try to explain it orally to a non-lawyer. If you cannot give an easy explanation, your writing will probably reflect that. Try this out on your partner or spouse – they are secure enough to offer honest critiques.

Impress yourself

The effective skeleton is one that puts you in a winning position before the judge enters the court. It persuades the court to follow your analysis of the problem and rely on the authorities you have cited. It must be sufficient by itself to convince the judge, so that if other side does not file one, you should win: you will have satisfied any doubt the tribunal may have and sated its appetite for asking questions.

So finally stand well back, metaphorically speaking, as you consider the overall impact of what you have created. Allow yourself to be impressed. If you feel not just happy with what you have produced, not merely that it will pass muster, but that you have fashioned a really good piece of work, so will the judge.

There are a number of occasions when you are required to settle and file your written skeleton well in advance of the hearing. It is when you come to read it through again, not having seen it for some weeks or months, that there will be instances when you stop and think 'Wow! Did I write that!' So try to impress yourself! Often.

Part 3
What Successful Advocates Provide: Worked Examples

9 Introduction to Worked Examples

In order to establish what successful advocates provide I considered the views and work of 15 highly respected silks (QCs) from the pinnacle of the profession, and 17 juniors, some of whom worked with the same leaders. This was not a focus group, and those members of the Bar concerned were highly individualistic and strong willed. They knew what they wanted to do. The question of compliance, whether strict or otherwise, with the requirements of the CPR, Family Proceedings, General Criminal or Supreme Court Practice Directions did not arise. However for our purposes, we should take it as read that successful advocates will not deliberately risk antagonising a judge by failing to comply with recognised rules of practice. Even with considerable stylistic differences it became possible to connect their experiences, and to find some commonality of approach in preparing their written advocacy. Each was asked about methodology, style, format and content and, of course, what it is that makes a skeleton argument succeed.

I am extremely grateful to the following for having provided samples of their written advocacy and kindly granted me permission to select from among these worked examples: Lord Faulks QC (with Andrew Warnock, Charles Brown, Sarah Paneth and David Thomson), Simeon Maskrey QC, John Norman, Lord Pannick QC (with Dinah Rose QC, Louise Mably and James Segan), Michael Pooles QC, Spike Charlwood, Roger Stewart QC, Lord Sumption QC (with Guy Philipps QC, David Anderson QC, Rodri Williams QC, Jemima Stratford and Martin Chamberlain), Richard Lissack QC with Keith Morton, Clare Baker and Oliver Assersohn, Ronald Walker QC with Catherine Foster, William Evans and Nigel Lewers, Sue Carr QC with Jonathan Hough, Andrew Hochhauser QC with David Craig and Andrew Mitchell, Dr Michael Powers QC, Simon O'Toole and Thomas Crockett.

In some cases they were concerned to protect the identity of their lay clients, or specific witnesses and locations, and accordingly I have concealed such information. However in cases where this material has been used in open court and any appellate process has been exhausted, and where no objection is taken, I have used the material verbatim. I have provided a very brief introduction, which gives the outcome in each case and says where, if at all, it has been reported. I have indicated the total length of each document since in some examples I have used extracts only, but also to impress upon you how short a good skeleton may be.

The brief commentary I have added in annotated form is intended to highlight the points made earlier in the main text. The use of white space is also intended to enable you to add your own notes, which you should feel free to do, particularly where it is helpful for you to refer back to pages in Parts 1 and 2. At the conclusion of each example I include in bold type a concise 'good practice suggestion' which I hope will be something you either carry out already or may wish to. While there is no standard approach to preparing written submissions, these are matters which, if omitted, the judge is likely to notice.

These are examples of what is essentially an art. They are not intended to be models or precedents, nor could they be. I wanted to show good advocacy in a reasonably wide range of different but effective personal styles of writing, which deal with both facts and law at different levels of tribunal. I have included examples of representation for different sides.

Please remember neither my interviewees nor I can offer a template. Why? Because skeleton arguments are significantly different depending on the purpose for which they are being prepared. That which is required for a case management conference with contested directions will not be the same as one supporting or opposing an application for summary judgment. Written submissions to open or close a trial will not be the same as those needed when the time comes to appeal the outcome of that trial. And in each of these the perspective from the viewpoint of the claimant or defendant is different. These differences in scope and approach are seen in the worked examples from actual cases.

Visual advocacy at trial

One of the advantages of putting submissions into writing, even if skeletal, is the medium of communication itself. It may be that some of the points being advanced are better expressed when reduced to writing, matters which may be difficult to convey in the course of oral argument. Naturally the reverse is true. So, at an early stage of preparation, trial counsel may wish to consider whether the points available are more easily communicated in written or oral form.

At this juncture the judge can be made to use his eyes as well as his ears to promote the better understanding of a case. For example, the use of visual aids – fairly common in the United States – can be a significant tool. Judges do tend to think in literary terms but diagrams are occasionally effective, as has been the experience in construction, technology and admiralty claims, particularly when a method, process or mechanism and its failure, or a very precise course or passage has to be shown. In clinical negligence claims a diagram of parts of the human body, now available on CD-Rom or online with digitally-enhanced 3D imagery is often used to enable judges to see how bodily functions work, and where and how the problem in issue has occurred.

Worked examples

The 16 examples in Part 3 provided are drawn from a wide range of subject matter, types of practice and levels of tribunal. Some arise from well know incidents – for example, the Hillsborough disaster; parliamentary privilege and the prosecution of MPs over expenses claims – some are much more obscure. Represented are both interim and preliminary applications and full opening notes for trials and appeals in the High Court, Queen's Bench and Chancery Divisions, the Commercial Court, the Central Criminal Court and the Crown Court sitting at a regional centre, the Court of Appeal (Civil and Criminal Divisions), the Supreme Court and the Judicial Committee of the Privy Council.

The tribunal in question

Good advocates have a healthy regard for the capability, background and former practice, likes and dislikes of the particular judge before whom they appear and try to cater for anything specific of which they are aware in pursuing their client's case. Since the essence of advocacy – *ad vocare* – is to call the tribunal towards a particular viewpoint, it makes sense to do so. However, in most trials and appeals the advocate will rarely know the composition of the tribunal before the skeleton is to be filed. Chancery, Family and Queen's Bench judges and their deputies, and members of the Court of Appeal operate in a general pool system which may make it impossible to customise a skeleton argument, much as he might wish to.

Where the courts have a much closer case management system in which a trial Judge is designated at the outset of proceedings, for example in the Technology and Construction Court or the Commercial Court, the likes or dislikes of a particular judge can be catered for insofar as to do so is consistent with the case. Counsel will be most often in a position to do this at the conclusion of any trial where he is asked to provide closing submissions in writing, or if he has a substantial interim hearing before an assigned master, and will welcome the opportunity of being able to tailor argument to the particular Judge. By likes or dislikes, I refer to submissions which the individual judge is more likely to find attractive or unattractive given his background or past expressions on the law. For example, if it is known that a certain Queen's Bench master will not accept a skeleton argument of more than two sides in length, that is how the submissions must be compressed; equally if a trial judge encourages an advocate to provide as full a closing submission in writing as he may wish, he need not worry unduly about the strictures of the practice rules and the costs implications. He is being asked to contribute to no small part of the judge's judgment.

Customising is even more important when one has to try to cater for a judge's likely familiarity with the particular area of law with which the case is concerned. The Ministry of Justice likes its judges as generalist as possible. This is good both for the Lord Chancellor, who wishes to ensure that judges are always fully occupied, and, to an extent, for cohesion in the law, since judges will apply first principles to areas outside their immediate discipline.

Even within the divisions of the High Court, the deputy system means that one may have a trial judge with no experience of the law in the particular case. You can try to accommodate this by preparing a short appendix to your skeleton,[1] which sets out the existing law and most recent authorities as neutrally as is consistent with your case. This sits well with the idea of counsel acting as a judicial assistant helping the court, rather than necessarily being a partisan figure.

---

1 See Example C at p.96 *et seq*.

Example A

Queen's Bench trial – Personal injuries – Quantum only – Claimant's skeleton opening by Lord Faulks QC in 1998 – 10pp.

Brittle v Chief Constable of South Yorkshire Police was an action arising from the Hillsborough disaster of April, 1989. The Defendant admitted liability. At the trial for the assessment of damages, the live issues concerned the nature of the Claimant's injuries and causation.

The writer uses a relaxed narrative style with short sentences, and commands great simplicity of expression, much desired by most trial judges. The effect is not unlike a judgment by Lord Denning. As a skeleton it is almost entirely fact orientated. There is no separate chronology and no summary, as these are encompassed in the narrative, although the issues are set out at paragraphs 17 and 18. The facts are all laid out for the judge, and while the Claimant's case is asserted, note that it is deliberately understated. The technique of being undemonstrative is effective: the writer is telling the judge that the facts speak for themselves, subject to what he will find.

The action settled at the door of the court.

CLAIMANT'S SKELETON OPENING

1. The Claimant, Robert Brittle, was born on the 7th March 1962 in Walsall. West Midlands. On the 15th April 1989, when he was 27, he attended Hillsborough Stadium to watch Nottingham Forest versus Liverpool in the semi-final of the FA Cup. He suffered physical and psychological injuries as a result. The Defendant has admitted liability and the Court is concerned with the assessment of damages only. A chronology is available with this skeleton opening.

2. *Bundles*

   A master index of bundles will be provided to the Court. The bundles are as follows:

   Bundle 1 (red) – pleadings
   Bundle 2 (blue) – witness statements
   Bundle 3 (green) – medical reports
   Bundle 4 (grey) – accommodation and needs reports
   Bundle 5 (black lever arch) – GP/Hospital/Clinic Notes
   Bundle 6 (black) – miscellaneous correspondence
   Box 7 – various videos

(References in this skeleton opening are to the Bundles eg. 6.1 (Bundle 6, page 1).)

3. *The Facts*

The Claimant was crushed against a perimeter fence. Many of those around him were killed or seriously injured. He suffered from a prolonged crush and probably lost consciousness. On examination at the Northern General Hospital, Sheffield immediately after the event he had signs of diminishing air entry on the left side of his chest. He had a small right pneumothorax, which required a chest drain. There was also air in the pericardium. He was transferred to the Intensive Care Unit and required a considerable amount of intravenous pain relief. His mental state was such that the Claimant was transferred to the Psychiatric Department. His lack of orientation was attributed partly to crush asphyxia and partly due to an acute stress reaction. By the 19th April his pain relief was reduced and chest drains were removed. It was noted that he was unable to bear his own weight and clinical examination showed weakness in both arms and legs. X-rays showed no fractures. It was originally thought that he might have had hypoxic spinal cord damage. A consultant in A & E, Mr. Wardrope (1.18), considered that the extent of his chest injury and muscle enzyme increase showed that he had suffered prolonged crush for some time. The weakness experienced in the muscles of the arms and legs was considered to be unusual although previously described in traumatic asphyxia.

4. On the 26th April 1990 the Claimant was transferred to Manor Hospital, Walsall. A physician treating him (report at 1.10) noted that he had not walked in the Northern General Hospital and that he still did not do so. On observation muscles of the lower limbs were moderately tender on pressure. Muscle tone was normal. Muscle power in the lower limbs appeared to be diminished considerably although this was attributed to severe pain caused by movement to the limbs. Both tendon and superficial reflexes were normal. There was subjective diminution of appreciation of sensations over the left arm. There was no obvious wasting of any muscle group. The physician referred the matter to a neurologist who could find no neurological problem and to a psychiatrist who thought that the problems were attributable to depression and acute grief following a massive traumatic experience superimposed on an emotionally immature personality. The Claimant was still not mobile when discharged on the 2nd June 1989 and left in a wheelchair.

5. He was seen by a neurologist in November 1989 (1.16). The Claimant was still completely unable to walk. The neurologist also reported stiffness and aching in the right shoulder, pins and needles and

numbness in the right hand, and widespread emotional problems of the kind often associated with post traumatic stress disorder. He said: "Despite the virtually normal signs on examination on the bed, he was completely unable to walk. Even the prospect of walking made him agitated. When he was stood up at the side of the bed he started shaking and clung on to people or objects around as would a drowning man. He was unable to make even small steps and, unless supported, would have fallen to the floor." The neurologist was in no doubt that all the symptoms were a direct result of the injuries sustained at Hillsborough Stadium. This emotional state was entirely explicable by reference to other survivors of horrific disasters. He considered that the characteristics of the Claimant's inability to walk indicated the problem was of a psychological origin and due to his emotional state.

6. Since 1989 the Claimant has been seen by a number of doctors instructed by solicitors on either side. Their reports are in bundle 3 (green). The medical notes themselves are in bundle 5 (lever arch black). It has been agreed between counsel that all medical notes in relation to the Claimant can be admitted into evidence without the need to call the authors of any notes and the Court is entitled to attach such weight if any as to the contents of the same as the Court thinks proper in the circumstances. The parties' expert witnesses who are called can comment upon all medical notes and draw such inferences from them as they consider appropriate. The relevant experts are:

For the Claimant –	Dr. Robin Jacobson (psychiatrist) and Dr. David Park (neurologist).
For the Defendant –	Dr. J. Swift (psychiatrist) and Surgeon Captain O'Connell (psychiatrist)

7. It is the Claimant's case that he was confined to a wheelchair until about the middle of 1996. He became able to drive a car and to swim. He could even stand up in a swimming pool because of the buoyancy of the water. However, he was unable to walk unaided; this he found frustrating and upsetting. He attempted suicide on one occasion.

8. He has had a number of the problems generally associated with post traumatic stress disorder such as depression, intrusive thoughts, nightmares, sleeping difficulties, irritability, hypervigilance and poor concentration. He has shown some obsessional features.

9. Dr. Jacobson saw him in July 1991 and then again in January 1993. By the latter date there was some sign of improvement in his symptoms of PTSD. Although he was still confined to a wheelchair with the aid of physiotherapy he was beginning to be able to stand for a few seconds. Otherwise he continued to crawl around the house and was unable to weight-bear or walk. Dr. Jacobson's view of his prognosis was that

there was some sign of improvement of his hysterical conversion reaction (i.e. his inability to walk) but that he required more intensive rehabilitation.

10. He received rehabilitation at the instigation of the Defendant's insurers who paid for him to attend a course at the Department of Psychiatry, Royal Naval Hospital, Gosport administered by Surgeon Commander O'Connell. The Claimant attended the course, living in a complex of flats away from the hospital with other members of the group. He apparently came to be less reticent as the course proceeded but remained in a wheelchair and still pre-occupied by the Hillsborough Disaster. Dr. O'Connell concluded in April 1984 that he continued to display the symptoms of post traumatic stress disorder. (3.104).

11. In January 1995 he went to RAF Headley Court, once again under the auspices of the Defendant's insurers, who paid for the course. Whilst at Haslar the emphasis was on post traumatic stress disorder. At Headley Court the Claimant was an in-patient at the Rehabilitation Unit. Attempts to mobilise him apparently caused him anxiety and a tendency to hyperventilate. It is said that he did not wish to co-operate with certain assessments proposed and he discharged himself after 13 days.

12. When Dr. Swift saw the Claimant in January 1996 he concluded that there was an unwillingness to give up what has been described as a "sick role" he said: "My impression is that he has made a good adjustment to the sick role and is not sufficiently discontented with his limitations to bear the emotional discomforts associated with change." (3.97). He considered that Mr. Brittle might actively resist change until there had been a financial settlement of his claim. He described his motivation as "suspect".

13. In his report of 1st May 1997 Dr. Jacobson also concluded that any residual temporary increase in symptoms was likely to diminish on resolution of his Court case. By the time Dr. Jacobson saw him Mr. Brittle was able to get around with crutches and for short periods without any crutches.

14. Dr. Jacobson has recently reviewed his opinion in the light of video evidence, the Defendant's exchanged medical reports and certain documents (viz the RAF Headley Court notes) and is now of the view that there is a deliberate element in Mr. Brittle's continued inability to walk normally which may well be motivated by a desire for financial gain.

15. The most recent reports of Dr. Swift (dated the 15th September 1997) and Dr. O'Connell (dated the 16th September 1997) indicate a

hardening of their views of the Claimant's genuineness. Dr. Swift concluded that rhe Claimant was able to walk at some time between the accident and April 1993. He concludes (3.69) that the inability to walk initially was genuine "i.e. an unconscious process, conversion hysteria, associated with psychological trauma" but this has changed over the years and "that there is now a conscious element determining the maintenance of a state of invalidity." Similarly Dr. O'Connell concludes that "at a very early stage he developed a sick role, in part reflecting guilt, however I would say that the major reason that he continued to present with the bizarre symptoms of a physical nature was with a view to achieving financial compensation – in other words he was malingering." (3.108)

16. The only neurological evidence comes from Dr. Park who saw the Claimant for the second occasion in June 1995. He noted that his legs were weak but that there was no evidence of disability from the neurological point of view. He concluded; "I have discounted the possibility that the disability is factitious or feigned, and I believe it to be a consequence of a neurotic disorder, which is a direct consequence of the incident at Hillsborough."

17. *The Issues*

The principal issues concern the nature of the Claimant's disability and its causation. The Claimant had a vulnerable personality as is evidenced by his personal and medical history. He was undoubtedly involved in a horrific incident in which he might well have died. It is also common ground that he has suffered from post traumatic stress disorder albeit that this has improved. It is further accepted that at least initially the Claimant's inability to walk was genuine i.e. caused by some form of hysterical conversion and was not; a deliberate attempt to feign disability.

18. Where the issue lies is when, if at all, he was in fact able to walk but deliberately did not do so. The Claimant maintains that his disability has been entirely genuine and that his improvement, also genuine, is something that he has welcomed. In the medical reports there is reference to malingering, hysterical conversion and a "sick role". The difficulty in this case may be disentangling the relative contribution of any of these factors. Specifically the doctors disagree as to when there was a conscious element on the Claimant's part, involved in his failure to improve.

19. *Damages*

General Damages
The Claimant is entitled to general damages for post traumatic stress disorder.

The JSB Guidelines suggest that the brackets are;

(a) Severe – £27,000 to £37,500

(b) Moderately Severe – £11,000 to £21,500

(c) Moderate – £3,250 to £8,000

(d) Minor – £1,600 to £3,250

It is the Claimant's case that (even apart from the inability to walk) his problems can probably be described as severe. The inability to walk is clearly an aggravating feature. It affected every aspect of his life and for a period of approximately 7 years he was confined to a wheelchair. He is now only able to walk with crutches. The Court will award an appropriate sum to reflect his physical disability. Account will also be taken of his undoubted physical injuries in the incident, the period of hospitalisation and the continued pain and discomfort in various parts of his body since the accident.

20. *Loss of Earnings*

The Claimant's early life was unpromising. But when he came out of prison in 1983 he began to settle down. From 1983 to 1989 he lived with his girlfriend and kept out of trouble. He had various forms of employment, mostly on a cash basis until 1988 when he obtained full-time employment with Mr. Owen. This was a highly satisfactory period of his life. Mr. Owen speaks highly of him (2.18). He was earning £154.62p net. Unfortunately he was made redundant towards the end of 1988 through circumstances unconnected with any dissatisfaction on his employer's part with the Claimant. His employment consisted of driving substantial goods vehicles around the country. The Claimant had a provisional HGV licence. He had taken his test once and failed and was due to take it again shortly after the Hillsborough Disaster but was unable to do so. Although he was unemployed when the accident took place, he had been offered a job by Peter Marriott which would have started in 1989 (2.31) at the rate of £300 per week for a 5½ day week. On any view of the evidence the Claimant was out of work as a result of the accident. The Defendants suggest the relevant period is 18 months (1.62). The Claimant says it was for much longer.

21. Employment: consultants have analysed Mr. Brittle's prospects now (see Keith Carter's updated report dated 28th October 1997 Bundle 1). The Claimant must now expect a difficult and lengthy job search having regard to his limited physical ability, his moderate ability generally, the job market and the period for which he has been out of work. The Claimant has made a few attempts to obtain employment

but it is submitted that given the extent of his disability there was never any realistic chance of his obtaining a job.

22. It is the Claimant's case that the accident happened at a crucial time in his life when he was beginning to sort himself out. The likelihood is that be would have obtained work and continued working had it not been for the accident. That he has not been able to do so has been as a result of the accident which has also affected his position on the labour market for the long-term. The Claimant has provided a Schedule of Loss of Earnings to assist the Court. (1.30).

23. *Care*

The Court is referred to the report of Rachel Bush (4.28) and in particular page 35 and the following. The costing of the Claimant's care is contained at page 53 and reflected in a voluntary schedule (1.58).

24. *Other Losses*

The Schedule at 1.58 refers to the cost of a gardener/handyman. The Claimant was effective with his hands before the accident. There are also references to the need for physiotherapy, aids and equipment, travel cost, holidays and the need for investment advice.

Good practice suggestion

Writing style

Style may be unimportant where your aim is to bring the attention of the judge directly to the relevant matter or point. However in a longer document, particularly where the facts need explanation, the use of a narrative style in good English is most effective. You should avoid defined terms and use the language one would find in a novel in a straightforward story telling technique. In this way you reduce the case to its essence and arouse the human interest of the judge. If you use short sentences, words that are not too long (which makes the occasional lengthy word stand out), non-legal words and adjectives from other sources (but not clichéic or slang expressions) you will capture the attention of the reader and carry him forward to your argument expeditiously and confident of his understanding of your position.

Example B

Queen's Bench trial – Clinical negligence – Quantum only – Claimant's skeleton opening by Simeon Maskrey QC in late 1998 – extract from 15pp.

Newton v Hereford Hospitals NHS Trust was an action for damages for 'wrongful birth' arising from a failed sterilisation. The Defendant admitted liability. At the trial for the assessment of damages, the parties filed a schedule that summarised their respective contentions. The Claimant's skeleton is specifically produced to highlight the major differences between the parties and summarise their rival contentions (para 3). As an exercise it is worth contrasting the style with the preceding case of Brittle.

The writer uses the technique of close comparison throughout. Although you may find defence counsel using this it is unusual in a claimant's opening, and therefore very specific to the situation. Its particular strength is clarity: the judge can focus directly on the issues to be decided without diversion.

The language is informal. Paragraphs are single issue and generally kept short. Key financial figures and citations are put in bold font. Much use is made of white space.

The action was compromised during the hearing.

CLAIMANT'S SKELETON OPENING

Introduction

1. This is a claim for damages for "wrongful birth". Liability has been admitted and interlocutory judgment entered on the 21st July 1998. The action proceeds as an assessment of damages. Put shortly, the claimant was sterilised on the 10th April 1995. The sterilisation failed because the left fallopian tube was not occluded properly. In August 1995 the claimant discovered she was pregnant with her 5th child. She declined the offer of an abortion. C was born on the 15th February 1996.

2. The rival contentions of the parties are summarised in the revised schedule served on the 11th January 1999 (page 52 bundle A) and the undated counter-schedule in reply (page 86 bundle A).

3. The purpose of this opening is to highlight the major differences between the parties and summarise the rival contentions.

Pain and suffering

4. The claimant seeks £40,000. The defendant admits £20,000 (page 91 bundle A). The claimant relies on the following matters in support of her contention.

    4.1 The pregnancy was complicated (report from Mr. Jarvis dated 3rd September 1998 (page 102 bundle B)).

    4.2 The labour and delivery were difficult although in the event the baby did not suffer HIE (page 103, bundle B). An episiotomy was required.

    4.3 The claimant was obliged to undergo a re-sterilisation under general anaesthetic on the 26th September 1996. She suffered vomiting as a consequence of the anaesthetic (page 104, bundle B).

    4.4 As a consequence of the pregnancy and birth of C the claimant suffered "notable and disabling evidence of depression" (report from Dr. Seifert dated 26th October 1998 (page 86, bundle B). "severe depression" (report from Dr. Bradley dated the 2nd November 1998 (page 231, bundle B).

    4.5 By July 1999 the claimant's psychiatric symptoms had lessened and both experts felt that there was no psychiatric reason why she should not return to work (page 236, bundle B).

    4.6 The court should take account of the recommendations contained in the Law Commission's Report, Law Com No. 257 that such awards should be increased by a factor of between 1.5 and 2.0 and that it is open to the courts (albeit via Court of Appeal guidelines) to do so. *Alsford v British Telecommunications plc* (1986) CA October 30th is not authority to the contrary.

Loss of congenial employment

5. The claimant seeks £5,000. The defendant concedes £1,000 (page 91, bundle A). The claimant will rely upon *Ministry of Defence v Hay* [2008] IRLR 928, [2008] UKEAT 0571 07 2107, [2008] ICR 1247, in support of her contention. She has had to give up employment that she enjoyed and that provided her with stimulation and social intercourse. It is unlikely that she will ever return to work of a similar nature.

Expenses to date of trial

6. The claimant has sought:

    6.1 £3,773 in respect of "recorded expenses"

6.2 £1,192 in respect of estimated expenses

6.3 £3,813 in respect of general household expenditure.

See pages 56 and 81 Bundle A

7. The defendant has allowed £4,611 + £1,080 = £5,691 (page 92, bundle A). The defendant has reached this figure by reference to NFCA rates, reduced by one-third and child benefit received. Apparently this has been done because Mrs. Convey has not seen the claimant's supporting documentation. She makes much complaint about the failure to "release" documents (see page 113, bundle B for example). The complaint is misconceived (see pages 87 and 15 – in that order – bundle F).

8. The reduction of one-third from the NFCA rates has been made because the defendant contends that the Newton family's income and expenditure was below the average used by the NFCA (see page 121 bundle B). The claimant does not accept this contention and it amounts to one of the significant disputes between the parties. The claimant contends that the NFCA rates are appropriate for future expenditure and is prepared to rely on the rates for past expenditure. However, she does not accept a one-third deduction. Therefore the claimant will accept £5,691 × 133.3% = £7,586 under this head of claim.

Future maintenance costs

9. The claimant seeks £64,085 under this head of claim (page 57, bundle A). The defendant allows £26,759 (page 93, bundle A).

10. The claimant has used the NFCA rates to the age of 18 (page 7 bundle B). It is accepted that no allowance has been made for accelerated receipt. Accordingly the claimant is prepared to accept the multipliers put forward by the defendant (page 110, bundle A) provided that the correct up to date NFCA rates are used (page 7, bundle B). Thus, the claimant seeks £44,058.

11. The defendant relies upon Mrs. Convey's report in order to establish that NFCA rates are inappropriate. In essence it is said that the family income in 1999 would have been £17,717 pa; that £7,269 would have been spent on the adults and running the car; thus leaving £10,447 for the children or £2,089 pa for each child (page 141, bundle B). As NFCA rates amount to an average of £4,336 pa spent on each child it can be demonstrated that they are an inappropriate benchmark in this case.

12. The claimant contends that Mrs. Convey's approach is misconceived. First, one has to look at the likely expenditure by the Newtons in 1995. Prior to C's birth the claimant had resumed full time work. Her net

income was £8,931. Her husband earned £10,715 net. The family received £1,859 pa child benefit. Thus, £21,505 was available for the family. If NFCA rates for 1995 are used it can be seen that £12,780 would be spent on the 4 children, leaving £8,725 pa for the two adults (see page 11B, bundle B)(the witness evidence supporting these figures is at pages 4 and 51, bundle C. The documentary evidence is at pages 35 and 37 of bundle E and page 139, bundle B). Therefore it can be demonstrated that the family expenditure on the children was at or about the rate used by the NFCA. The same exercise can be carried out at 1999 rates assuming that C had not been born. Once again, the family income would have been sufficient to spend the NFCA average figure on each child (page 11C, bundle B).

13. The errors made by Mrs. Convey can thus be summarised;

    13.1 Using the RPI to reach the assumed 1999 income of Mr & Mrs Newton.

    13.2 Assuming that Mrs Newton would have remained in part time work but for C's birth.

    13.3 Dividing the money available for the children by 5 rather than by 4.

Losses consequent upon forced house move

14. As a consequence of the birth of C (a) the claimant had to give up work (b) her husband was unable to earn at previous levels and (c) there was additional expenditure. In order to make ends meet the claimant was forced to sell her house at The Haven, Green Lane, Eardisland, near Leominster, and the building plots that went with the house (see page 12, bundle C). The need to sell quickly meant that the sales were at an under-value (see page 13, bundle B).

15. Moreover, the claimant incurred expense moving from The Haven to 'X' Avenue, Leominster (page 29, bundle C).

16. The move to 'X' Avenue was forced upon the claimant by the birth of C. As soon as she is in a position to do so she will move back to accommodation of a comparable standard to The Haven and which will be large enough for the whole family. costs associated with running a larger house (page 81, bundle A). Furthermore the cost of such a property has increased more rapidly than the value of The Haven (page 53, bundle B).

17. The claimant abandons the claim for the cost of a further move back to a smaller home (page 98, bundle A). The claim therefore amounts to £62,936 (plus interest)(page 57, bundle A).

18. The defendant's approach has been to accept the costs of moving from The Haven and the costs of moving to a larger house insofar as it is established that it has been necessitated by C's birth (page 97, bundle A). The sum admitted on that basis is £15,169. No other costs are accepted. In particular it has been denied that the sales of The Haven and the building plots were forced or were at an undervalue (see page 184, bundle B) and it is denied that it was in fact necessary to sell The Haven (see page 191, bundle B).

19. The observation that it was unnecessary for the claimant to sell The Haven is based upon a misapprehension of the claimant's case. It was necessary to sell and then buy a cheaper property so as to pay off debts which had accumulated and to be closer to the amenities of Leominster (see pages 5 and 13, bundle C).

Claimant's loss of earnings

20. But for the birth of C the claimant would have continued working for Barclays Bank on a full time basis (pages 36 & 37, bundle E)(pages 4, 11, 12, bundle C). The calculation is at page 64, bundle A. The claim amounts to £34,109 to date.

21. The defendant appears to accept that but for C's birth the claimant would have remained in employment with Barclays (page 88, bundle A). Therefore the claim has been admitted (page 99, bundle A) but presumably with the caveat that she would have incurred child care expenditure.

22. The claimant says that she would have worked full time at Barclays Bank but for C's birth; that she would probably have worked in the customer and sales department at a net salary of £11,650 pa rising each year for 5 years (page 65, bundle A); that she has been prevented from doing so; and that her earning potential has now been reduced by (a) her child care commitments and (b) her absence from the labour market. A multiplier of 17.17 is sought which reflects a working life to age 65. The claim on that basis amounts to £145,386.

23. The defendant has accepted that but for C's birth:

    23.1 the claimant would have been able to work full time at a net salary of £10,590 pa (pages 112 and 114, bundle A) until the year 2003. A loss of earnings for that period (subject to child care costs) is therefore accepted with a multiplier of 4.

    23.2 From the year 2003 to 2014 the defendant accepts a partial loss of earnings on the basis that the claimant will now only obtain part time work (pages 113 and 114, bundle A). A multiplier of 8.5 is used. However, the defendant concedes that in order to work the claimant will incur child care costs for C's and will make an additional payment in respect of such costs.

23.3 From 2014 to 2018 (the claimant's 60th birthday) a small loss of £582 pa is accepted on the basis that the claimant would by then have been able to work full time work at a comparable salary. A multiplier of 2.5 years is accepted.

24. On this basis the defendant concedes a loss of earnings of £77,093.

25. The major dispute between the parties is, therefore, (a) the extent to which it is likely that the claimant will be able to obtain work from 2003 and (b) what her likely salary will be (c) what it would have been had she remained at Barclays and (d) whether she would have worked to age 65 but for C's birth.

26. The claimant accepts that her psychiatric condition is unlikely to prevent her from working from the year 2003. It is highly unlikely that she would be able to obtain work in the banking sector (report from Keith Carter page 80, bundle B). It is possible that she could obtain part time clerical work at a salary of £4,385 gross (say £4,000 net) and the claimant is prepared to revise her claim accordingly (page 72, bundle B; page 214. bundle B). It is accepted that after 2 years her income would begin to rise as she gained in experience and worked longer hours. From 2005 she could be expected to earn £8,723 gross (say £6,990 net) and from £2014 she could earn £10,815 gross (say £8,100 net) (see page 72, bundle B). On that basis the claim falls to £137,204.

27. The claimant disputes the assertions contained in the defendant's employment report that (a) she would not have been a candidate for promotion within Barclays (page 204, bundle B) (b) she could expect to earn the median salary of a counter clerk on her return to full time employment (page 213, bundle B) (c) she would probably have retired at the age of 60.

Mr. Newton's loss of earnings

28. The claim to date is £12,124 (plus interest). The future claim is £8,030 (pages 58 and 82, bundle A).

29. The claimant does not understand the defendant to be challenging the fact of this loss or that it flows from the birth of C. As the claimant understands it the defendant disputes the claim simply because it is the loss of Mr. Newton and not hers.

30. The claimant accepts that her husband left his job because he was unable to work shifts following the birth of C. She accepts that this is his loss rather than hers. However, his loss of overtime to the date of trial and into the future is a consequence of (a) assisting the claimant whilst she

suffered from severe depression and (b) assisting her with child care in the future. Therefore this is a loss sustained by Mr. Newton in order to assist the claimant and it is recoverable according to ordinary *Housecroft v Burnett* principles. Thus the claimant reduces her claim to £5,900 (plus interest) to the date of trial and £8,030 until 2003 (see page 82, bundle A).

Loss of pension and other benefits

31. The claimant abandons her claim for loss of preferential borrowing and disability on the labour market. However, she maintains her other claims and awaits the response of the defendants in respect of the loss of pension claim (see page 104, bundle A).

32. The claimant abandons the claims made in respect of her husband's losses.

Care of C

33. The claim amounts to £57,822 to date and £48,241 for the future (page 59, bundle A). The defendant admits travel costs paid to Mrs. Newton senior (£427) but has denied all of the other claims (page 105 & 106, bundle A). The denial is based upon the premise that the claimant is not entitled to the cost of caring for C as this is counterbalanced by the positive elements of bringing up a child (see *Thake v Maurice* [1986] QB 644) (page 90, bundle A).

34. The claimant asserts that the cost of caring for C is recoverable provided that there is no double recovery when also claiming loss of earnings.

35. That the claim is allowable in principle is clear from the court of appeal decision of *Emeh v Kensington AHA* [1985] QB 1012. See, in particular, the judgment of Waller LJ @ 1022. In *Thake v Maurice* [1986] QB 644 the court of appeal agreed that the joy of having a healthy child could cancel out the time and trouble spent looking after that child (see, for example, page 683). But (a) these cases were decided before *Housecroft v Burnett* [1986] 1 All ER 332 and the modern practice of evaluating care provided by family by reference to commercial care costs, discounted by 20–33% (see Kemp 5-025) and (b) there can be no doubt that in this case the birth of C did not result in joy and comfort, but in severe depression that is still continuing. Moreover it is illogical to allow a loss of earnings claim and not a gratuitous care claim.

36. The claim made in respect of care provided by Mrs. Newton senior is recoverable subject to the normal *Housecroft v Burnett* principles.

37. The claim for the care provided by the claimant is subject to a deduction in respect of the loss of earnings claim. Thus the claim

should be reduced by (say) 50 hours per week and the calculation should be as follows:

> 168-50 =118 hours per week × £1.80 per hour × 177 weeks = £37,595 (see page 8. bundle B and page 83, bundle A).

38. For the future the claim is based on the report prepared by Mrs. Sweeting (see page 9, bundle B).

Transport

39. The claim is for the cost of a VW Sharan at £18,587. The defendant argues that a set off is required in respect of the sale of two old vehicles. The principle of the contention is accepted but the discount sought of £11,000 is too high (see page 107, bundle A). The claimant is prepared to concede a discount of £5,000 reducing the claim to £13,587 plus interest for past losses and £13,587 for the future.

Financial advice

40. If multipliers are assessed on the basis of a 3% discount rate when a net return of 2% is all that has been achievable for the past 12 months it is appropriate to seek financial advice and assistance. The claim is therefore maintained. The cost of £1,200 pa represents 10 hours advice each year and is a modest claim. Therefore the claim remains £32,219 (see page 83, bundle A).

Conclusion

41. The defendant admits by its counter-schedule £197,404 plus interest and pension loss but subject to (a) an adjustment for child care costs and (b) proof that moving from The Haven was justified. As amended in this opening the claimant seeks an award of £546,990 plus interest.

Good practice suggestion

Try to break down issues into small bites.[1] Make issues as simple as is consistent with accuracy – but be wary of oversimplification. In doing so try to avoid stylised language. Accuracy in dealing with the facts and the case is more important than worrying about simplification.

---

1 See also Example P.

Example C

Queen's Bench trial – Employer's duties – Defendant's skeleton opening by John Norman in July, 2004 – 6pp together with appendix on the law of 12pp. (NB The law is taken as at 2004.)

Martindale v Oxford County Council was a stress at work claim brought by a teacher. The Defendant contested liability on the issues of breach of duty and causation.

In his overview of the facts the writer uses short sentences in non-legal language with few technical terms. He has a narrative style which contains cross-references to the trial bundles. A close perusal of the document reveals that the defence case is not actually stated in terms; the ground is merely laid under paragraph 3. This gives defence counsel considerable flexibility depending on how the evidence comes out.

The opening contains an integrated chronology. The events of four years are confined to three-quarters of a page. Key dates are selected and highlighted with bold face.

Analysis of the law is relegated to a separate appendix. This enables the narrated opening to be advanced as unbroken prose. It is designed to assist a judge who may be unfamiliar with – or have no knowledge at all of – what is a specialist area, and should be contemplated when your case goes into a general list or if there is a likelihood of a deputy judge. This is a useful technique when you want to compartmentalise the facts and the law.

At trial the claim failed and was dismissed. Permission to appeal was refused by the Court of Appeal.

OPENING SUBMISSIONS OF THE DEFENDANT

At Trial: 8th July 2004

1. *Overview*

    1.1 This is a stress at work claim. Liability and quantum are in issue. The focus of events is really in the early part of 1999, although there are elements of the history which are important.

    1.2 The Claimant was an experienced teacher at X Middle School. His subjects were Art, and Design and Technology ("D&T"). He first went sick with depression in September 1997, and although he complains that he was 'bullied' by Mr Y (Particulars of Claim §15 – p.5) he makes no claim in respect of that episode (Particulars of Claim §18 – p.5).

1.3 He returned to work in May 1998, with a structured return starting with part time work. Almost exactly a year later, in April 1999 (the beginning of the summer term), and long after he had returned to full time working, he went sick again. He was then 43 years old. He claims damages only in respect of this episode. The report of the Defendant's psychiatric expert, Prof. F, is agreed (p.93). The condition was an adjustment disorder, with anxiety and depressed mood (p.109).

1.4 The essence of his pleaded case is that the pressures of work were too great for him, the Defendant knew this (or ought to have known this), and the Defendant ought to have reduced them. The Claimant also characterises the Head's executive decision in 1998 as to what he should teach in the coming year as 'bullying' (p.7 §24) – but no adverse consequence comes from this. Those pressures in part seem to be related by the Claimant to difficulties which the school was having generally – despite the 'new broom' introduced in April 1997. He disagreed with the management decisions on allocation of resources. There is no recognisable overwork claim pleaded. Although breaches of the Working Time Regulations appear in the immensely lengthy list of broken duties, no facts in support are pleaded – i.e. it is not said he had to work too many hours, merely that those hours limited what he could usefully achieve. His witness statement makes complaint about the hours worked, but does not reach any relevant threshold.

1.5 The Defendant's pleaded case is that the Claimant returned to work after careful discussion with the Defendant, the Defendant also spoke to his GP, and took advice from Occupational Health. In short, the Claimant returned to work with advice that he was fit. He retained ready access to suitable sources of medical/welfare advice, including counselling, and his return to work went well – with support from his Head Teacher and from LEA advisers. His sudden illness immediately after the Spring holiday was unexpected and was not caused by any breach of duty. The Claimant had made an appointment to seek advice from Occupational Health shortly before this (p.9, §32). It appears that neither he nor his advisers foresaw impending illness – or, as he had done before, the Claimant chose to ignore either his own view and/or the advice he was receiving.

1.6 It is apparent from the history given that there was a conflict between the Defendant's managerial decisions and what the Claimant felt ought to have been done. See also Prof F on p. 108–9. This appears to be at least partly related to his union activities. He was unable to accept the decisions of the new Head and failed to adjust or cooperate fully. Although he knew he could not and would not get his way, he chose to ignore the situation and stay put, but built up enormous anger over this. Worse, he had no medical support: his own GP was pleased with the progress he made after returning to full time work. The Defendant involved the Claimant's own GP and the Occupational Health adviser, but made it clear that the Claimant's job could not and would not be adjusted, and that the Claimant had to be fit for the job he would be required to do before he would be allowed back. Once the Claimant decided to return and started work the Defendant was not advised that he had to have any special regime. Although some 9 months later in March 1999 he had concerns about his health (see GP notes), but he fell ill before any material advice could be given to the Defendant (apparently he received none either), and well before any advice could have been effectively acted upon.

Key Dates:

20.10.95 GP Note: heart/palpitations; v anxious; change of routine – chat [described as 'sea-change' – F p.7]

20.9.96 GP Note: exhausted, work – 'stress/burnout' diagnosed [semble, ignored by the Claimant – no time off]

Sept '96 re-monitoring of C; upset, proposed leaving; job applications unsuccessful;

Apr '97 Change of management. Acting Head = Mr R; Dep = Mrs S 2+5.6.97 review meetings with R; request for C's 'back of envelope' plans for new workshop layout for Sept;

?6.6.97 to GP; told he should take time off for stress; rejected GP advice [F p.3]

30.6.97 referral by D for health monitoring (headaches; 11 days off this year)

1.9.97 C off sick from beginning of term – 7m – cut hand + reactive depression; Occ H and offered free [confidential] counselling – which he took up

8.10.97 GP Note: 'constructive dismissal, lawyer'

Nov '97 Ofsted – D&T unsatisfactory, Art satisfactory

17.3.98 note: S and OccH (J A) interview C with John L, Paul Mc, George

H and C's friend R S; make it clear he is not to return until he is fit. Apr 1998 GP to Ms T (Snr Educ Officer) = 'fit as anyone + fit as he'll ever be' (recorded in letter 1.5.98 to Head, Mrs S)

May '98 C returns to work – support and short hours;

25.11.98 GP Note – much better; medication to continue for 3m

5.3.99 GP Note: 'work pressures again', possible depression – prescribed Temazapan [not sleeping]

consulted union rep. who told him work pressures were excessive

23.3.99 meeting with Head

12.4.99 training day (day before term starts); request from Head for scheme of work – C felt he could not cope and went to GP [F p.5]

13.4.99 first day sick

2. *Preliminary Matters*

2.1 The Claimant has very recently served a report from Prof. G. The substance as well as the flavour of the report is not appropriate for forensic circumstances. It improperly attempts to address many issues which are the exclusive province of the trial Judge.

2.2 It may greatly assist if some of the witness statements were simply excluded. Several of the Claimant's witnesses do not address pleaded issues, but rather make complaints or give histories of quite different matters. In particular events prior to 1998 would seem wholly (or largely) irrelevant {W, Ws, L, A, S}. Ms T seems to have a different agenda – her own complaint. A great deal of the matters referred to by the Claimant's witnesses do not appear admissible, in particular the Claimant has neither sought nor obtained permission to adduce the extensive opinion evidence.

2.3 The Claimant also proposes to call his solicitor, Ms N. The wrong statement appears in my bundle – p.386. The statement relied upon appears to go to the credit of a witness the Defendant may call, Mr P. The Defendant submits this evidence is inadmissible – it seeks to impugn the credit of a witness. In any event the Claimant can call Mr P if he wants to, or can cross-examine him if and when the Defendant calls him. Further:

a. it is accepted that he would not sign the statement prepared for him;

b. he was expressly told he could alter or amend what the Claimant prepared as he saw fit;

c. Ms N's evidence of what he meant cannot be admissible.

3. *Legal Principles*

3.1 In stress cases there are some important differences or additions to the standard approach to the duty of care owed by an employer to an employee. These can easily be overstated. To assist there is an annexe to these submissions dealing with recent cases and the overall approach in this area of the law.

3.2 Whether the issue is the first episode of stress or, as here, a return to work, the standard of care is the same: to take reasonable steps to avoid exposing the Claimant to unreasonable risk of injury because of the requirements of his work.

3.3 Once there has been an extended period of psychiatric illness all sides recognise that there is a significant risk of relapse. There may be just as much (or more) adverse psychiatric influence from not working, or from seeking a new job, as there may be from returning to work. The options are usually for the Claimant to remain off work, to be a part timer or subject to special duties (with reductions in pay and status), or getting back to full time work with no special restrictions.

3.4 The fact that a relapse may occur does not in any way mean there has been a breach. It is the nature of the Claimant's condition that relapses are likely, and are not readily avoidable, but that the risk for the Claimant is worth taking. The employer does not underwrite the risk any more than the Claimant's medical or other advisers warrant that the risk is low.

3.5 The risk is kept within reasonable bounds partly because the alternatives carry similar risks, and partly because the Defendant has ensured that the Claimant has ample means of avoiding pressures when they get too much – i.e. not just unpleasant, but where he can see the build up of a pathological reaction. He can take days off, he can return to his GP for treatment or advice (or seek and follow advice from any other relevant source), he can approach his counsellor. What he cannot expect to do is to impose a special regime on his employer. That sort of claim falls exclusively within the jurisdiction of the Employment Tribunal under the Disability Discrimination Act.

3.6 The primary responsibility for an individual's health lies on the individual himself. This is particularly so where the person concerned is mature, educated and responsible, and where the subject condition is one which necessarily he will be best placed to assess and address – and one which many people wish to keep confidential. "People must accept responsibility for their own actions and take the necessary care to avoid injuring themselves or others" – *Gorringe v Calderdale BC*, [2004] UKHL 15, [2004] 1 WLR 1057; *Tomlinson v Congleton Borough Council* [2003] UKHL 47, [2004] 1 AC 46.

4. Quantum: it is the nature of cases with psychological injury that there is often a great number of variables which need to be resolved. Stress cases particularly give rise to these problems. It may be helpful to resolve the primary issues before addressing the detail of issues on quantum.

Appendix

Actions for Stress at Work – A Summary of Applicable Law

1. Although claims of this character are essentially the same as any other claim concerning occupational injury, there are a number of important and unavoidable special factors.

2. The material factors and principles have been summarised by the Court of Appeal in *Hatton*,[1] whose conclusions in turn have been approved (with a small distinction) by the House of Lords in *Barber v Somerset CC*.[2] The detail of these decisions appears at the end of this summary.

The duty of care

3. It is essential to bear in mind in every case that the employer's duty is not simply to take care, and is not proved to have been broken simply because someone becomes ill because of his or her work.

4. The employer's duty is to take reasonable care to ensure that the Claimant is not exposed to unreasonable risk of injury by reason of the requirements of his/her work – see *Hatton* §43(7)+(8). The material duty relates to health and safety. It is no good identifying stress generated by a breach of some obligation which is not within the scope of any arguable duty of health and safety (e.g. non-payment of wages, lack of promotion, selection for transfer).

5. There are many competing duties owed by employers, especially public bodies, and these competing duties inform the nature and limits of the relevant duty of care owed to the Claimant. Conflicts between employees, or between employees and customers, are likely to bring into play a whole range of competing contractual and statutory duties.

---

1 *Hatton v Sutherland* [2002] 2 All ER 1 CA (Brooke, Kay, Hale LJJ) – comprising four appeals: *Jones v Sandwell MBC; Bishop v Baker Refractories; Barber v Somerset CC*.

2 *Barber v Somerset CC* [2004] UKHL 13.

The public duty to fulfil certain statutory requirements regardless of resources can also give rise to difficulties.

6. For example, seen only from the Claimant's position it may be wholly unreasonable to keep the irritating Mr. Bloggs in the same post, or even to keep on employing him at all, but Mr Bloggs has his own rights, many imposed on the employer by statute, all of which the employer must also honour. While it may be upsetting to the Claimant not to get the changes he or she thinks would best assist, the employer may quite reasonably consider that the Claimant's special demands are bad for morale (and for the stress of other employees), or may reasonably value Mr Bloggs' contribution far more highly than the Claimant's (indeed the employer's obligation to his shareholders or to good financial conduct may oblige him to do so). In any event most employees agree that conflicts at work will be resolved by various types of grievance procedures. This in itself not only serves to reduce the risk of injurious conflict, but may be said to inhibit both the employee's right to claim and the employer's scope for response. See *Hatton* §43(9).

7. The reality of many situations is that even if there is something that the employer can do, he has a wide discretion as to how he manages his employees and especially how he manages an individual employee, and if the Claimant does not like it he/she is always free to leave the job and seek other employment. It is a false submission that this is not merely 'unfair' but actionably so:- fairness is material to unfair dismissal only. See *Hatton* §43(8),(9)+(10).

8. It also has to be borne in mind that Parliament has expressly provided for the sort of 'accommodation' which an employer is obliged to provide in response to an employee's health problems – and has specified the remedy available where he fails to do so. The Disability Discrimination Act 1995 applies to defined health problems, mental health only being included where particular criteria are met. Breaches of duties under the Act lie within the exclusive jurisdiction of the Employment Tribunal and have very tight time limits – 3 months.[3] It is submitted that:

   a. the common law had provided no significant remedy in relation to mental health caused by stress at work prior to 1995 (*Walker v Northumberland*[4] was reported in 1995);

   b. it would be unusual if Parliament had provided for an unnecessary remedy;

---

3 Section 8, applying to discrimination in the employment field.

4 *Walker v Northumberland CC* [1995] 1 All ER 737.

c. employment law is a closely regulated and highly sensitive political area; the common law should be very slow to impose any obligation or confer any remedy which Parliament has not thought appropriate when addressing the material area of activity (cf. the House of Lords' decision in *Johnson v Unisys*[5]).

Foreseeability

9. Mental health issues necessarily give rise to special problems of foreseeability. Employment problems will be included in almost any list of potential injurious stressors, thus there will rarely be any issue that psychological injury is a foreseeable consequence of stress at work. However, that does not address the issue of foreseeability with which the law is concerned. What has to be foreseeable by the employer is that the combination of this employee and this job is such that there is an unreasonable risk of injury – see *Hatton* §43(3). Until that stage is reached the employer can have no obligation to investigate steps to reduce the particular and unusual risk back to a reasonable level, still less to have put them into place.

10. All health matters are necessarily personal, and are usually confidential. People tend to be particularly sensitive about mental health matters, both employers and employees. Employees may react very badly to any suggestion that their mental health is not good. Conduct by an employer even by concerned inquiry about mental health may be characterised as intrusive and wrongly critical, and may provoke allegations of breach of the underlying duty of trust and confidence, or of discriminatory conduct. Merely revealing to an employee that the employer is concerned about his mental health may itself be stressful and corrosive to an effective working relationship.

11. An employer may well be best advised to rely upon the employee to be responsible enough to seek and follow their own medical advice, and at most to do little more than suggest that if they have any health concerns they should seek advice from their own GP. If there are employees who cannot be treated as responsible enough to look after their own health and/or to take their own decisions about it, good or bad, this will be an extremely rare situation. See *Hatton* §43(6). An employer who provides an independent confidential counselling service will usually have discharged any material duty of care – see *Hatton* §43 (11); necessarily this is an effectively passive arrangement on the part of the employer, which reflects the employee's primary responsibility for his own health.

---

5 *Johnson v Unisys* [2001] UKHL 13; [2001] 2 WLR 1076.

12. As Lord Reed put it in *Rorrison v West Lothian College* 1999 Rep LR 102, Ct of Sess [an application to strike out the action – "debate on Procedure Roll"]:

> *"I can find nothing in these matters (or elsewhere in the pursuer's pleadings) which, if proved, could establish that Andrews and Henning ought to have foreseen that the pursuer was under a material risk of sustaining a psychiatric disorder in consequence of their behaviour towards her. They might have foreseen that she would at times be unsatisfied, frustrated, embarrassed and upset, but that is a far cry from suffering a psychiatric disorder. Many if not all employees are liable to suffer those emotions, and others mentioned in the present case such as stress, anxiety, loss of confidence and low mood. To suffer such emotions from time to time, not least because of problems at work, is a normal part of human experience. It is only if they are liable to be suffered to such a pathological degree as to constitute a psychiatric disorder that a duty of care to protect against them can arise; and that is not a reasonably foreseeable occurrence (reasonably foreseeable, that is to say, by an ordinary bystander rather than by a psychiatrist) unless there is some specific reason to foresee it in a particular case. I can see no such reason in the present case."*

13. In *Petch v Customs & Excise* [1993] ICR 789 CA – the Claimant clerk of many years had a "mental breakdown" (manic depression) in 1974. He returned to work and then suffered an episode of "hypomania" in January 1975. In 1983 to 1986 he was ill again. His employers were aware of his health history. He complained that his episodes of illness were caused by improper pressure of work. His claim was dismissed, Dillon LJ stating:

> *"I take the view ... that, unless senior management in the Defendant's department were aware or ought to have been aware that the Plaintiff was showing signs of impending breakdown, or were aware or ought to have been aware that his workload carried a real risk that he would have a breakdown, then the Defendants were not negligent in failing to avert the breakdown."* [p.796H].

Particular duties – e.g. to diagnose problems; to give sympathy, etc.

14. It was also argued in *Petch* that the employer had a duty to counsel or give sympathetic support. Dillon LJ said:

> *"[the Plaintiff] submits that [his manager's] duty ... was to have counselled him, and endeavoured by leisured discussion to soothe away his worries ... For my part I do not believe that there was any such duty in law on Mr Woolf."* [p.799D].

15. On the submission that the employer owed a duty to give special weight to the views of the Claimant in making executive decisions when he knew that the employee was vulnerable:

> *"I cannot think that the duty of care owed to the plaintiff required that the chairman should subordinate his own views on the correct tactics to the plaintiff's views ... But I cannot see what other outcome from the impasse favourable to the plaintiff there could have been."* [p.800C]

16. This decision was approved by CA in *Garrett v LB Camden* [2001] EWCA Civ 395 where Simon Browne LJ observed:

> *"63. Unless, however, there was a real risk of breakdown which the claimant's employers ought reasonably to have foreseen and which they ought properly to have averted, there can be no liability."*

> *"67. It seems to me hardly surprising that Mr Garrett's claim should in those circumstances be held to fail. The combined effect of those twin findings was that he knew materially more than his employers about his propensity to work-related stress and breakdown, and can hardly, therefore, blame them for not recognising the particular difficulties attendant upon his continued employment."*

17. Accordingly, although there may well be concurrent duties upon the employer and on the Claimant himself, the Claimant cannot simply refuse to take responsibility for his own health. Where he chooses to work knowing that his work puts his health at risk he will be accepting the risk of injury at work, and his employer may well be in no position to deny him the opportunity to take that risk. If the employer were to do so he not only would risk a claim for injury from the stress of stopping the Claimant from working, but would also risk claims in respect of unfair dismissal, discrimination, and defamation: *Spring v Guardian Assurance*.[6]

The duty after medical advice is disclosed

18. Whether the material duty has been breached is tested by asking whether the Claimant has proved that the Defendant obliged him/her to suffer an unreasonable risk of injury – i.e. an unreasonably high risk. If the employer has medical advice that the employee is at special risk from certain factors at work, and then imposes those factors regardless, he will often be in breach, but not necessarily so.

19. First, what is the nature of the medical disclosure? It is a matter of fact and degree whether there has been sufficient disclosure. An employee may claim a need for special treatment because of his health, but an employer who has no medical report is hardly obliged to comply with the employee's request – it may be common for employees to try to get light or favourable duties in this way. The employee may be vague in his description, or he may agree to do the very work which on one view

---

6 [1994] 3 All ER 129; [1995] 2 AC 296.

he has suggested he should not be doing. An employer with clear advice directly from a medical source is much more likely to be obliged to respond – see *Hatton* §43(10).

20. However, the response which the law requires is not necessarily to follow the medical advice – as the above passages cited from both *Petch* and *Garrett* demonstrate. If it is evident to the employee that his employer cannot or will not put the special measures in place, the employee must still decide (i) whether he is prepared to risk his health by continuing to work in the known adverse conditions, (ii) whether he should go to his GP to obtain a sick certificate (i.e. unfit at this time to work in this job), or (iii) whether he should seek a different job. Many disputes involve questions of this kind.

21. There are also cases where the employer agrees to act in a particular way aimed at reducing the adverse factors at work. Mostly this is by giving an employee a graduated return to work. Sometimes some quite specific steps are agreed. The question then often arises: "When are the steps to be taken?" or "How long are these steps to remain in place?" In *Walker v Northumberland CC* [1995] 1AER 737 Colman J rejected a claim for damages for injury arising from fairly extreme pressures upon an employee who was contemporaneously complaining to his employer that those pressures would injure his health. However, he awarded damages in respect of the injury arising after Mr Walker's return to work. On his return there was specific medical advice as to what was needed, and the employer agreed to put the necessary structure in place. Having done so for a brief period, the employer then reverted to the pre-existing system and the Claimant had a further breakdown. This decision has been regularly referred to and either approved or not criticised in the Court of Appeal

Overwork

22. To a degree psychological stress injuries can readily be compared to physical ones. There are recognised limits to physical endeavour, and if an employer asks an employee to lift too great a weight he will be liable for ensuing damage. Similarly if an employer obliges someone to work too hard and causes injury thereby, he will be liable.

23. In lifting cases there is a quite specific statutory threshold – albeit relaxed in cases of farm labourers. The corresponding regulation for stress may be said to be the Working Time Regulations 1998: an excess of 48 hours per week on average for over 17 weeks breaches the regulation, unless the parties have contracted out. Of course in both cases the coincidence of a breach of duty and an injury does not prove causation, that is quite a separate matter.

24. It must also be borne in mind that there is no such thing as an impossible job – see *Hatton* §43(4) – it is the combination of a vulnerable employee with an onerous job that may result in injury. To establish a breach of duty the Claimant must prove that the work demanded of this particular employee was such that he/she was foreseeably exposed to an unreasonable risk of injury (cf. *Walker*, above).

Injury/causation

25. Lastly there are very complex issues of causation. It must be borne in mind that 'stress' is not a medical condition; it is the function of various factors in a given person's environment. 'Stress' at work is usually considered to be beneficial: it focuses attention, promotes efficiency, and generally is therapeutic to mental health.

26. It is not enough for the Claimant to prove he has suffered an injury caused or contributed to by stress at work; he must prove it was caused by an identified breach – see *Hatton* §43(15). With a condition such as ptsd (post traumatic stress disorder) there is usually no great problem: there is an identifiable index event. However, psychological injury associated with 'stress' is a far more complex beast.

27. First, there is invariably a problem in that the psychiatrists relate the cause to the Claimant's perception of the material events, as opposed to the events themselves. This is a perception which in many cases will have become distorted by reason of the psychological condition – i.e. both after the onset of the condition and in the prodromal state individuals tend to have a heightened and unreliable or unrealistic perception of events.

28. Second, the events referred to at work as the source(s) of the injurious stress almost invariably include matters which are not-actionable (such as personality conflicts; disappointment at the way resources are administered, frustrations at an inability to do one's job in a different way, resentment at more favourable treatment of other employees, etc.).

29. Third, there is usually a catalogue of stresses which exist outside work, whether emotional, financial, environmental, or otherwise (although many of these may not be revealed and/or may prove difficult to discover).

30. Another common problem is that one of the important stressors identified by the Claimant and/or her psychiatrist is often the employer's response to the primary complaint, rather than the subject matter of the complaint itself. For example, the conduct of another employee may well have been upsetting – albeit not pathologically so – but the Claimant may be even more upset by the grievance procedure

and the ensuing decisions, although it will be very rare that the employer's conduct in this regard is actionable in the civil courts (as opposed to the Employment Tribunal).

31. The Claimant then has to unravel all the concurrent stressors and prove on the balance of probabilities that a stressor which the court holds to have amounted to a breach of duty has actually caused an injury – see *Hatton* §43(15). This is not straightforward. The concurrent factors may be such that the material stressor (i.e. that which flows from any breach that the Claimant may have proved) simply cannot be identified with sufficient certainty as a potential and separate stressor. Even once identified, it is usually still difficult to prove causation to the necessary standard: psychiatrists often do not feel able to say with any certainty that the removal of this stressor from the environment would probably have left the Claimant in good health, or to a measurable degree in better health. This is not a *Fairchild* problem, there is only one Defendant – all the other stressors tend to be non-actionable.

32. That is not the end of the problem. The Claimant also has to prove that, absent the proven breach of duty, some different and more beneficial consequence would have ensued. In many cases the options for the employer would in fact have made no material difference (cf. Dillon LJ's comments in *Petch*, above). In some cases the options will have been such although it is possible that the employer might have acted in a way which would have helped avoid some or all of the subject injury, the *likely* non-tortious alternative course that the employer would have taken would also have made no difference. In many cases the best solution would have been for the employer to have dismissed/retired the Claimant for incapacity/ill-health before the injury arose. Not only is there no duty to do this – see *Hatton* §43 (12) – but where this feature is present it will often reflect the fact that this is the course that the Claimant ought to have taken – impacting on questions of *volenti* or on contributory negligence, or both.

Extent of injury

33. Once an injury is proved to have been caused by the identified breach, there is also the question of how significant or persistent it is. Psychological injuries from stress often simply reveal a vulnerable personality. Current thinking is that vulnerability to many psychological disorders is usually a constitutional matter, even where there has been no reported (or recorded) psychological problem before. In short, the employee will often be increasingly at risk of developing psychological problems – whether in response to work or to other factors – and the condition for which damages are claimed may be seen either as an acceleration of the onset of the condition, or one which would in any event have been superseded by a subsequent episode

within a given period. In *Hatton* the problem was resolved in one case in this way – see §43(16).

The recent cases: Hatton, and Barber

34. The Court of Appeal in Hatton conveniently set out a list of key features:

> "43. From the above discussion, the following practical propositions emerge:
>
> (1) There are no special control mechanisms applying to claims for psychiatric (or physical) illness or injury arising from the stress of doing the work the employee is required to do (para 22). The ordinary principles of employer's liability apply (para 20).
>
> (2) The threshold question is whether this kind of harm to this particular employee was reasonably foreseeable (para 23): this has two components (a) an injury to health (as distinct from occupational stress) which (b) is attributable to stress at work (as distinct from other factors) (para 25).
>
> (3) Foreseeability depends upon what the employer knows (or ought reasonably to know) about the individual employee. Because of the nature of mental disorder, it is harder to foresee than physical injury, but may be easier to foresee in a known individual than in the population at large (para 23). An employer is usually entitled to assume that the employee can withstand the normal pressures of the job unless he knows of some particular problem or vulnerability (para 29).
>
> (4) The test is the same whatever the employment: there are no occupations which should be regarded as intrinsically dangerous to mental health (para 24).
>
> (5) Factors likely to be relevant in answering the threshold question include:
>
> (a) The nature and extent of the work done by the employee (para 26). Is the workload much more than is normal for the particular job? Is the work particularly intellectually or emotionally demanding for this employee? Are demands being made of this employee unreasonable when compared with the demands made of others in the same or comparable jobs? Or are there signs that others doing this job are suffering harmful levels of stress? Is there an abnormal level of sickness or absenteeism in the same job or the same department?

(b) Signs from the employee of impending harm to health (paras 27 and 28). Has he a particular problem or vulnerability? Has he already suffered from illness attributable to stress at work? Have there recently been frequent or prolonged absences which are uncharacteristic of him? Is there reason to think that these are attributable to stress at work, for example because of complaints or warnings from him or others?

(6) The employer is generally entitled to take what he is told by his employee at face value, unless he has good reason to think to the contrary. He does not generally have to make searching enquiries of the employee or seek permission to make further enquiries of his medical advisers (para 29).

(7) To trigger a duty to take steps, the indications of impending harm to health arising from stress at work must be plain enough for any reasonable employer to realise that he should do something about it (para 31).

(8) The employer is only in breach of duty if he has failed to take the steps which are reasonable in the circumstances, bearing in mind the magnitude of the risk of harm occurring, the gravity of the harm which may occur, the costs and practicability of preventing it, and the justifications for running the risk (para 32).

(9) The size and scope of the employer's operation, its resources and the demands it faces are relevant in deciding what is reasonable; these include the interests of other employees and the need to treat them fairly, for example, in any redistribution of duties (para 33).

(10) An employer can only reasonably be expected to take steps which are likely to do some good: the court is likely to need expert evidence on this (para 34).

(11) An employer who offers a confidential advice service, with referral to appropriate counselling or treatment services, is unlikely to be found in breach of duty (paras 17 and 33).

(12) If the only reasonable and effective step would have been to dismiss or demote the employee, the employer will not be in breach of duty in allowing a willing employee to continue in the job (para 34).

(13) In all cases, therefore, it is necessary to identify the steps which the employer both could and should have taken before finding him in breach of his duty of care (para 33).

(14) The claimant must show that that breach of duty has caused or materially contributed to the harm suffered. It is not enough to show that occupational stress has caused the harm (para 35).

(15) Where the harm suffered has more than one cause, the employer should only pay for that proportion of the harm suffered which is attributable to his wrongdoing, unless the harm is truly indivisible. It is for the defendant to raise the question of apportionment (paras 36 and 39).

(16) The assessment of damages will take account of any pre-existing disorder or vulnerability and of the chance that the claimant would have succumbed to a stress related disorder in any event (para 42)."

35. In *Barber* the House of Lords unanimously held that these propositions were correct, but the majority held that the Court of Appeal had misdirected itself in applying them in the case of Mr Barber. The majority held that the findings of fact which the trial judge had made were within the range of findings he could properly have made, without any of the House observing that they would have found the facts in the same way. It is difficult to divine any material proposition of law which alters the concise direction given by the Court of Appeal; at this stage the commentators do not appear to have found any.

Good practice suggestions

The brief chronology

The essence is to keep it brief, aiming for no more than a half to three-quarters side of A4. If possible never create a chronology which the judge has to turn over. To succeed in this you must be highly discriminating with the facts, so that only the dates and events with which the hearing is concerned are listed. If it is reliable the judge is likely to prefer to use the shorter chronology should both sides produce one.

Do not hold back any of your basic argument – certainly never anything essential. Retain some colour to bring it to life orally. Oral argument is for dialogue, explanation, and amplification but the court should receive no serious surprises. Withhold any particular angle of an argument which may be received better if advanced orally.

Example D

Queen's Bench application to vacate trial – Claimant's skeleton submissions by Ronald Walker QC March, 2009 – 4pp.

Alison Cardy (Executrix of the Estate of Kevin Hegarty Deceased) v BBC was a mesothelioma claim – Need for permission to call epidemiologist as evidence in rebuttal of recently served evidence by Defendant.

The writer's skeleton is a model of succinctness. Applications to vacate are notoriously difficult but this was a designated category 'A' case with implications for other mesothelioma claims. It concerned what has to be proven in causation for liability to be established.

The application was successful. The claim was settled within six months.

CLAIMANT'S SKELETON ARGUMENT FOR APPLICATION: 24 MARCH 2009

[References in bold are to the Application Bundle]

Introduction

1. This is the Claimant's application (**36**) for an Order (1) vacating the trial window (commencing 2 April 2009), and (2) permitting the Claimant to rely upon the evidence of an epidemiologist.

2. There is an Application Bundle, but it has been sent from Newcastle and is likely to have reached the court only this morning. In support of the application the Claimant relies upon the witness statement of Andrew Venn dated 23 March 2009 (**409**).

Adjournment of trial

1. As appears from Mr Venn's statement there are two grounds for this application. The first is the Claimant's wish to instruct an epidemiologist; the second is the recent service by the Defendant of (a) a further expert's report, (b) the software programme upon which its expert's opinion is based, (c) a further witness statement, and (d) further documents (3 lever arch files).

2. This case has been listed as Category A by the Senior Master because it raises a point of general importance in mesothelioma claims. The point is whether a claimant who can prove occupational exposure has to prove that his tumour is more likely than not to have been caused by

that exposure (as opposed to environmental exposure) or whether it is sufficient to prove that the occupational exposure materially increased the risk. If the former is the case the claim will fail if the calculated occupational exposure is no greater than the calculated environmental exposure.

3. Defendants have recently argued this point successfully in the Liverpool County Court in *Sienkiewicz v Greif (UK) Ltd*.[1] The judgment (which is understood to be subject to appeal) is in the bundle at **362**. The defendants in that case (as in this) relied upon the evidence of Dr Jones, while the Claimant had only a plumbing and heating engineer. The judge (unsurprisingly) regarded the evidence of Dr Jones as "more authoritative…in epidemiological terms" (judgment, para. 46 (**390**).

4. When the present case was commenced it was perceived to be a run-of-the-mill mesothelioma claim. The point above referred to had not arisen before and was not considered. It was not raised in the Defence, nor at the CMC on 7 April 2008 (**32–5**), when directions for expert evidence were given (**25**). It emerged in Dr Jones's report of 17. 9.08 and was expressly raised by the Defendant at the CMC on 6 October 2008.

5. The Defendant contends that the Claimant could and should have sought evidence from an epidemiologist at this stage, rather than assume that the issue could be adequately dealt with by Mr Plumb and/or Dr Rudd. There is obviously force in this argument. Mr Venn deals with it in paragraphs 7–13 of his witness statement.

6. The salient points are that Mr Venn (a) had not until 9 March seen the judgment in *Sienkiewicz*, and (b) had not received the advice then given to him by Frank Burton Q.C. As to (a) Mr Feeny e-mailed the draft judgment to Master Whitaker on 27 November, and also attempted to do so to Thompsons. However it has now emerged that he did not have the correct e-mail address for Thompsons, which no doubt explains why the judgment did not reach Mr Venn.[2]

7. Quite apart from the wish to instruct an epidemiologist, there are further legitimate grounds for seeking an adjournment, *viz.*

   (1) the recent disclosure (18 March) of the software programme upon which Dr Jones's calculations are evidently based.[3] Dr Rudd is not due to return from annual leave until 30 March, and will not have adequate time to consider the programme, discuss

---

1 HH Judge Peter Main QC (25.11.08).

2 Andrew Venn w/s para.16.

3 Andrew Venn w/s paras.7–9.

the same with the Claimant's legal team and prepare a supplemental report;

(2) the late disclosure (9–10 March) of 3 further files of documents, relating to the deceased's exposure, which need to be analysed and upon which instructions, and possibly further witness statements, will be required from the Claimant's witnesses;

(3) the recent service (11 March) of a further witness statement from the Defendant's principal lay witness, and of a further report from Dr Jones (18 March) based upon this new evidence. The evidence of Mr Bean is obviously highly significant because it has caused Dr Jones to revise his estimate of occupational exposure by a factor of 5.[4] This is in breach of the Order of 2 December 2008 (**29–31**)[5] and it is submitted that this alone would entitle the Claimant to an adjournment to deal with this evidence.

Permission to rely upon epidemiologist

8. Obviously if the trial window is not vacated this application falls away.

9. However if the trial is adjourned it is submitted that there are good reasons why, in fairness, the Claimant ought to be entitled to rely upon the evidence of an epidemiologist, and no good reason why she should not.

Good practice suggestion

The skeleton was sufficiently clear and terse that the judge had to read no other material to get into the case and understand what was wanted, and needed very little material with which to support the argument. This directness of approach is business-like and wastes very little judicial time. However if the judge is not with you on the point, it gives little room for manoeuvre.

4 Andrew Venn w/s paras.20–21.

5 Which was made upon the Defendant's submission that it would like "a short period of time, say to 31 January 2009, to serve further witness evidence if so advised".

Example E

Queen's Bench Commercial Court trial – Claimant's opening skeleton submissions by Ronald Walker QC, September 2010 – 18pp.

Greene Wood & Mclean LLP (In Administration) v Templeton Insurance was a claim for an insurance indemnity in respect of costs due under an ATE policy of insurance arising from part of the British Coal Respiratory Disease Litigation.

Such complications as derive from the relationship between multiple parties and in a group action are skilfully diffused by the use of a clear narrative of events as a precursor to argument.

The claim succeeded. The case is reported at [2010] EWHC 2679 (Comm) and at [2010] All ER (D) 274 (Oct), Lawtel ref AC0126468.

CLAIMANT'S SKELETON OPENING

[References in bold are to the Trial Bundles and pages therein]

Background to the litigation

1. This litigation arises out of the wrongful refusal of the Defendant (hereafter "Templeton") to indemnify its insureds, 64 former coal miners, against liability under an interim costs order in the sum of £600,000 made against them by Sir Michael Turner on 18 May 2006.

2. The Claimant ("GWM") was a firm of solicitors who had acted for the miners in those proceedings, which consisted of an application for a Group Litigation Order ("GLO") the Respondents to which were 5 firms of solicitors, the Union of Democratic Mineworkers and a claims handling company associated with that Union.

3. Templeton was the ATE insurer of the miners, who were entitled to indemnity under the ATE policy against the costs order. When it became apparent that Templeton was not going to indemnify, and that the GLO Respondents were proceeding to enforce the order against the miners, GWM, by its professional indemnity insurers, the Seventh Party ("QBE"), satisfied the interim costs order and settled the costs claims of the GLO Respondents, paying in total the sum of £1,160,000.

4. QBE then sought to recover its outlay from Templeton. GWM had obtained from the miners assignments of the latter's rights under the policy. GWM therefore commenced arbitration proceedings against Templeton (the policy contained an arbitration clause). However

Templeton took the point that GWM had no rights under the policy because the same contained a prohibition against assignment.

5. This point was met by adding two of the miners ("Beardall and Cooke") to the arbitration proceedings. Templeton then argued (successfully) that Beardall and Cooke could not recover under the policy an indemnity against their costs liability because that liability had been satisfied by GWM. The only remaining liability against which Beardall and Cooke could be entitled to indemnity under the policy was their liability to pay disbursements, namely the fees of counsel who had represented them on the GLO application.[1]

6. The arbitration proceeded in relation to the disbursements claim and eventually Beardall and Cooke succeeded and on 20th October 2008 were awarded £152,127.86 (plus interest).

7. The Claim Form in this action was issued on 31 March 2008. Templeton (which is incorporated in the Isle of Man) refused to submit to the jurisdiction, so that it was necessary for GWM to apply for permission to serve out of the jurisdiction. The application succeeded and the decision was appealed to the Court of Appeal (**A1 3–11**).

Narrative of events

8. In 1998 two groups of actions against the British Coal Corporation[2] were tried; the first was the British Coal Respiratory Disease Litigation[3] (which was tried by Turner J.) and the second a group of vibration white finger claims.[4]

9. Following these judgments, in 1999 the Department of Trade and Industry set up two compensation schemes to deal with the hundreds of thousands of claims which were expected to be (and were) made by former miners who had contracted respiratory disease or VWF. Each scheme involved a Claims Handling Arrangement (CHA) which was made either between the DTI and the Claimants' Solicitors Group (CSG) or between the DTI and the UDM/Vendside Limited.

10. It was a feature of the CHAs that the costs of successful Claimants were paid by the DTI to the CSG or Vendside (usually on a tariff basis) and

---

1 Two of whom are the Fifth and Sixth Parties. The original leading counsel (now H. H. Judge Powles Q.C.) has not been joined to these proceedings.

2 Statutory successor to the National Coal Board. The occupational health liabilities of the British Coal Corporation were transferred to the Department of Trade and Industry on 1 January 1998.

3 *Griffiths v British Coal Corporation* (unreported 27.1.98).

4 *Armstrong v British Coal Corporation* [1998] CLY 2842.

that the Claimants themselves could not be ordered to pay any costs. The schemes proved to be hugely profitable to solicitors, some of whom had many thousands of cases. Nevertheless many miners were persuaded to enter into agreements whereby some part of their compensation was deducted and paid over to their union or Vendside.

11. In due course this state of affairs attracted publicity and complaints were made to Members of Parliament, some of whom in 2004 approached Mr Wynne Edwards, who was then with a firm specialising in class or group actions, for advice as to what could be done. No arrangements were made at that time but in the Spring of 2005 the approach was renewed, by which time Mr Edwards had been introduced to, and was doing business with, Templeton.

12. The essential feature of the miners' potential claims was that, while individually they were likely to be small, it was anticipated that there were potentially thousands, or even tens of thousands, of such claims. It was also essential that the miners who agreed to instruct GWM to act for them should be assured that they would not be at any risk of having to pay costs personally. It was Mr Edwards' perception that the best way of managing these claims would be via a Group Litigation Order.

13. Mr Edwards deals with the arrangements which were made in 2005, leading to the issue of the GLO application on 27 October, in paragraphs 4–15 of his witness statement (**B1 2–5**).

14. In summary Templeton, who were providing ATE insurance for two other group actions in which GWM were acting,[5] agreed to provide ATE insurance for the miners' claims. The agreement was reached in principle at a meeting in Douglas, Isle of Man, at the end of June, albeit details remained to be agreed (such as policy wording and premium) and were subsequently agreed, most of them at a further meeting on 7 July. The policy commencement date was 13 July 2005[6] (the policy is at **E2 12–22**).

15. On 29 June 2005 Mr Edwards attended a consultation with Stephen Powles Q.C. at his chambers (Henderson Chambers) and Oliver Campbell; it is the Claimant's case that the final decision to apply for a GLO was taken following, and as a result of, that consultation.

16. Mr Edwards then proceeded to prepare the documents to be used for the miners to enter into CFAs. These documents are at **E1 36–47**. They were sent to Templeton on 26 August (**E1 56**).

---

5 But neither of these actions (referred to as the British Biotech and Claims Direct litigation) was the subject of a GLO.

6 Albeit Templeton did not provide the completed version until 13 March 2006 (**E2 11**).

17. The Application Notice was issued on 27 October (**E1 70**), supported by Mr Edwards' witness statement dated 26 October (**E1 72–99**).

18. There was a directions hearing before Sir Michael Turner[7] on 7–8 December which resulted in the Order at **D2 71–5**.

19. Because the Respondents were querying the existence of effective ATE cover and calling for disclosure of the policy (which Templeton had still not issued) paragraph 3 of the Order (**D2** 72) required the Applicants by 16 December to state whether they were prepared to disclose the ATE policy. On 16 December Mr Edwards confirmed to the judge that the Applicants were prepared to do so (**C11 247**) but Templeton (having said they hoped to produce the policy wording by 31 December[8]) failed to do so. This led to applications by the Respondents for disclosure of the policy and to the Applicants consenting to an order for disclosure by 10 March (**D2 77**). The policy was eventually sent to GWM by Templeton on 13 March 2006 (**E2 11**) and then forwarded to the Respondents.

20. The GLO Application was heard on 3–5 April 2006. Judgment was handed down on 18 May (**E2 76–89.13**). On that occasion there was no information available as to the extent, if any, of the indemnity which Templeton would provide; accordingly the judge made an order for an interim payment of £600,000 "to force insurers' hands" (**D5 162**).

21. On 23 May Brooke North LLP (who acted for the UDM and Vendside) wrote to Templeton (**E2 92**) seeking confirmation that the policy was in force and that Templeton would satisfy the costs order. Mr Maule of Templeton replied to Brooke North on 25 May (**E2 94**) stating, for the reasons set out in his letter, he was "declaring the policy void ab initio". He did not, however, write to GWM or to any of the insureds.

22. Mr Maule's response to Brooke North's letter was e-mailed to GWM, who wrote to Templeton on 2 June (**E2 99**) asking for details of the grounds of the purported policy avoidance and for a clear statement of Templeton's position. Templeton did not reply to that letter; chasing letters of 13 and 23 June produced a holding response (**E2 104**). GWM sent a detailed letter to Templeton's nominated solicitors, Hannah & Mould, on 26 July (**E2 105**) but this produced only a holding reply (**C23 69**). GWM wrote again to Hannah & Mould on 6 September (**C23 110**) which resulted in another holding reply (**C23 124**). The next letter was from CMS Cameron McKenna (instructed by QBE) to Hannah & Mould on 10 November 2006 (**C23 245**).

---

7 Who was the supervising judge for the BCRDL.

8 **E1 150**.

23. Meanwhile, during this period, while Templeton was refusing to tell GWM whether it was avoiding the policy or not, there was a great deal of activity. On 27 June Brooke North obtained 27 interim Charging Orders on miners' homes (**C23 23**).[9] On 6 July Mishcon de Reya, who had by now been instructed by a number of the miners, wrote to Cameron McKenna citing the GWM "guarantee to clients" (**C22 138**) and on 11 June sent a pre-action protocol letter to GWM (**E2 118**).

24. On 7 and 9 June Brooke North and Weightmans issued applications for wasted costs orders against GWM (**C23 27, 45**) and directions for a hearing before Sir Michael Turner were agreed (**C23 101**).

25. In September and October Cameron McKenna negotiated settlements with the GWM Respondents. (**E2 141, 144**) and with the miners (**E2 147, 158**).[10]

26. No reply was received from Hannah & Mould to Cameron McKenna's letter of 10 November (referred to in paragraph 22 above) but on 21 November a holding letter was received from Manches LLP (who had evidently replaced Hannah & Mould) and by a further letter dated 22 December Manches stated that they were still not in a position to confirm indemnity (**B1 99**).

27. On 11 January 2007 Cameron McKenna commenced arbitration proceedings in the name of GWM. As stated above Templeton disputed GWM's entitlement to rely on the policy, because the same contained a prohibition against assignment (**E2 21**).The arbitrator upheld this objection in his First Partial Award (**F1 18**) and the arbitration proceeded in the names of Beardall and Cooke. By his Second Partial Award (**F1 43–4**) the arbitrator decided that the claim in respect of costs payable to the GLO Respondents could not succeed, because they had been paid by GWM, but the claim in respect of disbursements could continue.

28. The remaining issues were dealt with in the Third Partial and Final Awards. The disbursements claim succeeded (**F1 68–77**).

GWM's claims against Templeton

29. There are two claims; (1) for damages for breach of contract; and (2) for a contribution under the Civil Liability (Contribution) Act 1978.

---

9 And a hearing, of applications for final Charging Orders, was fixed for 1 August.

10 The circumstances in which these settlements were negotiated are set out in the witness statement of Peter Maguire, partner in CMS Cameron McKenna, at **B1 97–101**.

30. In the proceedings arising out of GWM's application to serve out of the jurisdiction Templeton's position was that neither claim was sustainable. In relation to the contract claim (which depends upon the implication of a term) Templeton denied that any term of the kind contended for could be implied. In relation to the claim under the 1978 Act Templeton contended that the element of "same damage" was absent, so that no claim for a contribution could lie.

31. These arguments, if accepted, would have produced an extraordinary result, i.e. that even though Templeton had a liability under the policy to indemnify the miners in respect of the costs order made in the GLO proceedings (a) the miners could not enforce that liability (because GWM had satisfied it), and (b) GWM would have no claim either. In short, Templeton's liability under the policy would have disappeared into a legal "black hole" (as Longmore LJ observed in the Court of Appeal, at paragraph 13) (**A1 7**).

32. The Court of Appeal held that GWM's contract claim raised a serious issue to be tried (i.e. on its merits).

33. However, on the "same damage" point the Court decided that the liability of both GWM and Templeton was in respect of the "same damage" (namely the liability of the miners to pay the costs of the respondents to the GLO application). Longmore LJ said this in terms (at paragraph 22), while in paragraph 24 he said

> *What is clear is that insurers' failure to pay the respondents' costs and the miners' own disbursements has rendered GWM in breach of their contractual obligation to the miners. The damage suffered by the miners is exactly the same damage as suffered by them as a result of insurers' failure to honour their obligations under the ATE policy.*

and in paragraph 27

> *But in the present case for the reasons given, the damage is not just substantially or materially similar. It is, in fact, the same damage.*

(1) GWM's contract claim

34. It is beyond question that there was a contract between GWM and Templeton, the essential term of which was that Templeton would provide ATE insurance to cover the potential liabilities of miners with whom GWM entered into Conditional Fee Agreements.

35. The version of events set out in Mr Edwards' witness statement (**B1 2–5**) (which forms the basis of the pleading at paragraphs 4–8 of the Re-Amended Particulars of Claim (**A1 13–14**) and the further information at **A1 154–5**) is uncontradicted by any evidence from Templeton, who

have never served any witness statement from Brunswick, Maule or Fresson.

36. It is GWM's case that, applying either or both of the business efficacy test and the officious bystander test, in agreeing with GWM that the latter would (a) be authorised to bind its clients to contracts of ATE insurance with Templeton and (b) give its clients the "GWM Guarantee"[11] Templeton must be taken to have agreed that it would meet valid claims under the Policy, and that this was an obligation assumed to GWM, and not merely to the individual miners.

37. By its contract with Templeton GWM effectively agreed to guarantee Templeton's performance of its obligations to the miners. If Templeton defaulted on those obligations, with the consequence that the miners looked to GWM for indemnity (as they were obviously highly likely to do, rather than seeking to proceed against a company outside the jurisdiction to enforce an insurance policy they had never even seen), it would be a strange result if GWM had no contractual claim over against Templeton.

38. As Longmore LJ observed (judgment, paragraph 14) if GWM have no subrogated right (as Templeton has maintained) or the existence of a subrogated right is doubtful (as it is)

> *that in itself must be a pointer to the necessity of the alleged implied term*

39. The absence of logic, let alone merits, in Templeton's position can be gauged by considering what actually happened. Because of Templeton's refusal to indemnify, the miners were facing the enforcement proceedings referred to in paragraph 19 of the Re-Amended Particulars of Claim. They had an apparently cast iron case against GWM for breach of the warranty contained in the GWM Guarantee. So GWM's PI insurers, QBE, satisfied the costs orders. When the miners claimed under the policy they were met, in the arbitration, with the defence that their loss had already been satisfied by GWM.

40. Accordingly it is contended that it must have been contemplated by the parties, when concluding their contract, that if Templeton wrongly refused indemnity and GWM was called upon to, and did, indemnify the miners against their costs liabilities, GWM would have a claim over against Templeton.

---

11 Pleaded in paragraph 7 of the Re-Amended Particulars of Claim (**A1 13**). The document itself is at **E1 36**.

41. Succeeding on its contract claim, as well as on the claim under the 1978 Act, is important to the Claimant for two reasons. First, its damages are not limited by the limit of indemnity under the policy, so that it can recover the sums claimed in the Particulars under paragraph 25 (**A1 17–18**). Secondly its claim is not susceptible to reduction for contributory negligence (if such were established).

(2) GWM's contribution claim

42. As stated above the "same damage" point has been decided by the Court of Appeal and Templeton cannot re-open it.[12] In any event the decision was obviously correct.

43. Since GWM was put in breach of its warranty to the miners by Templeton's fault, the contribution should amount to a complete indemnity. It is, of course, accepted that Templeton's contribution is subject to the limit of indemnity under the policy, £152,127.86 of which has already been paid.

44. It is a constant theme in Templeton's pleaded case that GWM's settlement with the GLO Respondents was in reality a settlement of its own potential liability for wasted costs. This is not so (although of course the settlement agreements did settle these potential liabilities). GWM had to indemnify the miners against their costs liabilities by reason of the GWM Guarantee. Whether or not they had also been negligent in the conduct of the litigation was nothing to the point.

45. In fact (if it arises) it is GWM's case that no wasted costs order would have been made against GWM (or if Sir Michael Turner had made one, the same would have been susceptible to successful appeal), not least because client privilege would have precluded GWM from giving evidence as to what advice it had received from counsel and the court would have been bound to give GWM the benefit of any doubt which it had.

46. But in any event there was no misconduct on the part of GWM which could plausibly have justified the making of a wasted costs order.

47. Finally on this point, the wasted costs applications were only made because of Templeton's wrongful failure to meet the interim costs order, but for which it is clear that no application would have been made (see **D5 142–3, 162**).

12 The words in brackets in issue 7(a) in the List of Issues at **A1 313** were included at the Defendant's request.

Templeton's additional claim against GWM

48. The issues which arise on this claim are set out as 9–13 of the List of Issues (**A1 314**).

49. The first issue is what, if any, relevant duties GWM owed to Templeton. It is pleaded by Templeton (**A1 94**) that the terms of the policy imposed duties, but this is an impossible argument; GWM was not a party to the contract of insurance.

50. The alternative pleading is that GWM owed a duty to Templeton (a) to advise upon the form and nature of any proposed proceedings, and (b) to conduct those proceedings with due care and skill. Neither proposition is accepted.

51. As to (a) above, insofar as the alleged negligence lay in choosing to apply for a GLO in the first place (which was Sir Michael Turner's view) Templeton chose to provide insurance knowing that this was the course which was to be adopted. As an experienced ATE insurer it was well able to decide whether this was a risk that it was prepared to insure, and to fix the premium accordingly; if it needed advice it would no doubt have asked for it (from GWM or elsewhere).

52. As to (b) GWM's duties were to its clients.

53. If there was duty owed to Templeton this gives rise to an extensive factual enquiry as to whether GWM was negligent in any respects and, if it was, what damage that has caused to Templeton.

54. Templeton appears to do no more than adopt the criticisms that Sir Michael Turner made in his judgment. It is GWM's case (and also that of the Fifth and Sixth Parties) that these criticisms were all misplaced (save perhaps those arising out of Templeton's repeated failure to produce the policy, the ambiguities in the policy and its changing and evasive explanations of how the premium was to be funded).

55. Mr Edwards deals with all of Sir Michael Turner's criticisms in paragraphs 37–61 of his witness statement (**B1 12–20**). He had dealt fully with the points raised in the wasted costs applications in his fifth witness statement (**D2 41**). The Fifth and Sixth Parties, both of whom arte extremely experienced in group litigation, give evidence to similar effect in their witness statements.

56. It is suggested that, in the face of this evidence, Templeton face a mammoth task in proving that the barristers, or GWM, were negligent.

57. In relation to both (a) the decision to apply for a GLO, and subsequently to pursue that application, and (b) the conduct of the

proceedings, GWM were also entitled to rely upon the advice of counsel. The only issues between counsel and Mr Edwards appear to be whether they were asked for and/or gave positive advice, and whether Mr Edwards in fact relied upon them at all. As to reliance, it is clear that he had decided that a GLO was the appropriate course in advance of instructing counsel. But if they had advised against it he would not have proceeded in the face of that advice.

58. Whether or not Mr Edwards relied upon counsel in relation to the initial decision to proceed by way of a GLO application, there can be no doubt but that he relied upon them in relation to the conduct of the proceedings, once the decision to proceed by way of a GLO application had been taken (in relation to such matters as the drafting of the Application, Generic Particulars of Claim and witness statements and the decisions as to which parties to join and which not to join).

59. As to whether positive advice was given, whether or not Mr Edwards' recollection of what Mr Powles said at the first consultation is accurate, it is clear that the barristers did in fact give positive advice in writing (see **E1 22–4** and **54**).

60. Therefore if Templeton have any tenable claim in relation to the costs or disbursements incurred, it will be necessary for the court to determine which items of costs or disbursements were incurred as a result of a particular act or omission, and then to determine whether that particular act or omission on the part of GWM was negligent. This exercise will necessarily involve a detailed enquiry which it will probably not be possible to undertake within the framework of the present trial.[13]

Beardall and Cooke's additional claim against GWM

61. This claim is contended to be misconceived, for the reasons pleaded in paragraph 17 of the Amended Reply and Defence to Additional Claims **(A1 127–8)**

62. Beardall and Cooke have suffered no damage. Their costs liability was discharged by GWM and they recovered their disbursements in the arbitration.

63. In relation to both costs and disbursements GWM's obligation was to ensure that they were at no risk by arranging ATE insurance, which obligation it performed. If the insurance was, in the event, inadequate in amount that has caused no loss to Beardall or Cooke.

---

13 Templeton have not so far sought to distinguish between different items, or even heads, of costs or disbursements.

64. It was a term of the retainer of GWM by Beardall and Cooke that the latter would be at no risk of having to pay costs or disbursements. Accordingly there was no duty to safeguard them against an adverse costs order or GWM incurring disbursements.

65. Finally, by the time each of Beardall and Cooke had retained GWM, the decision to apply for a GLO had already been made, and the proceedings were in train and there was no duty owed to each Applicant to reconsider the wisdom of decisions upon each becoming a party.

The Fifth and Sixth Parties' claims against GWM and QBE

66. At first sight these claims have a superficial attraction, inasmuch as QBE have retained the award which was made in the arbitration in respect of the barristers' fees, on the basis that Beardall and Cooke were obliged to pay them.

67. However, as a matter of law the claim is unsustainable, essentially for two reasons. The first is that QBE was entitled to sums payable under the policy by reason of its subrogated rights. The second is that, even if this were not so, the persons entitled to retain the fees would be Beardall and Cooke (and not the Fifth or Sixth Parties) – but for the fact that Beardall and Cooke had assigned their rights under the policy to GWM.

68. As to subrogation, the analysis is as follows.

    (1) GWM, by reason of the GWM guarantee (or, for that matter, negligence) was facing a potential liability to the miners.

    (2) That liability would have extended to whatever damages were recoverable by the miners, whether in respect of opponents' costs or disbursements or other heads of claim[14] (hereafter called "the damages claims").

    (3) QBE in turn were liable to indemnify GWM in respect of any claims the miners might make against them (whether in respect of the miners' liability for costs or disbursements).

    (4) QBE settled the damages claims. Upon so doing it became subrogated to whatever rights GWM had against third parties in respect of the subject matter of the damages claims. These rights included the right to claim damages against Templeton for not indemnifying their clients.

---

14 E.g. damages for distress.

(5) It cannot make any difference that some part of those damages was recovered in the arbitration rather than in the present action.

(6) But in any event, by the time of the arbitration, GWM had acquired by assignment the miners' rights under the policy (as part of the transaction whereby QBE discharged GWM's liabilities); so QBE became subrogated to those rights.

69. But if this analysis were incorrect the effect would be that the entitlement to the award would be that of Beardall and Cooke (were it not for the fact that they had already assigned their entitlement to GWM (see **E2 166**)).

70. There is no question of the claim for indemnity in respect of disbursements being impressed with a trust in favour of the barristers. If Beardall and Cooke had received the money they could have disposed of it as they wished. It will be recalled that it was this state of affairs[15] that led to the passing of the Third Party (Rights against Insurers) Act 1930.

71. Finally, by the time of the arbitration the barristers had obtained judgment against GWM in the sum of £148,081.25 in respect of their outstanding fees, so that they no longer had any rights to their fees (the same having been extinguished and replaced by the judgment).

Good practice suggestions

Providing the judge with a narrative rather than a chronology will appeal to his or her human interest as a reader, and engage him with the facts in a way that a list of dates will not.

Wherever possible simplify the subject matter, and use general principles with which to do so.

15 As exemplified by *re Harrington Motor Co Ltd* [1928] Ch 105 and *Hood's Trustees v Southern Union General of Australia* [1928] Ch 793.

Example F

Queen's Bench Commercial Court trial – Defendant's opening skeleton submissions by Sue Carr QC and Jonathan Hough, May 2010 – 41pp.

Persimmon Homes v Great Lakes Reinsurance was a claim to enforce a policy of insurance under the Third Parties (Rights Against Insurers) Act 1930 in unusual circumstances and raising some significant questions concerning legal principles and market practice relating to After-the-Event legal expenses insurance. Core factual issues involved findings of misrepresentation and non-disclosure in inducing the insurer to enter the policy.

The writer uses bold statements to interest the Court, and a clear and simple analysis of what has happened and what is required. Significant use is made of the sequential nature of the service of skeletons with issues being cross-referenced to the Claimants' position. Issues are numbered and addressed sequentially. Parties are referred to by name or acronym rather than by status.

The claim failed. The case is reported at [2010] EWHC 1705 (Comm) and at [2010] All ER (D) 114 (Jul), Lawtel ref AC0125342.

OPENING SKELETON ARGUMENT OF THE DEFENDANT

The structure of this skeleton argument is as follows:

A. Introduction
B. Factual Background
   - ATE Insurance
   - The RSA Pursuit Scheme
   - *CPH v Persimmon*: the Underlying Dispute
   - The Proposals for ATE Insurance
   - *CPH v Persimmon*: the Litigation
   - The Conduct of First Assist and the Decision to Avoid the Policy/Repudiate the Claim
C. The Issues
D. The 1930 Act and the Basis of the Claim
E. The Insurer's Right to Avoid the policy: Misrepresentations and Non-Disclosure at Inception
   - Misrepresentations and Non-disclosure
      (i) The dishonest statements of the Traceys in correspondence
      (ii) The dishonest note procured by Bernard Tracey and produced by Robert Dorin
      (iii) Paul Tracey's dishonest 'contemporaneous' note of the meeting on 1 December 1999

(iv) The bankruptcy of Bernard Tracey and the financial difficulties of the Traceys
(v) The dishonest account of the Traceys of the key meetings
– Materiality
– Inducement
– Persimmon's Submissions on ATE Insurance

F. The Insurer's Right to Avoid the Policy: Breach of the Post-inception Duty of Good Faith
G. The Insurer's Right to Repudiate the Claim: Policy Conditions
H. The Insurer's Right to Repudiate the claim: Fraudulent Claim/Illegality
I. Persimmon's Allegation of Waiver
J. Witnesses at Trial
K. Conclusion

A. Introduction

1. This case raises some significant questions concerning legal principles and market practice relating to After-the-Event legal expenses insurance ['ATE insurance'], a species of insurance which has developed in recent years to support litigation of various types. The Defendant's position is that conventional principles of insurance law governing avoidance and waiver apply to ATE insurance. The Claimant, by contrast, advocates an approach which is highly unorthodox both in legal and commercial terms.

2. In this case, an ATE policy branded 'Pursuit' ['the Policy'] was written in 2005 to cover the adverse costs liabilities of CPH Enterprises Ltd ['CPH'] in its proceedings against the Claimants ['Persimmon'][1]. The Policy was underwritten by Royal & Sun Alliance Insurance Plc ['RSA'], but it was administered for all practical purposes by FirstAssist Insurance Services Ltd ['FISL'] under a binding authority. The Defendant ['GLR'] has succeeded to the legal expenses insurance business of RSA as the result of a transfer under Part VII of the Financial Services and Markets Act 2000[2]. In order to obtain the insurance, CPH made a detailed presentation, comprising a proposal form, summary of claim, draft witness statements, etc. CPH signed declarations in the usual form confirming the accuracy and completeness of the material supplied.

3. The underlying proceedings between CPH and Persimmon involved a dispute over a property transaction concerning a substantial site in Birmingham. In those proceedings, CPH alleged that Persimmon had entered into an oral agreement in December 1999 to provide a series of

1 The Claimants will be referred to collectively as 'Persimmon', save where it is necessary to specify one of them.

2 The transfer took effect on 8 February 2006.

benefits in return for CPH having introduced Persimmon to the site. In the alternative, CPH alleged that the parties had reached an informal agreement in August 1999 which conferred upon it a *Pallant v Morgan* equity. In the further alternative, CPH claimed restitution on the basis of the 'free acceptance' principle. Persimmon resisted all the claims. It contested the factual account of CPH's witnesses, notably its director Paul Tracey and his father, Bernard Tracey. It also raised a series of legal objections to the claim, including arguments that any agreement found to exist would be both void and ineffective for want of consideration.

4. The trial in *CPH v Persimmon* took place in June 2008. In the course of the trial, Persimmon exposed a series of dishonest documents and statements made by the two men at the heart of CPH, Bernard and Paul Tracey. At the conclusion, the Judge (HH Judge Pelling QC) dismissed the claim with indemnity costs. He found that both the Traceys had been systematically dishonest and that they had put forward a claim which they knew was baseless. After receiving news of the result, FISL reviewed the Judgment and the transcripts of evidence. It then decided, on behalf of RSA, to avoid the Policy and to refuse the claim of CPH for an indemnity in respect of its costs liabilities. The decision to avoid was based upon a series of instances of material non-disclosure and misrepresentation. In addition, FISL relied upon breaches of various claims conditions. The decision to avoid was not taken lightly: this is one of only two cases in which FISL has taken such a decision[3].

5. CPH was not able to meet its liability to pay costs[4]. Persimmon has had the company wound up, and it now seeks to enforce the Policy for its own benefit, pursuant to the Third Parties (Rights Against Insurers) Act 1930 ['the 1930 Act']. For the purposes of this claim, it effectively stands in the shoes of CPH and the insurer is entitled to take any relevant policy defence. Thus Persimmon is now placed in the unusual position of seeking to espouse the rights of the adversary whose fraud it successfully proved. It is GLR's case that the Policy was avoided validly and/or that it was entitled to refuse to indemnify CPH by virtue of CPH's breach of conditions precedent within the Policy.

6. There are three central points of dispute between the parties. First, Persimmon seeks to defend CPH against most of the charges of misrepresentation and non-disclosure. In particular, it suggests that the

---

3 See statement of Mr Peter Smith at paragraph 66 [2/145].

4 Those costs have not been assessed, although a payment on account of £175,000 was ordered. Persimmon has produced a draft bill of costs. In the event that this claim were to succeed, declaratory relief would follow with the matter then proceeding through a detailed assessment procedure to ascertain the level of liability.

Traceys gave to FISL an account of events which was 'truthful to the best of their belief'[5].

7. Secondly, Persimmon denies that the insurer ever acquired the right to avoid the Policy. It maintains that the instances of non-disclosure and misrepresentation on which the insurer relies were not material and/or did not induce the insurer to grant cover. To support that submission, it says that a special approach is required to ATE insurance. In particular, it argues that what is material to the risk is not the detailed factual account of the events underlying the litigation but the risk assessment of the solicitors conducting the case[6]. In that regard, Persimmon's case is contradicted by its own expert's evidence. Persimmon also seeks to say that any misrepresentations/non-disclosure did not induce the insurer to offer terms at inception because the insurer did not avoid the Policy when presented, very shortly before trial, with some of the material used to discredit the Traceys[7].

8. Thirdly, Persimmon asserts that FISL on behalf of GLR is precluded from relying upon any misrepresentation, non-disclosure or breach of policy conditions. It says that Persimmon elected to affirm the Policy and that an estoppel arises. It appears that Persimmon is arguing that the knowledge of CPH's solicitors should be attributed to the insurer, although the legal basis for that attribution remains a mystery.

9. The position of GLR is based on established principles and on facts which cannot be seriously in dispute.

   (a) The basic proposition that ATE insurance is subject to the ordinary principles governing avoidance of cover is now well settled by authority. See: *Al-Koronky v Time-Life Entertainment Group Ltd* [2006] EWCA Civ 1123, [2007] 1 Costs LR 57; *Michael Phillips Architects Ltd v Riklin and Riklin* [2010] EWHC 834 (TCC), [2010] All ER (D) 164 (Jun). See also the Final Report of Sir Rupert Jackson's Review of Civil Litigation Costs at p92.

   (b) This case involves the starkest instances of misrepresentation and non-disclosure at the inception stage. CPH failed to inform FISL of a number of highly significant facts and misrepresented the key events with which the underlying litigation was concerned. The untruths of CPH were exposed at trial through careful cross-referencing of the documentary material and through cross-examination of the witnesses, notably Paul Tracey.

---

5 Claimant's Skeleton Argument, paragraph 79.

6 Claimant's Skeleton Argument, paragraphs 14 and 36.

7 Claimant's Skeleton Argument, paragraph 46.

It is extraordinary that Persimmon is now seeking to resile from the attack which it successfully mounted on the Traceys at trial.

(c) The instances of non-disclosure and misrepresentation on which GLR relies are individually and collectively material. Persimmon's position on the issue of materiality is contrary to its own expert evidence.

(d) Inducement is clearly made out, based on witness evidence and documentary evidence. Persimmon's submissions on inducement are based on logical flaws and a partial view of the facts.

(e) Quite apart from the question of avoidance for pre-inception misrepresentation and non-disclosure, the insurer was entitled to refuse this claim on various other grounds.

(f) The facts of this case do not come close to establishing the necessary conditions for waiver by election or waiver by estoppel. The insurer was never aware that the account it had been given was untrue, and it was not aware of much of the material which was used to establish the dishonesty. There was never any unequivocal representation that it would not exercise its rights based on the material now available. There was no reliance.

10. Persimmon's arguments at every stage seek to conflate two distinct duties: (i) the duty of the insured to inform an insurer of material allegations made against him; and (ii) the duty of the insured to tell the insurer whether the material allegations are true[8]. It was not enough for CPH to tell FISL what was being said against it. The company also owed a duty to give the insurer a true and complete account of what had really happened, within its knowledge. See Report of Mr Matthew Williams, underwriting expert for GLR at [2/194].

11. In its Skeleton Argument, Persimmon makes much of the notion that GLR's position in this case, if accepted, would mean that ATE insurance is valueless, at least in cases where factual disputes arise. There are three answers to that *cri de coeur*:

(i) The simple fact that a judge prefers one party's evidence over that of the other does not mean that the second party failed to make a full, accurate and honest presentation to insurers at inception. Self-evidently, a judge can reject a witness's evidence

8 See, for example, Claimant's Skeleton Argument at paragraph 56.

on a point of fact without finding that the witness did not tell him the truth from his perspective.

(ii) Even if an ATE insurer has a strict legal right to avoid a policy, it can be expected only to exercise that right in stark cases, like this one. That is because both regulatory obligations (considered below) and commercial pressures would prevent an insurer being too ready to avoid.

(iii) If Persimmon's submissions were accepted, the duty of utmost good faith would be deprived of most, if not all, of its content in the context of ATE insurance.

12. As this claim is brought under the 1930 Act, the litmus test is whether the Court would enforce the insurance contract for the benefit of the Traceys in an action brought by CPH. After their serial dishonesty at every stage, it is hardly surprising that the answer is 'no'.

B. Factual Background

ATE Insurance

13. Legal expenses insurance is a statutorily recognised class of insurance and it is regulated by the Insurance Companies (Legal Expenses Insurance) Regulations 1990 which protect against conflicts of interest between insurer and insured. The two forms of legal expenses insurance ['LEI'] are Before the Event legal expenses insurance ['BTE insurance'] and After the Event legal expenses insurance ['ATE insurance'].

14. BTE insurance is a form of insurance often sold as part of ordinary motor or household policies or as an adjunct to such policies. It covers the insured against his own costs and his liability for an opponent's costs in the event that he should suffer an uninsured loss and sue to recover damages. The premium for such insurance is usually very low. Its history is described in the judgment of Lord Philips in *Sarwar v Alam* [2001] EWCA Civ 1401, [2002] 1 WLR 125 at paragraphs [20]–[22].

15. ATE insurance developed in the early 1990s. The insured would take out the policy after having suffered a loss but before, or during, litigation to recover the loss. Such a policy would insure him against any liability to pay the opposing party's costs or his own disbursements. It would sometimes also cover any irrecoverable costs of the insured's own lawyers. When solicitors were permitted to enter into conditional fee agreements ['CFAs'] in 1995, the use of ATE insurance became more widespread. From April 2000, the ATE market expanded rapidly as a result of statutory changes to the funding of civil

litigation. Under these changes, litigants were permitted to recover against unsuccessful opponents: (i) success fees charged by their legal representatives under CFAs (Section 58A of the Courts and Legal Services Act 1990, as amended by Section 27 of the Access to Justice Act 1999); and (ii) premiums paid for policies to cover irrecoverable costs liabilities (Section 29 of the Access to Justice Act 1999). The operation of the statutory provisions and the market (including rating) is explained in some detail in *Callery v Gray (No 2)* [2001] 1 WLR 2142 (CA); [2002] 1 WLR 2000 (HL).

16. ATE premiums are often payable on a deferred and contingent basis. In some cases, this is achieved by the policy providing that the premium is itself one of the disbursements covered by the insuring clause. In other cases, the policy simply requires the premium to be paid at the conclusion of the litigation. Various models of premium calculation have been developed, including staged premiums: see *Rogers v Merthyr Tydfil* [2006] EWCA Civ 1134, [2007] 1 WLR 808.

17. The practical effect of the changes has been to protect the insured litigant against any liability in most cases where the insured's solicitor is acting under a full CFA. However, the litigant is not entirely immunised against personal risk. Most ATE policies contain claims conditions, including provisions which require the insured to co-operate with the ATE insurer and the solicitor handling the case and to follow their advice regarding settlement of the underlying litigation. Some ATE policies permit the insurer to withdraw cover for future stages of the litigation if the prospects of success are considered to have fallen below an acceptable level.

18. Because of the need to protect their position, ATE insurers often impose a contractual obligation on the insured to agree to his solicitor providing regular information regarding the case. As will be submitted below, an obligation of this type does not constitute the solicitor the agent of the insurer, nor does it fix the insurer with deemed knowledge of what would have been provided if it had all the information known to or ascertainable by the solicitor. Rather, its inclusion reinforces the fact that the insured's solicitor is not the agent of the insurer (since otherwise the clause would be otiose).

19. ATE insurance has, in the past, often been provided to support personal injury claims of relatively modest value. However, a number of insurers operating in the market also provide ATE insurance to support litigants in business disputes. The principles governing such policies are the same, but the premium will usually be higher and the insurer's process of commercial risk assessment will naturally be more meticulous. There are, as the experts agree, relatively few ATE

insurance providers who will underwrite substantial business disputes. The market is narrow and highly specialised.

20. Since ATE insurance is often taken out by litigants of limited means, the question has regularly arisen whether an ATE policy can afford adequate security for costs and thus provide an effective bar to a security for costs application. The Courts have repeatedly explained that there is no universal answer to this question. An ATE policy may or may not provide satisfactory security. In particular, the court will wish to ascertain whether the insurer could realistically avoid its contractual liability to pay the defendant's costs if the claim were unsuccessful. See *Michael Philips Architects Ltd* at paragraph 18.

The RSA Pursuit Scheme

21. The Pursuit scheme for ATE insurance was developed by FISL and RSA, who were already market leaders in BTE insurance. FISL administered the scheme under a binding authority from RSA, receiving the profits from the scheme and accounting for losses. The scheme was rolled out at a year before ATE premiums became recoverable. The Pursuit policy involves a deferred and conditional premium which is calculated by a formula based upon the fees of the insured's own solicitor. The terms of the Policy in this case will be considered in detail below, but it should be stressed at the outset that the Policy does not permit the insurer to terminate cover simply because prospects of success apparently fall during the course of the litigation.

22. Mr Smith, director of FISL, gives a full account of the genesis and development of the Pursuit scheme in his statement [2/132–36]. As he explains, the scheme was subjected to a wholesale attack by liability insurers in 2005. That litigation resulted in a detailed judgment of Senior Costs Judge Hurst: *The RSA Pursuit Test Cases* [2005] EWHC 90003 (Costs). In general terms, the scheme survived all the root-and-branch challenges (e.g. allegations of champerty) but the Court concluded that the premium ought to be based upon actual costs, rather than estimated costs. This is the basis which now applies.

CPH v Persimmon: the Underlying Dispute

23. London & Suburban Securities Ltd ['LSSL'] was a company controlled by Bernard Tracey. CPH was a company incorporated on 19 May 1999 and was apparently controlled by Paul Tracey. The underlying litigation was pursued by both CPH and LSSL, and it concerned the dealings of the Traceys with Persimmon regarding a site at Navigation Street, Birmingham ['the Site']. In late 1997, Bernard Tracey was introduced to the Site by Robert Dorin, an employee of National Car

Parks Ltd ['NCP'] which owned the Site and was contemplating selling it for development. Over the course of 1998, Bernard Tracey began to take an interest in the Site with a view to purchasing it. It appears that his initial intention was to persuade others to acquire parts of the site (or pre-let units) and to raise funds for the purchase on that basis. In any event, terms of sale were agreed subject to contract in August 1998, with the price set at £3.25M, a figure which was later dropped to £3.15M.

24. In March/April 1999, Steve Watt, the executive chairman of Persimmon (City Developments) Ltd, was introduced to the Traceys by Tony Edmunds, a mutual business acquaintance. The initial plan was that Persimmon should acquire a part of the Site for development of residential premises, while the Traceys (through CPH/LSSL) should develop the remaining part for commercial premises. The Traceys appear to have intended that their purchase of the Site should be simultaneous with the sale of part of the Site to Persimmon, and that their deposit payment for the Site should effectively be funded by Persimmon's deposit. However, on 21 June 1999, Bernard Tracey agreed to waive Persimmon's deposit.

25. In mid-August 1999, an arrangement was made between the Traceys and Persimmon that the latter should take over as purchaser of the Site. It was a matter of dispute in the litigation precisely how that arrangement was made and on what terms. CPH maintained that Bernard Tracey and Steve Watt had made the arrangement over a series of telephone calls on 11 August 1999. Its case was that the arrangement was not formalised, but was for Persimmon (a) to pay a 2% introduction fee; (b) to discharge fees of professionals engaged by CPH/LSSL; (c) to pay a 1% commission on the sale of all residential units to be constructed; and (d) to sell the commercial space to CPH 'at cost'. By contrast, it was Persimmon's case at trial that the arrangement had been made between Paul Tracey and Steve Watt in a meeting at the latter's office on 12 August 1999. According to its case, Paul Tracey had explained that he could not fund the acquisition of the site and had asked that Persimmon take over the acquisition of the Site and discharge the £50,000 to £60,000 in professional fees incurred to date.

26. Between August and December 1999, Persimmon negotiated directly with NCP regarding purchase of the Site. It was required to increase its bid for the Site to £3.6M and to agree that £2M of that sum should be a non-refundable deposit. It appears that Persimmon was aggrieved that it had been required to outbid another potential purchaser.

27. On 1 December 1999, there was a meeting between Paul Tracey and Steve Watt at Mr Watt's office. Mr Tracey claimed that he had initially requested a payment of £200,000 for the work done by CPH/LSSL in

introducing Persimmon to the Site and making preparations for development. He said that he and Mr Watt had gone on to agree formal terms that Persimmon would (a) pay professional fees incurred by CPH; (b) pay a fee calculated as 2% of the final purchase price; (c) make available to CPH 12,500 square feet of office space at cost; and (d) pay CPH a commission of 0.5% on the proceeds of any residential property sold by Persimmon. He said that he had made a contemporaneous manuscript note of the meeting [9/1926] and that, at the end, Mr Watt had shaken hands and said they had a deal.

28. By contrast, Mr Watt's account and Persimmon's case was that nothing had been formally agreed at the meeting. It was accepted that there was some discussion of the professional fees and the possibility of letting the Traceys have commercial space at cost. Mr Watt could not recall Mr Tracey having kept a note during the meeting.

29. After December 1999, CPH and LSSL played no material part in the arrangements for purchase and development of the Site. In May 2001, Persimmon completed its purchase of the Site. However, by that stage it had been acquired by the Beazer Group and there was a commercial incentive for it to sell the Site on. Accordingly, in September 2001, Persimmon exchanged contracts with Beaufort Western for the sale of the Site to that company. Following the sale of the Site, there was a series of increasingly heated correspondence between Paul Tracey and Steve Watt in which the former asserted a right to remuneration.

30. In June 2003, Edwin Coe LLP were instructed by CPH/LSSL. The firm obtained an Advice from counsel (Andrew Butler) [3/419–428] which put at 60% the prospect of successfully claiming damages against Persimmon on the basis of breach of an oral contract concluded on 1 December 1999. The Advice also indicated that, even if an oral contract could not be proved, the client should succeed in a restitutionary quantum meruit claim (with a 70% prospect of success). In January 2004 [9/2131], Edwin Coe sent a letter of claim to Persimmon. It received a response to the effect that a meeting had taken place in which an introduction fee had been discussed, but nothing agreed [12/2834–2936]. A formal letter of claim was sent on 14 May 2004 [10/2167] and a response was received from Nabarro Nathanson ['Nabarro'], Persimmon's solicitors, dated 17 June 2004 [9/2136–2141].

The Proposals for ATE Insurance

31. In May 2004, Joanna Osborne of Edwin Coe explored the possibility of arranging ATE insurance with RSA/FISL under the Pursuit scheme. She discussed the nature of the Pursuit policy with Emma Knights of FISL, and she advised her clients. On 9 June 2004 [11/2522–2523], she

submitted to FISL a completed insurance proposal form in the name of CPH, together with the following documents:

(i) Status reports for the Persimmon companies;

(ii) Edwin Coe's CFA (and risk assessment);

(iii) A 'Chronology of Facts' document;

(iv) A 'Summary of Claim' document;

(v) A 'Summary of Evidence in Support' document;

(vi) An 'Indications from the Defendant' document;

(vii) A copy of Andrew Butler's Advice and a note on his concerns;

(viii) A set of pre-action correspondence between the parties.

As will be explained below, those documents contained a full and detailed account of CPH's version of events. In particular, they contained a narrative of an informal agreement made in mid-August 1999 and an oral contract made on 1 December 1999. They made reference to the manuscript note of the meeting on 1 December 1999. They made reference to an agreement on 15 October 1998 between LSSL and Robert Dorin for payment of an introduction fee of 2%.

32. The proposal form contained an 'Important Notice' on the first page which included the following statement:

> 'All material facts must be disclosed. Failure to do so may give the Insurer the right to avoid the policy. A material fact is one that may influence the acceptance or assessment of this proposal. If you are in any doubt as to whether something constitutes a material fact you should disclose it.' [3/215]

It also contained a 'Declaration' signed by Paul Tracey and Ms Osborne in the following words:

> 'We declare that the above statements made by us or on our behalf are to the best of our knowledge and belief true and complete and we agree that this proposal will form the basis of the contract between us and the Insurer.' [3/225]

33. Following receipt of the proposal form by FISL, it was considered by Mike Fallon at FISL, who requested and received the letter from Nabarro responding to the letter of claim. On 19 August 2004, Mr Fallon sent an email [11/2536] to Ms Osborne stating that FISL's

concerns were that the insured required a large amount of cover and that the case was heavily dependent upon oral evidence. He indicated that cover could not be offered unless counsel was prepared to enter into a CFA.

34. In July 2005, Edwin Coe arranged a conference with Mr Butler, who agreed to act on a CFA [12/2923]. Following that conference, the firm supplied a completed proposal form to TheJudge, a legal expenses insurance broker, for submission to the market[9] [12/2970] [3/210–522]. The form was dated 1 August 2005 and included as annexes all the material supplied in 2004 to FirstAssist and various additional documents:

(i) Counsel's CFA risk assessment;

(ii) Further inter-partes correspondence;

(iii) Witness statement of Paul Tracey;

(iv) Witness statement of Bernard Tracey;

(v) Witness statement of Gordon Allison.

The statements of the Traceys contained, in essence, the account which they later gave to the trial judge.

35. That form included a note on the first page to the following effect:

> 'All material facts must be disclosed. A material fact is one that may influence the acceptance of the proposal, or the terms offered. If you are in any doubt as to whether something constitutes a material fact you should disclose it. The insurers which take part in this service provide quotations or indications of quotations based on the information you provide…' [3/210]

It concluded with a declaration in the following terms, signed by Ms Osborne on behalf of her firm and her client.

> 'I declare that the information contained in this form and accompanying enclosures is true to the best of my knowledge and belief.' [3/213]

36. TheJudge submitted the proposal form to FISL and three other ATE providers. Within days, the broker informed Edwin Coe that the other providers had refused to offer terms but that FISL had yet to consider the proposal [12/2985].

---

9 The use of a broker can assist a litigant in showing that he has obtained a competitive premium quotation.

37. On 2 December 2005, FISL offered terms for cover [11/2555]. It also required that a quotation be signed containing a declaration that the information already disclosed in the proposal form was true and complete, that it was unchanged and that it would form the basis of the insurance contract. The obligation of continuing disclosure from the date on which the proposal form was signed was expressly identified. Paul Tracey and Ms Osborne duly signed that declaration [11/2559]. The policy schedule and wording were sent to Edwin Coe on 19 December 2005 [11/2560], and a Notice of Funding served on Nabarro a few days later [10/2191].

CPH v Persimmon: the Litigation

38. CPH and LSSL issued protective proceedings on 1 August 2005, shortly after the conference with counsel and on the same day as the proposal form was submitted to TheJudge. Proceedings were served on 30 November 2005. The Particulars of Claim [4/563] pleaded breach of an oral agreement concluded on 1 December 2005 and, in the alternative, put forward the quantum meruit claim. The Defence [4/571] was served on 19 January 2006. It denied that any binding agreement had been reached for payment to be made to CPH. It also pleaded that, if any such agreement had been reached, it was an agreement relating to an interest in land which was not in writing and was thus void under Section 2 of the Law of Property (Miscellaneous Provisions) Act 1989 ['LP(MP)A'].

39. While the initial pleadings were being exchanged, an argument over security for costs was brewing. On 30 August 2005, Nabarro wrote to Edwin Coe asking CPH/LSSL to provide security for costs in the sum of £60,000 [10/2180]. After serving the Notice of Funding (which made reference to the ATE insurance), Edwin Coe wrote on 18 January 2006 to ask whether Nabarro still intended to seek security, having regard to the existence of the Pursuit policy [10/2197]. On 16 February 2006, Nabarro responded to the effect that their client wanted security in the sum of £110,000 and that the ATE insurance did not provide satisfactory security because of the risk of avoidance by insurers [10/2209]. There were further exchanges of correspondence in which Edwin Coe asserted that the policy provided adequate security (and that an application for security would be opposed by their clients and insurers on that basis). Nabarro denied that proposition [10/2230–32]. It is also clear from the disclosure given in these proceedings that Nabarro was advised by counsel that in view of the decision in *Al-Koronky* the policy would not provide security if there were, on the facts of the case, a likelihood of the policy being avoided or indemnity refused [12/3026(a)]. Nabarro passed on that advice to Persimmon [12/3028a]. It then obtained the ATE policy documents and considered

them. A decision was taken in April 2006 not to pursue a security for costs application [10/2242].

40. In November 2006, CPH served draft Amended Particulars of Claim [4/588(a)] which added the contention that an informal arrangement had been entered into between Bernard Tracey and Steve Watt on 11 August 1999 which was sufficient to give rise to a *Pallant v Morgan* equity even if there was no subsequent formal contract. Other amendments provided further colour to the restitutionary claim. The initial response of Persimmon was to object to those amendments as demurrable [10/2266].

41. A CMC was scheduled for 17 April 2007 at which the application to amend was to be considered. In the event, it was adjourned to permit a mediation to take place. Some limited disclosure was given by both parties in advance of the mediation. The mediation itself was held on 25 June 2007 and it failed to achieve any settlement. Persimmon, which had previously offered £30,000 to settle the claim, increased its offer by only £3,000. CPH, which had previously offered to accept £180,000, made clear that its claim was now £1.2M in view of the evidence as to the potential of the Site.

42. In August 2007, Persimmon agreed to directions, including a facility for the Particulars of Claim and Defence to be amended. An Amended Defence [4/602] was served in September 2007 which pleaded that the discussion in mid-August 1999 had been between Paul Tracey and Steve Watt and had resulted in a distress arrangement. In early October 2007, a CMC was held before Master Bowles at which Persimmon pressed for punitive costs orders based upon the amendments. The Master refused that application and, in the course of the hearings, described Persimmon's defence as 'congenitally aggressive', awarding CPH its costs[10].

43. The parties exchanged lists of documents on 6 December 2007 and they exchanged witness statements on 7 March 2008. Then, on 14 April 2008, Nabarro gave disclosure of evidence that Bernard Tracey had been made bankrupt on 20 April 1999. On the same day, it served a Re-Amended Defence [4/736(a)] adding a further argument that, even if there was a concluded agreement on 1 December 1999 between Paul Tracey and Steve Watt, that agreement was not binding for want of valid consideration. Edwin Coe responded by serving a supplemental statement of Bernard Tracey and a Re-Amended Reply [4/736(dd)] answering the argument on consideration.

---

10 See report of Edwin Coe on the hearing at [11/2693].

44. The trial took place between 4 and 13 June 2008, opening Skeleton Arguments[11] having been exchanged on Friday 30 May 2008. The principal witness for CPH/LSSL was Paul Tracey, as his father was by this stage too unwell to give oral evidence. The principal witness for Persimmon was Steve Watt. In the course of cross-examination, counsel for Persimmon repeatedly challenged the honesty of both Paul and Bernard Tracey. In his closing oral submissions and his closing skeleton argument, he made clear that Persimmon's case was that both men had been systematically dishonest:

    (i) '[The skeleton highlights] the points where both Paul Tracey and Bernard Tracey are shown to be seriously falling below any standard of truthfulness… We are talking here about much more serious things where people are going out to dishonestly deceive, fabricating documents, behaving in a way which is dishonest… We are in that territory, and I say that in relation to both Paul Tracey and Bernard Tracey.' (Oral submissions [7/1637])

    (iii) 'The extent of the falsehoods engaged in by Paul Tracey and indeed by Bernard Tracey render the whole of their evidence unreliable. Not only did they create false documents. Paul Tracey in the witness box was clearly not telling the truth about a whole range of issues.' (Closing skeleton [13/3404])

    Given the way Persimmon now puts its case[12], it will be necessary for the Court to read the full cross-examination of Paul Tracey [6/1319 – 7/1420] and the oral closing submissions of Persimmon at trial [7/1637–1659].

45. HH Judge Pelling QC gave judgment orally on 19 June 2008 [4/523–560]. He dismissed all the claims, accepting Mr Watt's evidence on all points and rejecting that of the Traceys. He made clear that the reason he was rejecting their evidence was that he regarded them as untruthful witnesses. In relation to Bernard Tracey, the Judge said that he had 'lied in business correspondence… wherever and whenever he perceived it to be in his best interests to do so' and that, because of his various untruths, his statement was 'virtually valueless' (paragraphs 17 and 23 [4/527, 531]). In relation to Paul Tracey, the Judge said that his evidence was to be 'treated with enormous caution' because he had given various untruthful answers and had acted deceitfully on various occasions (paragraph 26 [4/531]). At the end of his judgment, Persimmon applied for costs to be awarded on the indemnity basis. In

---

11 See: Claimant's document [6/1218]; Defendant's document [6/1288].

12 For example, Skeleton Argument at paragraph 81.

acceding to that application, the Judge gave a clear summary of the findings he had made:

> 'I have had, in the course of this case, to make some wide-ranging findings, frankly of dishonesty in the way in which the evidence has been given and of documents which have been created after the event for the purpose of creating a false impression... This trial lasted for the number of days it took up and had to be rigorously defended essentially because of that dishonest conduct.
>
> ... It seems to me that the defendants have been put to the expense of defending this claim which, to the knowledge of the Traceys, was a claim that could not succeed.' (paragraphs 112–113 [4/558–559])'

Persimmon now says that these comments by the Judge were 'unnecessary and unjustified by the evidence'[13]. It also makes the courageous submission that the Judge did not really make findings of dishonesty (so he cannot have meant what he said in the passage above)[14]. GLR disagrees on both points.

46. The Judge's conclusions were based on a careful analysis of the documentation (notably correspondence) and the oral evidence. The following points arising from the Judgment should be emphasised at this stage:

    (i) He drew attention to the fact that Bernard Tracey had repeatedly made statements in correspondence to the effect that CPH/LSSL had a 'Fund', meaning a major financial institution committed to providing financial backing for their purchase of the Site. As Paul Tracey had admitted in oral evidence, there was no Fund and all those references were untruths (paras. 17 – 18).

    (ii) He relied upon the fact that Bernard Tracey had sent a fax to Robert Dorin on 12 August 1999 in which Mr Tracey had asked Mr Dorin to produce a letter dated October 1998 saying that Dorin had agreed an introduction fee of 2% payable to him. In fact, the agreement had been for a 1% fee for services. Mr Dorin had complied with that request, drafting a misleading letter which was dated 15 October 1998 (paras. 19 – 22).

    (iii) He relied upon further correspondence which demonstrated that Paul and Bernard Tracey had referred to parts of the Site having been pre-let or pre-sold when that was not the case (as Paul Tracey accepted was the case) (paras. 18f and 26c)).

---

13 Skeleton Argument at paragraph 16.

14 Skeleton Argument at paragraph 82.

(iv) He concluded that the supposedly contemporaneous note of the meeting of 1 December 1999 was not made at that meeting, because (a) it made inappropriate reference to solicitors' fees having been 'paid off', (b) it referred to architects who had not been instructed as in early December 1999 and (c) the writing on the note suggested that different parts had been written on different occasions (paras, 77 – 99).

(v) He set out a paper-trail of documentary evidence which showed that the Traceys were in dire financial straits in August 1999, including evidence that they were not paying modest professional fees and were trying to borrow money on unfavourable terms to pay such fees. This supported the contention of Persimmon that the Traceys were keen to enter into a distress arrangement in August 1999 and militated against the argument of CPH that it had been prepared to hold out for satisfactory terms (paras. 28 – 40).

The Conduct of FirstAssist and the Decision to Avoid the Policy/Repudiate the Claim

47. When the proposal for insurance was first made in 2004, it was considered by Mike Fallon and also by the senior manager, Peter Smith[15]. FISL was wary about underwriting a piece of litigation based upon an oral agreement. This was despite the fact that counsel had put the prospect of success at 60% for the contractual claim and higher for the restitutionary claim. It was despite the fact that reputable commercial solicitors were willing to act on CFA terms. It was despite the fact that the client claimed to have a contemporaneous note of the key meeting. Mike Fallon of FISL therefore insisted that it had the additional reassurance of counsel entering into a CFA.

48. When the proposal was re-submitted in 2005, Mr Fallon requested the full file from archives and reviewed all the material, which was considerable (it fills bundle 3 of the trial bundles in this case). One month after the proposal, FISL confirmed that terms would be offered[16].

49. After going on risk, FISL was entitled to be provided with regular progress reports, as well as specific information (see Condition 8 [3/205], discussed below). It was provided with such reports by Edwin Coe, but it did not receive (and would not have expected to receive) all correspondence and evidence in the case. It received the following information and documents without prompting Edwin Coe:

---

15 See: [11/2535].

16 See email at [11/2541] and letter at [12/2999].

(i) It was provided with the statements of case when they were served.[17]

(ii) It was provided with details of settlement offers.[18]

(iii) It was given information about the security for costs application.[19]

(iv) It was told when Nabarro entered into a CFA, as a question had to be answered as to whether the Policy should be extended to cover any success fee of Nabarro[20].

(v) It was informed of the mediation, supplied with the parties' position statements and told of the outcome[21].

(vi) It was informed of procedural decisions and directions.[22]

(vii) It was notified of the disclosure of documents evidencing Bernard Tracey's bankruptcy[23].

(viii) It was provided with a supplemental statement from Bernard Tracey and given the opportunity to review other witness statements[24] (see further below).

(ix) It was provided with the skeleton arguments (two working days before trial)[25].

(x) It was notified of the result of the trial[26].

50. In addition to receiving some information without prompting, FISL made requests for information and documents from time to time. In particular:

---

17 The pleadings were forwarded as follows: Particulars of Claim [11/2553]; Defence [11/2563]; Amended Particulars of Claim [11/2616]; Amended Reply [11/2698]; Re-Amended Defence and Amended Reply [11/2745].

18 E.g. CPH's Part 36 Offer of £180,000 [11/2543]; Persimmon's Part 36 Offer of £30,000 [11/2588].

19 See correspondence at [11/2564-2171].

20 See [11/2578].

21 See [11/2660] and [11/2689].

22 See, for example, the report on the CMC before Master Bowles [11/2693].

23 See [11/2739].

24 See [11/2739].

25 See [11/2766].

26 See [11/2767].

(i) In early January 2007, Mike Fallon left FISL. Ian Coleman took over from him and a full file review was undertaken [11/2604–2605b]. At that stage, Mr Coleman requested and received an updated case assessment from Edwin Coe [11/2606–2607].

(ii) In advance of the mediation in June 2007, Ian Coleman exchanged emails with Joanna Osborne as to CPH's expectations in settlement negotiations [11/2664–2666].

(iii) After the CMC of October 2007, Mr Coleman expressed concern about rising costs and asked for a case review meeting with solicitors and counsel. The meeting took place on 12 December 2007 and is recorded in an attendance note [13/3229]. At that meeting, counsel advised that prospects of success were 65% and Paul Tracey was described by the lawyers as a 'genuine' person.

(iv) On 6 May 2008 (two months after exchange of witness statements), Edwin Coe wrote to FISL to notify the insurer of Bernard Tracey's bankruptcy [11/2739]. The solicitors expressed the view that this new information would not affect the 'contractual aspects' of the case but would be used by Persimmon to bolster its argument that CPH was in financial difficulties and had therefore begged Persimmon to take over as purchaser of the Site. The letter asked whether FISL would wish to see copies of the witness statements. In response, Mr Coleman said that he did not need to be supplied with the statements, but that he did require an overview of the evidence [11/2742]. He received a positive response, which contained statements to the effect that the evidence of Persimmon was at odds with that of independent witnesses and with various documents [11/2745]. Nothing was said of the dishonest documents and statements which were ultimately exposed at trial.

51. It is important to appreciate that FISL did not receive everything which Edwin Coe received. This is entirely conventional in ATE insurance: the insurer will wish to receive the key information and to understand the underlying events, but will not expect to receive every document in the case. FISL did not receive, at any time, the voluminous documentary disclosure in the case. It did not receive the substantial correspondence between Edwin Coe and the Traceys.

52. After receiving news of the trial, FISL (on behalf of the insurer) undertook a careful review before finally making the decision to avoid the Policy and refuse indemnity to CPH. Edwin Coe notified FISL of the result on the day of the judgment, 19 June 2008 [11/2767]. More information about the judgment was set out in a letter dated 23 June 2008 [11/2767]. Mr Coleman of FISL sent an email reserving insurers'

rights on the same day [11/2762], and he also requested copies of the full trial transcripts [11/2772]. After consideration of those, he provided a report on the trial to his managers, including Mr Smith [11/2779] which recommended a continued reservation of rights and gave the following summary:

> 'There is nothing readily to be seen in the submission [i.e. the proposal for insurance] or the subsequent papers to forewarn insurers of this approach though there is a hint of what is to come in the Defendants' skeleton argument dated 30th May 2008. It must be assumed that at trial the extent of the potential dishonesty has been "outed".' [11/2785]

After that report, FISL on 30 June 2008 sent an email to Edwin Coe maintaining the reservation of rights and requesting a transcript of the judgment [11/2796]. After consideration of the judgment, FISL made the decision to avoid the Policy and repudiate the claim and it communicated that decision by a letter from Hextalls solicitors to Edwin Coe dated 1 August 2008 [13/3477].

53. After that decision was made, Persimmon took steps to enforce an order for payment on account of costs against CPH and LSSL. When the companies failed to pay, it had them wound up[27] as a preliminary to bringing this claim under the 1930 Act.

C. The Issues

54. The following key issues arise for resolution by the Court.

    (1) Was the insurer prima facie entitled to avoid the Policy for material misrepresentation and/or non-disclosure? Having regard to the classic principles in *Pan Atlantic Insurance Co v Pine Top Insurance Co* [1995] 1 AC 501, that question resolves itself into the following sub-issues:

        (a) Did CPH make the misrepresentations and fail to disclose the facts alleged?

        (b) Were the representations and facts in question material?

        (c) Was the insurer induced to enter into the contract by the representations or failures of disclosure?

    This issue requires consideration of Persimmon's novel submissions about the legal test for materiality and inducement in relation to ATE insurance.

---

27 See: [13/3471]; [13/3483].

(2) Did CPH breach the post-inception duty of good faith so as to justify avoidance?

(3) Is the insurer entitled to repudiate the insurance claim based upon the particular conditions of the Pursuit policy?

(4) Is the insurer entitled to repudiate the claim on the basis that it is tainted by fraud?

(5) Can Persimmon establish that the insurer has waived all rights to avoid the Policy and/or repudiate the claim?

D. The 1930 Act and the Basis of the Claim

55. Section 1 of the 1930 Act (as material) provides as follows:

'(1) Where under any contract of insurance a person (hereinafter referred to as the insured) is insured against liabilities to third parties which he may incur, then –

...

(b) in the case of the insured being a company, in the event of a winding-up order or an administration order being made...;

if, either before or after that event, any such liability as aforesaid is incurred by the insured, his rights against the insurer under the contract in respect of the liability shall, notwithstanding anything in any Act or rule of law to the contrary, be transferred to and vest in the third party to whom the liability was so incurred.

...

(4) Upon a transfer under subsection (1) or subsection (2) of this section, the insurer shall, subject to the provisions of section three of this Act, be under the same liability to the third party as he would have been under to the insured, but –

(a) if the liability of the insurer exceeds the liability of the insured to the third party, nothing in this Act shall affect the rights of the insured against the insurer in respect of the excess;

(b) if the liability of the insured is less than the liability of the insured to the third party, nothing in this Act shall affect the rights of the third party against the insured in respect of the balance...'

56. Thus, Persimmon steps into the shoes of CPH for the purposes of this claim. It can be in no better position as against the insurer than they could have been if they had sued on the Policy. That follows from two separate strands of reasoning. First, Section 1(1) transfers only those rights which the insured enjoyed under the Policy. Secondly, Section 1(4) makes clear that the insurer should be under the same liability to the third party as to its own insured. See: *Post Office v Norwich Union Fire Insurance Society Ltd* [1967] 2 QB 363 at 374 (Lord Denning MR), 376 (Harman LJ); *The 'Padre Island'* [1984] 2 Lloyd's Rep 408 at 410 and 414 (Leggatt J). The insurer can take advantage of any right to avoid or any condition of the policy (including notice clauses, arbitration clauses, etc.), because it is not a claim but the contractual rights of the insured which will be transferred.

E. The Insurer's Right to Avoid: Misrepresentations and Non-disclosure at Inception

Misrepresentations and Non-Disclosure

57. Reliance is placed upon all the misrepresentations and instances of non-disclosure which are pleaded in paragraphs 26–27 of the Defence [1/19–24]. These can conveniently be grouped into five categories:

(i) the repeated dishonest statements of Bernard and Paul Tracey about their financial backing and the parts of the Site which had been pre-sold or pre-let;

(ii) the production of the dishonest note by Robert Dorin at the instigation of Bernard Tracey;

(iii) the spurious 'contemporaneous note' of the meeting of 1 December 1999;

(iv) the bankruptcy of Bernard Tracey and the financial difficulties faced by the Traceys in mid-1999;

(v) the dishonest account of Bernard and Paul Tracey regarding the key events on 11–12 August 1999 and 1 December 1999.

58. For the avoidance of doubt, there can be no question of Bernard Tracey's dishonesty being taken out of the equation, on the basis that he was not a formal director or shareholder of CPH:

(a) Bernard Tracey was a directing mind of the CPH for the purpose of the relevant transactions in 1999, for the purpose of instructing Edwin Coe and for the purpose of placing insurance (see, for example [12/2911–2914]). Under the usual principles of attribution, CPH is fixed with his knowledge – see *El Ajou v Dollar Land Holdings* [1994] 2 All ER 685 CA; *PCW Syndicates v PCW Reinsurers* [1996] 1 Lloyd's Rep 241 at 253R–254L.

(b) Section 18 of the Marine Insurance Act (applicable to non-marine insurance) provides that the assured will be deemed to know every circumstance which ought to be known by him in the ordinary course of his business[28]. Even if Bernard Tracey were not a directing mind of CPH, CPH will nonetheless be deemed to know of the correspondence which he wrote in relation to the Site and of matters which he discussed continuously with the company's director.

(c) Bernard Tracey was CPH's agent to insure – he approved the summary of claim in the proposal form [12/2876], and participated in the July 2005 conference preparatory to the second proposal for insurance – and his knowledge was imputed to CPH for the purpose of insurance at least (see Section 20 of the Marine Insurance Act).

(d) It is as a matter of fact impossible to draw any distinction between the knowledge of father and son – see eg. [12/3145]. The Judge certainly took that view (see Judgment, paragraphs 4, 112).

(i) The Dishonest Statements of the Traceys

59. During 1998 and 1999, the Traceys made multiple dishonest statements in correspondence with various parties to the effect that their purchase of the Site was supported by a specific financial institution, to which they referred as their 'Fund'. In some of those statements, they indicated that the 'Fund' had solicitors and was taking an active interest in the negotiations. The Traceys also repeatedly made dishonest representations that parts of the Site had been pre-let or pre-sold.

(a) In a letter of 22 January 1998 to the architects, Bernard Tracey referred to discussions with a merchant bank which was supposedly funding acquisition of the Site [8/1665]. Paul Tracey accepted that there never was any Fund, or any funding arrangement [6/1328].

---

28 *ERC Frankona Re v American National Insurance* [2006] Lloyd's Rep IR 157 at 181R.

(b) In a letter of 11 August 1998, Bernard Tracey told Julian White of NCP that funding had been agreed with a German bank [8/1669].

(c) In a conversation with Mr Dorin on 1 February 1999 (documented in a letter from Mr Dorin of that day), Paul Tracey said that the 'Fund' would not entertain a payment above a certain level [8/1735].

(d) In a letter of 12 April 1999, Bernard Tracey told Mr Dorin that he had spoken to the 'Fund' about various items [8/1743].

(e) In or before May 1999, Paul Tracey had told CPH's solicitors that a deal had been struck with Persimmon for use of most of the residential space in the Site. This was recorded by the solicitors in a letter to Paul Tracey dated 11 May 1999 [8/1755]. In cross-examination, Mr Tracey accepted that no such deal had been struck and could provide no honest explanation [6/1347].

(f) In a note to CPH's solicitors dated 13 July 1999, Bernard Tracey falsely stated that CPH/LSSL had pre-sold an 8-storey block of flats at the Site and that the hotel element of the scheme had been sold to Cladon Ltd for £8M [8/1813]. As can be seen from a letter one week later from the project manager, Mr Bignell, the hotel element of the scheme had not been sold to anyone [8/1815]. Bernard Tracey had previously made similar statements on 12 May 1999 to the property agents [8/1762]. Paul Tracey accepted that those statements amounted to a lie [6/1349].

(g) In a note to Mr Dorin dated 3 August 1999, Bernard Tracey made false statements that CPH had pre-let or pre-sold: a public car park to NCP; a block of 145 residential apartments; a 6-floor hotel to Holiday Inn Express Group [8/1824]. At trial, Paul Tracey accepted that those statements were untrue [6/1359].

(h) In a letter to Mr Watt dated 22 September 1999, Paul Tracey said that he had been telephoned regularly by Mr Allison of NCP seeking assurances as to Persimmon's intentions [9/1885]. This passage from the letter was actually quoted in the proposal documents as an instance of documentary evidence supporting the Traceys' account [3/416]. Mr Allison convincingly denied that he had made such calls, and his evidence was (quite correctly) accepted by the Judge.

CPH failed to tell the insurer at any time that its key management personnel had made dishonest statements or that these specific statements in correspondence were not true.

(ii) The Dishonest Note Produced by Robert Dorin

60. On 14 July 1998, Bernard Tracey wrote to Robert Dorin, agreeing to pay him a fee of 1% of the acquisition price of the Site to represent LSSL in the purchase negotiations [8/1667]. There was never any suggestion that that arrangement was actually changed before mid-1999. On 12 August 1999, Bernard Tracey sent a fax to Robert Dorin telling him that Persimmon was taking over the negotiating position of CPH and asking Mr Dorin to provide a letter, dated early 1998, stating that CPH had agreed with Dorin an introduction fee of 2% [9/1856]. The letter was duly produced by Dorin and dated 15 October 1998 [6/1701], who confessed in the course of his evidence that he had produced a back-dated letter as requested. He accepted the proposition that he had 'picked out a date… and created a letter that looked authentic' [7/1463]. Paul Tracey could provide no honest explanation of the arrangement [6/1322]. Thus, it was clearly established at trial that Bernard Tracey and Robert Dorin had conspired to create a document which was misleading both as to its date and as to the terms of the arrangement it recorded.

61. At no time did CPH inform the insurer that a dishonest document had been created in this way, on Bernard Tracey's instructions. In the proposal documents, the misleading letter of 15 October 1998 was included in the Chronology of Facts as if it were a genuine document produced on that date: [3/229]. CPH did not tell FISL about the dishonest arrangement. Although it was picked up by leading counsel for CPH at the mediation stage [12/3095], it was not identified to FISL before the Defendant's skeleton argument was forwarded two working days before trial [6/1304]. Even then, no explanation was given by the insured.

(iii) The Spurious 'Contemporaneous Note' of the Meeting on 1 December 1999

62. Throughout the *CPH v Persimmon* litigation, CPH placed great reliance on a note supposedly made by Paul Tracey at the meeting with Mr Watt on 1 December 1999 [9/1926]. That note was referred to in the proposal documents as a contemporaneous document which supported CPH's case [3/416], and the statement of Paul Tracey supplied to insurers at the proposal stage in 2005 says that the note was made at the meeting [4/488]. Paul Tracey must have known whether that statement was true or untrue.

63. At trial, the note was subjected to a careful forensic analysis and the Judge (correctly) concluded that it was not made at the meeting, but at a later time and in unexplained circumstances. His conclusion was based on three matters:

(a) The note referred to the fees of Wedlake Bell (CPH's solicitors) having been paid off. In fact, they were not paid until later, as Paul Tracey knew at the time (see letter of Paul Tracey [9/1936]. Paul Tracey's only explanation was that Mr Watt had lied to him for no very obvious reason [7/1402–1403].

(b) The note referred to Corrigans, a firm of architects who were not instructed until January 2000, as is plain from their initial quotation [9/1942]. Paul Tracey said that Mr Watt had told him that Corrigans were to be the architects [7/1403]. However, as the Judge found, it was most unlikely that Mr Watt would have told Mr Tracey that before instructing the architects themselves.

(c) The note was written with multiple different writing implements, a point discovered when the Judge called for the original to be produced. Paul Tracey was re-called and sought to explain this by saying that there had been a gap in the meeting during which a pencil had been provided [7/1612]. However, there had been no reference to such a gap during his account of the meeting in the body of his evidence.

CPH failed to tell the insurer the truth about this document and misleadingly presented it to the insurer as an honest document written at the meeting.

(iv) The Bankruptcy of Bernard Tracey and the Financial Difficulties of the Traceys in Mid-1999

64. Bernard Tracey was declared bankrupt on 20 April 1999, a fact first made known to Edwin Coe by Persimmon on 14 April 2008 [13/3289]. As mentioned above, Edwin Coe informed FISL of this fact on 6 May 2008 [11/2739]. This had not been disclosed to insurers at the time of the proposal for insurance. By the same token, it had not been disclosed to insurers that Bernard Tracey had committed criminal offences, in continuing to play a part in the management of CPH and LSSL after his bankruptcy (under the Company Directors Disqualification Act 1986).

65. In addition to that specific point, CPH had failed to disclose that the company (and not just Bernard Tracey) was in serious financial difficulties by mid-August 1999, a fact which was (correctly) relied upon by Persimmon and by the Judge to support the conclusion that Paul Tracey had indeed sought a distress arrangement at that time. In the statement of Paul Tracey which was supplied at the time of the 2005 proposal, it was said that by August 1999, although CPH had 'not had enough time to organise the funding for the development aspect of the project', the company <u>did</u> have 'sufficient funding in place to cover exchange' [3/482]. This statement was untrue, and compounded the

failure to disclose the true state of affairs. In fact, both the Traceys and their companies were in dire straits in August 1999 and did not have the funds to cover any further stages of the project, including the deposit payable on exchange of contracts. This was established at trial by careful cross-examination of Paul Tracey by reference to the correspondence. Mr Tracey ultimately accepted that neither he nor the companies had money to cover the purchase, the deposit, the professional fees already incurred or the professional fees required for further work [7/1371].

(v) The Dishonest Account of the Traceys of the Key Meetings

66. In its proposal documents, CPH made the following representations of fact:

(a) that there had been an outline agreement on 11/12 August 1999 under which Persimmon agreed to pay CPH a 2% introduction fee, a profit percentage from the commercial elements of the scheme and a further payment geared to the ultimate success of the development project [3/409, 513];

(b) that that outline agreement had been made over the telephone between Bernard Tracey and Mr Watt [3/513];

(c) that, although Paul Tracey had met Mr Watt on 12 August 1999, that had not been a substantive meeting [3/482];

(d) that, at a meeting on 1 December 1999, an oral agreement had been entered into between Paul Tracey and Mr Watt providing for a 2% payment, a 0.5% commission on residential sales and a purchase option relating to the commercial elements of the development [3/410, 487–89].

67. Those statements about the key meetings were untruthful, as Judge Pelling found in his Judgment [4/523][29]. Those were, in summary (references to the judgment appear in parentheses):

---

[29] For the avoidance of doubt, as a general point, the Defendant would submit that the findings of HH Judge Pelling are binding as *res judicata* since they were findings made on the same subject-matter in litigation between Persimmon and CPH, with whom the insurer had a privity of interest. See: *Phipson on Evidence (17th edn.)* at paragraphs 43–27 to 43–29. It is obviously logical that such findings should be binding as between insurer, insured and opposing party. However, the submission on *res judicata* is unnecessary, given that the documentary evidence, coupled with the transcripts, convincingly show that the Judge was right. Moreover, Persimmon sensibly does not dispute the findings of the Judge – nor could it, without there being an abuse of the process of the Court: having sought the relevant findings of dishonesty against Paul and Bernard Tracey for purpose A in proceedings A, it cannot now invite the court to reach different findings on the same facts for purpose B in proceedings B.

(a) Mr Watt's evidence was generally to be preferred over that of the Traceys, given their systematic dishonesty (paragraphs 23 and 26);

(b) his account of Paul Tracey begging for Persimmon to take over as purchaser of the Site was consistent with the evidence of the parlous financial position of CPH and the Traceys (paragraph 40);

(c) the account of Paul Tracey that he had attended Persimmon's office solely to deliver the solicitors' invoices was incredible (paragraph 42) – a conclusion supported by the poor explanation given by Paul Tracey in cross examination [7/1375–1377]

(d) the account of the Traceys regarding the arrangement made in August 1999 was belied by correspondence in September 1999 (paragraphs 49–51 and 62–3);

(e) it was inherently unlikely that Persimmon would agree to provide such generous remuneration to CPH in view of the slender value of the work it had actually done (paragraph 58);

(f) the dishonest presentation of the supposedly contemporaneous note of the meeting on 1 December 1999 told against Paul Tracey's credibility in relation to that meeting;

(g) the correspondence in the months and years after the 1 December 1999 meeting was entirely inconsistent with the notion that CPH had entered into a binding agreement with Persimmon (paragraphs 88–99) – another conclusion supported by the unsatisfactory answers given by Paul Tracey when cross-examined (e.g. at [1407–1415]).

68. While FISL had been put on notice that Mr Watt did not accept the Traceys' account of the key meetings, it had not been given a true account by the insured of what actually happened. As the Judge expressly concluded, the Traceys put forward (through their companies) a claim which, to their knowledge, could not properly succeed (Judgment, paragraph 113 [4/559]).

69. Persimmon now argues that the true account of the key meetings did not need to be disclosed by virtue of Section 18(3)(b) of the Marine Insurance Act[30]. That subsection provides that an insured need not disclose 'any circumstance which is known or presumed to be known to the insurer'. Here, the insurer, unlike the Traceys, did not know that

---

30 Skeleton Argument, paragraph 56.

their account was false, much less that it was dishonest in important respects. The insurer only knew that the account of the Traceys was not agreed by Persimmon. Like any other insurer, FISL/RSA was entitled to an honest and accurate presentation of the underlying facts at inception.

Materiality

70. The test of materiality, which applies equally to misrepresentation and non-disclosure, is whether the fact in question would influence the judgment of a prudent insurer in fixing the premium or determining whether to take the risk[31]. Like the concept of utmost good faith from which the duty of full and honest disclosure derives, that duty arises in relation to the full range of insurance contracts: see *The 'Star Sea'* [2003] 1 AC 469 at paragraphs 41–60 (Lord Hobhouse); *Good Faith and Insurance Contracts, ed MacDonald Eggers et al (2nd edn.)* at paragraphs 1.29 to 1.33.

71. In the usual way, the parties have put forward expert evidence on this issue. What is perhaps less commonplace is that both parties' experts have agreed that each of the instances of non-disclosure and misrepresentation pleaded by the Defendant was material in the relevant sense. See the report of Mr Smart (Claimants' expert) at paragraphs 6.8 to 6.9 [2/162–165] and the report of Mr Williams (Defendant's expert) at [2/184–185]. As Mr Smart makes clear, any one of those instances would have been material.

72. The experts are obviously right: each of the misrepresentations and instances of non-disclosure relied upon was plainly material, for three reasons. First, the relevant facts undermined each aspect of the Traceys' case and made the insured risk one which would be unacceptable to any sane and honest ATE underwriter. For example:

    (a) The dishonest accounts of their funding and what parts of the Site they had sold suggested that they were having to lie about the project to retain control of it.

    (b) In failing to give an honest and complete account of their true financial position in August 1999 they prevented the insurer from appreciating how readily Mr Watt's account of the meeting in that month could be supported.

    (c) The manufacture of misleading documents was indicative of the fact that the Traceys could not support their position honestly.

---

31 The test from sections 18 and 20 of the Marine Insurance Act 1906 which applies equally to contracts of non-marine insurance – *Pan Atlantic* at 518.

(d) If a simply honest account had been given of the two key meetings, it would have been apparent that the claims were hopeless.

73. Secondly, the misrepresentations and non-disclosure supported the general conclusion that the evidence of the Traceys was not to be accepted, save where it was independently corroborated or against the interest of CPH. In a case where oral evidence was always understood to be significant, this powerfully influenced the quality of the insured risk.

74. Thirdly, the misrepresentations and non-disclosure were relevant to the general question of moral hazard. Circumstances relevant to that matter are generally to be regarded as material. As Mance J acknowledged in *ICCI v Royal Hotel Ltd* [1998] Lloyd's Rep IR 151 at 156–158, an insurer is entitled to disclosure of facts which suggest that the insured is dishonest, even if those facts are not directly relevant to the subject-matter of the insurance. See, in particular 156R:

> 'It is important to realise what is embraced by "risk". It is not simply the peril of the possibility of loss or damage occurring within the scope of the policy. It embraces other matters which would, if known be likely to influence a prudent underwriter's decision. It includes what is known as "moral hazard", which may merely increase the likelihood of it being made to appear (falsely) that loss or damage has occurred falling within the scope of the policy.'

In *Gate v Sun Alliance* [1995] LRLR 385 at 406R–407L, 408, the Court again stressed that the dishonesty need not relate directly to the risk. Although the passage quoted above from the *ICCI* case is in the context of property insurance, it can readily be applied to the context of legal expenses insurance. A prudent legal expenses insurer would naturally be averse to providing cover to a litigant who was congenitally dishonest, since the insurer could not rely upon such a person to provide accurate information about the claim or to co-operate honestly and fairly during the proceedings. The central importance of moral hazard as an aspect of the duty of utmost good faith also shows the absurdity of any suggestion that an insurer can cover the assured against the risk that its own latent dishonesty will be discovered.

Inducement

75. The test of inducement is whether the insurer would have offered cover on precisely the same terms if a full and accurate presentation had been given: *Pan Atlantic* at 549–50; *Drake Insurance Plc v Provident Insurance Plc* [2003] EWCA Civ 1834, [2004] QB 601 at paragraph [63] (Rix LJ). For the presumption of inducement see *Pan Atlantic* at 542A and 551.

76. In this case, the evidence shows beyond question that FISL would not have offered cover on the same terms if the true and complete picture had been presented. Peter Smith, who was the senior manager responsible for the Pursuit scheme and for oversight of the CPH case, describes the process by which a proposal is assessed (paragraph 31 [2/136]). As he explains, FISL would never contemplate covering a fundamentally dishonest claim (paragraph 61 [2/143–44]). He also provides a commentary on Mike Fallon's dealings with Joanna Osborne, in which he notes that Mr Fallon was repeatedly pressed with the facts and circumstances supporting the case of CPH and formed a positive view based on those matters (paragraphs 35–50 [2/137–141]).

77. The evidence of Mr Smith is also supported by the contemporaneous documents. In August 2004, Mr Fallon was not prepared to cover the case without obtaining a file review from Mr Smith [11/2529]. After that review, he told Ms Osborne that FISL's concerns were that the amount of cover required was large and the case was heavily dependent on oral evidence. He was not prepared to cover the case without counsel having entered into a CFA. That communication strongly supports FISL's case that it would not have provided cover (especially cover without limit of indemnity) if it had known of any of the matters set out above. If Mr Fallon had been told that the oral evidence on which the case was dependent was fundamentally dishonest or was from people who had written a series of dishonest letters in the context of the same deal, he would obviously not have offered terms.

78. FISL's case is also supported by the actual views expressed by the underwriters at FISL as the case approached trial. On 2 March 2007, Mr Smith annotated a file review note expressing concern about the fact that this was a finely balanced case based on oral evidence [11/2615]. On 26 October 2007, Mr Coleman indicated that he hoped to consider at the case review meeting in December the weight of the evidence supporting CPH's factual account [11/2699]. When confronted with the information about Bernard Tracey's bankruptcy, the immediate concern of FISL was to ascertain whether it affected the credibility of the witnesses [11/2742]. Can it seriously be suggested that FISL would have underwritten a case which it knew to be founded on the evidence of dishonest people?

79. In any event, this is a case in which a presumption of inducement arises, since the Court can properly infer that FISL would not have offered cover on the same terms if it had received a full and accurate presentation at inception. See: *Pan Atlantic* at 551; *St Paul Fire & Marine Insurance Co Ltd v McConnell Dowell Constructors Ltd and ors* [1995] 2 Lloyd's Rep 116 at 127R (Evans LJ).

80. On the question of inducement, Persimmon argues that the fact that FISL did not immediately avoid the Policy when presented with (for example) evidence of Bernard Tracey's bankruptcy, shows that FISL's decision to propose for insurance would not have been influenced by evidence of the Traceys' dishonesty or evidence seriously undermining their case[32]. There are two key fallacies in this argument. First, it fails to distinguish between the approach taken by an insurer when proposing for cover and the approach taken when presented with new information during the period of insurance. A decision to avoid a policy is much more dramatic, and damaging to the assured, than a decision not to offer terms of cover. Secondly, the argument fails to acknowledge that FISL was not, at any stage before trial, presented with either an accurate account of the underlying facts or full details of the evidence which was ultimately used to establish the dishonesty of the Traceys.

Persimmon's Submissions on ATE Insurance

81. Persimmon's pleaded case is that a different approach to materiality and/or inducement applies in the context of ATE insurance (see Particulars of Claim, paragraphs 4.1–4.2; Reply, paragraphs 3–5; Skeleton Argument, paragraphs 11, 14, 36). On both questions, it contends that a prudent underwriter 'would be unconcerned about individual facts being disclosed at inception of the policy' and would only have any real interest in the view of the solicitor/counsel conducting the case as to its overall legal merits. It is also implicit in Persimmon's case on waiver that, at most, the obligation of the insured only extends to telling the insurer what each party alleges in the proceedings, as opposed to what actually happened to the knowledge of the insured. These contentions are unsustainable.

82. First, there is no support in authority for the proposition that ATE insurance is not governed by conventional principles of good faith. Over the centuries, it has been established that those principles apply across the board – see *The 'Star Sea' (op cit)*. An ATE policy may be avoided for a material mis-presentation of the risk at inception just as any other policy may. In some extreme cases, this may mean that, if the claim fails the insurer is likely to have good grounds for avoidance. See the comments of Sedley LJ in *Al-Koronky* at paragraphs [33]–[36].

83. Secondly, Persimmon's arguments are entirely at odds with the understanding and practice of the market. The experts both agree that an ATE insurer expects from the insured a detailed, complete and honest presentation of the facts of the case, especially when covering a complex business dispute. Persimmon's expert is at pains to point out

---

32 Skeleton Argument, paragraphs 38, 45.

that the ATE insurer will wish to form its own view of the case based on that presentation. See: Williams at [2/187]; Smart at paragraph 6.10.1 [2/166].

84. Thirdly, the argument proves too much. If correct, it means that an insured who diligently and successfully misleads his own legal team as to the facts of the case and then confesses the truth at trial is entitled to the full benefit of ATE insurance.

85. Fourthly, as submitted above, the right of an ATE insurer to avoid for material non-disclosure does not (as Persimmon has argued) make the policy worthless in any case where there is a central dispute of fact. The right to avoid will only arise if it can be shown that the assured failed to make a full and accurate presentation at inception. Even where the right does arise, an ATE insurer will only in practice exercise that right if presented with the clearest evidence of dishonest conduct, because of the commercial and regulatory[33] damage it could suffer if it were to be perceived to have avoided on purely technical grounds.

86. Fifthly, the present case was not one where CPH's failure in the underlying litigation would necessarily have been based upon findings of dishonesty against the Traceys. Viewed from the perspective of those reviewing the case at FISL, it was entirely possible that a trial judge would prefer the evidence of Mr Watts without making the coruscating findings of fraud which were in the event made by Judge Pelling. Furthermore, CPH's factual account could have been accepted but its case could have failed for legal reasons, e.g. by virtue of the defences based on the LP(MP)A and/or lack of consideration (defences which were still pursued at trial).

F. The Insurer's Right to Avoid: Breach of the Post-Inception Duty of Good Faith

87. Throughout the course of the underlying litigation, the Traceys regularly sent communications to their solicitors[34] asserting the version of events which, as the Judge found, was untrue and known by them to

---

33 An insurer or underwriting agent is required to abide by the Insurance Conduct of Business Sourcebook, which requires that claims be handled fairly (ICOBS 8.1.1(1)) and that claims should not be unreasonably rejected, including by the exercise of rights of avoidance (ICOBS 8.1.1(3)). It is also required to apply the principles of the full FSA Handbook, which include obligations to conduct its business with integrity, observe proper standards of market conduct, pay due regard to the interests of its customers and treat those customers fairly (PRIN 2.1.1). Breaches of these obligations can render the insurer or agent liable to FSA disciplinary sanctions (PRIN 1.1.7).

34 See, for example, the communications at: [12/3020-21]; [13/3198].

be untrue. They persisted in their dishonest account at the case review meeting attended by Mr Coleman in December 2007.

88. This persistent dishonesty in dealings with the insurer (including dealings through CPH's innocent agent, Edwin Coe) constitutes breach of the post-inception duty of good faith. It would therefore also entitle GLR to avoid the Policy. See: *The 'Star Sea'*; *The 'Mercandian Continent'* [2001] EWCA Civ 1275, [2001] 2 Lloyd's Rep 563 at paragraph [35].

G. The Insurer's Right to Repudiate the Claim: Policy Conditions

89. It is submitted that, apart from the non-contractual remedy of avoidance, this claim must fail by reason of various specific terms in the Pursuit policy.

General Exclusion 12

90. General Exclusion 12 of the Policy provided as follows:

> 'This insurance does not cover any payment by the Insurer under the Policy where there has been misrepresentation or material non-disclosure by the Insured Litigant or the Insured Solicitor.'

This exclusion operates to absolve the insurer from the duty to pay a claim in circumstances where there has been material misrepresentation or non-disclosure by the insured or his agent. The exclusion, which has a more limited effect than the remedy of avoidance, does not require inducement. In this case, there is the clearest evidence of material non-disclosure and misrepresentation (see above). GLR is entitled to rely upon General Exclusion 12 to repudiate this claim even if (contrary to all the arguments set out above), inducement were not established.

Breach of Claims Conditions

91. The Policy contained the following further Conditions:

> '4. Minimising Claims or Legal Proceedings
> The Insured must take all reasonable measures to minimise the cost of Legal Proceedings.'

> '6. Fraudulent Claims
> If the Insured Litigant or Insured Solicitor makes any request for payment under the Policy knowing it to be fraudulent or false in any respect (or in circumstances where it ought reasonably to be known to be so)... the Policy shall be voidable at the Insurer's option.'

'8. Provision of Information
The Insured Solicitor must

(a) provide to Us regular progress reports on the Legal Proceedings and associated costs and when specifically requested by Us

...

(f) provide Us promptly with any requested information

...

The Insured Litigant or Insured Solicitor must advise Us of any material changes to the prospects of success in the Legal Proceedings.'

'10. Conduct of Legal Proceedings
(a) All information to be given to the Insured Solicitor
The Insured Litigant must give all information and assistance required by the Insured Solicitor. This must include a complete and truthful account of the facts of the case and all relevant documentary or other evidence in the Insured Litigant's possession. The Insured Litigant must obtain or execute all documents as may be necessary and attend any meetings or conferences when requested. The Insured Litigant must co-operate fully with the Insured Solicitor.'

The following condition made the compliance of CPH with those terms a condition precedent to the liability of the insurer.

'7. Due Observance
The due observance of and compliance with the terms provisions and conditions of the Policy insofar as they relate to anything to be done or complied with by the Insured Litigant or Insured Solicitor shall be conditions precedent to the liability of the Insurer to make any payment hereunder.'

CPH breached each of Conditions 4, 6, 8 and 10(a), as explained below. Because those were conditions precedent, it is not necessary to demonstrate prejudice[35] (although that could easily have been proven in each case here).

92. As regards Condition 4, CPH breached that term by failing to provide full and accurate information to Edwin Coe. If such information had been provided, it is inconceivable that that firm would not have advised settlement (e.g. by acceptance of one of Persimmon's offers) or discontinuance. That, in turn, would have reduced the cost of the legal proceedings.

---

35 See, for example, *Pioneer Concrete (UK) Ltd v National Employers' Mutual General Insurance Association Ltd* [1985] 1 Lloyd's Rep 274 at 281.

93. As regards Condition 6, any insurance claim by CPH would have been barred by that term because it would have been fraudulent, for the reasons given above. As the Judge held, the Traceys had pursued a claim which they knew could not properly succeed. Any request for payment by them would have been made in the knowledge that it was 'false or fraudulent in any respect'.

94. Taking Conditions 8 and 10(a) together, those terms imposed on CPH a duty to provide full and accurate information to Edwin Coe at every stage and to instruct Edwin Coe to pass on that information to FISL in accordance with the reporting obligations in Condition 8. In breach of those terms, CPH provided (directly and through Edwin Coe) inaccurate accounts to insurers throughout the litigation (e.g. at the case review meeting in December 2007).

H. The Insurer's Right to Repudiate the Claim: Fraudulent Claim/Illegality

95. In addition to the grounds elaborated above, the insurer was also entitled to repudiate the insurance claim on the basis that it was tainted by fraud and gave rise to the remedy of forfeiture. An assured who makes a dishonest insurance claim (or uses fraudulent devices to support a claim) forfeits the entire benefit of the policy. See: *Orakpo v Barclays Insurance Services* [1995] LRLR 443; *The 'Aegeon'* [2003] 1 QB 556 at paragraphs [13]–[46].

96. In this case, CPH pursued litigation which was (to the knowledge of its directing personalities) baseless. Therefore, the insurance claim by CPH on which this action is founded would be fraudulent.

97. Furthermore, to permit CPH to recover would be objectionable under the illegality principle, given that its entire claim was founded on a fraud. See the recent statements of the principle in *Stone and Rolls (in liquidation) v Moore Stephens (a firm)* [2009] UKHL 39, [2009] 3 WLR 455 and *Nayyar and ors v Denton Wilde Sapte* [2009] EWHC 3218 (QB), [2010] Lloyd's Rep PN 139 at paras 75 to 82[36].[37]

---

[36] Due to be heard on appeal next month.

[37] Although the point has not been taken by Persimmon, it is right to acknowledge that there is an obiter dictum of Mance J in *Total Graphics Ltd v AGF Insurance Ltd* [1997] 1 Lloyd's Rep 599 at 606R to the effect that a pure public policy defence (unlike, say, a defence based on breach of the pre- or post-contractual duty of good faith) cannot be taken to a claim based on the 1930 Act. It is respectfully submitted that that view is wrong and is not supported by authority. Indeed, it is at odds with the opinion of Lord Brown in *Stone & Rolls* at para. 195.

I. Persimmon's Case of Waiver/Estoppel

98. Persimmon alleges that the insurer in this case waived all rights it ever gained to avoid the Policy or repudiate the claim. See: Amended Particulars of Claim at paragraph 4.2.2 [1/18]; Reply at paragraphs 12–16 [1/45–46]. It is important that the Court should decide first precisely what rights the insurer attained and the basis of those rights, since Persimmon will bear the burden of showing that the insurer waived each and every basis for avoidance, and each and every breach of conditions precedent.

Legal Principles

99. Persimmon's Skeleton Argument (though not its statements of case) makes clear that it is relying upon both waiver by election and waiver by estoppel.

    (a) Waiver by election/affirmation arises where the insurer acquires a legal right and has to choose whether or not to exercise it. The insurer must have actual knowledge of the facts on which the right is based. Constructive knowledge is not sufficient[38]. The insurer must then unequivocally[39] act in such a way as to evince an intention not to exercise that right. It is not necessary that the assured should have relied upon the insurer's conduct. Election is final.

    (b) Waiver by (promissory) estoppel arises where the insurer possesses a legal right or defence and unequivocally represents (by words or conduct) that it will not rely upon its legal rights. The insured must have relied upon the representation for the equitable estoppel to be established[40]. The consequence must be that it would be inequitable for the insurer to rely upon the rights in question. Waiver by estoppel has a suspensory effect.

    See: *MacGillivray on Insurance Law (11th edn)* at paragraphs 10-103 to 10-105; *Good Faith and Insurance Contracts* at paragraphs 17–16 et seq.

100. Whichever basis is relied upon for the plea of waiver in this case, it is hopeless.

---

38 See: *ICCI v Royal Hotel (op cit)* at 161–163; *Callaghan v Hedges* [2000] Lloyd's Rep IR 125 at 133L (David Steel J).

39 See *Kosmar Villa Holidays Plc v Trustees of Syndicate 1243* [2008] EWCA Civ 147, [2008] 1 Lloyd's Rep IR 489 at 508–9 (Rix LJ).

40 See *HIH Casualty and General Insurance Ltd v Axa Corporate Solutions* [2002] EWCA Civ 1253, [2003] Lloyd's Rep IR 1 at para. 29.

Waiver by Election

101. To make good its case on this ground, Persimmon must show, in respect of each particular ground for avoidance of the Policy or repudiation of the claim, that (i) the insurer actually knew the facts underlying the particular ground and (ii) the insurer unequivocally demonstrated an intention not to rely its right. It fails at both stages.

Requirement of Knowledge

102. The first objection to any argument based on waiver by election is that RSA and its agent, FISL, did not before trial acquire actual knowledge of the facts founding the right to avoid or the right to repudiate the claim.

(a) They did not know that Bernard and Paul Tracey had repeatedly lied about 'the Fund' and about the fact that parts of the Site had been pre-let or pre-sold.

(b) They did not know that Bernard Tracey and Robert Dorin had conspired to produce a document which was dishonest both as to its date and as to the agreement recorded.

(c) They did not know that Paul Tracey's note of the 1 December 1999 meeting was not contemporaneous (or even near contemporaneous).

(d) They did not know that, in August 1999, CPH was entirely without the means to go on as lead developer.

(e) They did not know that the Traceys' account of the meetings in August 1999 and December 1999 was fundamentally dishonest. They knew that Persimmon's witnesses disagreed with the Traceys, but not that the Traceys' account was untruthful.

103. It is Persimmon's pleaded case that the knowledge of the insurer 'extends to those matters which it would have discovered if it had exercised its rights to access material' and 'all material in the possession of [Edwin Coe]'[41]. That amounts to a contention that constructive knowledge is sufficient for waiver by election, which is not the case (see authorities cited above). In any event, GLR rejects the notion that a reasonably diligent ATE insurer would have conducted the minute analysis and cross-referencing of documents which was embarked upon at trial. Even if that were wrong, the pervasive dishonesty of the

41 Reply, paragraph 13 [1/45].

Traceys was only firmly established when Paul Tracey was cross-examined.

104. In its Skeleton Argument (at paragraph 50(1)), Persimmon seeks to put a modified version of the same argument: that the insurer should be deemed to know all facts about which it has been put on inquiry. *CTI v Oceanus* [1984] Lloyd's Rep 476 at 498 and *ICCI* are cited in support of that proposition. In fact, neither authority supports that broad proposition. Kerr LJ in *CTI* at 497R made the specific point that knowledge of a material fact is not to be deemed on the basis that the underwriter could have extracted the fact from material to which he has access or which was 'cursorily shown to him'. As Mance J said in *ICCI* at 162L, knowledge for these purposes is a simple question of fact (a 'jury question').

105. Persimmon also argues (Skeleton Argument, paragraph 50(2)) that the insurer should be fixed with knowledge of all matters known to (and all documents in the possession of) Edwin Coe[42]. This, again, is a hopeless point.

(a) Persimmon is unable to cite any authority for this novel and striking proposition.

(b) The solicitors were not the agents of the ATE insurer, but of the insured (their client). This is confirmed by the policy definition of "insured solicitor" [3/201]. Clause 8 of the Policy required the insured to instruct his solicitors to provide assistance and information to the insurer upon request, but it did not establish the solicitor as the agent of the insurer. Such a relationship would create a serious structural conflict of interest. As Mr Williams explains in his report the market would not regard the solicitor as the agent of the insurer, but as the agent of the insured [2/188–89]. This is not to say that the insured's solicitor may not carry out tasks for the benefit of the insurer on the instruction of the insured (e.g. reporting to the insurer, recovering the premium, seeking to resist or minimise adverse costs orders).

(c) Persimmon argues that Edwin Coe was a party to the insurance contract and bound to report matters to the insurer. For the record, GLR disputes that contention[43]. In any event, even if Edwin Coe were a party to the contract, the primary obligation

---

42 See, for example, the comments at [13/3497].

43 Although the policy wording refers to the insured solicitor as being bound under the policy, that should be construed as obliging the insured to instruct his solicitor to do certain things and as meaning that the solicitor is expected to comply.

of the firm would be to its client and it could not be made to report matters save with its client's approval. Even if that were wrong and there was an obligation to report to the insurer irrespective of the client's wishes, that would not support the conclusion that the insurer had actual knowledge of the circumstances which should have been reported.

Requirement of Unequivocal Conduct

106. To satisfy this requirement, Persimmon must show that the insurer's words or conduct unequivocally demonstrated to CPH an intention not to rely upon any of the rights acquired. In fact, at no point did FISL give any indication to CPH that the insurer would not rely upon any of the various grounds for avoidance/repudiation.

107. Persimmon argues that FISL's failure to avoid the Policy or announce its intention to rely on a breach constitutes the necessary conduct. In other words, it relies upon silence or inactivity. As is well established, mere silence will not amount to an election in normal circumstances[44].

108. Persimmon makes much of three points: (i) that FISL did not avoid the Policy when told of Bernard Tracey's bankruptcy in early May 2008; (ii) that Mr Coleman did not ask for the witness statements when they were offered in early May 2008; and (iii) that FISL did not avoid the Policy when provided with the Skeleton Argument of the Defendant on 30 May 2008. None of these points can provide the basis of an argument that FISL elected to affirm the Policy. As explained above, FISL did not have actual knowledge of the points now relied upon until after trial. In any event, the fact that FISL did not immediately avoid the Policy or announce an intention to repudiate any claim at this late stage in the proceedings cannot be regarded as unequivocally demonstrating an intention never to avoid the Policy or rely upon a breach of claims conditions. To the contrary, Mr Coleman's response to Edwin Coe of 7 May 2008[45] indicated that he was concerned with the accuracy of the Traceys' version of events, not that he was announcing an intention not to rely upon any dishonesty on their part or any untruths or serious omissions in the proposal documents. He did not comment on the skeleton arguments at all, and his silence cannot be construed as any kind of unequivocal representation in any event but particularly given the very short time between the provision of the documents and the trial[46].

---

44 *Clough v LNWR* (1871) LR 7 Ex 26 at 35; *Allen v Robles* [1969] 1 WLR 1193; *Callaghan v Hedges* (supra).

45 [11/2742].

46 For the relevance of timing, see the judgment of Rix LJ in *Kosmar* at paras.79 and 80.

109. Persimmon also suggests that the failure to act at an earlier stage than May 2008 should be regarded as an election. It bases that suggestion on the fact that it had repeatedly contested the Traceys' factual version of events. However, the critical point is that the insurer did not know that the Traceys' version was false or that it had been bolstered with the series of lies which were admitted by Paul Tracey at trial.

110. In this context, it is important to appreciate the commercial realities. FISL could not too readily announce an intention to avoid the Policy or repudiate any claim. The regulatory obligations of an insurance agent such as FISL require that the greatest care be taken in such decisions. It was no doubt with those obligations in mind that FISL took great care before making its decision even after the judgment had been given. The Pursuit policy does not permit the insurer to withdraw cover either prospectively or retrospectively simply because prospects of success in the litigation have apparently fallen, a feature which is no doubt of real value to policy-holders. Allegations of waiver must be seen against that background.

Waiver by Estoppel

111. To establish an estoppel, Persimmon would have to demonstrate that, in respect of each particular ground for avoidance of the Policy or repudiation of the claim, (i) the insurer unequivocally represented an intention not to rely upon its rights; (ii) CPH acted in reliance upon that representation; and (iii) it would be inequitable to allow the insurer to rely upon its rights. Once again, it fails at every stage.

Requirement for Unequivocal Representation

112. This criterion is, on the facts of this case, the same as the requirement of unequivocal conduct discussed above. In these circumstances, the insurer would have to have known of the material bases for avoidance/repudiation and given a clear indication that it would not rely upon any. That proposition cannot be supported on the facts here (see above under 'Waiver by Election').

Requirement for Reliance

113. CPH did not rely upon any representation made by FISL. Even supposing that the silence of Mr Coleman in May 2008 constituted the necessary unequivocal representation, Persimmon adduces no evidence to prove that CPH acted in reliance upon it. By the later stages of the litigation, CPH was fully committed to pursuing its claim. It is most unlikely that it would have discontinued the litigation whatever noises the insurer had made. It would not have been able to secure insurance elsewhere, since any announcement of FISL that the Policy was to be

avoided or an indemnity refused would have had to be disclosed to any other insurer.

Equity

114. The final criterion for a waiver by estoppel is that it should be inequitable to allow the insurer to rely upon the right which it has represented will not be exercised. The equitable doctrine must be applied having regard to the position of the insured, CPH. Here, it cannot seriously be suggested that it would be inequitable to deprive CPH of the benefit of insurance which it obtained by a fundamentally dishonest presentation to support a fundamentally dishonest claim.

J. Witnesses at Trial

115. The following witnesses of fact are to be called:

(a) for Persimmon, Mr Gerald Francis, company secretary and legal director of Persimmon [2/1/99–107];

(b) for GLR, Mr Ian Coleman, ATE technical manager at FISL [2/1/109–127], and Mr Peter Smith, director of FISL and First Assist Legal Expenses Insurance Limited [2/3/129–145].

The following expert witnesses are to be called, as indicated above:

(a) for Persimmon, Mr Jason Smart of Elite Insurance Company Limited [2/4/147–174];

(b) for GLR, Mr Matthew Williams of AmTrust Europe [2/5/175–199].

As already apparent (and as can be seen from the experts' joint statement), there is almost no disagreement between the experts[47]. In particular, Mr Smart accepts in its entirety GLR's case on individual and collective materiality.

K. Conclusion

116. Persimmon stands in the position of the insured and it can only succeed if CPH could have successfully enforced the Policy. Applying conventional principles, the insurer was entitled to avoid that Policy. It

---

[47] And GLR will say no material disagreement at all. The issue of whether or not a prudent underwriter could have written the Policy in the first place is irrelevant: this is not a trial of whether or not the insurer acted competently but what the insurer's obligations and rights are under the Policy once incepted.

was also entitled to refuse to indemnify CPH for breach of policy conditions and because CPH's claim was fraudulent. The insurer (through its agent, FISL) did not lose its rights by any form of waiver.

117. Persimmon seeks to avoid that ineluctable conclusion by crafting new rules or tests for avoidance and waiver in the context of ATE insurance. There is no support in principle or authority for that attempt.

Good practice suggestions

Sequential service of skeletons

If you are defending a claim or responding to an application or to an appeal always seek the opportunity to have skeletons delivered sequentially, either voluntarily from your opponent or as a CMC direction. Prepare the core features and argument of your own document before having sight of the other side's. Then adapt it so that your skeleton reads as a complete answer to what has been said, rather than an independent document.

Structure

Provide the reader with plenty of signposts dealing with the structure of the document: a contents page for longer documents, or introduction; use headings and sub-headings. Make sure paragraphs are short, where possible deal with a single point only, and are numbered for ease of reference and reply.

Example G

Chancery Division – Application for summary judgment – Skeleton argument of 2nd Defendant by Spike Charlwood, March 2009 – 10pp.

Wave Lending v Al-Ansari and Another was a lender claim brought against both borrower and solicitor alleging fraud. In this skeleton summary judgment for fraud against the solicitor is strongly resisted.

The writer has a very structured approach, dealing with events, facts and legal argument. His use of footnotes is fairly striking, de-cluttering the text but also creating the opportunity to give depth to his argument by enabling the reader to choose when to take in that detail in respect of the points made. This style is not for everyone, but is effective. It enables you to convey a substantial amount of information in a relatively small number of pages.

The application was refused.

SKELETON ARGUMENT ON BEHALF OF D2

Introduction

1. This is a lender's claim in which C seeks summary judgment on an allegation of fraud.[1] D1 was the borrower. No application is made against him. D2 is a firm of solicitors and acted for C and D1 on the relevant transaction.

2. The allegation of fraud against D2 is on p.13 of the Particulars of Claim [A/3/13]. It relates to a single alleged representation "that the sum of £1,950,000 was to be applied to the purchase and secured upon 26 P Place", said to be "known" to be false because C's advance was disbursed in part to purchase 9 O Square and in part to D1.

3. D2 admits that it acted in breach of its common law duties of care to C (although not to the extent alleged by C), but strenuously denies the allegation of fraud/dishonesty. It relies in support of that denial on a witness statement from R S [A/14], who will give evidence at any trial of this matter.

---

[1] But not, subject to the possible exception dealt with in paragraph 20ff, below, in relation to its other claims against D2. See paragraph 44 of Ms B's statement [A/13/15]: "[C] has decided to seek summary judgment in respect of its claim in fraud."

Summary judgment: the law

4. A claimant may obtain summary judgment under CPR Part 24 only if two criteria are met:

    4.1 that the defendant has no real prospect of success; and

    4.2 there is no other compelling reason why there should be a trial.

    See CPR Part 24.2(a) and (b).[2]

5. As to the former:

    5.1 "The criterion which the judge has to apply under CPR Pt 24 is not one of probability; it is absence of reality."; and

    5.2 a mini-trial[3] is to be avoided.

    See *Three Rivers DC v Bank of England* [2001] UKHL 16, [2001] 2 All ER 513, HL, paras.[158] (Lord Hobhouse) and [95] (Lord Hope), respectively.

6. As to the latter:

    6.1 the risk of a finding of dishonesty may itself provide a compelling reason for allowing a case to proceed to trial;

    6.2 that is because "Experience teaches us that on occasion apparently overwhelming cases of fraud and dishonesty somehow inexplicably disintegrate"; and

    6.3 that experience is a factor always to be borne in mind in such cases; but

    6.4 will not "always, or inevitably" provide a compelling reason for allowing a case to proceed to trial.

    See *Wrexham Association Football Club Ltd v Crucialmove Ltd* [2006] EWCA Civ 237, CA, paras.[57–8] (from which the quotations above are taken).[4]

---

2 White Book, volume 1, page 557.

3 With its risk of summary injustice.

4 Insofar as it might be suggested that *Nationwide Building Society v Dunlop Haywards Ltd* [2007] EWHC 1374 (Comm), [2007] All ER (D) 393 (Jul), para.9 means that an allegation of dishonesty cannot by itself amount to a compelling reason for trial, it is submitted that that would be incorrect. *Wrexham*, para.57 expressly states that "the risk of such a finding [being a finding adverse to a party's integrity] may provide a compelling reason for allowing a case to proceed to a full oral hearing".

7. Summary judgment on an allegation of dishonesty will therefore be very rare.[5] Indeed, in cases such as this one, it should not be granted. Lewison J's comments in *Nigeria v Santolina* [2007] EWHC 437 (Ch), at para.71(i)[6] are apposite:

> "An allegation of personal corruption in public office is probably the most serious allegation that can be made against an elected officer of government. Only in exceptional circumstances[7] would it be right to enter judgment against him without giving him the opportunity to confront his accusers and to have his side of the story heard." (footnote added)

Legal issues relating to fraud and dishonesty

8. D2 relies on four further points of law relating to fraud and dishonesty:

    8.1 fraud requires dishonesty;[8]

    8.2 such dishonesty requires conscious wrongdoing;[9]

    8.3 to be made good an allegation of fraud must be proved to the heightened burden of proof; and

    8.4 C must prove reliance.

---

5 C accepts (B, para.43 [A/13/15]) that allegations of dishonesty will not "ordinarily" be suitable for summary judgment, but that understates the matter.

6 There were two applications for summary judgment in fraud in this case. The first, [2007] EWHC 437 (Ch), [2007] All ER (D) 103 (Mar), Lewison J, was refused. The second, [2007] EWHC 3053 (QB), Morgan J, was allowed following the relevant defendant pleading guilty to various criminal charges.

7 Which would have to involve something beyond any apparent strength the claim was said to have.

8 See, in particular, *The Kriti Palm* (below), para.256: "As for the element of dishonesty, the leading cases are replete with statements of its vital importance and of warnings against watering down this ingredient into something akin to negligence, however gross."

9 And NB that, although recklessness (taking care not to equate that with gross negligence) can suffice for this purpose, C does not allege recklessness, but only knowing misrepresentation. See p.13 of the Particulars of Claim [A/3/13].

See, for example, *Cheshire Building Society v Dunlop Haywards (DHL) Ltd* [2008] EWHC 51 (Comm), [2008] PNLR 19, David Steel J, para.46, summarising *The Kriti Palm* [2007] 1 All ER (Comm) 667, CA, paras.[251–260].[10]

9. Findings of fraud/dishonesty are therefore rare even at trial, a point which reinforces the inappropriateness, at least in the vast majority of cases, of a summary finding, especially against a professional man.

Dishonesty: D2's submissions

10. D2 denies dishonesty and submits that summary judgment should not be granted. It makes six submissions.

11. First, a summary finding of fraud/dishonesty should not be made against a practising solicitor (which R S[11] is) who strenuously denies dishonesty and is willing to give evidence[12] in support of that denial at trial and for whom the consequences of the finding would be very severe. This submission speaks for itself, but if necessary D2 will rely on the following matters in support of it.

    11.1 Mr S is a practising solicitor.

    11.2 As in *Nigeria v Santolini* (above), the allegation made, dishonesty in the course of his practice as a solicitor, is probably the most serious allegation that could be made against him.

    11.3 The SRA may intervene into a practice if it has "reason to suspect dishonesty" (Solicitors Act 1974, schedule 1, para.1(a)) (and has not intervened into Mr S's practice).

---

10 (i) Further to point 2 (dishonesty requires conscious wrongdoing), see also *Bryant v The Law Society* [2007] EWHC 3043 (Admin), Richards LJ and Aikens J, paras.[137–155], confirming that, in solicitors' disciplinary proceedings at least, the test for dishonesty involves subjective dishonesty. Whether this applies more widely may be a matter of debate (see, for example, the authorities referred to in *Bryant*), but D2 submits that it does and, in any event, that it could not summarily be determined that it did not.

(ii) The heightened burden of proof was recently discussed by the House of Lords in *R (D) v Life Sentence Review Commrs* and *In Re B* [2008] UKHL 33 and 35 respectively, but those decisions do not impact here.

11 Although p.13 of the Particulars of Claim [A/3/13] (where the allegation of dishonesty is contained) does not state which natural person is alleged to have acted dishonestly, para.9 of the Particulars of Claim [A/3/8] and paras.45–7 of Ms B's statement [A/13/16-7] refer to R S. Accordingly, D2 proceeds on the basis that C seeks to attribute Mr S's acts to it. If that is not correct, then C is required to state its position.

12 Mr S is not D2's only intended witness.

11.4 That is a much lower threshold than is required for summary judgment.

11.5 Although Mr S was arrested, the charges against him were dropped at a plea and case management hearing (statement, para.17 [A/14/5]).[13]

11.6 The relevant criminal and regulatory authorities therefore clearly do not consider the position as clear as C now contends it is, even after (in the case of the criminal authorities) what must have been a full investigation.

11.7 A finding of fraud/dishonesty would, in all likelihood, leave Mr S unable to practice.

11.8 Although it obtained a freezing order against D1 [A/7/14], C has neither sought judgment against D1 nor given any evidence as to why it has not. C did not seek a freezing order against D2.

11.9 This case is readily distinguishable from the very few recent cases in which summary judgment has been granted on an allegation going to the defendant's integrity. For example:

(1) Mr S's denial of dishonesty distinguishes this case from *Cheshire Building Society v Dunlop Haywards (DHL) Ltd* (above), in which David Steel J noted (at para.45(i)) that: "far from vigorously denying the allegation of fraudulent misrepresentation, [the defendants] merely make 'no admission'".

(2) Likewise, Mr S's willingness to assist D2 distinguishes this case from *Cheshire.* See especially para.[52]: "the circumstances of M's appearance at this hearing [he appeared only on the second day and then only briefly: paras.7–17] make it plain that no assistance, or at least none worth having, will be forthcoming."[14]

---

13 Cf. *Nigeria v Santolina* (above), where the relevant defendant had pleaded guilty to various criminal charges by the time of the second, successful application.

14 These points appear to have been less clear at the time of the *Nationwide v Dunlop Haywards* hearing, but that case involved the same person, Mr M, and it is submitted that the same points apply in relation to that judgment.

(3) The fact that the allegation in this case is one of dishonesty (and not the lesser[15] allegation of breach of fiduciary duty) distinguishes it from the *Wrexham* case.

(4) In *Nigeria v Santolina* (above) the relevant defendant had pleaded guilty to various offences in criminal proceedings against him.

12. Second, the Court should not conclude that Mr S was dishonest without hearing from him. Again, this submission speaks for itself, but D2 will rely on the following matters if necessary.

12.1 "Negligence, however gross" is not dishonesty.[16]

12.2 Carelessness is precisely what Mr S says occurred.

12.3 His case in that regard is supported by his witness statement [A/14/1–7], referring to external pressures (family and work), his practice (he was not a specialist/regular conveyancer), being taken in by D1, instructions from D1,[17] possible explanations for the certificates of title he signed and specific responses to each of the allegations contained in Ms B's statement under the heading "Evidence of Dishonesty".

12.4 Carelessness, incompetence or even stupidity, as opposed to dishonesty, are common conclusions once all the evidence in a case has been weighed.

12.5 The conscious/subjective element of fraud (see paragraph 8.2, above) renders evidence and cross-examination particularly necessary.

12.6 C's Request for Further Information illustrates that the case against D2 is not as clear as C contends; were it so, the request would have been unnecessary.

13. Third, the specific matters relied on by C as justifying summary judgment (set out in paragraph 44 of Ms B's statement [A/13/15]) do not do so.

---

15 In the sense that breach of fiduciary duty does not require dishonesty. See, for example, *Bristol & West Building Society v Mothew* [1998] Ch 1, CA, at 19E: "Conduct which is in breach of this duty need not be dishonest but it must be intentional."

16 The quotation is an extract from the longer quotation from *The Kriti Palm* (above) in footnote 8, above.

17 As to which, see also para.1 of the Further Information [A/6/2].

13.1 "Overwhelming strength", even if apparently made out at a summary judgment hearing (and the Court should not find that it is), is not sufficient. See the quotation from *Wrexham*, para.57 set out in paragraph 6.2, above.[18]

13.2 Mere reference to other allegedly similar cases cannot assist C. Mr S denies any allegation of dishonesty/fraud (statement, para.18 [A/14/5]), no other summary judgment application has been made and repetition is not to be equated with proof.

13.3 Alleged lack of explanation likewise cannot assist. D2 has filed a defence and Mr S has given a witness statement and will give evidence at trial. In the circumstances, any point C may have about delay is at best one for cross-examination.

14. Fourth, D2 will if necessary rely on the principle that C may rely only on allegations of dishonesty properly made.[19] It mentions this because of the references to honesty in C's Request for Further Information which go beyond the single allegation of dishonest misrepresentation on p.13 of the Particulars of Claim [A/3/13].

15. Fifth, even if dishonesty is made out, C has not established reliance – generally a matter for trial[20] – to the standard required for summary judgment. Thus: the Particulars of Claim (at para.11 [A/3/9]) plead reliance on the certificate of title, not the representation pleaded to have been fraudulent; Mr B (at para.14 of his statement [B/1/5]) refers to the certificate of title only as "the trigger" for the advance, again without referring to the relevant representation; the issue is not otherwise dealt with; and disclosure has not been given.[21] Further, in the light of the availability of mortgages in excess of 100%, the regular diet of media reports describing reckless lending by mortgage lenders, C's asserted reliance on D1's statements as to his wealth (B, para.29 [B/1/8]) and C's plea that D2 failed to submit a certificate of title in relation to 9 O Square,[22] it cannot be assumed that C would not have made the loan it did on the lesser security represented by 9 O Square.

---

18 For ease of reference: "Experience teaches us that on occasion apparently overwhelming cases of fraud and dishonesty somehow inexplicably disintegrate."

19 See, for example, *Three Rivers* (above), paras.[51–[53] (Lord Hope) and [183–[190] (Lord Millett).

20 See paragraphs 20ff, below.

21 See footnote 29, below.

22 PoC, para.12(2)(vii). C could not properly complain that it had not received a certificate of title in relation to the property "to which [D2] was intending to apply [C's] funds" if there was no possibility that it would have lent on that property.

16. Sixth, C has served no (proper) evidence as to loss. With the court bundles it served for the first time a statement from Mr G [15/1-3] purporting to deal with certain questions of loss, but that statement is mere assertion unsupported by evidence and is plainly inadequate. In any event, the extreme lateness of the evidence, which should have been served with the application, has prevented D2 from giving it any proper consideration. Given the amount at stake (the sums referred to being very nearly £240,000), D2 therefore objects to this evidence.

17. For all these reasons therefore, D2 submits that it has a real prospect of defending the allegation of fraud against it and/or that there are compelling reasons for a trial in this case.

C's other claims

Introduction

18. As already noted,[23] C does not, with one possible exception, seek summary judgment on the remainder of its claim. This is entirely logical. The allegation of fraud must have been included by C for a reason and will, if it is not summarily determined, require a trial. In any event, C would no doubt not have set itself the hurdle of seeking summary judgment in fraud if it thought it could summarily establish its claim by some other route.

19. Nonetheless, Ms B refers (statement, paras.39–42 [A/13/14-5]) to various matters of causation and contributory negligence allegedly consequential on D2's limited admission of breach of its common law duties. If that is merely consequential on C's application for summary judgment in fraud, then D2 refers to its submissions on reliance in paragraph 15, above.[24]

20. If, however, Ms B's comments are intended to go further, it is denied that C is entitled to summary judgment on the points referred to. D2 makes, in outline, four points:

    20.1 a trial will be required in any event;

    20.2 insofar as it may be suggested that contributory negligence is not available in this case, that would be incorrect;

---

23 See paragraph 1, above.

24 And has already confirmed (Defence, para.24.2 [A/4/12]) that it does not assert that contributory negligence would be available to it if C established fraud.

20.3 the issues of causation and contributory negligence raise factual issues about C's conduct which cannot be summarily determined; and

20.4 C has served no (proper) evidence on loss.[25]

Background and law

21. As the Court may well be aware:

21.1 there was a protracted round of "lender litigation"[26] following the property market crash of the early 1990s;

21.2 that round of litigation included a number of managed claims;

21.3 such managed claims were described[27] as giving "a more balanced view of the way that the [relevant lender] operated than if I had tried a single claim only";

21.4 having considered a number of applications for summary judgment in the first of the managed claims, Chadwick J concluded:[28]

> "... I have no doubt that, generally, it would be unsafe to act on the basis of untested assertions in the society's affidavits that the society 'would not have touched the transaction with a bargepole'. I think it may well turn out at a trial that, in the relevant period (1988 to 1991), the society was a good deal less fastidious in choosing its borrowers than it would now wish to recall.
>
> Accordingly, where the question, 'what would the society have done if it had been asked for authority to proceed to completion', is a relevant question, it is a question which needs to be tried. If, as I suspect, that will necessitate very extensive discovery – ... – that will have to be faced; ..."; and

21.5 it is clear following the last round of lender litigation that contributory negligence can, and can very markedly, reduce the damages to which a lender might otherwise be entitled – a

---

25 See paragraph 16, above.

26 i.e. claims by secured mortgage lenders against the professionals who acted for them in relation to their secured lending.

27 Specifically by Blackburne J in *Nationwide v Balmer Radmore* [1999] Lloyd's Rep PN 241 at 247, col.1, but the point is submitted to be of general application.

28 See *Bristol & West Building Society v May May & Merrimans* [1996] 2 All ER 801 at 828f–h.

particularly graphic example is *Nationwide v Archdeacons* [1999] Lloyd's Rep PN 549, in which contributory negligence was assessed at 90%.

This case

22. D2 submits that the above principles are applicable in this case; issues as to what C would have done are not suitable for summary judgment and contributory negligence is available to D2. Indeed, in the present climate Chadwick J's observation that lenders may turn out to have been less fastidious than they assert is particularly apposite.

23. In addition, D2 relies on the following matters:

    23.1 C has not yet given disclosure;[29]

    23.2 issues as to C's conduct should not be determined without the opportunity to test C's evidence by cross-examination following disclosure and, probably, expert lending evidence;

    23.3 that is especially so in the present context, that of a mortgage lender making assertions about its lending practices against a regular diet of media reports describing reckless lending by such lenders;

    23.4 quite apart from anything else, an assertion that C's solicitors have taken instructions (B, para.40 [A/13/14]) is an insufficient basis for a summary finding of fact; and

    23.5 numerous specific allegations of contributory negligence are set out in paragraph 26 of D2's Defence [A/4/13-5], they cannot be dismissed on the basis of untested assertion on behalf of C and in any event this is an issue on which further disclosure will be relevant.[30]

---

[29] It has now provided a copy of its lending file in relation to 26 P Place, but no list of documents or any of the other disclosure that it would be required to give. For example: its files on 9 O Place and 24 P Place (PoC, paras.2–3 [A/3/1-2]; B, para.18 [B/1/6]); its lending criteria (including policy documents to and from its credit committee (B, para.11 [B/1/3])); communications with the Council for Mortgage Lenders and fraud prevention bodies; its arrears, repossession and sales files; and any documents relating to D1.

[30] Thus, for example, the post default investigations referred to at Spilsbury, para.17 [B/1/162] could have been carried out before the advance was made.

24. Any application for summary judgment on the issues of causation and/or contributory negligence should therefore be dismissed on the basis that D2 has a real prospect of succeeding on those points and/or that there are compelling reasons for a trial in this case.

Conclusion

25. C's application should therefore be dismissed.

> **Good practice suggestion**
>
> A sound structure is essential in producing a lucid and compelling argument. Here a list of enumerated points is highly effective. It demonstrates organised thought and enables the reader to deal with the argument in the same structured way. It also facilitates comments from other parties.

Example H

Chancery Division trial – Defendant's opening skeleton by Spike Charlwood, January 2008 – 14pp.

Aishah v X was a claim against solicitors for alleged breach of retainer and negligence in the conveyance of beneficial interests on the purchase of a property. The claim was resisted as to breach/negligence, causation, loss, or the recoverability of any loss within the scope of the duty owed.

There is a strong emphasis on detail and cross-referencing to the trial bundles. The text is de-cluttered by placing heavy reliance on footnotes. The language used is not formal, occasionally idiomatic but not conversational. There is a real sense of completeness – the judge can base his entire judgment on this written skeleton should he wish to. As a document it is designed for the judge to take away and use to formulate his opinion after the evidence has concluded. The writer uses a chronological narrative that is sufficiently detailed to avert the need for a separate chronology.

Note that the writer deals with the Claimant's pleaded case without preempting the way evidence may come out in relation to certain issues. No formal conclusion is offered.

The claim was adjourned on day four of the trial.

OPENING SKELETON ARGUMENT ON BEHALF OF THE DEFENDANT

Introduction

1. In this case C alleges professional negligence against D, a firm of solicitors. Negligence, causation, loss and that any loss that may have been suffered fell within the scope of D's duty are all denied.

2. In short: the claim arises out of a residential property purchase by C and her late husband ("the King") in 2001; the property purchased was 2–3, Regent's Park, London ("the Property"); and the claim relates to how the joint ownership of the Property was dealt with.

3. C's case is not, however, that D effected the wrong type of joint ownership – it could not be: C was registered as the sole proprietor of the Property as she says she should have been. Rather, C alleges, in effect, that in the course of acting on the purchase D failed to create certain pieces of evidence that would, she says, have been useful to her

in a subsequent dispute between her and her late husband's estate ("the Estate").

4. D's case is that it did what C instructed (had her registered as the sole proprietor of the Property) and thereby complied with its obligations to her, or was not in material breach of those obligations. In any event: C's dispute with the Estate existed independently of any failing by D; protecting her from that dispute (a claim by, in effect, her co-purchaser) was not part of what D was retained to do; any failing by D did not impact on the settlement; and C cannot make out any loss, having chosen to assert privilege over documents relating to the mediation and the costs claimed by her.

The factual background

5. D was instructed in early July 2001. Those instructions came via CF of Standard Chartered Grindlays ("the Bank").[1] What C and her husband had discussed with the Bank and what, if anything, they had then agreed as to the beneficial ownership of the Property, if purchased, are in issue. In outline, however: C and her husband had made some enquiries about London property with the Bank in May 2001;[2] the possibility of purchasing the shares of the company which then owned the Property, as opposed to the Property itself, was canvassed as early as 4 June 2001;[3] that was the scheme in place by 13 July 2001;[4] the final decision to proceed with the purchase was not taken until after 17 July 2001;[5] and all of the Bank's discussions after the initial enquiries in May were with C.

6. D reported on title to C and her husband on 8 August 2001 [2/157–62]. It is unclear when this was first forwarded to C by the Bank,[6] but it was faxed to C by Ms F on 29 August 2001 [2/198] and again on 3 September 2001 [2/199], not having gone through properly on 29 August 2001. As the report and faxes make clear, the intention to purchase the shares in the then owner of the Property subsisted until early September, but D

---

1 NB that, although part of the Bank's file has been disclosed, it is incomplete. See, for example, footnote 6, below.

2 See e.g. Ms F's fax of 29/5/01 [2/89].

3 See Ms F's fax of 4/6/01 [2/91].

4 By 3/7/01 it had seemed that a share purchase would be possible [2/95] and on 13/7/01 Mr S wrote that "we will have saved on the … heavy Stamp Duty" [2/106].

5 See Ms F's fax of 17/7/01 [2/109]. On 11/6/01 Ms F had asked if C/her husband wished to go ahead [2/93], C asked the Bank to take the next step in a conversation with Ms F on 25/6/01 [2/94] and C discussed the price with Mr S on 13/7/01 [2/97, 106].

6 The second paragraph of Ms F's fax of 29/8/01 [2/198] begins, "I am attaching again the property report from [D] …", but the first sending is not in the trial bundles.

was unable to obtain the guarantees necessary to support such a scheme and in her fax of 3 September 2001 Ms F noted that:

> "The alternative is to purchase the property itself which as you are aware would lead to a stamp duty liability of £100,000. ... You could then either purchase the property in your joint names or we could form a new company to acquire the property on your behalf."

7. Those issues were discussed in a conversation between Mr S and C on 8 September 2001 [2/202] and C instructed Mr S that the Property should be purchased via a company. There was not, however, time to form the new company prior to exchange of contracts and so it was agreed that exchange would take place in C's and her husband's personal names and that completion would be in the name of the new company.[7]

8. On 26 September 2001 Ms F specifically confirmed D's authority to exchange on that basis [2/235]. Then, or probably shortly afterwards, Ms F also instructed D that if the new company was not set up, then C/her husband would hold the Property as beneficial joint tenants. Whether that reflected an agreement to that effect between C/her husband is in issue, but after more than 2 years' equivocation on the point[8] C now accepts that D did indeed receive such instructions.[9] There is therefore no claim against D on the basis that it did not receive instructions on this point.

9. Exchange of contracts (in C's/her husband's personal names, but on the basis that completion would be to a company) took place on 28 September 2001, with completion scheduled for 31 October 2001 [2/268–75].

10. On or about 2 October 2001 C's husband was hospitalised[10] and this, his illness and death ultimately lead to the Property being transferred into C's/her husband's personal names and then into C's sole ownership. In more detail:

---

7 See [2/214, 218, 219, 226, 229].

8 See the amendments to the Particulars of Claim.

9 See paragraph 23 of the Re-Amended Particulars of Claim [1/2/7]. NB that although the words containing this plea were in the original Particulars of Claim, they were conditional until the re-amendment on 9/11/07.

10 See e.g. Ms T's fax of 2/10/01 [2/290].

24.1 on 26 September 2001 the Bank had sent documents necessary for the formation of the anticipated new company to C's husband;[11]

24.2 D had sought details of the company on 2 October 2001 [2/289];

24.3 Ms F in turn chased the information on 10 October 2001 [3/1];

24.4 D again chased on 17 October 2001 [3/5], but was advised by Mr G on 19 October 2001 that it would be difficult to obtain C's husband's signature before completion [3/14];[12]

24.5 C/her husband had not chosen the name of the new company by 22 October 2001 [3/13] and Mr G was by then concerned as to whether completion would be able to take place on 31 October 2001 [3/15];

24.6 as a means of dealing with the difficulties caused by the illness, D suggested leaving the name of the transferee blank on completion, so giving more time for C's husband to deal with the necessary company creation issues [3/14, 16–7, 23, 30];

24.7 completion took place on 31 October 2001 on that basis;[13]

24.8 D then sought details of the new company [e.g. 3/34, 39, 40];

24.9 Mr G tried to have the necessary documents completed [3/47], but this never occurred;

24.10 C's husband died on 21 November 2001;

---

11 The covering letter is at [2/236], the documents at [2/237-266]. The Court is referred specifically to [2/250], where the intended shareholdings of C/her husband are given as 50% each.

12 Thus D's advice that there were no further documents that needed to be signed by C's husband (if completion was into C/her husband's personal names) (see e.g. paragraph 30A of the Re-Amended Particulars of Claim [1/2/9]) did not come out of the blue, but was a response to the difficulty created by C's husband's illness.

13 See Mr C's letter of 31/10/01 [3/28] and in particular point 3 in that letter. Despite asserting at paragraph 2 [1/2/3] that "This claim arises out of the joint purchase ... on 31st October 2001", paragraph 36 of the Re-Amended Particulars of Claim [1/2/10] now describes this as "purported" completion. D's case, as set out in paragraph 33 of the Re-Amended Defence [1/3/36], is that the contract was completed on 31 October 2001 (both parties having done everything required of them under the contract and the vendor having agreed to leaving the name of the transferee blank) and that the disposition of the Property was completed on registration. See e.g. *Elements of Land Law* (Gray & Gray, 4th edn, 2005), para.12.52.

24.11 C began to chase the Bank as to the position in relation to the Property, according to her, 2 days later[14] and began the process of re-selling the Property no later than 4 December 2001;[15]

24.12 D immediately put in hand the steps required to have the Property registered in C's sole name and this was done, the process being completed on 8 December 2001 [3/60, 61, 63–5, 82, 83, 88, 91–3, 95]; and

24.13 in so acting, D acted in accordance with instructions from C given on 6 December 2001 [3/85].

11. D repeated its understanding of the position in letters dated 30 January 2002 [3/120] and 1 February 2002 [3/123], but the Estate disputed C's ownership and on 24 May 2002 applied to register a caution over the Property [3/135–7]. That application:

24.14 asserted that the whole of the Property was held on trust for the Estate; and

24.15 relied on five matters in support of that proposition:

(1) the husband's provision of the whole of the purchase price;

(2) evidence from the husband's personal and private secretaries;

(3) the applicant's (the husband's son) own knowledge;

(4) Sharia law, the husband having been a Muslim and, according to the caution, duty bound to leave his estate in accordance with that law; and

(5) the existence of 10 other beneficiaries to the Estate (the husband's children).

12. C's present solicitors were instructed on about 30 May 2002,[16] D therefore has little direct knowledge of matters after this date and the following brief chronology is derived from such disclosure as has been given.

---

14 See paragraph 26 of her statement [1/10/118]. At paragraph 27 she says that her first conversation with D was on 6 December 2001.

15 See the letter from Knight Frank at [3/73].

16 See paragraph 29 of C's statement [1/10/119].

19 July 2002	Malaysian letters of administration granted [3/158]
28 January 2003	An offer of £2.15m was made for the Property [3/212]
15 April 2003	C issued a claim against the Estate seeking removal of the Estate's caution [3/276]
6 May 2003	The caution was removed by consent on the basis that the proceeds of sale of the Property would not be paid out pending resolution of the Estate's claim [4/41]
18 November 2003	English letters of administration granted [4/93]
December 2003	C and the Estate agree to mediate [4/102–3]
3 March 2004	C and the Estate exchange mediation papers [4/180, 191]. In addition to the matters set out in the caution, the Estate's paper referred to the following matters:[17] (6) C's entitlement to a share of the husband's "substantial worldwide estate" (para.5); (7) the insertion into one of the company creation documents of an indication that C/her husband were to hold the company 50/50 (paras.7.6 and 12);[18] and (8) Mr G's knowledge (para.10).
11 March 2004	Estate's claim settled at mediation on terms which saw C agreeing to pay 61.6724% (£650,000) of the then disputed share of the Property to the Estate [4/214]

13. A letter of claim was sent by C on 28 June 2005 [4/224], more than 15 months later. D's letter of response was served on 28 September 2005 [4/226].

17 Continuing the numbering from paragraph 11.2, above.

18 The document appears at [2/250].

The issues[19]

14. There is presently no agreed list of issues in this case, C having declined to serve a draft list in advance of the exchange of skeleton arguments. D suggests, however, that the primary issues are likely to be as follows.

    (1) Did D fulfil its obligations, or its material obligations, to C by registering her as the sole owner of the Property?

    (2) If not, was D negligent in any of the respects alleged in paragraph 64 of the Particulars of Claim?

    (3) If (which is denied) C suffered any loss by reason of her dispute with the Estate, was that loss within the scope of D's duty of care?

    (4) If (which is denied) D was negligent in any respect, did that negligence have any causative effect?

    (5) What, if any, loss has C suffered?

15. Further to issue (4), above, four primary sub-issues are likely to arise.

    (a) Has C proved any case as to causation?

    (b) Was the Estate's claim caused by any act or omission of D?

    (c) What was the husband's intention in relation to the ownership of the Property/the common intention of C/the husband?[20]

    (d) Was C's position in her dispute with the Estate weakened by any negligence proved by C, if necessary weighing the impact of any such matter in the light of the file as a whole and the evidence given to C's solicitors by D,[21] and including, for example, whether D could have obtained the husband's signature to the TR1?

16. More generally in relation to issues (4) and (5), above, C's claim is at best a loss of a chance claim and so two further issues may arise.

---

19 For the avoidance of doubt, the entirety of this section of this skeleton is without prejudice to D's case as to C's failure to prove causation or loss, as set out in paragraphs 25–27, below.

20 See e.g. paragraphs 5 and 8, above.

21 A statement and supplemental statement from Mr Watson appear at [4/162 and 207].

(6) Did C have any real prospect of improving on the settlement?

(7) If so, what was her chance of doing so?

17. In summary, D's case on each of those issues is as follows:

    (1) D did fulfil its obligations, or its material obligations, to C by registering her as the sole owner of the Property.

    (2) D was not negligent.

    (3) Any loss suffered by C was not within the scope of D's duties to her.

    (4) Any negligence by D had no causative effect.

        (a) C has proved no case as to causation.

        (b) The Estate's claim was not caused by any act or omission of D.

        (c) The husband intended a tenancy in common/there was no common intention for a beneficial joint tenancy.

        (d) C's position in the dispute was not weakened and D could not have obtained the husband's signature.

    (5) C has suffered no loss.

    (6) (For reasons nothing to do with D) C had no, or no real, prospect of improving on the settlement.

    (7) If that is wrong, then any impact of any negligence by D on the settlement was small and any loss of a chance award should be correspondingly small.

Issues (1), (2) and (3): negligence and scope of duty

In general

18. C has had trouble deciding what her case on negligence is. Even leaving aside her oscillation as to whether she accepted that D had received instructions as to the required form of ownership of the Property: two of the original allegations of negligence have now been abandoned;[22] four of the ten allegations now made were first made only

[22] What were paragraphs 64A(1) and (2) of the Particulars of Claim [1/2/16].

in November 2007;[23] and one of the remaining allegations was substantially amended at that time.[24]

19. D submits that this reflects a real difficulty in C's case: D registered C as the sole proprietor of the Property in accordance with her instructions. C therefore cannot (and does not) say that D failed to implement its instructions. Rather, D submits, C has in effect sought (on now 4 occasions[25] and with the benefit of hindsight), but failed, to turn her dispute with the Estate into a claim against D.

20. Thus, D's first submission as to negligence in this case is that D was not, or not materially, negligent – in accordance with his instructions it registered C as the sole proprietor of the Property and thereby fulfilled his obligations, or his material obligations, to her.

21. Further or alternatively, D submits that the losses claimed by C are not within the scope of the duties of care it owed. They are losses caused by a dispute raised by the Estate, not any failure of registration, and it was not part of D's retainer to protect C from claims by the husband or the Estate.

22. Turning to C's specific allegations of negligence:

    24.16 it is submitted that negligence is not something to be considered in a vacuum, but against the particular circumstances of the case and D refers in particular to the following matters:

        24.16.1 C's/the husband's decision to act via the Bank;

        24.16.2 the ongoing desire to purchase the Property via a Company; and

        24.16.3 the complications caused by the husband's health; and

    24.17 otherwise, they will be a matter for evidence and submissions, as appropriate.

---

23 What are now paragraphs 64(5), (7), (9) and (10) of the Re-Amended Particulars of Claim [1/2/17-8].

24 What is now paragraph 64(4) of the Re-Amended Particulars of Claim [1/2/17].

25 The draft Particulars of Claim accompanying the letter of claim, the Particulars, the Amended Particulars and the Re-Amended Particulars.

The evidence of Mr Freedman

Admissibility

23. D's case is that conveyancing evidence of the sort given by Mr Freedman is inadmissible for the reasons given by the Court of Appeal in *Bown v Gould & Swayne* [1996] PNLR 130.

Content

24. This will be dealt with by cross examination in the first instance.

Issue (4): Causation

(a) Has C proved any case as to causation?

25. In this case C claims 2 heads of loss: £650,000 paid in settlement of her dispute with the Estate; and various legal fees said to have been incurred in relation to that dispute. Despite that, she has consistently refused to disclose any material from either her Malaysian or her English lawyers, asserting that it is privileged; even the very bills of which payment is, in effect, sought have been withheld.[26] Accordingly, D submits that C's claim must fail or should be rejected for want of proof.

26. Further or alternatively, the Court has before it no proper evidence as to the basis of the settlement and, for example:

    26.1 it seems that C's dispute with the Estate was not limited to the Property: [4/209A] refers to "a wider dispute in terms of [C] being unhappy with regard to how the estate was being run in Malaysia and also matters in America";

    26.2 even though the Estate accepted that any part of the Property not owned by C would be dealt with subject to the English law of intestacy,[27] C seems to have settled for an amount less than she would have been entitled to under the intestacy rules;[28] and

---

26 See p.2 of C's disclosure list at [1/8/64].

27 See paragraph 5 of its mediation paper [4/193-4].

28 As his wife, C would have been entitled to: (i) personal chattels; (ii) £125,000; and (iii) a life interest in one half of the residuary estate: s.46 of the Administration of Estates Act 1925. If, as the Estate contended, it was entitled to half of the value of the Property, that would have amounted to £1,053,956.20 (half of the sum in paragraph C of the settlement agreement [4/214]). Less the £125,000 referred to above, that leaves £928,956.20, of which half is £464,478.10. For a 30 year old (as C was) a life interest in that sum would have been worth at least 84.9% of the total (see the sheet attached to this skeleton), i.e. £394,341.91. In total, therefore, C's interest on an intestacy would, on the Estate's case, have been worth £519,341.91 (£394,341.91 + £125,000). By contrast, C in fact received only 38.3276% of the disputed share of the Property, i.e. £403,956.20.

26.3 C's case simply ignores the numerous matters relied on by the Estate independently of anything D did, as set out in paragraphs 20 and 21, above.

27. Thus, D will if necessary say that the settlement does not speak for itself, alternatively that it is, or should be taken to be, C's assessment of her chances of proving that the husband truly intended a beneficial joint tenancy based on her knowledge of her dealings with him.

(b) Was the Estate's claim caused by any act or omission of D?

28. D denies that it was. The dispute between C and the Estate was initiated well before the Estate received D's file[29] and was not caused by anything D did or did not do, but by the Estate's belief that the husband had not intended to give C the entirety of the Property – see, for example, the terms of the caution set out in paragraph 11.2, above.

(c) What was the husband's intention in relation to the ownership of the Property/the common intention of C/her husband?

29. This will be largely a matter for cross-examination in the first instance, but D's case is that the husband intended a tenancy in common and that there was no common intention for a beneficial joint tenancy.[30]

(d) Was C's position in her dispute with the Estate weakened by any negligence proved by C?

30. Paragraph 65 of the Re-Amended Particulars of Claim makes numerous assertions as to the impact of the matters alleged against D. There is, however, no evidence as to those matters and could not be any proper evidence on them without disclosure by C of matters relating to the mediation and her dispute with the Estate more generally.

31. Subject to paragraph 30, above, D denies that C's position was weakened by it. For example:

31.1 in the light of the matters set out in paragraph 10, above, it is denied that D could at any material time have obtained the husband's signature to the TR1 for the Property;

---

[29] So, for example, the Estate applied for its caution on 24/5/02 [3/135], but did not receive D's file until 28/11/03 [4/98].

[30] And, for the avoidance of doubt, that the husband would not have signed any document to the contrary.

31.2 D gave evidence in support of C's position in the dispute with the Estate;[31]

31.3 the documents referred to in paragraph 10.12, above, would have supported, and do support, D's evidence that it was instructed that there should be a beneficial joint tenancy;[32] and

31.4 C accepts that evidence.[33]

Issue (5): Loss

32. D denies that C has suffered any loss. In particular, there is no evidence of any loss and the settlement sum does not amount to/cannot be taken as a loss.

Issues (6) & (7): Loss of a chance

33. D submits that C's claim is at best a claim for the loss of a chance, *viz.* the chance of obtaining a better settlement with the Estate. Further:

33.1 for the reasons given above, C had no, or no real, prospect of obtaining, or has not proved that she could have obtained, any such settlement; and

33.2 if (contrary to D's case) such a chance has been proved, then it was a small chance and D will rely in that regard on the fact that matters arising from its file were only one of the nine[34] matters relied on by the Estate.

---

31 It appears at [4/162 and 207].

32 Indeed, paragraph 28 of the Re-Amended Particulars of Claim [1/2/13] expressly asserts that D's letters of 23 November 2001 [3/60, 61] could only have been written "in the belief that [C and her husband] had held the beneficial interest in the property as joint tenants and that the right of survivorship operated on the death."

33 See paragraph 23 of the Re-Amended Particulars of Claim [1/2/7].

34 The other eight are set out in paragraphs 11.2 and 12, above.

Good practice suggestions

Length

You should be very conscious of length. Make sure the document is not too long. While it may be that some cases demand skeletons in excess of the 20-page guidance, more often than not the longer the written submission, the less well received it will be. As a suggestion, be as brief as you sensibly can. It should not be necessary to re-write to reduce length, but do so where you can.

Abbreviations

Most advocates dislike the use of abbreviations and use them only because they believe (wrongly) that the court wants them, or they are under pressure to shorten their written submissions and this feels like a way of helping to do so. In fact abbreviations interfere with the readability of the text because, unless the reader is very familiar with their use, he must make a mental note to stop and check to whom the contraction is referring. Sometimes a judge will physically have to stop and look back some pages. It is irritating to have to do so.

You should distinguish between skeleton arguments, where brevity is expected in the form of abbreviated parties, personal names – particularly corporations – and statutes, and fuller written submissions, where these are not. Use only familiar or recognised short forms. Do not create your own abbreviations or create new terms of art. The court will not appreciate it. Where being concise is important you should use established nomenclature, contract full names, and refer to parties' status or occupations, such as 'the complainant', 'the donor,' 'the driver,' 'the doctor.' After first setting out the full title of a piece of legislation or delegated legislation, reduce it to 'the Act' or 'the Rules'; contracts, disciplinary codes or proposals can be 'the Code' or 'the Scheme'. If parties' names are being used, do not use initials but do give a title.

Textual emphasis

No consensus has emerged on the question of textual emphasis, although opinions extended only between those who advocate none at all (preferring headings and subheadings) and those using bold or italic type very sparingly. The overuse of textual enhancement may be seen by some judges as an intellectual challenge to their ability to spot the point. They think it is spoon-feeding a little too far. Some advocates wish to use italics only for sub-headings or the citation of authority.

Ideally you should use bold only for topic headings, the title, and central dates and events in the chronology. Use italics very sparingly as a contrast to impress something on the judge.

Example I

Central Criminal Court – Defence skeleton for preliminary legal issues – David Etherington QC with Shaun Murphy, Jeremy Benson QC and Gillian Jones, October 2010 – 8pp.

In Reg. v Ali and Ali the defendants were convicted of attempted murder following a trial at Snaresbrook. They contested the charge, but admitted their guilt at the point of sentence. Some two years later the victim died, not as a direct result of the injuries, but as a consequence of bed sores caused almost certainly by his immobility which was a result of the injuries. The complicating feature was that he had not cooperated with treatment to a degree that, by the end, virtually all the agencies declined to treat him except a saintly district nurse. The judge, following argument which he decided to hear before summing-up, allowed the defence to argue that the victim's behaviour was of such a type and character that it broke the chain of causation, although the judge made clear that the defendants had to take their victim as they found him and that if their behaviour had caused his character to become as it did then that was their responsibility. There was evidence that his character was always of that kind. On the face of it the defendants were trapped between the "rock" of egg-shell skull (as applied to character) and the "hard place" of being the cause of his character change. Nevertheless, the judge did allow the jury to consider whether, notwithstanding, that the victim's behaviour did break the chain of causation.

The skeleton is devised very much in the form of a case management checklist for the court. Brevity and simplicity in the development of the argument are the key features of this document, which is highly effective in taking the judge straight to the key points.

It may be noted that written material in criminal trials have not yet developed the degree of sophistication seen in the Court of Appeal or in civil claims. There is no reason why they should not do so (save for questions of proper remuneration for advocates).

The defendants were both acquitted.

SKELETON ARGUMENT OF THE DEFENDANTS ON CERTAIN PRELIMINARY LEGAL ISSUES

Mathew Ali and Philip Ali (hereinafter "the Defendants") are indicted for the Murder of Richard Cabby (who died on February 14, 2008) having been previously convicted of his Attempted Murder (Date of Offence – December 25 2005; Date of Conviction February 2007) and sentenced to fifteen years imprisonment.

1. In this case, there are two potential legal issues:

   a. Is there a defence at all?

   b. Is it an issue for the judge or the jury?

2. There are a number of secondary issues:

   a. Is the character of the accused relevant?

   b. Is the character of the deceased relevant?

   c. Can the accused give any relevant evidence and does the issue of adverse inferences arise?

3. Broadly, the Defence contends that the correct answer to these questions is as follows:

   a. There is a defence.

   b. The issue of whether there is a defence is for the judge and the issue of whether it succeeds is for the jury on the criminal burden and standard of proof.

   c. The character of the Defendants is irrelevant.

   d. The character of the deceased is relevant.

   e. The Defendants cannot give any relevant evidence on the issue for the jury and the question of adverse inferences should not arise.

4. MURDER is when a man of sound memory and of the age of discretion unlawfully killeth within any county of the realm any reasonable creature *in rerum natura* under the king's peace with malice aforethought, either expressed by the party or implied by law so the party wounded or hurt dies of the wound within a year and a day after the same (Coke's *Institutes*, 47).

5. The only relevant issue in this case is whether the Defendants killed the deceased.

6. By virtue of the Law Reform (Year and a Day Rule) Act 1996, the rule that death must occur within a year and a day of the act inflicting injury has been abolished, subject to certain consents which were obtained in this case.

7. Adopting the learned editors of Smith & Hogan's *Criminal Law* [12th Edition] at page 478: *if an act can be shown to be the cause of death, it may now be murder...however much time has elapsed between the act and the death.*

8. *Is there a defence on the facts of this case?*

   a. If an accused's acts caused the deceased's death, then he has no defence.

   b. The question, if raised by plea, is a matter for the jury.

   c. The jury must apply legal principles which it is the duty of the judge to explain to them: *R. v. Pagett* (1983) 76 Cr App R 279 CA.

   d. Where, at one end of the scale, the jury is simply applying the law to admitted facts the judge is entitled to state what the result will be: *R. v. Blaue* [1975] 3 All ER 466; *R. v. Malcherek* [1981] 2 All ER 422.

   e. In other cases the jury may have a primary role in establishing the facts: *R. v. Cheshire* [1991] 3 All ER 670.

   f. It is not for expert witnesses to decide the ultimate issue but to give such evidence as lies within his or her expertise about the issue. This, put more simply, in a causation case permit an expert to say *what* caused death, but not *who* caused it.

   g. A defendant's acts need not be the sole cause of death, but the culpable element in the defendant's conduct must contribute to the end result. Included in other causes of death may also be the deceased's negligence.

   h. A defendant's conduct must be a "not negligible" cause of death. Where there is an intervening cause, a defendant's act must be a substantial and continuing cause: see Smith & Hogan, page 78 and the authorities cited therein.

   i. For reasons of public policy, the negligence of health care professionals will not cause a break in the chain of causation.

   j. The general principle of liability is that a defendant must take the victim as he finds him (*Blaue* – the Jehovah's witness refusing blood). *Blaue* extended the principle from taking someone as you find him physically to taking him as you find him altogether.

k. The editors of Smith and Hogan (p 88) are unclear whether the same view would be taken if a deceased chose not to accept the blood merely to spite the defendant.

l. It is further well-established law that causing a person to behave in a way detrimental to themselves will not deflect liability.

m. The test is whether the deceased's behaviour in response to the defendant's unlawful act is within a range of responses which might be expected from someone in his situation: cf *Blaue* with *R. v. Williams & Davies* (1991) 95 Cr.App.R. 1; Corbett [1996] Crim L.R. 594.

n. However, the chain of causation is *not* broken if the defendant's act is a continuing and operative cause.

o. There is a degree of conflict between the authorities as to whether the deceased's subsequent omissions may break the chain of causation, assuming the omission is of the unreasonable or "daft" kind.

p. The general principle at common law was that they would not: see *Wall* (1802) 28 State Tr 51 and *Holland* (1841) 2 Mood & R 351, which line of reasoning was expressly followed by *Blaue*. However, in all three cases the defendants' acts were still a continuing and operative cause of death.

q. In any event, the acts of the deceased in this case are a mixture of acts of commission and omission and the cause of death is not the original injury.

r. It would be peculiar if different principles applied to acts and omissions.

s. Thus, it is submitted that the preferred approach should be that the deceased's acts may break the chain of causation if:

   i. The cause of death was not the injury caused by the unlawful act but was an intervening cause.

   ii. The deceased produced (or, reflecting the criminal burden and standard of proof *may have produced*) this intervening cause by behaving in a way which was outside a range of normal responses as judged by the jury – behaving, for instance, in a wholly unexpected or "daft" way either by doing or by not doing certain things, or both.

iii. The deceased's response was not a response to the defendant's act: *R. v. Dear* [1996] Crim L.R. 595

t. In this case, the cause of death is said to be septicaemia (blood poisoning) due to chronic osteomylitis (infection of the bone marrow) due to decubitus ulcers (bed/pressure sores). In his summary, Dr Simon Poole states that the inflammation was a response to infection of the deep, soft tissue and the bones and that the causative micro-organisms (which originated from faecal matter and the surface of the skin) gained access to the subjacent tissues via the ulcers.

u. This runs the possible danger of eliding different causes. It would appear that the cause was septicaemia. The gateway was the pressure ulcers and the agent was the penetration of the micro-organisms. If this is correct, then it is a "but for" case rather than direct operative causes. Without the ulcers in the state they were, the fact of immobility even added to faecal incontinence would not have caused septicaemia.

v. Ulcers may be caused by prolonged immobility. The likelihood of their proving fatal is greatly increased by poor personal hygiene (see the defence expert Maureen Bingham).

w. It is arguable that the deceased both in what he did and what he did not do caused his own demise.

x. The deceased did not die from the injuries inflicted by the Defendants, upon which they would have to take his personality as they found it, but because of a new event. The new event *may* have occurred without the deceased's contribution to it. It *may* have proved fatal. But, it is submitted, the Crown cannot establish this beyond reasonable doubt.

y. It follows, therefore, that the jury is entitled to consider whether this "new" event was caused or contributed to by such a degree of unreasonable behaviour on the part of the accused, that it serves to extinguish their liability for murder.

z. There is a considerable gap of time between the act causing injury and the subsequent death of the deceased. The reason the problem may not have risen so acutely hitherto is that the "Year and a Day" rule operated to make it likely that death would flow from the original injury and that common lawyers in the past apprehended a problem not analysed sufficiently or at all by modern legislators.

aa. It is submitted, therefore, that each Defendant has a defence if the jury concludes that the cause of death was not the injury caused by the Defendants (upon which they would have to take the person and character of the deceased as they found it) but was the micro-organisms operating through the gateway of the decubitus ulcers such that the jury cannot be sure that it was not the deceased's unreasonable and unresponsive behaviour, caused by his own acts of commission and omission, that broke the chain of causation and caused his own death.

bb. The Defence cannot argue the Defendants are Not Guilty of Murder except by inviting the jury to conclude upon the evidence that the chain of causation is not secure, mirroring the discussion above.

9. *The character of the deceased is relevant*

a. If the deceased responded in hospital in the way he did, it would not break the chain of causation if his response were caused by a personality change effected by the Defendants' original acts.

b. If it were that original injury which killed the deceased then his character would be irrelevant, following *Blaue*.

c. However, where a new cause of death has arisen, the deceased's behaviour is relevant provided it is not a response to, or caused by, the Defendants' original act.

d. It may be suggested, and even if not suggested it may be considered by the jury, that the deceased's behaviour was, in effect, a personality change effected by the Defendants' act.

e. The extensive bad character of the deceased, which is contained in the draft Admissions and which the Defence seeks to admit, shows that the deceased was a violent, belligerent, anti-social criminal whose unreasonable behaviour following his injuries, was merely a continuation of his old habits.

10. *The character of the Defendants is irrelevant*

a. Mathew Ali has no previous criminal conviction before this event. It is, strictly speaking, irrelevant on the issues. However, it is submitted that a defendant is always entitled to place his good character before a jury – if for no other reason to avoid speculation that he has a bad one. However, no directions would be appropriate on these facts.

b. Philip Ali has one conviction which it is submitted is irrelevant. The principal of "tit for tat" does not apply on these facts.

11. *The defendants can give no relevant evidence and no adverse inference should be drawn*

a. Whilst this may seem obvious on the facts, the Criminal Justice and Public Order Act 1994, §35, does not appear to contemplate the situation faced on the present facts and under a strict interpretation of §35 (1) it would appear that the judge would be obliged to give the usual direction.

b. However, it is submitted that this would be unfair and fly in the face of common sense on these particular and unusual facts and the Court will be invited to explain to the jury in common-sense terms why the Defendants will not be giving evidence, assuming some unconsidered eventuality does not arise which causes either Defendant to give evidence.

Good practice suggestions

Think about the layout of your document and the visual impact it will have on the reader.

Ask yourself, 'is this easy to read?' 'Is it a document I can keep with me, make notes on, and use for the purpose of my own argument/judgment?' If the answer is 'no', you will not be assisting the court.

Example J

Crown Court at A – Wasted costs application – Respondent's skeleton argument by Sue Carr QC, July 200[ ] – 15pp.

R v X Y was a wasted costs application initiated by the trial judge, brought against leading counsel for the defence. Counsel had introduced remarks in his closing speech to the jury concerning previous acquittals of the Defendant, whereupon the judge discharged the jury and ordered a retrial. The application was heard only after the High Court directed the trial judge to recuse himself and have the application heard at a different crown court centre.

The writer uses a narrative style to deliver a difficult and brave argument, (brave in the sense of the great tradition of the Bar to advance fearlessly direct criticism of a judge).

Narrative is used to compel the reader to a conclusion which appears both right and obvious.

The substantive wasted costs application was dismissed at this hearing.

SKELETON ARGUMENT ON BEHALF OF THE RESPONDENT FOR HEARING ON 31 JULY 200[ ]

A: Introduction

1. This skeleton argument is made on behalf of Z QC ("the Respondent"), the respondent to an application that he pay wasted costs ("the Application"). The Application was originally initiated in November 200[ ] by His Honour Judge B QC sitting in the [ ] Crown Court.

2. References in the following form are references to pages within the hearing bundle prepared by RPC solicitors for use at the hearing: [1.1] means tab 1, page 1.

3. Disposal of the Application has been greatly delayed because HHJ B refused to recuse himself from hearing the Application, which refusal was only quashed on 22 May 200[ ] by Mr Justice Hickinbottom after a successful claim for judicial review against the [ ] Crown Court. As a result of Hickinbottom J's decision the matter was transferred to [ ] Crown Court.

4. This is the first time the matter has come before this Court and the first time that there has been an opportunity to consider the Application and its management absent the issue of recusal.

5. Accordingly, the Respondent anticipates that the purpose of the hearing is to consider whether the Application ought to proceed and, if so, to give directions for its conduct.

6. The Respondent invites the Court to dismiss the Application at this stage; his reasons are detailed below.

7. If, contrary to his request, the Application is to proceed, directions should require proper particularisation of the complaint against the Respondent and in particular clarification of whether it is alleged the Respondent acted to deliberately mislead the jury.

B: Background

8. This is addressed briefly, the detail is in the witness statement of N B to which the Court is referred.

9. The Application arose from the trial of X Y. Mr Y's original trial took place in July 200[ ] before HHJ B. He was accused of 15 counts of money laundering under section 93(c)(2)(b) of the Criminal Justice Act 1998. He was acquitted on 2 counts but convicted on 13 counts and sentenced to 4 years imprisonment.

10. In June 200[ ] the Court of Appeal quashed Mr Y's convictions and ordered a retrial on the basis of a misdirection as to the mental element of the offences. In particular, the jury had incorrectly been told that in order to convict Mr Y it was sufficient that they believed that there were reasonable grounds for him to suspect that the goods were being paid for with the proceeds of crime and he knew of those grounds.

11. The re-trial of the 13 counts took place between 14 October and 3 November 200[ ]. Mr Y was represented by the Respondent. Before the re-trial an application was made on behalf of Mr Y for the jury to be told not only that there had been a previous trial, but also of his acquittal on 2 counts and the quashing of his convictions on the 13 counts that were the subject of the re-trial. HHJ B QC rejected this application, ruling that the previous trial could be referred to, but not its verdicts.

12. However, during cross-examination Mr Y broke down and told the jury that there had been a previous trial and that he had been acquitted on two counts. The judge addressed the disclosure of the two acquittals by amending his draft direction (with the agreement of both defence and prosecuting counsel) which made it clear to the jury that the two acquittals were entirely irrelevant to its considerations.

13. Following the Respondent's closing speech on 30 October 200[ ] HHJ B raised concerns as to a statement made to the jury in relation to Mr Y's first trial. On 3 November 200[ ] HH J B heard submissions from the Respondent and counsel for the prosecution, D QC on whether the trial could proceed in the light of the Respondent's closing speech. Both the Respondent (on instructions from Mr Y who had received independent advice from his solicitor who had in turn consulted his partners) and D QC indicated that they wished the trial to continue [4.45] to [4.51].

14. However, in the teeth of the submissions of both leading counsel and despite the fact Mr Y had always wished his quashed convictions to be revealed to the jury, HHJ B discharged the jury and immediately warned the Respondent to inform his insurers. [ ] Crown Court followed this up on behalf of the judge in writing by letter dated 13 November 200[ ].

15. Through letters sent by his solicitors, RPC, the Respondent asked HHJ B QC both to particularise his complaint against him and either to recuse himself from hearing it or to pass the matter of recusal to one of his brother judges in accordance with principles set out in *El Faragy v El Faragy* [2007] EWCA Civ 1149. The request for recusal was made because the Respondent's defence to the Application was to include – and does include – a direct attack upon reasonableness of HHJ B's own decision to discharge the jury.

16. Despite these attempts to deal with recusal and particularisation informally, the Respondent was required to make formal application to HHJ B which was heard on 18 March 200[ ].

17. On 18 March 200[ ] both counsel for the Respondent and D QC, who attended at HHJ B's request to assist the Court, stated that the judge should recuse himself. It was emphasised that the judge could not possibly decide the Application without giving at least the appearance of bias because doing so would entail him deciding upon the reasonableness of his own actions.

18. However, again in the teeth of shared submissions, HHJ B followed his own course and refused to recuse himself by a judgment handed down on 27 March 200[ ] [9.141]. In addition, he declined to particularise the complaint against the respondent saying that the complaint was clearly set out in his judgment of 3 November 200[ ], despite the judgment leaving it unclear whether the Respondent stands accused of acting in bad faith by deliberately misleading the jury and undermining the Judge's ruling on admissibility.

19. In the absence of a right of appeal, the Respondent made an application for permission for judicial review of HHJ B QC's decision not to recuse himself on 29 April 200[ ] [10.147] and [11.155].

20. Following a rolled up hearing on 15 May 200[ ], Mr Justice Hickinbottom granted the Respondent permission to apply for judicial review, allowed his application and quashed HHJ B's decision to refuse ordering that the Judge should not hear any issue arising from the Application and that the Presiding Judge of the [ ] Circuit should allocated the Application to another judge and determine which court it should be heard [17.257].

21. The above history explains the listing of the hearing on 31 July 200[ ] in [ ] Crown Court. The Respondent expects its purpose will be to consider whether the Application ought to proceed and, if so, for directions to be given for its conduct.

D: The Nature of the Complaint

22. As recognised by Hickinbottom J in paragraph 54 of his judgment [15.235], the focus of HHJ B's concern was a particular statement in the Respondent's closing speech given on 30 October 200[ ]. In the course of this speech, the Respondent attempted to rebut evidence of potential bad character and deal with the evidence as to the previous acquittals of Mr Y on two counts that had come out in his cross-examination. In particular, the Respondent stated that:

> *"...There is no evidence that he has ever, for example, given evidence and been disbelieved by a jury. Bear in mind he gave evidence in a case in front of a jury, which was last year, he was believed..."*

23. In giving his reasons for discharging the jury, the HHJ B stated that this comment:

> *"...was frankly an outrageous thing for any counsel, let alone leading counsel, to say to a jury. Not only was it incorrect, but it totally undermined any proper direction the court was going to give the jury. The previous jury clearly disbelieved Mr Y because they convicted him on 13 counts. To invite this jury to say that the previous jury believed him was doing exactly what the direction that was to be given said they should not do, as it made clear they should not speculate about what had or had not happened at that trial...If this jury would retire to consider their verdicts with the false impression that the previous jury had only considered two counts and had believed Mr Y when he had given evidence on oath, the question is whether or not this can be repaired without prejudice to Mr Y or the Crown."* [4.56]

24. In the event, the Judge took the view that it was not possible to repair the position without causing prejudice to Mr Y, reasoning that if the

jury were given the full picture of the original trial (i.e. that Mr Y had originally been convicted of 13 counts) and Mr Y were convicted and instructed different lawyers to appeal, he had little doubt that the Court of Appeal would quash the conviction. Accordingly, he discharged the jury.

25. As set out above, the Judge has been asked to particularise his complaint against the Respondent and in particular to make clear whether it is alleged that the Respondent acted deliberately so as to mislead the jury or to undermine the ruling on admissibility. This is because from passages in his judgment on 3 November 200[ ] it appears this may be alleged [4.55]:

    a. *"...Not only does Mr Z's submission attempt to undermine the direction he knew I was going to give the jury, but it also gives the strong impression that the jury had only dealt with [the 2 counts on which he had been acquitted]..."*

    b. *"...The accumulative effect of the above confirms the impression I had at the time that Mr Z was attempting to suggest to this jury that the previous jury had only been considering the two...counts..."*

26. However, despite attempts to obtain clarification as to whether *male fides* is alleged, HHJ B refused to provide any more particularisation than in a letter of 2 December 200[ ] from [ ] Crown Court, which stated:

    "...[The respondent's conduct in his closing speech to the jury in the case of R v Y on 30th October 200[ ] was improper, unreasonable and/or negligent resulting in the Court discharging the jury and ordering a retrial. Full details of the conduct alleged are contained in the judgment of 3 November 200[ ]..." [1.7]

27. Therefore, the complaint appears to be that:

    a. The Respondent acted improperly and/or unreasonably and/or negligently in stating to the jury in his closing speech of 30 October 200[ ] *"...There is no evidence that he has ever, for example, given evidence and been disbelieved by a jury. Bear in mind he gave evidence in a case in front of a jury, which was last year, he was believed..."*; and

    b. As a consequence of that statement it was necessary to discharge the jury meaning the costs associated with the re-trial were wasted as a result of the Respondent's culpable conduct.

E: Substantive Legal Principles

28. Section 19A(1) of the Prosecution of Offences Act 1985 provides that:

> *"In any criminal proceedings…the Crown Court…may...order the legal or other representative concerned to meet, the whole of any wasted costs or such part of them as may be determined in accordance with regulations."*

29. Sub-section (3) defines "wasted costs" as:

> *"…any costs incurred by a party –*
>
> *as a result of any improper, unreasonable or negligent act or omission on the part of any representative or any employee of a representative; or*
>
> *which, in the light of any such act or omission occurring after they were incurred, the court considers it is unreasonable to expect that party to pay."*

30. Regulation 3 of the Costs in Criminal Cases (General) Regulations 1986 (SI 1986 No 1335), made under section 19A, is in similar terms. The costs in respect of which an order can be made must, therefore, be "as a result of" (i.e. caused by) the representative's misconduct as defined in section 19A(3)(a).

31. There is a three-stage test (*Re A Barrister (Wasted Costs Order) (No 1 of 1991)* [1993] QB 293 @ 301 ("*Re A Barrister*"), *Ridehalgh v Horsefield* [1994] Ch 205 @ 231 and the Practice Direction on Costs in Criminal Proceedings, para VIII.1.4(iv)). The questions to be addressed are:

    a. Has there been any improper, unreasonable or negligent act or omission?

    b. As a result have any costs been incurred by a party?

    c. Should the court exercise its discretion to order the lawyer to meet the whole or any part of the relevant costs?

32. Only if all three questions are answered in the affirmative will an order be made. A causal link between the conduct complained of an the wasted costs is essential. Where the conduct is proved but no waste of costs is shown to have resulted it is not one for exercise of the wasted costs jurisdiction (see in particular *Ridehalgh* @ 237).

F: The Respondent's substantive position

33. Should this court decide to invoke the wasted costs jurisdiction and the Application proceed the Respondent will defend the Application at all three stages of the test: conduct, causation and discretion.

Conduct

34. As set out above, the Respondent does not know whether it is alleged that he deliberately sought to mislead the jury in saying that Mr Y had not been disbelieved by the jury at his trial and deliberately sought to undermine HHJ B's ruling on admissibility. If this is alleged then it is strenuously denied. The Respondent said on 3 November 200[ ]: *"I said what I said with absolutely no intention of misleading the jury or anything of that kind...I am extremely sorry if I have caused anxiety to others. It was wholly unintentional."* [4.49–4.50] That remains his position.

35. Furthermore, the Respondent maintains that his statement cannot fairly be characterised as negligent. The Judge's ruling on admissibility had left the parties to walk a tightrope where the jury could know about the previous trial, but not its verdict. This was made even more difficult by the fact that because Mr Y had revealed his acquittals, those could be referred to and it was legitimate refer to them to rebut the evidence of bad character that was relied on by the prosecution.

36. The court should be especially slow to conclude that there was negligence in this case since the conduct complained of was in the course of advocacy. A judge invited to make or contemplate making an order arising out of an advocate's conduct of court proceedings must make full allowance for the pressures and difficulties advocacy entails and only conclude that his conduct is culpable when after making all allowances made, an advocate's conduct of court proceedings is quite plainly unjustifiable (see *Ridehalgh* @ 236).

Causation

37. However, even if the Respondent's statement was made negligently, it did necessitate the discharge of the jury and did not cause the costs of the re-trial to be wasted. Rather, as detailed below, the costs were wasted because of HHJ B's wholly unreasonable decision to discharge the jury.

Discretion

38. Further, or alternatively, the even if the first two stages of the test are considered satisfied, the respondent maintains that given the pressured circumstances of the conduct and the obvious existence of alternatives to discharging the jury, it would not be just for the Court to exercise its discretion to make a wasted costs order against him.

G: Why the Application ought to be dismissed

39. The Application ought not to be dismissed now. To proceed would not be a proper use of the wasted costs jurisdiction.

The Nature of the Wasted Costs Jurisdiction

40. Where a representative may have misconducted himself in the terms of section 19A(3)(a) of the Prosecution of Offences Act 1985 then, either following an application or on its own motion, the court needs to consider whether to invoke the wasted costs jurisdiction and require a representative to show cause why he should not pay the wasted costs.

41. As was emphasised by Hickinbottom J in the postscript to his judgment (paras 57 to 61 [15.236]), in deciding whether or not to invoke the wasted costs jurisdiction, the court must keep in mind the essential characteristics of the jurisdiction and in particular its *"quintessentially summary nature"*.

42. The authorities show that the jurisdiction should only be invoked where the proceedings can take place on or very soon after judgment, there is a plain and obvious case for a wasted costs order and the proceedings can be addressed swiftly and economically:

> *"Unless wasted costs proceedings can take place in summary form, on or very soon after delivery of judgment, they are unlikely to be appropriate."* (Rose LJ in *Re Freudiana Holdings,* Unreported 28 November 1995, para 16)

> *"The jurisdiction to make a costs order is a summary jurisdiction. It follows, first that the hearing should be short, secondly that the procedure should not be unduly elaborate; thirdly that the jurisdiction should only be exercised in a reasonably plain and obvious case."* (Millett LJ in *Re Freudiana,* p.28)

> *"...it is...important, in the public interest and in the interests of the legal profession to have a wasted costs procedure which is swift, economical and effective. That means that it must retain its summary form..."* (para 52, Kennedy LJ in *Re P (A Barrister)* [2001] EWCA Cim 1728)

43. In addition, the authorities make it clear that allegations of dishonesty on the part of legal representatives are not capable of summary determination (see *Jackson & Powell on Professional Liability,* 11-133, note 22; *Re Freudiana, per* Millett LJ, p.30 and [*Manzanilla Ltd v Corton Property & Investment Ltd* [1997] 3 F.C.R. 389]).

Submissions

44. It is plain that Hickinbottom J, when reviewing the above principles, was concerned that the time and expense spent on this matter had already exceeded a level appropriate to the wasted costs jurisdiction:

> *"...It will be for the judge assigned to deal with this wasted costs application to determine whether this case is one where the jurisdiction should be invoked. Nothing I say should or, I am sure, will influence him to other than to exercise his independent judicial mind on the facts and circumstances of this case. However, looking at the four files of papers which have been lodged in relation to this interlocutory application within a wasted costs matter – and without laying any blame on anyone for the costs and time expended on this wasted costs application to date, which is at a relatively preliminary stage – I should like to underscore the essential characteristics of this jurisdiction...I would urge courts to be sensitive both to the summary nature of the procedure and to alternative ways of dealing with apparent misconduct of representatives."* (paras 57 and 61, [15.236])

45. Similarly, Mr Justice Davis, when ordering a rolled up hearing of the claim for judicial review echoed these sentiments:

> *"This whole case is most unfortunate. It is also troubling that so much as been incurred already by way of costs even before any substantive wasted costs hearing."*

46. The Court ought to heed the comments of these two judges and take the opportunity both to prevent the waste of more time and costs and to underscore the summary nature of the jurisdiction by dismissing the Application.

47. The Respondent relies on the following points:

    a. As things stand there is an allegation of bad faith against the Respondent and that is unsuited to summary determination;

    b. Even if it is only alleged that the Respondent acted negligently, there is no strong prima facie case against the Respondent;

    c. There has already been excessive delay and this will be increased by continuation of the Application; and

    d. Continuation of the Application will mean yet more money will be spent when too much has been spent already.

(a) Allegation of bad faith unsuited to summary determination

48. As set out above, it is not appropriate to consider serious allegations of dishonesty in a wasted costs, summary context. As set out above, part of the reasoning given before the jury was discharged suggests that it is alleged that the Respondent acted deliberately to mislead the jury and to undermine the HHJ B's ruling on admissibility. Hickinbottom J accepted that the Respondent was entitled to know whether this allegation is being made (see para 55 of his judgment [15.235]). However, HHJ B failed to clarify this.

(b) No clear and obvious case

49. The Respondent takes issue with each part of the three stage test. There are significant arguments to be had at each stage. However particularly significant is the critical issue of causation.

50. Previous case law shows that a wasted costs application can be successfully defended on the basis that costs have been wasted because the decision by a judge to discharge a jury was unreasonable (see *Re A Barrister (Wasted Costs Order) (No 1 of 1991)* [1993] QB 293).

51. Here the decision to discharge the jury was plainly unnecessary and unreasonable. It was made despite the fact that:

    a. Both prosecution and defence wished the trial to proceed with an amended direction;

    b. Mr Y requested that it proceed on 3 November 200[ ] after receiving independent advice from his solicitor, who had consulted with his partners and from junior counsel (see page 3 of the transcript of 3 November 200[ ] [4.47]. In this regard, it is surprising that HHJ B seems to have held the view that this did not amount to sufficiently independent advice; and

    c. All the judge was being asked to do was to reveal to the jury what the Mr Y had always wished to be revealed long before the alleged negligence of the Respondent, namely his conviction of the 13 counts and subsequent quashing of those convictions. Therefore, the Judge's view that revealing this information might make any conviction unsafe was perverse.

52. It must be remembered that for present purposes the Court need not be certain that these arguments will succeed after a full inquiry into a hearing should the Application proceed. Rather, it is sufficient for dismissal of the Application if, in the light of these arguments, the Court takes the view that it is not plain and obvious that the Respondent was the cause of wasted costs, rather than HHJ B QC.

53. Apart from the above arguments, the following also point to the cause on causation being far from plainly and obviously against the Respondent:

    a. In his submissions at the recusal application on 18 March 200[ ], D QC made it clear that never before had he experienced a jury being discharged because of something which all parties were agreed, in terms of the conduct of the previous trial, was not relevant to the issue of determination and in any event capable of rectification, and in circumstances where it had always been the case that the material relevant to rectification was material that the defence had always argued should be before the jury in any event [7.111];

    b. Mr Justice Hickinbottom, whilst being careful not to tie this Court's hands:

        i. In paragraph 42 of his judgment described the suggestion that HHJ B was the true cause of wasted costs as being *"more than meritless"* [15.231]; and

        ii. In paragraph 49(ix) of his judgment, rejected HHJ B's opinion that the Respondent's case was not exceptional on the basis that the decision to discharge the jury was made *"in circumstances in which the Crown and the defendant in the criminal trial were ad idem in considering that the jury need not and should not be discharged..."* [15.234].

(c) Continuation will involve further delay

54. Through no fault of the Respondent, it will be 9 months since the relevant events by the time of the first valid hearing in this matter. On any view this is a serious infringement of the Rose LJ's guidance that *"Unless wasted costs proceedings can take place in summary form, on or very soon after delivery of judgment, they are unlikely to be appropriate."* (*Re Freudiana*, Unreported 28 November 1995, para 16).

55. Plainly, if this matter proceeds there will be further delay to allow: HHJ B QC to particularise his complaint properly, until a hearing to be listed on a date that all parties can attend, and sufficient time for the Respondent to prepare evidence on his behalf, which he anticipates will include a statement from his junior as well as transcripts of the re-trial (in particular the preliminary hearing on admissibility).

56. This delay has and will continue to impact upon the second re-trial of Mr Y. Mr Y wishes the Respondent to represent him and therefore no trial is to take place until it the Application has been disposed of

because otherwise the ongoing prosecution of the Application initiated by HHJ B might be said to affect the Respondent in the performance of his duties before that judge. This delay was cited as a matter of concern by D QC for the prosecution before Hickinbottom J, where he emphasised that the Court of Appeal when quashing Mr Y's convictions stated that they hoped to see his re-trial dealt with swiftly. As it is, over a year has passed since the Court of Appeal's decision and Mr Y is no further forward.

57. Therefore, the Application has not merely created create unwieldy, slow and costly satellite litigation, but has also impinged upon the expeditious and just disposal of the second re-trial of Mr Y.

(d) Costs on costs all about wasted costs

58. The Application, brought because of alleged wasted costs has, thus far, served only to waste costs itself.

59. Thus far, the Respondent has spent around [£...] simply in trying to get a fair hearing and clarification of the complaint against him and preparing for the hearing of 31 July 200[ ]. Of these, [£...] were spent in the judicial review proceedings.

60. Although 75% of the judicial review costs were ordered to be paid by [ ] Crown Court, that does not represent full recovery and it should still be a matter of concern that the 75% ordered has to be borne by the public purse.

61. In addition, the prosecution has incurred around [£...] because of D QC's attendance – on both occasions at the request of the Court – at the recusal hearing and the judicial review hearing. The Treasury Solicitor also incurred [£...] in the judicial review proceedings.

62. Therefore, without the matter having got any further forward, the Application has cost [£...]. In addition, judicial time has also been spent which is obviously of value to the other court users.

63. Should this matter proceed then yet more costs will be incurred in preparing for a substantive hearing, including the briefing leading counsel, preparing and filing evidence and bundles etc. It is estimated that costs will be in the region of [£...].

64. On any view, the Application has not been economical and the position will only be made worse if it proceeds.

Why the Application should be dismissed – conclusion

65. Continuation of the Application would offend the essential characteristics of the wasted costs jurisdiction. There is no plain and obvious case against the Respondent, it has been slow not swift and it has been extremely expensive not economical. Now is the time to stop this spiralling, satellite litigation by dismissing the Application.

H: Directions

66. Should the Court decide to proceed with the Application, it is suggested that it should:

    a. Require HHJ B QC properly to particularise his complaint and in particular to clarify whether ot not it is alleged that the Respondent acted deliberately to mislead the jury and/or to undermine the preliminary ruling on admissibility;

    b. Give directions for the filing of witness statements and a skeleton argument on behalf of the Respondent; and

    c. Fix a 1 day hearing.

I: Conclusion

67. As a result of the defences available to the respondent, especially as to causation, this was never going to be a matter suitable for the wasted costs jurisdiction. However, through no fault of the Respondent, the position has been exacerbated by extraordinary delay, expense and wasted time. The Court ought to take the chance to bring an end to this unfortunate episode and allow the Respondent to get on with preparing to represent Mr Y at a second re-trial as soon as possible.

Good practice suggestion

Use structured argument in short paragraphs with argumentative headings: these can be in the form of questions or statements e.g. *Why the application should be dismissed* or *How the Judge fell into error*. Be bold in making assertions which you think can properly be advanced on the evidence and the law.

Example K

Court of Appeal – Renewed permission hearing – Skeleton argument of the Appellant Defendant by Andrew Hochhauser QC with David Craig, April 2006 – 16pp.

Keen v Commerzbank AG concerned whether a term of a contract of employment relating to the requirements for payment of a discretionary bonus by a bank fell within the scope of the Unfair Contract Terms Act 1977 s.3. The Court of Appeal held the employee did not deal with the bank as a consumer and the bank's business was not entering into contracts of employment with its employees.

Here the writer commits himself to a reasonably lengthy and compelling argument that one imagines leave little room for oral development. The style is forceful, in some places quite abrupt. In the context of an application for permission it is highly effective.

The application succeeded, as did the substantive appeal.

The case is reported at [2006] EWCA Civ 1536 CA (Civ Div) (Mummery LJ, Jacob LJ, Moses LJ) 17/11/2006; LTL 17/11/2006; (2006) 2 CLC 844; (2007) ICR 623; (2007) IRLR 132; *Independent*, November 23, 2006; Lawtel AC0112184.

SKELETON ARGUMENT OF COMMERZBANK

[References below are to the Appeal Bundle by: divider/page number]

Introduction

1. Commerzbank seeks permission to appeal from the Order of Morison J [4/31] who dismissed Commerzbank's application for summary judgment under Part 24 of the CPR in respect of the Claimant's claims for bonus. Permission to appeal was refused by Morison J on 7 April 2006, on the grounds that the matter was "best left to [the] Court of Appeal to decide whether it wishes to look at my decision," and "a trial is to take place (unless mediation is successful)" [5/34].

Background

2. The Claimant was employed by Commerzbank from November 2002 until June 2005 as the manager of a trading desk known as special situations 2 ("SS2") in the Investment Banking Division of Commerzbank's London branch, pursuant to a contract which provided for:

   (1) a basic annual salary of £120,000 [11/82];

   (2) a generous benefits package (including eligibility for pension, life assurance, private medical insurance and permanent health insurance) [11/83]; and,

   (3) participation in a discretionary bonus scheme [11/83].

3. The Claimant's claims arose from the operation of Commerzbank's discretionary bonus scheme which, pursuant to his contract of employment, the Claimant was eligible to participate in. The Claimant's right was set out in the following terms [11/83]:

> *"You are eligible to participate in the Bank's discretionary bonus scheme. The decision as to whether or not to award a bonus, the amount of any award and the timing of any award and the form of the award are at the discretion of the Bank. Factors which may be taken into account by the Bank in deciding whether or not to award a bonus and the amount of any bonus include:*
> - *The performance of the Bank*
> - *The performance of your business area*
> - *Your individual performance and your contribution to the Bank's performance and the performance of your business area*
> - *The strategic objectives of the Bank*
> - *Whether you will be remaining in the employment of the Bank*
>
> *No bonus will be paid to you if on the date of payment of the bonus you are not employed by the Bank or if you are under notice to leave the Bank's employment whether such notice was given or received by you."*

4. Commerzbank's obligation under the contract was essentially to exercise a discretion: (1) as to whether to award the Claimant a bonus, and (2) as to the amount of any such bonus. That discretion was not absolute. Commerzbank was subject to an implied contractual fetter that it would not exercise its discretion irrationally or perversely (see *Clark v Nomura International plc* [2000] IRLR 766 [para. 40]; *Mallone v BPB Industries plc* [2002] EWCA Civ 126, [2002] ICR 1045 CA, para. 37 and *Horkulak v Cantor Fitzgerald International* [2004] EWCA Civ 1287, [2005] ICR 402, para. 56 CA). Commerzbank was entitled, in exercising its discretion, to take into account the factors expressly set out in the contract (see para. 3 above). The weight to be given to any particular factor was a matter for Commerzbank (see *Reda v Flag* [2002] UKPC 38, [2002] IRLR 747 PC at [91]).

5. As set out in more detail below, the Claimant was awarded bonuses of close to €3 million for the 2003 and 2004 bonus years, and was awarded no bonus for 2005 because he was not in employment on the payment date. For the sake of simplicity, this Skeleton Argument firstly addresses the 2003 and 2004 bonus claims, and then the 2005 bonus claim.

The Claimant's claim in respect of the bonus award made to him for 2003

6. Pursuant to the operation of the discretionary bonus scheme, in March 2004 the Claimant was awarded a bonus for the 2003 calendar year of

c.€2.8 million[1], some 15 times more than his annual basic salary. That resulted in his being the 4th most highly remunerated employee not only in Commerzbank's London office (where there were approximately 1,000 employees at the time) but also across Commerzbank's banking divisions globally (which employed about 24,000 people at the time). The Claimant earned more for 2003 than any of Commerzbank's Board of Directors[2].

7. The Claimant's pleaded case in respect of this bonus award of €2.8 million (POC, paras. 12–14 [7/51]) was predicated on the following factual assertions (which for the purposes of the summary judgment application only were accepted): (1) SS2 made a profit of approximately €40 million that year; (2) his line manager recommended a bonus pool for SS2 of 15–18% of profit; and, (3) Commerzbank instead decided on a reduced bonus pool for SS2 of 10% of profit.

8. The Claimant claimed (POC para. 15, [7/51]) that the exercise of the discretion to make a bonus pool of that size was in breach of contract because:

   (1) the exercise of the discretion was irrational or perverse. It was asserted that *"no rational bank in the City faced with the performance of SS2 (and thereby the Claimant) and the recommendation of Mr McCreadie would reduce the bonus pool in this way"*; and,

   (2) Commerzbank *"failed to take any or any adequate account of the performance of SS2 (and thereby the Claimant) and of Mr McCreadie's said recommendation"*.

9. Commerzbank's response to this claim, as set out in the Defence [8/55–65] and addressed in the witness statements of John Benson, Commerzbank's Joint Head of Legal[3] was, inter alia, as follows:

   (1) There was no contractual obligation on Commerzbank to accept the recommendation as to the size of the bonus pool for the SS2 team made by Mr McCreadie (see in particular Defence, para. 14(3) [8/58]; JB1, paras 12.3 and 15.1 [11/77 and 79]; JB2, para. 14 [13/180]). That is clear from:

---

1 This comprised a cash bonus of €2,238,670 (paid in March 2004) and 35,897 shares (awarded in March 2004, but vesting on 1 June 2006).

2 See the second witness statement of John Benson at paragraph 11 [13/180].

3 Mr Benson served three witness statements. A witness statement in support of the application [hereinafter referred to as JB1 – at tab 11, p.74–80]; and two statements in reply to the statements produced by the Claimant. Mr Benson's second and third witness statements are referred to as "JB2" [13/178–187] and "JB3" [15/209–210] respectively. The Claimant's witness statements are referred to as "JK1" [12/138–146] and "JK2" [14/203–204].

(a) the provisions of the discretionary bonus scheme itself [11/83], which make no reference whatsoever to the recommendation of a line manager as a matter that the Bank was required even to take into account, far less that it was obliged to accept[4];

(b) the manner in which Mr McCreadie himself made his recommendations as to the size of the bonus pool[5]. That is evidenced by his email to Mr Rock in early 2004 in which he described his bonus proposals for the 2003 year as a "*first fly past*" reflecting the "*aspirations of managers*" [11/133].

In any event Commerzbank did take into account Mr McCreadie's recommendation as to the size of the bonus pool for SS2 but did not accept that recommendation.

(2) In 2003 the Investment Banking Division of Commerzbank made a loss of €32 million, and Commerzbank AG made a loss of €2.32 billion. These were matters that were taken into account by Commerzbank and, having regard to those matters amongst others (including the performance of SS2 and of the Claimant), which Commerzbank was entitled (although not bound) to take into account, it could not be said that the decision to award a bonus pool of €4 million for SS2, and a bonus of €2.8 million for the Claimant, was outside a range of reasonable awards such that no reasonable employer could have come to this determination.

(3) The Claimant's claim was based on a fundamental misunderstanding as to the bonus process. The Claimant complained (POC para. 15(a) [7/51]; JK1 para. 4.7 [12/141]) that Commerzbank acted irrationally or perversely in that it "reduced" the bonus pool from the amount recommended by Mr McCreadie in each year to the amount actually awarded by the Defendant. Insofar as this suggests that the recommendation of Mr McCreadie served to fix the bonus pool and that the pool was later reduced, this is simply wrong. As set out by Mr Benson (JB2 para. 15 [13/181]) until the board set the bonus pool there was none.

(4) The manner in which the amount of the bonus pool was calculated was a matter for Commerzbank. The protection

---

4 Contrast *Clark v Nomura International plc* [2000] IRLR 766 where there was an express obligation to take into account individual performance.

5 In fact, Mr McCreadie's recommendation was not strictly speaking as to the size of a bonus pool. His recommendation was as to the bonuses that each individual manager should receive. It is acknowledged that the total of these amounts could sensibly be described as a bonus pool.

afforded by the fetter on an employer's discretion so that it must not be exercised irrationally or perversely, was not intended to permit an employee to second-guess the method of calculation or the weight accorded to various factors by an employer by seeking to use the court as a forum for an appeal against an extremely generous bonus award in order to improve further upon that award (JB1, para. 15 [11/78]).

(5) There was no obligation on Commerzbank to create a bonus pool at all; its obligation was to exercise a discretion as to a bonus award for the Claimant (Defence para. 15(2) [8/60]; JB2, para. 14(4) [13/181]).

(6) The Claimant's claim was articulated (see JK1 para 4.7 [12/141]) on the basis that no rational explanation had been given as to how the bonus pool of €4 million for 2003 was reached or why Mr McCreadie's recommendation was not followed. That was simply incorrect – see in particular: Defence para. 14 [8/58]; JB1, para. 15 [11/78]; and JB2, para. 14 [13/180]. Moreover, the burden of proof was on the Claimant. It was for him to establish that Commerzbank exercised its discretion in a way that no reasonable employer would have exercised it. He would not succeed in this claim if he were able to establish that there was another way in which Commerzbank could reasonably have exercised its discretion, or that Commerzbank could reasonably have awarded him the bonus which he claimed that it ought to have done. Rather, he would have to establish that no reasonable employer ***could*** have exercised its discretion in the manner in which Commerzbank did.

(7) Further, the Claimant (as team leader) was responsible for determining the percentage that he took of the total bonus pool for SS2 and for the bonus awards to be made to the other members of the SS2 team.

The Claimant's claim in respect of the bonus award made to him for 2004

10. In March 2005 the Claimant was awarded a bonus for the 2004 calendar year of c.€2.95 million[6]. That resulted in his being the 3rd most highly remunerated employee across Commerzbank's banking divisions globally (again when it employed some 24,000 people, 1,000 of whom

6 This comprised a cash bonus of €1,524,635 (paid in March 2004) and 81,249 shares (awarded in March 2005 but vesting on 1 June 2006). Again it was about 15 times more than the Claimant's annual salary.

were employed in London). Once again the Claimant earned more for 2004 than any of Commerzbank's Board of Directors[7].

11. The Claimant's pleaded case (POC, paras. 17–21 [7/52]) in respect of this award was effectively the same as for the previous year. He asserted that: (1) SS2 made a profit of approximately €57.5 million in 2004; (2) his line manager recommended a bonus pool for SS2 of the order of €10 million (equating to c.17.5% of profit); and, (3) Commerzbank instead decided on a reduced bonus pool for SS2 of less than 10% of profit [€5.35 million]. Again for the purposes of the summary judgment application only these factual assertions were accepted.

12. The Claimant pleaded that Commerzbank was in breach of contract because:

    (1) the exercise of the discretion was irrational or perverse. It was asserted that *"no rational bank in the City faced with the performance of SS2 (and thereby the Claimant) and the recommendation of Mr McCreadie would reduce the bonus pool in this way"*; and,

    (2) Commerzbank failed *"to take any or any adequate account of the performance of SS2 (and thereby the Claimant) and of Mr McCreadie's said recommendation"*.

13. Commerzbank's response to the claim (as set out in the Defence paras. 16–19 [8/60–62] and Mr Benson's witness statements) was the same as for the previous year, save that in 2004 the Investment Banking Division of Commerzbank, of which SS2 was a part, made a loss of €279 million – although Commerzbank made a profit of €393 million. Taking into account those factors, along with factors such as the performance of the Claimant and of SS2, it could not be said that the decision to award a bonus pool of €5.35 million for SS2, and a bonus of €2.95 million for the Claimant, was outside a range of reasonable awards such that no reasonable employer could have come to this determination.

The Judgment in respect of the 2003 and 2004 bonus claims

14. The learned Judge's reasons for dismissing Commerzbank's application for summary judgment in respect of the Claimant's claims for bonus for 2003 and 2004 are set out at paragraphs 24–27 of the Judgment [5/43–44]. Morison J held:

---

7 See JB2, para. 20 [13/183].

(1) the Bank had not adduced any compelling case as to the making of the bonus decisions for either year. The witness statements of Mr Benson contained very little positive material;

(2) it must have been the common intention of the parties that the Claimant would receive a bonus in some way commensurate with the success of his Desk;

(3) the Claimant believed that his manager's recommendation was fair and reasonable and he had been given no satisfactory explanation as to why that figure was reduced by the decision makers at the Bank. That fact together with anecdotal material as to conversations that the Claimant had about bonus raised a claim which had some real prospect of success;

(4) the fact that the Claimant was highly paid was not of much significance;

(5) the wording of the contract suggested a scheme under which the bonus would be calculated and paid to him on an individual basis but instead the scheme was operated on a Desk basis. Although this formed no part of the Claimant's pleaded case it was bound to arise in the evidence and called for an inquiry as to whether the Bank took account of the Claimant's own performance and if so how;

(6) the case in favour of dismissing the application was enhanced by the fact that there was to be a trial anyway – in relation to the claim regarding the vesting of shares in respect of which no Part 24 judgment was sought.

Grounds of Appeal in Respect of 2003 and 2004

15. The learned Judge erred in law in dismissing Commerzbank's application for summary judgment for the following reasons.

A. An erroneous approach to the employment contract and the Claimant's pleaded claim

(1) The formulation of the Claimant's pleaded claim that Commerzbank was in breach of contract in relation to the bonuses awarded to him for 2003 and 2004 are set out at paragraphs 8 and 12 above. That formulation does not reflect the contractual obligations of Commerzbank. Commerzbank's obligations to the Claimant in relation to the awarding of bonuses were set out under the terms of the discretionary bonus provision in the Claimant's contract. There is no reference in that provision to the recommendation of a line manager as a matter

that Commerzbank was either obliged to take into account or to accept. The learned Judge failed properly to address this matter or Commerzbank's submissions in this regard.

(2) Insofar as there is any analysis in the Judgment of the obligations contained in the Claimant's contract relating to the discretionary bonus, it is inaccurate. Contrary to the finding at paragraph 24 of the Judgment, there was no contractual obligation on Commerzbank to award the Claimant a bonus in a manner that was commensurate with the success of his Desk, nor can a common intention to this effect be divined from the contract or the Claimant's pleaded claim. In holding the contrary, the learned Judge fell into error.

(3) Further, there was no obligation on Commerzbank to create a bonus pool for SS2. The absence of such an obligation is ignored in the Judgment, and in so doing the learned Judge failed properly to construe the contract. Commerzbank's obligation was to exercise a discretion in a non-irrational, non-perverse fashion as to whether to award the Claimant a bonus and if so how much to award him and the learned Judge wrongly failed to have regard to the nature and extent of that obligation.

(4) In addition, at paragraph 26 of the Judgment, the learned Judge appears to have taken into account in deciding to dismiss the application, an assumption that an issue was bound to arise in the evidence at a trial as to whether Commerzbank had failed to comply with its obligations under the discretionary bonus scheme on the basis that the wording of the contract suggested a scheme under which the bonus would be calculated and paid to the Claimant on an individual basis but instead the scheme was operated on a Desk basis. However, this was no part of the Claimant's case. In any event the analysis was wrong. A discretion was exercised as to what the Claimant's individual bonus should be; it was the Claimant himself who, as team leader, was responsible for the division of the pool amongst the members of his team, including the amount of his own bonus award (subject to what Mr Benson described as a sanity check[8]). For 2003 the Claimant awarded himself 70% of the pool for SS2 and for 2004 he awarded himself 55% of the pool for SS2. The fact that the discretion as to how much the Claimant should be awarded was delegated to the Claimant himself was not a breach of contract. The learned Judge should have decided the application for summary judgment on the basis of the Claimant's pleaded case. He failed to do so. That amounted to an error of law.

---

8 JB2, para. 13 [13/180] and para. 22 [13/183].

(5) The learned Judge also wrongly failed to take any or any sufficient account of the fact that the Claimant was largely responsible for determining the size of his own bonus.

(6) The learned Judge also erred in failing to take into account the fact that the Claimant's assertions about discussions that he had in relation to the bonus award for 2003 and 2004: (a) emerged for the first time in his witness statement for the summary judgment application; (b) formed no part of his pleaded case; and, (c) in any event fell foul of an entire agreement clause in the contract. Further and/or alternatively the learned Judge was wrong to find that this "anecdotal material" weighed in favour of the matter going to trial or that the claim had a real prospect of success for the reasons set out above[9].

B. Size of bonus awards

(7) In addition, when considering whether the claim as formulated stood a real prospect of success, as can be seen from paragraph 25 of the Judgment, the learned Judge wrongly failed to take any or any sufficient account of the fact that the Claimant received a bonus for 2003 and 2004 of close to €3 million, which resulted in his being one of the most highly remunerated employees throughout Commerzbank's global banking operation. Unlike the decisions in *Clark v Nomura International plc* [2000] IRLR 766 and *Mallone v BPB Industries plc* [2002] ICR 1045, this was not a case in which no award whatsoever was made. The size of the Claimant's bonus awards, in absolute and in relative terms (i.e. the Claimant was one of the most highly remunerated employees across Commerzbank AG), was a plainly relevant factor in determining whether the Claimant had a real prospect of success in establishing that Commerzbank had acted irrationally or perversely in exercising its discretion.

C. Burden of proof

(8) The Court also failed to have any or any proper regard to the fact that the burden of proof in establishing that Commerzbank had behaved irrationally or perversely and thereby in breach of contract was on the Claimant; it was not for Commerzbank to disprove the same or to adduce a compelling positive case that it had not behaved irrationally or perversely. Nor was it for Commerzbank to provide the Claimant with an explanation for its bonus decisions that he considered satisfactory. In any event,

9 Further detail regarding the new material adduced by the Claimant in his first witness statement is set out at paragraphs 25–27 and 33 of the Skeleton Argument of the Defendant in the Court below.

Commerzbank had explained that in exercising its discretion as to whether to award the Claimant a bonus and if so how much to award him for 2003 and 2004, it took into account the performance of the Bank, the performance of the Investment Banking Division, the performance of the Claimant's desk, and the performance of the Claimant. That led Commerzbank to award the Claimant close to €3million and thereby to make him one of the most highly remunerated employees in the Bank. The Court also erred in failing to take that explanation properly into account.

(9) The Court further failed to pay any or any sufficient regard in this respect to the tentative manner in which Mr McCreadie made his recommendation as to the size of the bonus pool for SS2, as can be seen from his email, which describes the exercise as being "a first fly-past", representing "the aspirations of managers".

D. Approach to summary judgment application

(10) In dismissing Commerzbank's application for summary judgment, the learned Judge erred in law in his finding [at paragraph 27] that the case in favour of dismissing the application was enhanced by the fact that there was to be a trial anyway. Part 24.2 of the CPR expressly provides for an application for summary judgment to be given on the whole of a claim *"or on a particular issue"*. The Claimant's claims for bonus were issues that were clearly suitable for disposal by way of summary judgment. The fact that there was another discrete issue in relation to the vesting of shares, which was to proceed to a trial, should not have affected the outcome of the Part 24 application on whether the Claimant's claims for bonus had a real prospect of success (see, e.g., *Adams v British Airways plc* (EWHC 27 April 1995 – unreported); *Bamford v Cordiant Communications Group plc* [2004] EWHC 552 (Comm); *Kong v Commonwealth & British Services Limited* [2003] EWHC 56 (Ch), [2003] All ER (D) 110 (Jan)).

The Claimant's claim for a bonus for 2005

16. The Claimant has not been paid a bonus for the period of his employment between January 2005 and June 2005 when his employment was terminated. The express terms of the discretionary bonus scheme set out at paragraph 3 above made it clear that the Claimant was entitled to be paid a bonus only if he was in employment on the payment date (which for the 2005 calendar year would have been March 2006). Notwithstanding the express provisions of the contract, the Claimant asserts that Commerzbank was in breach of contract in not awarding him a bonus for 2005.

17. The factual basis of that claim (accepted for the purposes of the summary judgment application only) is that SS2 made a profit of €46.5 million over that period (POC para. 23 [7/53]). The Claimant claims that Commerzbank was in breach of contract in stating that it will not pay him a bonus for 2005, and that insofar as that decision was based on the exercise of a discretion such discretion was exercised irrationally or perversely (POC paras. 25 and 26 [7/53]).

18. Commerzbank, in its Defence to the claim (Defence para, 22 [8/62]) relies on the clear wording of the discretionary bonus provision in the Claimant's contract which sets out that no bonus would be paid to the Claimant if, inter alia, he was not employed on the payment date (which was March 2006 for the 2005 year).

19. In his Reply [9/66], the Claimant asserts that on a proper construction of the bonus provisions the Bank was not entitled to make no bonus payment to the Claimant (Reply para. 6 [9/67]); alternatively, that the provision was caught by section 3 of the Unfair Contract Terms Act 1977 ("UCTA") on the basis that the bonus provision rendered a contractual performance substantially different from that which was reasonably expected of Commerzbank or rendered no performance at all, and that the clause did not satisfy the test of reasonableness (Reply para. 8 [9/67]).

The Judgment in respect of 2005

20. In his judgment dismissing Commerbank's application for summary judgment under part 24 in respect of the 2005 bonus claim Morison J held (paragraphs 28–30 [6/44]):

    (1) The construction and UCTA points relied on by the Claimant could (in a sense) be decided on the application for summary judgment, but that the reasonableness of the clause would still remain live and therefore resolving the two issues would not necessarily resolve the claim.

    (2) The UCTA point was better dealt with a trial. If the Court was going to have to look at reasonableness it would be better equipped to do so after the evidence had been heard including, possibly, expert evidence.

    (3) If the Claimant had known that his Desk was to be closed down mid-year and that he would not thereby have been entitled to a bonus he would not have worked assiduously or at all over the period; the Claimant must have been working on the assumption and in the expectation that he would receive a bonus for the work that he did. It was arguable that the Bank had behaved irrationally in refusing to pay a bonus for 2005.

Grounds of appeal in respect of 2005 bonus claim

21. The issue as to whether s.3 of the UCTA applied to this contract was a discrete issue. It should have been determined on the application for summary judgment. Morison J was in as good a position as the trial judge to determine this issue. The fact that the learned Judge observed that expert evidence might be needed in respect of the 'reasonableness' issue were UCTA held to apply, was itself a compelling reason for the applicability of UCTA to be determined on the application for summary judgment. A ruling that UCTA did not apply on the facts of this case will narrow considerably the issues that will have to be determined by a trial judge, with a considerable saving of time and expense (see, e.g., *Adams v British Airways plc* – supra)[10].

22. There is no proper basis for the Claimant's claim in respect of a bonus for 2005. The contract provided [11/83] that no bonus would be paid to the Claimant:

    > *"if on the date of payment of the bonus you are not employed by the Bank or if you are under notice to leave the Bank's employment whether such notice was given or received by you."*

    The meaning of that provision is clear[11]. Bonuses were paid by Commerzbank in March of the year following the period in respect of which they were paid. Thus the Claimant was awarded his bonus for 2003 in March 2004, and for 2004 in March 2005. Any bonus for the calendar year 2005 would have been paid in March 2006. The Claimant was dismissed in June 2005. He has no entitlement to be paid any bonus[12].

23. In his witness statement in response to the application for summary judgment ([12/143] para. 6.6) and in his Reply ([9/67] para. 6), the Claimant appeared to suggest that events subsequent to the contract being entered into should have some bearing on the interpretation of the bonus provision set out above. It is trite law that the Court may not look at the subsequent conduct of the parties in order to interpret a

---

10 A trial has now been fixed for 6–8 days commencing on 29 January 2007.

11 Although the Claimant at para. 6.6 contends that "My position is that the employment contract does not so provide" [12/143].

12 One of the factors that Commerzbank was in any event entitled to take into account in determining whether to award a bonus to any employee (i.e. someone still in employment on the payment date) was whether that employee would be remaining in the employment of the Bank [11/83]. Commerzbank would have been entitled on that basis alone to determine that the Claimant should not receive a bonus – as has been set out by Mr Benson the purpose of paying bonuses is to incentivise employees (JB2, para.26 [13/184]).

written agreement (see, e.g., Schuler (L.) *AG v Wickman Machine Tool Sales Ltd* [1974] AC 235 HL), although in any event the meaning of the contractual provision is clear. Moreover part of the conduct to which the Claimant refers, relates to without prejudice discussions and for that reason alone cannot be relied upon. The reason why that material is without prejudice is set out at paragraph 28 of Mr Benson's second witness statement [13/184]. Having been invited to excise reference to this material from the witness statement and the evidence, the Claimant has declined to do so. At the hearing before Morison J the learned Judge indicated that he did not regard such material as being determinative and therefore the issue was not considered at first instance. No objection is taken to this Court considering the material de bene esse. Should it become necessary to do so, the Defendant will make submissions that the material is without prejudice and not admissible. In any event, the existence of negotiations between Commerzbank and the Claimant about paying the Claimant a severance package, which included an element for bonus, does not assist in determining whether there was a breach of contract in not awarding the Claimant a bonus for 2005 (which there was not).

24. The Claimant's second argument in relation to his claim for a bonus for 2005 is that the provision that he would only be entitled to a bonus if he was in employment on the payment date is an unfair contract term upon which Commerzbank is not entitled to rely (Reply para. 8 [9/67]). In this regard the Claimant seeks to have declared unlawful a provision which, as this Court will be aware, is a near universal feature of discretionary bonus schemes in the City (see, for example, *Clark v Nomura International plc* [2000] IRLR 766 [para. 7]; *Horkulak v Cantor Fitzgerald International* [2005] ICR 402 [para. 11]). Further, there is authority (albeit not at Court of Appeal level) directly against the Claimant on this issue.

25. In *Peninsula Business Services Ltd v Sweeney* [2004] IRLR 49 (EAT), Rimer J (giving the judgment of the Employment Appeal Tribunal) allowed an appeal from an Employment Tribunal which had held that an employee was entitled to all commission which was outstanding when his employment was terminated, notwithstanding the fact that the rules of the commission scheme expressly provided that "an employee has no claim whatsoever to any commission payments that would otherwise have been generated and paid if he is not in employment on the date when they would normally have been paid". In so doing, Rimer J rejected the argument that the clause fell foul of the UCTA. He stated [para. 37]:

> *"...From the moment [the employee] signed the commission rules document, he could have had no expectation, reasonable or otherwise, of being paid post-resignation commission, since section B made it clear that he would not be entitled to such commission. In that respect, it was akin to the type of clause*

that Morland J and Judge Clark respectively considered in Brigden *and* Brennan, *namely ones that set out his entitlement and the limits of his rights. In our view it was not a contract term falling with section 3(2)(b) of the 1977 Act, and we hold that the tribunal were in error in deciding that it was. That being so no question of the reasonableness or otherwise of section B under s.11 of the 1977 Act arose."*

26. From the moment that the Claimant signed the contract in this case he cannot have had any (reasonable) expectation of being paid a bonus if he was not employed on the payment date. The provision could not be clearer (see also *Brigden v American Express Bank Ltd* [2000] IRLR 94 at para. 22; *Brennan v Mills and Allen Ltd* 13 July 2000 EAT (unreported) at p.16).

Disposal

27. Commerzbank seeks permission to appeal the judgment of Morison J, and thereafter an Order that the appeal be allowed, that the Order of Morison J be substituted with an Order that the Claimant's claims in respect of bonus be dismissed, and that the Claimant do pay the Defendant's costs in relation to the dismissed claims, including the costs of the appeal and the application below.

Good practice suggestion

If you have compiled a truly persuasive argument it should leave the reader with the impression that what you have said is not only correct but also obvious – that there is no room for any opposing view. When you have completed your work try it out on someone with no knowledge of the case in order to seek that reaction.

Example L

Court of Appeal – Skeleton argument of the Appellant by Ronald Walker QC with Nigel Lewers, May 2010 – 18pp.

Dalling v Heale concerned whether a trial judge had properly assessed whether an individual who had sustained head injuries that left him with executive dysfunction through a fall at work had acted voluntarily in becoming intoxicated so that he sustained further injuries through another fall.

Here the writer uses pace and concision to great effect. He puts up the issue early on and there is a sense of great focus throughout the document.

The Appeal was dismissed.

The case is reported at [2011] EWCA Civ 365 CA (Civ Div) (Sir Anthony May (President QB), Smith LJ, Aikens LJ) 5/4/2011; [2011] All ER (D) 54 (Apr); Lawtel AC0128297.

APPELLANT'S SKELETON ARGUMENT

Estimated length of hearing: 4 hours
Estimated reading time: 4 hours

[References in bold are to Trial Bundle/Appeal Bundle page nos.]

The award

1. The award was made up as follows:

(A) General damages for pain, suffering and loss of amenities[1]
£110,000

(B) Special damages[2]

(1)	Travel expenses	£797.00	
(2)	Loss of earnings	£58,500.00	
(3)	Care	£19,181.86	
(4)	Household expenditure	£250.00	
(5)	Court of Protection	£1,348.75	
(6)	Miscellaneous	£55.00	
(7)	Gym membership	£500.00	
(8)	Case management/treatment	£5,375.00	
			£86,007.61

1 Judgment, para.198.

2 Judgment, para.199.

(C)	<u>Future losses</u>		
(1)	Loss of earnings		
		£217,128.06	
(2)	Job coach	£45,000.00	
(3)	Care	£118,576.09	
(4)	Case management	£75,060.00	
(5)	Aids and appliances	£900.00	
(6)	Household expenditure	£3,000.00	
(7)	Home decoration costs	£8,700.00	
(8)	Court of Protection	£100,000.00	
			£568,364.15
Total £764,371.76 x 75%			£573,278.82
Plus interest (agreed)			**£580,006.00**

Essence of the appeal

2. The Claimant suffered the index accident on 4 March 2005. Prior to the commencement of proceedings liability was admitted with an agreed reduction of 25% for contributory negligence. Thereafter the action proceeded towards an assessment of damages. However on 25 October 2008 the Claimant suffered another accident when he fell over in a public house, the fall being due to his becoming drunk.

3. The Defendant's case was (and is) that the second accident was a *novus actus interveniens* so that the Defendant should not be held liable for the injury, loss and damage that the Claimant would have suffered as a result of the second accident if the first accident had not occurred (in accordance with *Jobling v Associated Dairies Ltd*[3]).

4. The judge found that (a) the impairments caused by the index accident "played a causative part" in the Claimant's excessive drinking on the day of the second accident;[4] and (b) that the second accident was not a *novus actus interveniens*.[5]

5. The central issue on this appeal is whether the judge was entitled, on the evidence before him, to make finding (b) above. If he was, there are no other grounds of appeal; if he was not, his judgment should be set aside and the damages re-assessed on the basis of stripping out losses that the Claimant would have suffered in consequence of the second accident had the index accident not happened.

---

3 [1982] AC 794.

4 Judgment, para.97.

5 Judgment, para.98.

The essential facts

6. These are contended to be as follows:

(1) Prior to the index accident there were occasions when the Claimant would go out for a drink with his friends and become drunk;[6] (his own evidence was that he would typically drink 5–6 pints of beer).[7]

(2) The index accident occurred on 4 March 2005.

(3) In November 2005 the Claimant's partner, Ms Harris, went back to work two days a week, leaving the Claimant to look after their baby child Caitlin (d.o.b.24.4.05).on those days.

(4) During 2007 and 2008 the Claimant on occasion drank to excess. It was the evidence of his partner that his drinking problem surfaced towards the end of 2007[8] albeit the judge noted, in June 2007, a history in Professor Wood's first report of drinking to excess "over the last 12 months."[9] This evidently subsided for a while but there was a recurrence and deterioration of drinking to excess in the latter part of 2008[10] (the evidence of both the Claimant (**70**) and Miss Harris (**83**) was that this happened in September).

(5) On 25 October 2008 the Claimant, with Miss Harris, went to a funeral. She then left him at about lunch-time, following which he went to a public house with his friends and then continued drinking until the time of his accident at about 11.45 pm.[11] It is common ground that he had consumed alcohol to excess, and that this was what caused him to fall and sustain a head injury.[12]

(6) After this accident the Claimant again resumed drinking to excess[13] in December. However, following a period of separation from his partner the Claimant gave up drinking to excess. He was able to do so without apparent difficulty, and he has not

---

6 Judgment, para.6.

7 Claimant Transcript, p.20D–F.

8 Harris Transcript, p.22D–E.

9 Judgment, para.25; Wood Report (**225**).

10 Claimant w/s, para.37 (**70**); Harris w/s, para.22 (**83**); Harris Transcript, 23E–H.

11 Harris Transcript 24E–25B.

12 And the judge so found (judgment, para.44; cf the A & E note (rehearsed in the judgment, para.48)).

13 Claimant w/s, para.39 (**71**); Harris w/s, para.24 (**84**).

drunk excessively since the early part of 2009, albeit he goes to public houses and drinks in moderation.[14]

(7) The second accident caused bleeding into the same area of the brain as had the index accident. Although, of course, it would be impossible to ascertain with certainty what would have been the consequences of the second accident standing alone, there was a substantial measure of agreement between the experts. Thus:

i. Mr Redfern and Dr Schady were agreed that the 2008 injury would have led to comparable symptoms in terms of their nature (right-sided hearing loss, anosmia, postural vertigo and a frontal lobe syndrome); whether their severity would have been the same is speculative (**506**).

ii. They also agreed that the October 2008 injury would, in isolation, have led to a similar risk of epilepsy (**506**)

iii. Professor Wood and Dr Powell agreed that Mr Dalling would probably have exhibited a range of problems associated with left frontal brain injury (disturbance of mood, cognition and personality) (**509–10**).

iv. Dr Upton and Professor Dolan agreed that the 2008 injury was a "significant head injury" which would, taken alone, have had a "significant impact upon his functional abilities" (**519**). Professor Dolan considered it would have produced a significant handicap in employment, and that he would not have been able to continue his former employment (**519**); it would also have given rise to a need for care (**520**). Dr Upton considered that the 2008 injury would probably have had an impact on employment, but "there would have been a potential spread of outcomes from mild to possibly the extent described by Professor Dolan."

The law

7. The judge accepted, on the basis of the decision in *Jobling*, that *Baker v Willoughby* had no application[15] and therefore, implicitly, that if the second accident was a *novus actus interveniens* the Claimant could not recover damages in respect of the injury and losses that he would have sustained in that accident, had the index accident not happened.

---

[14] Claimant w/s, para. 42 (**72**); Claimant Transcript, 6D–F, 32G–33E; Harris Transcript, 27G–28D.

[15] Judgment, para.69.

8. As to the principles relevant to *novus actus interveniens* there are two lines of cases; the first are cases where the first accident causes a physical infirmity which plays a part in the second accident, but the chain of causation may or may not be broken by the claimant's behaviour at the time of the second accident The second line of cases are those in which the second accident (typically suicide) is the result of the deceased's ostensibly voluntary act, but it may or may not be the case that the first accident can be said to be the cause of that voluntary act, because of the disturbance of mind brought about by the first accident. The principles applicable are, of course, similar in both types of case.

9. The leading case of the first kind is *McKew v Holland & Hannen & Cubitts (Scotland) Ltd.*[16] In that case the House of Lords held that the act of the appellant in attempting to descend a steep staircase without a handrail without assistance, when his leg had previously given way, was unreasonable and broke the chain of causation between the tort and the consequences of the second accident. Lord Reid stated the principle as follows (at p.1623):

> In my view the law is clear. If a man is injured in such a way that his leg may give way at any moment he must act reasonably and carefully. It is quite possible that in spite of all reasonable care his leg may give way in circumstances such that as a result he sustains further injury. Then that second injury was caused by his disability which in turn was caused by the defender's fault. But if the injured man acts unreasonably he cannot hold the defender liable for injury caused by his own unreasonable conduct. His unreasonable conduct is novus actus interveniens. The chain of causation has been broken and what follows must be regarded as caused by his own conduct and not by the defender's fault or the disability caused by it. Or one may say that unreasonable conduct of the pursuer and what follows from it is not the natural and probable result of the original fault of the defender or of the ensuing disability. I do not think that foreseeability comes into this. A defender is not liable for a consequence of a kind which is not foreseeable. But it does not follow that he is liable for every consequence which a reasonable man could foresee. What can be foreseen depends almost entirely on the facts of the case, and it is often easy to foresee unreasonable conduct or some other novus actus interveniens as being quite likely. But that does not mean that the defender must pay for damage caused by the novus actus

10. The *McKew* principle was considered by the Court of Appeal in *Spencer v Wincanton Holdings Ltd.*[17] In that case the trial judge had held[18] that

---

16 [1969] 3 All ER 1621.

17 [2009] EWCA Civ 1404, [2009] All ER (D) 194 (Dec).

18 See Court of Appeal judgment [21].

> The Claimant was carrying out an everyday task that he had done a number of times before without incident. He was seeking to act without reliance on others; in general terms his determination to live his life as normally as possible is to be commended. His conduct fell far below what could be described as Mckew unreasonable.

11. The Court of Appeal dismissed the defendant's appeal against that finding. Sedley LJ (at [14]) quoted the following passage from Lord Nicholls' speech in *Kuwait Airways Corp v Iraqi Airways Co*

> How then does one identify a plaintiff's "true loss" in cases of tort?...I take as my starting point the commonly accepted approach that the extent of the defendant's liability for the plaintiff's loss calls for a twofold enquiry; whether the wrongful conduct causally contributed to the loss and, if it did, what is the extent of the loss for which the defendant ought to be held liable. The first of these enquiries, widely undertaken as a simple "but for" test, is predominantly a factual inquiry… The second inquiry, although this is not always openly acknowledged by the courts, involves a value judgment ("ought to be held liable"). Written large the second inquiry concerns the extent of the loss for which the defendant ought fairly or reasonably or justly to be held liable…the inquiry is whether the plaintiff's harm or loss should be within the scope of the defendant's liability, given the reasons why the law has recognised the cause of action in question. The law has to set a limit to the causally connected losses for which a defendant is to be held liable.

12. Sedley LJ went on to state [15]

> Fairness, baldly stated, might be thought to take things little further than reasonableness. But what it does is acknowledge that a succession of consequences which in fact and in logic is infinite will be halted by the law when it becomes unfair to let it continue. In relation to tortious liability for personal injury, this point is reached when (though not only when) the claimant suffers a further injury which, while it would not have happened without the initial injury, has been in substance brought about by the claimant and not the tortfeasor

13. The second line of cases referred to in paragraph 8 above invoke the question whether harm caused by a voluntary act on the part of the victim of a tort, whose mental state has been affected by the tort, is to be regarded as caused by the tort, or whether the voluntary act is a *novus actus interveniens*. The question was considered, in the context of suicide, by the House of Lords in *Corr v IBC Vehicles Ltd*.[19] In that case it was held that the suicide had been the direct result of the depressive illness caused by the accident at a time when the deceased's capacity to make reasoned and informed judgments about his future had been

---

19 [2008] UKHL 13, [2008] AC 884.

impaired by his illness; accordingly the suicide was not a *novus actus*. Lord Bingham stated [15] – [16]

> The rationale of the principle that a novus actus interveniens breaks the chain of causation is fairness. It is not fair to hold a tortfeasor liable, however gross his breach of duty may be, for damage caused to the claimant not by the tortfeasor's breach of duty but by some independent, supervening cause (which may or may not be tortious) for which the tortfeasor is not responsible. This is not the less so where the independent, supervening cause is a voluntary, informed decision taken by the victim as an adult of sound mind making and giving effect to a personal decision about his own future. Thus I respectfully think that the British Columbia Court of Appeal were right to hold that the suicide of a road accident victim was a novus actus in the light of its conclusion that when the victim took her life "she made a conscious decision, there being no evidence of disabling mental illness to lead to the conclusion that she had an incapacity in her faculty of volition": *Wright Estate v Davidson* (1992) 88 DLR (4th) 698,705.
>
> In the present case Mr Corr's suicide was not a voluntary, informed decision taken by him as an adult of sound mind making and giving effect to a personal decision about his future. It was the response of a man suffering from a severely depressive illness which impaired his capacity to make reasoned and informed judgments about his future...

14. Lord Walker put it in similar terms [42]

> His severe depression produced feelings of hopelessness which became increasingly strong; they came to determine his reality; by the time of his suicide he was suffering from a disabling mental condition which (as the agreed statement of facts and issues records) impaired his capacity to make reasoned and informed judgments.

15. In the Canadian case referred to by Lord Bingham (*Wright Estate v Davidson)* the deceased, following a road accident, was found to have suffered "mental disturbance that culminated in suicide."[20] Nevertheless in allowing the defendant's appeal the Court of Appeal stated (p.705)

> What is determinative of liability in the case under appeal is that when Mrs Wright took her life she made a conscious decision, there being no evidence of disabling mental illness to lead to the conclusion that she had an incapacity in her faculty of volition. Accordingly her suicide must be taken as a *novus actus interveniens*

---

[20] Cf. p.701; the disturbance was described as Post Traumatic Stress Disorder and Major Affective Disorder (p.703).

16. An example of a case where the claimant's injury, consequent on addiction to drugs, following clinical depression consequent upon an accident, was held not to be caused by the accident is *Wilson v Coulson*[21] where the judge stated [69]

> Even if, however, it were right to say that the "but for" test of causation shows that the headaches from the road traffic accident brain injury led to the claimant's use of heroin, which led to the addiction, which led to the overdose, the use of heroin in those circumstances resulted from a voluntary and informed decision by him to take the illicit Class A drug...I accept Professor Griffith Edward's evidence that the claimant had not lost the power to say no. His decision was voluntary, deliberate and informed. As was pointed out, at a later stage, which was after additional brain damage had been caused by the overdose, he was able to exercise the will power, albeit with the help of other people, to come off heroin and cocaine, which is no mean feat and is to his credit.

The judge's erroneous approach

17. The submissions made above are the same as were advanced below. The judge (judgment, para. 73) quoted the extract from Lord Nicholls' speech in the *Kuwait Airways* case which Sedley LJ had cited in *Spencer*.

18. He then proceeded (judgment, paras. 75–96) to conduct the first stage of the enquiry – namely to determine whether the index accident causally contributed to the 2008 accident. On the basis of the evidence which he accepted, he concluded that it did (para.97). This he was clearly entitled to do. The "but for" test of causation was therefore satisfied.

19. But the second stage of the enquiry required the judge to apply the principles set out in *Corr v IBC* and to ask himself whether the Claimant's conduct in becoming so drunk as to cause his October 2008 injury was the result of his "own volitional conduct (in becoming drunk)"[22] or whether he had an "incapacity in his faculty of volition".[23]

20. Instead the judge evidently considered (in para. 98) that all he was required to do was to decide what he considered to be "fair". Had he properly considered what Lord Bingham had said in *Corr* (quoted in para. 13 above) he would have appreciated that he needed to address the "volitional conduct" question in order to decide *why* it would be

---

21 [2002] PIQR P300.

22 He identified this question in paragraph 71 of the judgment, when dealing with the Claimant's submissions on the law, but did not in the event pose it to himself in paragraph 98.

23 Cf. *Wright Estate v Davidson* (paras. 13 and 15 above).

fair (or unfair) to treat (or not treat) the Claimant's decision to drink to excess on 25 October 2008 as a *novus actus*.

The evidence

21. Had he asked himself the right question, the judge could not possibly have concluded that the Claimant's decision to drink too much was other than his own volitional decision. Both the direct evidence and the circumstantial evidence pointed ineluctably to this conclusion. As to the former the Claimant's own evidence was unequivocal; see Transcript 32G – 34D.[24] So also was that of his partner Miss Harris; see Transcript 27A – 28C. No other lay witness was called.

22. As to circumstantial evidence

- He was quite capable of not drinking when he chose not to (for example while looking after his child, or when he would have to drive).[25]

- Following the second accident he apparently continued drinking heavily until the early part of 2009, but then stopped when he realised that his drinking was putting his family relationships at risk. He was able to do so without difficulty.

- He does not now have to abstain completely from alcohol; he drinks in moderation and knows when to stop.

23. There was therefore no plausible case that he was in a position analogous to that of the deceased in *Corr* (cf paragraph 13 above) as opposed to that of the claimants in *Wright Estate v Davidson* and *Wilson v Coulson* (cf paragraphs 15, 16).

24. The judge evidently placed great store on the evidence of the Claimant's experts Professor Wood and Dr Upton (see judgment, paras.81–2, 84, 89–91, 93–6). This evidence clearly entitled the judge to reach the conclusion that he did in paragraph 97 (that the index accident played a "causative part" in the excessive drinking on 25 October 2008).

---

24 The judge referred to some of this part of the Claimant's evidence (judgment, paras. 76–77) but opined that "some caution" was necessary in relation to it. But the answers were clearly true, and they were supported by Miss Harris's evidence and uncontradicted by any other witness.

25 In their joint statement (**(2) 514**) Dr Upton and Professor Dolan agree that "alcohol misuse has not been a prevailing complicating factor".

25. However it equally clearly could not support a finding (if the judge had intended to make one) that the excess drinking was not the Claimant's own volitional act. The evidence of Professor Wood and Dr Upton, which so impressed the judge, was directed to the way in which brain injury can affect judgment/self-control/alcohol tolerance.[26]

26. But this is a far cry from justifying a finding that on 25th October either (a) the Claimant drank to excess for a reason other than because that is what he wanted to do (whether wisely or unwisely), or (b) that the amount of alcohol he consumed on that day had a disproportionate effect on him; but in any event the judge's finding was not that he had become unexpectedly drunk on a modest amount of alcohol, but rather that he had drunk to "very great excess" (judgment, para.97).

27. As to (a) above, in his evidence Dr Upton was constrained to accept that drinking to excess on 25th October had been the Claimant's choice (albeit unwise); see Upton Transcript 17A – 18F. To conclude (as Dr Upton did at 18E) that "his ability to make decisions with respect to his drinking is influenced by the index accident and matters flowing from it" is no basis for a finding that getting drunk was not a volitional act.

28. As to factor (b) referred to in paragraph 26 above (alcohol intolerance) there was indeed not a shred of evidence of this (i.e. becoming disproportionately drunk on a small amount of alcohol) and Dr Upton did not identify any; see Upton Transcript 14C – 15E. In any event, as stated in paragraph 26 above, the Claimant was drunk on 25th October because he had drunk to "very great excess" not because he overreacted to a modest consumption.

29. Dr Upton summarised his opinion as follows (Transcript 17H – 18A):

> What I'm stating is that I consider his capacity to make decisions over daily events has been impaired since the indexed accident, particularly when he's perhaps appraising risks and knowing when to stop and that combined with an intolerance of alcohol, which is almost invariable post head injury, I consider *contributed* to the events that occurred that day. (emphasis supplied)

30. This evidence too is no basis for a finding that getting drunk on 25th October was not a volitional act.

31. Finally the judge's finding (judgment, para. 103) of one third contributory negligence in relation to the second accident is inconsistent with a finding (had he intended to make one) that this accident was not attributable to the Claimant's own volitional act.

---

26 The evidence of Dr Upton summarised in para. 90 of the judgment is at Upton Transcript 9A–10H.

Grounds of appeal

(1) *The learned Judge erred in law and/or in fact in holding that the Claimant's accident on 25 October 2008 was caused by the Defendant's breach of duty on 4 March 2005.*

32. The errors of law and fact relied upon are set out in paragraphs 17, 19–20 and 24–30 above.

(2) *Having correctly directed himself that the issue of causation called for a twofold enquiry (judgment, paragraphs 73–4), in relation to the second enquiry the learned Judge ought to have directed himself that the question was whether the Claimant's drunkenness which caused the 2008 accident was attributable to his own voluntary, informed decision taken by him as an adult of sound mind making and giving effect to a personal decision about his future (in accordance with Corr v IBC Vehicles Ltd [2008] AC 884). Instead the Judge decided the second question solely on the basis of what he regarded as "fair" (judgment, paragraph 98).*

33. See paragraph 20 above.

(3) *While the evidence of Gemma Harris, Dr Upton and Professor Wood (which the learned Judge accepted and relied upon) was sufficient to justify his finding that the consequences of the 2005 accident were causative of the 2008 accident (applying a "but for" test) that evidence could not support a finding that the Claimant's drunken state on 25 October 2008 was not "the consequence of the Claimant's own volitional conduct " (cf judgment, paragraph 71).*

34. This is dealt with in paragraphs 21 – 30 above.

(4) *Had the learned Judge applied the correct criterion in relation to the second enquiry, he ought to have concluded that the case was indistinguishable from the decisions in Wright Estate v Davidson (which the House of Lords approved in Corr v IBC Vehicles Ltd) or Wilson v Coulson.*

35. This too is dealt with in paragraphs 21 – 30 above.

(5) *The learned Judge's finding that the Claimant was guilty of contributory negligence (to the extent of one third) in relation to the 2008 accident was wholly inconsistent with a finding (had he made it) that his drunken state was not the result of his own "volitional conduct".*

36. See paragraph 31. The point does not permit of, or require, much further elaboration. While it is not suggested that there could not be a

finding of contributory negligence in relation to an accident which was not a *novus actus* the finding of one third fault, as expressed in paragraph 103 of the judgment, does not appear consistent with a finding (had the judge intended to make one) that getting drunk was not the Claimant's own volitional act.

(6) *The learned judge apparently treated the perceived difficulty of assessing what would have been the extent of the Claimant's injuries and damage (in consequence of the 2008 accident) had the 2005 accident not occurred as a ground for not finding the 2008 accident to have been a novus actus interveniens (judgment, paragraph 102).*

37. This has not been dealt with so far. The "further consideration" referred to in paragraph 99 of the judgment is evidently the perceived difficulty of assessing damages if the Defendant's argument succeeds (see paragraph 102). No doubt there are such difficulties, but these cannot affect the question of whether the second accident is, or is not, to be regarded as having been caused by the first accident.

(7) *The learned Judge failed to have due or any regard to the uncontradicted evidence (and in particular the evidence of the Claimant himself) that*

- *The Claimant was quite capable of not drinking when he chose not to (for example while looking after his child, or when he would have to drive), which proposition the Claimant accepted (judgment paragraph 76).*

- *Following the second accident he apparently continued drinking heavily until the early part of 2009, but then stopped when he realised that his drinking was putting his family relationships at risk, and was able to do so without difficulty.*

- *He does not now have to abstain completely from alcohol; he drinks in moderation and knows when to stop.*

38. See paragraph 22 above.

(8) *The learned Judge accordingly erred in failing to (a) make an assessment of the injury, loss and damage that the Claimant would have suffered as a result of the 2008 accident, if the 2005 accident had not occurred and (b) to discount the awards of damages for (1) pain, suffering and loss of amenities, (2) special damages (loss of earnings, care and case management and Court of Protection costs), and (3) future losses (all heads) by taking account of such an assessment.*

39. This summarises what it is contended the judge ought to have done, had he found the second accident to have been a *novus actus*.

Order sought

40. If the appeal succeeds it will be necessary for damages to be assessed on the basis of deducting, in relation to most of the heads of damages, whatever sums are assessed as damages the Claimant would have sustained as a result of the second accident if the first accident had not occurred.

41. This is obviously not a task which permits of precision but, as in many other circumstances where hypothetical situations have to be dealt with, the court is required to do the best it can. In this case the experts specifically considered, and dealt with, this issue and there was a substantial measure of agreement; see paragraph 6 (7) above.

42. The maximum degree of agreement was contained in the joint statement of Professor Wood and Dr Powell at point 9 (**510**), which stated that "in the absence of the head injury on 4.3.05, he was likely to have evidenced the same or similar clinical picture and prognosis as set out in paragraph 5 above"; this comprised, effectively, all the sequelae of the head injury caused by the index accident.

43. Since the judge accepted the evidence of Professor Wood and Dr Powell on every other point of their evidence to which he referred, it is difficult to see why he would not have accepted this view. However, having referred to it in paragraph 100 of the judgment, he appears not to have accepted it, apparently because there was other evidence that the position was "speculative".

44. If the appeal succeeds the court is invited either to remit the matter to the trial judge for re-assessment of damages on the basis of the evidence given at the trial, alternatively (if it is prepared to do so) to assess the damages itself.

Permission to appeal

45. The Defendant needs permission to appeal. The judge refused permission. It is contended that the Defendant's prospect of success could not fairly be described as fanciful.

46. The judge, it is submitted, made a fundamental error in deciding the central issue simply on the basis of what he regarded as "fair" and specifically erred in the respects set out in the grounds of appeal.

47. If the decision were correct it would mean that the Defendant (and others who cause injury giving rise to frontal lobe damage and drinking alcohol to excess) would be liable for whatever accident and/or injury to himself or others that this Claimant (or others) might cause as a result of getting drunk. On Dr Upton's evidence (cf Upton Transcript 18D–F) there will in future be risks of similar occurrences for which the Defendant (on the judge's finding) would be liable – but for the rule that the Claimant cannot bring more than one action.

Authorities

48. The authorities cited in this skeleton argument are all referred to in the judgment. Where more than one authority has been cited, this is for the purpose of distinguishing between them and all citations are necessary for the proper presentation of the arguments.

Good practice suggestions

Make a conscious decision about whether to use quotations from authorities within the body of your text. Either make them as short as conceivably possible, relegate them to an end-note or footnote, or an appendix of authorities with pages pre-highlighted. Be conscious of how they will look.

Use a succinct summary of the argument – one or two sentences, no more – in support of each ground of appeal. This can be a stand alone introduction, or a conclusion.

Example M

Court of Appeal – Appellants' skeleton argument by Jonathan Sumption QC with Andrew Mitchell, 2010 – 26pp.

In Safeway Stores v Twigger and Others where an undertaking infringed provisions of the Competition Act 1998 relating to anti-competitive activity and was duly penalised by the Office of Fair Trading, that undertaking was not entitled to recover the amount of such penalties from its directors or employees who were themselves responsible for the infringement. Such recovery would be contrary to the maxim ex turpi causa as the undertaking would be personally liable to pay the penalties and the Act did not impose liability of any kind on the directors or employees for which it could be vicariously responsible.

This is a short skeleton in which the writer captures the reader's attention from the outset with an assertion about the importance of the case and its controversial subject matter. The argument is driven by logic. The use of short sentences and relatively short paragraphs gives real pace.

The appeal was allowed.

The case is reported at [2010] EWCA Civ 1472 CA (Civ Div) (Pill LJ, Longmore LJ, Lloyd LJ); [2011] 2 All ER 841; [2011] 1 Lloyd's Rep 462; [2011] 1 CLC 80; Lawtel AC0127171. The first instance report is at [2010] EWHC 11 QBD (Comm) (Flaux J); [2010] Bus LR 974; [2010] 3 All ER 577; [2010] 2 Lloyd's Rep 39; [2010] 2 BCLC 106; Lawtel AC0123301.

APPELLANTS' SKELETON ARGUMENT

Introduction

1. This appeal raises a controversial question of law. Can an undertaking, which is fined by the Office of Fair Trading for infringing the Competition Act 1998, recover an indemnity in respect of that fine from the individual directors or employees whose acts or omissions are alleged to have given rise to the infringement? The Defendants submit that a claim of this kind is barred by public policy: *ex turpi causa oritur non actio*. The point is a novel one, but in the relevant respects the Competition Act 1998 is fairly typical of current legislative techniques for the regulation of business practices. It is therefore likely that many other cases will be affected by the outcome.

2. The matter came before Flaux J. on an application by the Defendant directors and employees for summary judgment dismissing the claim. He dismissed the application.

3. The relevant facts are either admitted or pleaded by the Claimant and assumed to be true.

The statutory background

4. The Competition Act 1998 marked a radical break with the previous scheme of domestic competition law. Under successive enactments dating from 1956, the most recent of which was the Restrictive Trade Practices Act 1976, the statutory regulation of competition in the United Kingdom had been based on a requirement to register specified anti-competitive agreements and practices so that they could be scrutinised by a specialised tribunal and avoided if they were found to operate against the public interest. The Act of 1998 replaced this scheme by a general prohibition of anti-competitive agreements (Chapter 1) and abuses of a dominant position (Chapter 2) modelled on EC law and enforced by a system of regulatory penalties administered by the Office of Fair Trading. Section 60 of the Act provides that it is to be applied as far as possible in a manner consistent with the principles which would apply in EC law.

5. Under Section 2(1) of the Act, anti-competitive agreements between 'undertakings' are prohibited unless exempt. Under Section 36(1), the OFT 'may require an undertaking which is party to the agreement to pay a penalty in respect of the infringement', but only if it is 'satisfied that the infringement has been committed intentionally or negligently by the undertaking': see Section 36(3). A Section 36 penalty is normally assessed by reference to the turnover of the 'undertaking', the gravity of the infringement, the benefit which the 'undertaking' has derived from it, and the need to deter others, subject to an overall maximum of 10% of turnover fixed by Section 36(8): see the OFT's Guidance, summarised by the Judge at [39]–[42]. An infringement by an 'undertaking' of Section 2(1) is not technically a crime, nor is a Section 36 penalty a criminal sanction. But the Judge was right at [43] to treat an infringement as sufficiently serious to engage the *ex turpi causa* rule, and the Section 36 penalty as analogous to a criminal fine.

6. 'Undertaking' is not defined in the Act, but it has an established meaning in EC competition law from which these provisions are derived: see Bellamy & Child, *European Community Law of Competition*, 6th ed. (2008), paras. 2.003, 2.004 It means the entity carrying on the relevant economic or commercial activity in its own right, regardless of its legal status. A sole trader, partnership, company or group of companies are all, in respect of a businesses carried on by them, 'undertakings'. But an individual is an 'undertaking' only in so far as it engages in the relevant economic or commercial activity in its own right. An officer or employee is not, as such, an 'undertaking': Case 40/73 *Suiker Unie v. Commission* [1975] ECR 1663, at para. 539.

7. It will be apparent from the statutory provisions referred to above that the Chapter 1 prohibition is directed at the 'undertaking', and that the regulatory penalty may be imposed on the 'undertaking' alone. Liability is not strict, but dependent on proof of negligence or intention. There is, however, no provision for the imposition of a Section 36 penalty on an officer, employee or other agent of the 'undertaking', even if he was responsible for the intentional or negligent conduct in question. The legislative policy is plainly to subject the undertaking itself to the penalty, in order to induce it to apply effective controls to the conduct of its officers and employees. This is the usual basis on which criminal or quasi-criminal liability is imposed on principals for the acts of their agents: see *Tesco Supermarkets Ltd. v. Nattrass* [1972] AC 153, 193–4 (Lord Diplock), and *Director-General of Fair Trading v. Pioneer Concrete UK Ltd* [1995] 1 AC 456, 474 (Lord Nolan).

8. The scheme of the penalty provisions of the 1998 Act may be contrasted with that of Part 6 of the Enterprise Act 2002, which created for the first time a criminal offence (the 'cartel offence') of dishonestly agreeing with one or more other persons to make or implement specified kinds of anti-competitive arrangement broadly corresponding to those prohibited by Chapter 1 of the Act of 1998: see Section 188. This offence can be committed only by individuals and therefore directly affects officers, employees and other agents, but is more difficult to prove because it requires evidence of dishonesty.

The assumed facts

9. The Claimant, Safeway, operated a chain of supermarkets. Together with its various operating subsidiaries, it constituted the relevant 'undertaking' for present purposes. Some of the Defendants were directors of Safeway or its operating subsidiaries. The others were employees of varying degrees of seniority.

10. In 2002 and 2003, there was much public concern about the financial plight of farmers, who were making what were said to be excessively low margins on dairy products. Safeway and other supermarkets responded by raising the retail price of milk and cheese so as to enable the dairies to increase the price of milk paid to farmers.

11. In 2005, the OFT alleged that this policy was concerted between the supermarkets and involved a breach by Safeway of section 2(1) of the Competition Act 1998. Safeway entered into an 'early resolution arrangement' under which it admitted the infringement and forewent its right to make further representations. In return, the OFT indicated it would seek a reduced penalty. While the OFT is not bound by this indication, the penalty which might be levied once a Decision is adopted lies within the range £10–16,000. The early resolution

agreement has not been disclosed and the precise calculation of the fine is not known. But Safeway say that it is based on its turnover in milk and cheese products in 2006/2007.

Ex turpi causa

12. The rule of public policy prevents a Claimant from using the courts to obtain compensation for loss which he has suffered as a result of his own unlawful act, or to obtain a benefit from his own unlawful act, even if apart from the rule he would have a good cause of action. The underlying policy was explained by Lord Mansfield in a celebrated case in 1775, *Holman v Johnson* (1775) 1 Cowp 341, 343:

> No court will lend its aid to a man who founds his cause of action upon an immoral or an illegal act. If, from the plaintiff's own stating or otherwise, the cause of action appears to arise *ex turpi causa*, or the transgression of a positive law of this country, there the court says he has no right to be assisted. It is upon that ground the court goes; not for the sake of the defendant, but because they will not lend their aid to such a plaintiff.

The leading modern case about the ambit and rationale of the rule is the decision of the House of Lords in *Gray v Thames Trains Ltd* [2009] UKHL 33, [2009] 1 AC 1339.

13. In *Gray*, Lord Hoffmann (with whom the rest of the Committee agreed) distinguished between two forms of the rule, a 'wider' and a 'narrower' form, whose rationales were in some respects different [29]:

> In its wider form, it is that you cannot recover compensation for loss which you have suffered in consequence of your own criminal act. In its narrower and more specific form, it is that you cannot recover for damage which flows from loss of liberty, a fine or other punishment lawfully imposed upon you in consequence of your own unlawful act. In such a case it is the law which, as a matter of penal policy, causes the damage and it would be inconsistent for the law to require you to be compensated for that damage.

14. In relation to the narrower form of the rule, *Gray* is authority for the following propositions, all of which are derived mainly from the speech of Lord Hoffmann:

(1) A civil court will not entertain an action by an offender to recover an indemnity against the consequences of a punishment inflicted on him by a criminal court: [33], citing *Askey v. Golden Wine Co. Ltd.* [1948] 2 All ER 35, 38 (Lord Denning).

(2) At [36]–[42], Lord Hoffmann rationalised this as being based on the principle of consistency, which he expressed by adopting the formulation of Mummery LJ in *Worrall v. British Railways Board* [CA Transcript, 1999/684]:

> It would be inconsistent with his criminal conviction to attribute to the negligent Defendant in this action any legal responsibility for the financial consequences of crimes which he has been found guilty of having deliberately committed.

Or, as Lord Brown put it [93], 'the law cannot at one and the same time incarcerate someone for his criminality and compensate him civilly for the financial consequences.' Cf. Lord Rodger at [77]; *Hall v Hebert* (1993) 101 DLR (4th) 129, at 165 (McLachlin J), approved in *Stone & Rolls Ltd v Moore Stephens* [2009] 3 WLR 455, at [128] (Lord Walker).

(3) This is, as Lord Hoffmann observed at [41], because 'it must be assumed that the sentence was what the criminal court regarded as appropriate to reflect the personal responsibility of the accused for the crime he had committed.' Cf. Lord Rodger at [69].

(4) It makes no difference to the operation of the rule that the Claimant's crime was directly caused by the Defendant's breach of duty: see Lord Hoffmann at [43]–[44].

15. The wider rule precluded recovery of losses which did not necessarily arise from the imposition of a penalty by a criminal court. Lord Hoffmann said about it:

> It differs from the narrower version in at least two respects: first, it cannot, as it seems to me, be justified on the grounds of inconsistency in the same way as the narrower rule. Instead, the wider rule has to be justified on the ground that it is offensive to public notions of the fair distribution of resources that a claimant should be compensated (usually out of public funds) for the consequences of his own criminal conduct. Secondly, the wider rule may raise problems of causation which cannot arise in connection with the narrower rule. The sentence of the court is plainly a consequence of the criminality for which the claimant was responsible. But other forms of damage may give rise to questions about whether they can properly be said to have been caused by his criminal conduct.

The wider form of the rule simply depends on the application of rules of causation analogous to those applying in tort: i.e. on whether the criminal act of the Defendant had caused the Claimant's loss as opposed to merely providing the occasion for it [55].

Application to this case of the narrow form of the rule

16. The loss which Safeway is seeking to recover from the Defendants is damage flowing from the imposition by a public authority of a penalty for negligently or intentionally engaging in conduct prohibited by statute. Once it is accepted that the rule of public policy is engaged by an infringement of this kind, the claim is on the face of it directly contrary to the rule of public policy in its narrower form.

17. The Judge accepted that an infringement of Section 2(1) in principle engaged the public policy, but held that it had no application unless the acts giving rise to the infringement were acts for which Safeway was personally and not just vicariously liable. For this purpose they had to be authorised in accordance with the company's 'primary rules of attribution' (as that expression was used by Lord Hoffmann in *Meridian Global Fund Management Asia Ltd v Securities Commission* [1995] 2 AC 500), i.e. by persons constituting the company's directing mind and will: see [54]. He considered that he was bound to reach this conclusion by the reasoning of the House of Lords in *Stone & Rolls Ltd v Moore Stephens* [2009] 1 AC 1391. Since it was common ground that the acts giving rise to Safeway's liability to penalties under the Act were not authorised by the shareholders in general meeting or formally by the Board or anyone exercising the powers of the Board, the Judge concluded that the claim was not barred: see [77].

18. In the Defendants' submission, this analysis is mistaken, for the following reasons:

    (1) The rationale of the narrower rule is the need for consistency in any coherent system of law, between the principle on which the law visits penal consequences on those guilty of certain conduct, and the principle on which it allows the party suffering those consequences a remedy against a third party for the resulting loss. This principle applies irrespective of the distribution of personal fault whenever a party (whether it is a corporation or a natural person) has been fined and seeks to recover the fine. The point is well illustrated by the decision of Rowlatt J. in *Leslie v. Reliable Advertising and Addressing Agency Ltd.* [1915] 1 KB 652, where a fine imposed a moneylender for a contravention of the Moneylenders Act 1900 was held to be irrecoverable from the

independent contractor who was wholly to blame for the infringement.[1]

(2) Attribution in the sense which the Judge was considering is irrelevant in this situation. This is because the Competition Act itself answers the question of attribution. A legal rule which imposes a fine on a person for breaking the law, clearly posits that for the purpose of that rule the person fined is in law to be regarded as responsible for the breach. If Safeway is treated by Sections 2 and 36 of the Competition Act as responsible (indeed exclusively responsible) for the infringement, it would be inconsistent for a Court to treat it as not being responsible for the purpose of obtaining a remedy against its officers and employees. This is the very point made by Lord Hoffmann in *Gray* at [41] and by Lord Rodger in the same case at [69]: see para. 14(3) above.

(3) The difference between personal and vicarious liability has nothing to do with this question. Safeway has not been made to pay a penalty because it is vicariously liable for the acts of the Defendants. It has been made to do so because the Competition Act treats it as personally liable for the infringement and personally subject to a penalty by reason of its negligence or intention. Vicarious liability on the other hand depends on a rule of law which makes an employer strictly liable for the wrong of his agent committed within the scope of his employment. The company is liable not for its own wrong but for the agent's. But the Defendants is this case are incapable of committing the wrong in question. By definition only Safeway, as the relevant 'undertaking', can infringe Section 2(1) of the Act. Safeway cannot therefore be vicariously liable for the infringements of its officers and employees. It can only be personally liable.

(4) Another way of making the same point is that the scheme of the Act requires what Lord Hoffmann in *Meridian Global* called a 'special rule of attribution', because the primary rules of attribution would defeat its purpose. It has already been pointed out that Sections 2(1) and 36 apply only to undertakings, and that their purpose is to inducing them to organise their affairs in such a way as can reasonably them expected to prevent infringements: para. 7 above.

---

1 The Judge dealt most unsatisfactorily with this case. He sought to distinguish it on the ground that the moneylender was a one-man company. In fact (i) there is no basis in the report for the view that the moneylender was a one-man company, (ii) on the facts, he was not to personally blame for what happened, whether he was a one-man company or not, and (iii) this was no part of Rowlatt J's reasoning.

(5) For the same reasons it would be contrary to the policy of the Act to allow Safeway to pass on a liability intended to be specific to them, to its officers and employees. In particular, it would undermine the policy of deterring other undertakings, and requiring them to take proper steps to control the acts of their employees. Claims for indemnity in these circumstances have the additional, and unattractive consequence, of enabling them to access its officers' D&O insurance indirectly in circumstances where it would not have been entitled to claim a direct indemnity against the penalties from its own insurers.

19. The Judge seems, with respect, to have been misled by the discussion of attribution in *Stone & Rolls*. In the first place, that case did not involve the consistency principle, or the narrower form of the ex turpi rule, because Stone & Rolls was not seeking to recover from its auditors an indemnity in respect of a fine. Secondly, the House of Lords was not dealing with a statutory scheme which itself resolved the question of attribution. Most of the debate in *Stone & Rolls* arose from the need to determine whether the fraud in question in that case was that of the company itself or only that of its agent Stojevic. The tort alleged (fraud) could in principle have been committed by either or both of them. That is not a question that can arise in this case.

Application to this case of the wider form of the rule

20. In the circumstances of this particular case, the rule of public policy is also engaged in its wider form. The penalty and associated expenses payable by Safeway are the direct consequence of its infringement of Section 2 of the Act. The distinction between personal and vicarious liability is no more relevant in this context than it is in that of the narrower form of the rule. This is essentially for the reasons spelled out in para. 18 above. The statutory scheme visits personal and not vicarious responsibility on the undertaking.

Hampshire Land

21. Towards the end of his judgment the Judge considered Safeway's 'alternative' argument that because Safeway was a 'victim' of the Appellants' assumed breaches of duty, those breaches should not be attributed to Safeway so as to bar its claim. This argument was said to derive support from the so-called *Hampshire Land* principle. The Judge held [117] that Safeway's argument could not be dismissed on a summary application.

22. It is submitted that the attempt to apply the *Hampshire Land* principle to this case is plainly unsound:

(1) It is just as incompatible with the consistency principle as Safeway's primary case. The effect of the *Hampshire Land* principle is that a principal is not to have attributed to him responsibility for acts by his agent which were in reality directed by that agent against him. There is no scope for this exception to the ordinary rules of attribution under a statutory scheme which itself attributes responsibility to the principal, i.e. the undertaking which is engaging in the relevant business.

(2) The Judge's reasoning on this point has no regard to the very narrow scope given to the *Hampshire Land* principle by the Court of Appeal in *Stone & Rolls*, an aspect of the Court of Appeal's reasoning was not affected by the reasoning in the House of Lords. A company cannot be regarded as the victim of its employees, unless the acts of the officers and employees were directed against it. There is no prospect of establishing this. The fact that a company suffers a fine on account of the wrongful acts of its managers does not prevent the acts and knowledge of the managers from being attributed to it: see *McNicholas Construction Co. Ltd. v Customs & Excise Commissioners* [2000] STC 553 and *Bank of India v Morris* [2005] BCC 739, as applied by the Court of Appeal in *Stone & Rolls*.

Good practice suggestion

In appellate argument make sure that your criticism of the court below is planned and well thought out before committing pen to paper. It needs a structure and internal logic to get over the inherent bias of judges whose initial reaction will be to protect one of their own unless the error is obvious from a reading of the judgment without your assistance. Be bold in your criticism if it needs to be made.

Example N

Court of Appeal – Respondent's skeleton argument by Ronald Walker QC, January 2007 – 4pp.

Ellis v Bristol City Council was an appeal by a health worker against the dismissal of her claim for damages for personal injury sustained in an accident occurring in the course of her employment as a care assistant at a home for the elderly run by the respondent local authority. She had slipped in a pool of urine left by one of the residents on the floor of a corridor covered by non-slip mats. The issue was whether the Workplace (Health, Safety and Welfare) Regulations 1992 reg.12(1) and reg.12(2) required that the surface of a workplace floor must not be slippery, and that requirement applied not only to permanent states of slipperiness but also to states of slipperiness occurring with a sufficient degree of frequency and regularity.

This very short skeleton is an example of what can be done by a respondent who seeks to uphold the reasoning of the trial judge.

The appeal succeeded.

The case is reported at [2007] EWCA Civ 685 CA (Civ Div) (Smith LJ, Lloyd LJ, Wilson LJ); (2007) PIQR P26; (2007) ICR 1614; *The Times*, August 21, 2007; Lawtel AC0114181

RESPONDENT'S SKELETON ARGUMENT

[references in bold are to Appeal Bundle pages]

Appellant's Grounds of Appeal

Ground 1: The Approved Code of Practice

1. The ACOP to the Workplace Regulations was neither pleaded, nor referred to in the Claimant's opening skeleton (**A24–7**). It was first referred to in the Claimant's closing submissions (**A34**). Be that as it may, s.17 of the HSWA provides only for the use of approved codes of practice in criminal proceedings. It is not accepted that they are aids to construction of statutory provisions previously enacted.

2. Because the ACOP had not been canvassed during the hearing, there was no investigation of whether the floor was "unduly slippery" when wet. The Claimant adduced no evidence, either expert or lay, to support such a suggestion and, as the judge observed (**A52**), there was

no evidence from the Claimant relating to the unsuitability of the particular type of floor in use at that time.[1]

3. The judge was therefore right to disregard the code (**A53**).

Ground 2: the ambit of Regulation 12(1) and (2)

4. Regulation 12(1) is not engaged. The judge's reasoning at **A52–3** is unassailable. The Claimant's contentions are unsustainable in principle and on the authorities.[2] If they were correct they would render Regulation 12(3) virtually otiose and create a strict liability for transient conditions, for which Regulation 12(3) provides a "reasonable practicability" defence.

5. It can be accepted that the purpose for which the floor or surface is to be used is relevant to the suitability of its construction (so that, for example, a swimming pool surround should be constructed so as to minimise the risk of slipping when wet). However this was a corridor in an old people's home. It had no special features to distinguish it from corridors in similar premises, such as care homes or hospitals. There was no evidence, expert or lay, to suggest that the construction differed from that to be found in any similar premises.

Ground 3: breach of Regulation 12(1) and (2)

6. This was a typical corridor floor which might occasionally become wet if there was an accidental spillage of liquid or urine from an incontinent resident. There was in place an effective system to deal with such spillages, inasmuch as it was the duty of any member of staff who saw urine or other liquid on the floor to clean it up immediately (the judge accepted this evidence (**A48**)). There was evidence of a small number of accidents, almost all to residents, who were elderly an infirm, and which either were or were assumed to be due to slipping, and almost all of a minor nature.

7. Regulation 12 is, of course, concerned with the risk to employees and not to residents. The records showed only two previous falls by employees, Pat Theobald (**A210**) and the Claimant herself (**A219**), neither of whom sustained any significant injury.

---

1 Contrary to the Claimant's submission on this appeal, the content of the National Care Standards Commission Report (**A207, 209**) was not evidence to this effect; nor was it evidence at all as to the state of the floor (no Civil Evidence Act Notice was served to support an attempt to rely upon the opinion of the unidentified inspector, and any such attempt would have been resisted).

2 *Levesley v Thomas Firth and John Brown Ltd* [1953] 2 All ER 866; cf *Redgrave's Heath and Safety* (4th edn) **7.25, 7.26**.

8. The judge, in her conclusions in relation to both breach of statutory duty and negligence, took into account this history of accidents and, on the basis of them, made the value judgment that she did, and was entitled to do. It cannot be suggested that she erred in law.

   See *Searson v Brioland Limited* [2005] EWCA Civ 55, [2005] All ER (D) 197 (Jan), paragraphs 8, 27–8 (Buxton LJ) and 33–4 (May LJ).

9. The Claimant's reliance on the NCSC Report (published after this accident), seemingly as expert evidence, is misplaced for the reasons set out in fn 1 above.

Ground 4: Regulation 12(3)

10. It was, of course, accepted that the burden was on the Defendant to prove that it had kept the corridor (the traffic route) free from urine, so far as was reasonably practicable (**A30**).

11. Reasonable practicability is a question of fact, and has been described as "a matter of common sense fact to be determined by the trial judge".[3]

12. The judge's finding at **A53–4** is one of fact and is unassailable. Contrary to the Claimant's skeleton it did not rest upon a finding that the slipping risk was not known prior to October 2002.

Ground 5: negligence

13. Although the ground is more widely formulated in the Notice of Appeal, the Claimant's skeleton argument appears to rely solely on failure to install a floor with a non-slip surface prior to the accident.

14. The judge took into account all the relevant factors and gave full and adequate reasons for her finding that the Defendant exercised such care as was in all the circumstances reasonable (**A54–5**). She made no error of law and her finding of fact is not one with which the Court should interfere (cf *Searson v Brioland* (para. 8 above)).

Conclusion

15. This was a simple slipping accident, liability for which fell to be determined essentially by reference to questions of fact, which the judge was required to determine. She made no errors of law. Her primary findings of fact are all supported by the evidence and her inferential findings (that the Defendant was neither in breach of statutory duty nor negligent) were correct, alternatively at the very

---

[3] *Pratt v Intermet Refractories Ltd* (CA 21. 1.2000), May LJ.

least not obviously wrong, and there is no justification for this Court to reverse her decision.

Respondent's Notice

16. Having found against the Claimant, the judge did not go on to consider contributory negligence.

17. However, the judge did reject the Claimant's evidence as to the circumstances of the accident (in particular to the effect that there were no mats on the floor in the area where she fell). Furthermore the judge found as a fact (**A45–6**)

    (a) that the Claimant was fully aware of the need to be vigilant (in particular because one of the residents had recently taken to urinating at that location – which is why the mats were put down);

    (b) that she knew that it was her duty, if the floor was wet, for the floor to be cleaned immediately and warning signs put in place;

    (c) that she had seen the Risk Assessment and the Health and Safety Notice in the staff room; and

    (d) that there was a warning sign in place at this location (**A235**) of which she was aware.

18. It was the Claimant's own evidence had there been mats in place she would not have fallen (**A80, 83**).

19. The line of authority referred to in paragraph 13 of the Claimant's opening skeleton (**A26**) is not directly analogous. The Claimant was not guilty of mere inadvertence while carrying out a repetitive job; she was not looking where she was going in circumstances where there was a known hazard, the eradication of which was part of her duties.

20. Therefore if the appeal is allowed there should be a finding of a substantial degree of contributory negligence.

Good practice suggestion

Tribunals are likely to appreciate being direct and to the point. It reduces reading time, focuses attention on the real issues, and allows the advocate to expand argument orally.

Example O

Supreme Court – Printed case of the appellant local authorities by Jonathan Sumption QC with Rhodri Williams QC, December 2010 – 21pp.

Harrow LBC v Risk Management Partners Ltd sought the determination whether, where a public body exercised control over an entity similar to that which it exercised over its own departments, and at the same time the entity carried out the essential part of its activities with the controlling public body, that public procurement rules such as those contained in the Regulations did not apply by virtue of the exemption enunciated in Teckal Srl v Comune di Viano (Reggio Emilia) (C-107/98) [1999] ECR I-8121 ECJ being incorporated into English law; and if so, whether the exemption was applicable where the contract was for insurance; and whether, for the Teckal exemption to apply, individual control by a local authority was necessary or whether it was sufficient that the contracting authorities exercised that control collectively.

This is an example of arguing broad principles of law at the highest level, rather than seeking to do practicable justice between the parties on the facts. At the time of this appeal the principal appellant, Brent LBC, had settled its part of the claim. Harrow LBC was seeking a clarification of questions of wide importance. Unlike Examples A–N this example is given as printed, complete with the formatted first page, since it provides useful information for the Justices to locate reports of the judgments below.

The appeal was allowed. It was held that the Teckal exemption was incorporated into English law, it was applicable to contracts for insurance, and individual control by a local authority was not necessary.

The case is reported as *Brent London Borough Council (Appellant) v Risk Management Partners Ltd (Respondent) & (1) London Authorities Mutual Ltd (2) Harrow London Borough Council (Interested Parties) (2011)* [2011] UKSC 7 SC (Lord Hope (Deputy President), Lord Rodger JSC, Lord Walker JSC, Lord Brown JSC, Lord Dyson JSC); [2011] 2 AC 34; [2011] 2 WLR 166; (2011) PTSR 481; [2011] 2 All ER 209; (2011) BLGR 169; *The Times*, February 10, 2011; Lawtel AC0127604.

IN THE SUPREME COURT OF THE UNITED KINGDOM
APPEAL NO. UKSC 2009/0166

ON APPEAL FROM HER MAJESTY'S COURT OF APPEAL (CIVIL DIVISION)

Reports of proceedings below

High Court – Judicial review claim [2008] EWHC 692 (Admin); [2008] BLGR 331
High Court – Damages claim [2008] EWHC 1094 (Admin); [2008] BLGR 429; [2008] EuLR 660

Court of Appeal – [2009] EWCA Civ 490; [2010] BLGR 99

Time Occupied by Lower Courts

First Instance – 11 days
Court of Appeal – 4 days

B E T W E E N:-

HARROW LONDON BOROUGH COUNCIL
Appellant

– and –

RISK MANAGEMENT PARTNERS LIMITED
Respondent

CASE FOR THE APPELLANT

Introduction

1 The essential question on this appeal is whether a group of local authorities may lawfully insure with a captive mutual insurer created by them for that purpose, without putting the contracts out to competitive tender.

2 The appeal arises out of arrangements made in 2006 and 2007 by a number of London local authorities for mutual insurance against various classes of risk, in particular property, liability and terrorism. These arrangements were designed to reduce the cost of premiums and raise the standard of risk management. They are described in the judgments of the courts below, and are broadly in line with other schemes of mutual insurance which will be familiar to those of your lordships who have been concerned with shipowners' P&I clubs, the Bar Mutual Indemnity Fund or other non-life mutual insurers associated with specific economic sectors. In summary, they involved the incorporation of the London Authorities Mutual Ltd ('LAML'), a company limited by guarantee. Ten London local authorities subscribed the Memorandum and Articles of Association of the company, thereby becoming 'Members'. Seven of them, including Brent and Harrow, were insured by the company in the course of 2007 and 2008, thereby becoming 'Participating Members'.

3 The business of LAML was restricted to the provision of insurance to its 'Participating Members'. It was funded by (i) paid and guaranteed capital contributions from Participating Members, (ii) premiums, (iii) supplementary calls on Participating Members pro rata to their premiums for the relevant year up to a maximum of 100%, and (iv) reinsurance placed in the market. The management of the company's affairs was vested in a Board comprising a majority of directors appointed by Participating Members, with some independent directors. Many aspects of the management were delegated to professional managers, Charles Taylor & Co. Ltd., under the authority of the Board.

4 These arrangements were challenged by the Respondent, Risk Management Partners Ltd, a commercial insurer which claims that it might otherwise have obtained the business. The challenge was mounted on two distinct bases. First, in proceedings in the Administrative Court they sought judicial review of the decision of Brent to participate in LAML, on the ground that this was beyond its statutory powers. Harrow and LAML itself participated in these proceedings as interested parties. Secondly, in separate proceedings in the Queen's Bench Division against Brent, Harrow and LAML, the RMP claimed damages on the basis that by entering into insurance contracts the Defendants acted in breach of the Public Contracts Regulations 2006.

5 Burnton LJ (sitting as a judge of the Queen's Bench Division) declared in the judicial review proceedings that the arrangements were beyond the statutory powers of the participating local authorities. In the damages action, he gave judgment in favourt of RMP on liability. The Court of Appeal affirmed both decisions. Your Lordships gave permission to appeal on all issues on 2 August 2010.

6 Since the decision of the Court of Appeal, two developments have substantially narrowed the scope of the dispute. The first was the enactment of Section 34 of the Local Democracy, Economic Development and Construction Act 2009, which expressly empowered local authorities to enter into mutual insurance arrangements of the kind in issue in these proceedings. The section is expected to be brought into force shortly. The second development was the settlement between the Respondents and Brent, which resulted in Brent being permitted to withdraw its appeal to your lordships on 24 August 2010. Accordingly, the judicial review proceedings, which were exclusively concerned with the statutory powers of local authorities under earlier enactments and in which Harrow would have participated as interested parties supporting Brent, are no longer before your lordships. Because of the change in the law, they would in any event have been of limited practical importance.

7 The present appeal is therefore confined to the question of principle arising in the damages action, namely whether the making of contracts of insurance between Harrow and LAML was a breach of the Public Contracts Regulations 2006. This is an issue of considerable, and continuing importance. Until it ceased trading in 1992, most insurance provided to local authorities in the United Kingdom was provided by Municipal Mutual Insurance Ltd, a mutual insurer created on the initiative of a number of local authorities which had been in existence since 1903. Mutual insurance is potentially a source of significant financial savings for local authorities as well as providing other advantages which are not readily available in the commercial insurance market. If the decisions of Burnton LJ and the Court of Appeal in the damages action are allowed to stand, local authorities will in practice find it difficult to avail themselves of the expanded powers conferred on them by Section 34 of the Act of 2009. This is a source of serious concern not only to Harrow but to other local authorities who were insured by LAML or are potentially interested in obtaining mutual insurance on a similar basis. There are currently five other actions for damages pending in the High Court against local authorities who contracted with LAML, which have been stayed pending this appeal.

The Public Contracts Regulations and Directive 2004/18/EC

8 The Public Contracts Regulations 2006 were made under Section 2(2) of the European Communities Act 1972, in order to give effect in the United Kingdom to Directive 2004/18/EC on the Coordination of Procedures for the Award of Public Works Contracts, Public Supply Contracts and Public Service Contracts. The Directive is primarily an internal market measure, directed to the free movement of goods and services within the EU. Its object is to ensure that there is a level playing field between external providers of goods and services to

public authorities. Where public authorities award 'public contracts', they must do so only after fair and open competition and to the one making the best offer. The Directive of 2004 replaced earlier EC legislation on the same subject dating back to 1971, and some of the authorities are concerned with earlier versions. But the differences between them do not affect the present issue.

Teckal

9 Harrow does not claim to have observed the Public Contracts Regulations in its placing of insurance with LAML. The contract was not put out to tender. The question is whether the Regulations apply to the kind of collective provision of services involved in this case.

10 The Directive deals with 'public contracts', which are defined by Article 2(a) as 'contracts for pecuniary interest concluded in writing between one or more economic operators and one or more contracting authorities'.[1] The question what is a 'public contract' for the purpose of the EU public procurement regime is a question of EU law. It is irrelevant how the arrangement is classified by national law: Case C-220/06 *Asociación Profesional de Empresas de Reparto y Manipulado de Correspondencia-v-Administracion del Estado* [2007] ECR I-12175 (paragraph 50).

11 Self-evidently, under English law a contract requires agreement between two distinct juridical persons. The same appears to be true under the domestic law of contract of every other member state. But EU law has developed its own, autonomous concepts for determining whether the parties to an agreement are sufficiently distinct for it to constitute a 'public contract' under the EU procurement regime. This is because it is fundamental to the operation of that regime that it applies only to contracts awarded by public authorities to external contractors. It is not intended to prevent a public authority from procuring the relevant goods or services from its own resources. This qualification gives rise to no particular difficulty where a public authority manufactures goods for its own use or avails itself of services in-house, through its own employees, for example by using its own direct labour department to maintain buildings. The difficulties have arisen in cases where a public authority has procured goods and services from a distinct juridical entity which is closely associated with either with the

---

1 The corresponding definition in Regulation 2(1) the UK Regulations is a 'contract, in writing, for consideration'.

contracting authority or with a consortium of authorities to which it belongs. This is a question of considerable practical importance. In a number of EC member states, including the United Kingdom, local authorities have increasingly sought to obtain efficiency gains by resorting to collective arrangements for the provision of goods and services. These commonly involve a collectively controlled entity serving the needs of the participating authorities. Their status under the Directive, and that of other arrangements between public authorities for the collective provision of goods and services, has given rise to a substantial body of case-law in the European Court of Justice.

12 The leading decision is Case C-107/98 *Teckal Srl v. Comune di Viano* [1999] ECR I-8121. In this case, a consortium of Italian municipalities set up a separate corporate entity under their collective control to provide energy and environmental services to the participating authorities. The Court held that the Directive applied only to contracts between a public authority and a contractor which is 'formally distinct from it *and independent of it in regard to decision-making*.' (paragraph 51). It therefore had no application to a case where, although there is a formal contract with separate legal entity, the public authority

> exercises over the person concerned a control which is similar to that which it exercises over its own departments and, at the same time, that person carries out the essential part of its activities with the controlling local authority or authorities (paragraph 50).

13 The decision is accordingly authority for the proposition that two conditions must be satisfied if a contract is to be taken out of the scope of the Directive. First, the public authority must control the contractor. It is implicit in the fact that the contractor in *Teckal* was a consortium company that this control may be exercised by a public authority jointly with other public authorities. Secondly, the contractor's essential function must be to supply the controlling authority or authorities. In other words, it should not have other customers as well. It is convenient to refer to these as the 'control test' and the 'function test' respectively.

14 It will be seen from the way in which the law has been developed by the European Court since the original decision in *Teckal* that both tests have been subsumed in a broader principle which is essentially founded on the public interest in favour of certain forms of collective procurement by public authorities. This principle is that where a public authority contracts with a contractor (i) which is either itself a public authority or is wholly owned by one or more public authorities, and (ii) whose sole function is the provision of goods and services to public authorities for the performance of their public functions, the contract is treated as tantamount to the provision of

those goods and services 'in-house'. It is not therefore subject to the Directive. The reason is that in those circumstances the authority is not going into the market to satisfy its needs, which is the basic premise on which the Directive operates.

15 For want of a better label, this can conveniently be referred to as the '*Teckal* principle'. It is important to note that it is not to be found in terms anywhere in the language of the Directive. It is a judicial gloss on the language, which reflects (i) the Court's view of the Directive's wider economic purpose, and (ii) its traditional concern with economic substance as opposed to legal form. The effect is that agreements between a public authority and a controlled entity, although satisfying all the requirements of contractual validity imposed by the national law of contract, are nevertheless not to be treated as 'public contracts' for the purposes of the Directive, if the reality is that they are in-house arrangements made by a public authority or a group of public authorities acting collectively for their public purposes.

Does the *Teckal* principle apply to the Regulations of 2006?

16 The Respondents raised this threshhold issue at both stages below. They argued that the *Teckal* principle was a principle of EU law which was not been transposed into English law when effect was given to the Directive. This contention has so far been rejected by all four judges who have considered it. It is submitted that they were right to reject it. There is no reason to suppose that the draftsman of the Regulations intended to exclude the *Teckal* principle, and a number of reasons to believe that he did not.

17 In the first place, while there is no explicit reference to the *Teckal* principle in the Regulations, neither is there any in the Directive on which they are modelled. The omission is on the face of it no more significant in the one context than in the other.

18 Secondly, if the *Teckal* principle be excluded from the Regulations, it must follow that a significant class of contracts which are not required by the Directive to be put out to tender have been subjected to such an obligation as a matter of English law, by way of delegated legislation under the European Communities Act 1972. The power to make regulations under Section 2(2) of that Act is not limited to the literal implementation of Community obligations. Under Section 2(2)(b), it extends also to 'dealing with matters arising out of or related to any such obligation'. However, the imposition of a regime of competitive tenders on a category of transaction which is not the subject of any Community obligation, cannot be brought within the extended power

under Section 2(2)(b). The mere fact that the subject-matter is the same cannot justify so expansive an approach to the power.[2]

19 It is accepted that the United Kingdom would not have been in breach of its obligations under EU law if it had decided to introduce into its domestic law comparable rules about tenders applying to additional categories of contract. There is therefore no *Marleasing* point to be taken in this case. However, the Directive is intended to co-ordinate national procedures for the award of public contracts: see Recital 2. The Regulations, generally speaking, accurately transpose the language of the Directive into English law, with only the minimum of change necessary to fit in with the basic principles and terminology of the United Kingdom's domestic law of contract. The *Teckal* principle is a well established principle of EU law, which reflects the economic objectives of the public procurement regime. The natural inference to be drawn from the draftsman's undoubted intention to transpose the Directive into English law, is that he intended to transpose it together with the accumulated body of judicial exposition of the concepts that were being transposed. No plausible reason has been suggested why the United Kingdom government should have wished to do anything else. If it had, then the Regulations would surely have dealt with the point expressly (as well as by primary legislation).

The control test

20 There are two critical points to make under this head.

(1) The first is that the control test is in reality a test for determining whether the contractor is sufficiently closely identified with the public purposes and functions of the public authority to warrant treating it as if it were a department of the authority which contracts with it, although juridically it is not.

(2) The second is that where the contractor is controlled by a consortium of public authorities, and is sufficiently closely identified with their public purposes and functions, the control test will be satisfied even though it is in the nature of collective control that no single authority can be said to exercise the kind

---

2 There was much discussion in the courts below of Regulation 30(10), which treats as an 'offer' a bid by one part of a public authority to provide goods or services to another part of the same authority in competition with external bidders. This is not, however, an analogous situation. The provision was held to be within the power in *R (Coles) v Portsmouth City Council* (1996) 95 LGR 494. It is, however, a classic example of the proper use of Section 2(2)(b) of the European Communities Act, its purpose being to explain the operation of the public procurement rules in the context of English law, which would not otherwise have regarded an internal bid as an 'offer'.

of control which it would have over one of its own departments. In effect EU law treats the controlling group as if it were a single public authority dealing with a captive contractor.

21 The case-law of the European Court has become progressively clearer with the development of its jurisprudence on public procurement.

(1) The origin of the notion that the control test depends on the identification of the contractor with the public functions of the authorities with which it contracts, is the Court's decision in Case C-26/03 *Stadt Halle and RPL Recyclingpark Lochau GmbH v. Arbeitsgemeinschaft Thermische Restabfall-und Energie verwertingsanlage TREA Leuna* [2005] ECR I-1. This concerned a contract between a German municipality and a 'semi-public company' in which it indirectly held three quarters of the shares, leaving the other quarter in private hands. The issue turned entirely on the relevance of that private shareholding to the application of the control test. At paragraph 48 of its Judgment, the Court recognised that

> a public authority which is a contracting authority has the possibility of performing the tasks conferred on it in the public interest by using its own administrative, technical and other resources, without being obliged to call on outside entities not forming part of its own departments (paragraph 48).

However, it ruled that the mere existence of a substantial private shareholding in the contractor was inconsistent with the control test: paragraph 49. There were two reasons for this. First, the relationship between the public authority and the contractor must be governed exclusively by 'considerations and requirements proper to the pursuit of objectives in the public interest', and this was not possible if private capital was involved: paragraph 50. Secondly, such an arrangement was not consistent with the objective of achieving a level playing field between external contractors, because the preferential status of the contractor in its dealings with the municipality conferred on its private shareholder an advantage over its competitors: paragraph 51. In other words, the fact that the contractor is exclusively engaged in providing goods and services for the performance of the public functions of the public authority and owes no responsibilities to any private commercial interests is a critical factor in determining whether the control test is satisfied.

(2) The Court elaborated the control test in Case C-458/03 *Parking Brixen GmbH v. Gemeinde Brixen and Stadtwerke Brixen AG* [2005]

ECR I-8585. The Court held in this case that the question was whether the concessionaire was

> subject to a control enabling the concession-granting public authority to influence the concessionaire's decision. It must be a case of a power of decisive influence over both strategic objectives and significant decisions (paragraph 65).

Parking Brixen did not involve a consortium. The facts were that the municipality of Brixen in the Italian Tyrol granted a parking concession to a company which it wholly owned. However, the municipality's effective control over its subsidiary was held to be limited by the fact (i) that the latter's objectives included the performance of services on a commercial basis to third parties, and (ii) that its statute provided for the obligatory opening up of its capital to private interests. The Court considered that against this background, the independence from the municipality which the company's constitution conferred upon its Board was inconsistent with the control test. The decision was not based on the mere existence of discretions vested in the company's Board. It is apparent from later decisions that this is in itself unexceptionable. It was based on the need of the Board because of the prospect of private customers and private capital to take account of interests other than the exclusively public interests of the municipality of Brixen.

(3) The *Parking Brixen* case is relevant to the present issue mainly because of the way in which it was subsequently applied in consortium cases. Case C-340/04 *Carbotermo SpA and Consorzio Alisei v. Commune di Busto Arsizio* [2006] ECR I-4137 concerned a contractor of which the commune of Busto Arsizio held 99.98% of the shares, the remaining 0.02% being held by other local authorities. The Court repeated at paragraph 36 of the Judgment the 'decisive influence' test derived from *Parking Brixen*. It then, at paragraph 37, applied that test to a consortium company in the following terms:

> The fact that the contracting authority holds, alone or together with other public authorities, all of the share capital in a successful tenderer tends to indicate, without being decisive, that that contracting authority exercises over that company a control similar to that which it exercises over its own departments, as contemplated in paragraph 50 of *Teckal*.

It was nevertheless held that the control test was not satisfied, mainly because in spite of the commune of Busto Arsizio's possession of almost all the shares, the company's constitution made no provision for it to restrict any of the management discretions vested by the company's constitution in its board: see paragraph 38.[3]

(4) The proportion of the shares held by the relevant local authority in *Carbotermo* was particularly high, but that was not the reason why (but for the absence of a power in the shareholders to direct the board) contracts with the company would in principle have satisfied the control test. This is apparent both from the way that the test was formulated at paragraph 37 of *Carbotermo* and from the subsequent decision of the Court in Case C-295/05 *Asociación Nacional de Empresas Forestales (ASEMFO) v. Transformación Agraria SA (TRAGSA) and Administración del Estado* [2007] ECR I-2999. The position in the latter case was rather similar, except that the contractor (TRAGSA) was 99% owned by the Spanish state and the public authority which contracted with it was one of four local authorities (or 'Autonomous Communities') which together owned only 1% between them. The Court held that the control test was satisfied. Citing the test formulated in paragraph 37 of *Carbotermo*, it rejected the argument that only contracts made or procured by the Spanish state, with its 99% interest, could be said to satisfy the control test: paragraphs 57–59. It is therefore clear that the 'decisive influence' which the relevant authority must have over the decisions of the contractor may be present even if it is exercisable only in conjunction with the other public authorities involved.

(5) In reaching this conclusion the Court in *ASEMFO* attached importance to the fact that the arrangements were wholly directed to the performance of the public authorities' public functions. This was demonstrated in this particular case by the fact that the contractor, TRAGSA, was bound to provide its services to any participating authority on prescribed terms: see paragraph 60. The Court made this point in terms in commenting on this paragraph of the Judgement in another case, decided later in the same year, Case C-220/06 *Asociación Profesional de Empresas de Reparto y Manipulado de Correspondencia y Administración General del Estado* [2007] ECR I-12175. The Court identified as the critical factor in *ASEMFO*, that the contractor's obligation to deal with any of the participating authorities on prescribed terms showed that it was 'an instrument and a technical service of the General State Administration and of the

3 An additional reason is given at paragraph 39, namely that any control which the commune might have had by virtue of its shareholding would have to be exercised through a wholly owned intermediate holding company. This may reflect some principle of Italian company law. To an English lawyer, it seems surprising.

administration of each of the Autonomous Communities concerned' (paragraph 52).

(6) These principles were decisively developed by the Court in Case C-324/07 *Coditel Brabant SA v. Commune d'Uccle and Région de Bruxelles-Capitale* [2008] ECR I-8457, in which judgment was delivered some six months after Burnton LJ's judgment in the damages action. This case concerned a contract let by the Belgian municipality of Uccle to manage its municipal cable television network. It was awarded to a co-operative called Brutélé set up by a consortium of municipalities. Uccle joined the consortium in order to be able to contract with Brutélé. It was held that the contracts of Brutélé with participating municipalities were not 'public contracts' for the purposes of the Directive, for a combination of three reasons. First, membership of the co-operative was open only to municipalities and not to private entities (paragraph 32). Secondly, the governing council charged with the management of Brutélé's business was composed of representatives of the participating municipalities, who were thereby enabled collectively to exert 'decisive influence' over the consortium's affairs (paragraphs 33–4). Thirdly, and critically, although the governing council enjoyed the widest powers of management (paragraph 35), the real question was

> whether Brutélé has thus become market-oriented and gained a degree of independence which would render tenuous the control exercised by the public authorities affiliated to it (paragraph 36).[4]

The Court answered this question No, for reasons which are explained at paragraphs 37–9 of its Judgment. Under Belgian law, inter-municipal co-operatives were forbidden to have a commercial character.

> 38. It seems to be apparent from that Law, which is supplemented by Brutélé's statutes, that Brutélé's object under its statutes is the pursuit of the municipal interest – that being the raison d'être for its creation – and that it does not pursue any interest which is distinct from that of the public authorities affiliated to it.

4 The origin of the expression 'market-oriented' as a touchstone of control appears to be the opinion of Advocate-General Yves Bot in Case C-220/06 *Asociación Profesional de Empresas de Reparto y Manipulado de Correspondencia v Administracion del Estado* [2007] ECR I-12175. Commenting on the fact that the Spanish state postal service had been converted into a limited company with objects extending to the provision of postal services to private entities, he remarked (paragraph AG79) that it thereby 'became market-oriented, which renders the state administration's control tenuous'.

39. Subject to verification of the facts by the referring court, it follows that, despite the extent of the powers conferred on its governing council, Brutélé does not enjoy a degree of independence sufficient to preclude the municipalities which are affiliated to it from exercising over it control similar to that exercised over their own departments.

In other words, it was not the manner or extent of the control which mattered, but its nature, viz that it was exercised for the same exclusively public purposes as the powers which the municipality might have exercised over its own departments.

(7) It was implicit in this reasoning that it was enough to satisfy the control test that the participating public authorities could control Brutélé collectively. This became explicit later in the Judgment, when the Court turned to a further question posed by the national court, namely

> whether... it is necessary, in order for the control which those member authorities exercise over the co-operative to be regarded as similar to that which they exercise over their own departments, for that control to be exercised individually by each of those public authorities or whether it can be exercised jointly by them, decisions being taken by a majority, as the case may be (paragraph 43).

The Court's answer was:

46 According to the case law, the control exercised over the concessionaire by a concession-granting public authority must be similar to that which the authority exercises over its own departments, but not identical in every respect (see, to that effect, *Parking Brixen* at [62]). The control exercised over the concessionaire must be effective, but it is not essential that it be exercised individually.

47 Secondly, where a number of public authorities elect to carry out their public service tasks by having recourse to a municipal concessionaire, it is usually not possible for one of those authorities, unless it has a majority interest in that entity, to exercise decisive control over the decisions of the latter. To require the control exercised by a public authority in such a case to be individual would have the effect of requiring a call for competition in the majority of cases where a public authority seeks to join a grouping composed of other public authorities, such as an inter-municipal co-operative society.

48 Such a result, however, would not be consistent with Community rules on public procurement and concession contracts. Indeed, a public authority has the possibility of performing the public interest tasks conferred on it by using its own administrative, technical and other resources, without being obliged to call on outside entities not forming part of its own departments (*Stadt Halle and RPL Lochau* at [48]).

(8) These principles were taken to their logical conclusion in the Judgment of the Court in Case 480/06 *Commission v. Germany* [2009] ECR I-4747 issued, coincidentally, on the same day as the Judgment of the Court of Appeal in these proceedings. The facts were that four local authorities (or *Landkreise*) entered into a long-term contract for waste treatment services with the cleansing department of the city of Hamburg, without going to tender. The purpose of the contract was to enable the City of Hamburg to build a much larger waste treatment facility than it required for its own purposes, thus generating economies of scale for all five parties. The City of Hamburg was not of course a consortium company, and it was admitted that the four *Landkreise* had no control over it at all: see paragraph 36. The contract was nevertheless held to fall outside the public procurement regime, because (i) the contract was concluded solely by public authorities, no private interests being involved (paragraph 44); (ii) *Coditel Brabant* established that public authorities were entitled without calling on external contractors to perform their public functions by using their own resources, in co-operation with other public authorities if they chose (paragraph 45); and (iii) the *Landkreise* and the City of Hamburg could have achieved their purpose by setting up a joint venture vehicle, and their failure to do so made no real difference (paragraph 46). Summarising the principle at paragraph 47 of their Judgment, the Court said:

> It must be observed though, first, that Community law does not require public authorities to use any particular legal form in order to carry out jointly their public service tasks. Secondly, such cooperation between public authorities does not undermine the principal objective of the Community rules on public procurement, that is, the free movement of services and the opening-up of undistorted competition in all the Member States, where implementation of that cooperation is governed solely by considerations and requirements relating to the pursuit of objectives in the public interest and the principle of equal treatment of the persons concerned, referred to in Directive 92/50, is respected, so that no private undertaking is placed in a

position of advantage vis-à-vis competitors (see, to that effect, *Stadt Halle and RPL Lochau*, paragraphs 50 and 51).

The significance of this case is that it demonstrates that the control test is in fact no more than an indication of the contractor's exclusive identification with the public functions of the authorities with which it contracts. It may be dispensed with in a case where other circumstances sufficiently demonstrate that identification.

The function test

22 This can be dealt with quite shortly. It has been seen from the developing case-law on the control test that the absence of private capital and private customers are important indications that a contractor is not providing goods and services in the course of a commercial business, but doing so under arrangements which are entered into as part of the public functions of the authorities. The relevance of the function test is essentially the same. Unless the contractor 'carries out the essential part of its activities with the controlling local authority or authorities' it cannot readily be identified with the public purposes and functions of the authorities that it contracts with. A contractor which satisfies the control test is therefore likely to satisfy the function test as well.

23 In particular, where the contractor is owned by a consortium of public authorities, the function test will be satisfied if it 'carries out the essential part of its activities, not necessarily with any one of those authorities, but with all of those authorities together': Case C-295/05 *Asociación Nacional de Empresas Forestales (ASEMFO) v. Transformación Agraria SA (TRAGSA) and Administración del Estado* [2007] ECR I-2999 (paragraph 62).

Application to LAML

24 The constitution of LAML and the manner in which it is run, are conventiently summarised in the Witness Statement of Martin Fone, at paras. 35–55, and in the company's Memorandum, Articles and Rules.

25 The salient points are as follows:

(1) LAML is not a company limited by shares. It is wholly owned by its Members and has no external or private capital. It has been pointed out above that this was treated in *Carbotermo* (paragraph 37) as a strong indication of control, albeit not a decisive one.

(2) There is no private involvement in its affairs apart from that represented by the presence of a minority of independent directors on its Board. The latter is a standard feature of good corporate governance which is required by the Financial Services Authority as a condition of the authorisation of an insurer. It has no relevant implications for the purposes which LAML is designed to serve.

(3) The main objects of the company, recorded in its Memorandum, were to insure, by way of mutual insurance, 'Participating Members' and 'Affiliates'. 'Participating Members' meant Members who were insured by LAML. 'Affiliates' comprised specified categories of associated persons or bodies, namely school governors, the management committees of 'Arms Length Managed Associations'[5] and the boards of companies wholly owned by a Participating Member. The subsidiary objects of LAML fall under the terms of the Memorandum to be restricted by reference to the main objects. The evidence is that it has never been contemplated that LAML would insure any one other than Participating Members and Affiliates: Witness Statement of Martin Fone, para. 36. This is not consistent with LAML being treated as 'market-oriented'. The company does not carry on business in the market on a commercial basis, either actually or potentially. It exists only to serve the insurance needs of its Members.

(4) Participating Members are by definition public authorities. Affiliates are parties for whom insurance may be arranged by a Participating Member. They are insured only in their capacity as Affiliates, i.e. in respect of their contribution to the public functions of Participating Members.

(5) LAML is ultimately controlled by its Participating Members, who alone have the right to vote at general meetings. The Board has the normal powers of management: see Articles 2 and 36. But directors are elected by Participating Members. There is a majority of 'Member Directors' representing Participating Members. And no Board meeting is quorate unless a majority of directors present are Member Directors: see Article 39. The Board is also subject to direction by special resolution of the Participating Members in general meeting, which requires a 75% majority.

---

[5] This is a textual error. It means 'Arms Length Management Associations'. They are companies established by local authorities with ministerial consent under housing legislation to manage and improve the authority's public housing stock: see Witness Statement of Martin Fone, para. 38(b).

(6) The insurance that may be offered to Members is governed by the Rules of LAML. Under Rule 16, the company may offer only such insurance as Participating Members have agreed in general meeting may be offered. Correspondingly, LAML is bound to offer insurance within the approved categories on demand to any Member. Article 76 provides that the Rules may be altered by ordinary resolution by the Participating Members in general meeting, subject to the Board having first approved the change.

(7) This means that collectively the Participating Members have a decisive influence over LAML's 'strategic objectives and significant decisions'. That influence is of a different order to that which the shareholders of a commercial company would have over its affairs.

26 It is submitted that in these circumstances, contracts of insurance made with LAML were not 'public contracts' for the purpose of the Directive or the Regulations. They fall within the letter and the purpose of the *Teckal* principle, both as originally stated in that case, and as subsequently developed by the European Court of Justice.

27 It should be noted that all major contracts for the provision of goods and services to LAML from external sources, in particular reinsurance contracts, are put out to tender in accordance with the Public Contracts Regulations 2006.

The judgments below

28 Burnton LJ accepted that the *Teckal* principle applied to the Regulations in the same way as it applied to the Directive (paras. 63–65), and considered that there was no reason why it should not apply to contracts of insurance (paras. 66–68). However, he held that the control test was not satisfied, for reasons which are briefly summarised in paragraphs 78 of his Judgment. These were (i) that the management contract between LAML and Charles Taylor & Co. Ltd. constituted a form of private participation in the company comparable to that which was held in *Stadt Halle* and *Carbotermo* to be inconsistent with the *Teckal* principle; (ii) that Article 11 empowered the Board to terminate on notice the Membership of any Participating Member if it 'in its judgment determines that it is undesirable for a Participating Member to continue to be a Participating Member'; (iii) that Rule 22(1) excluded a Member Director from participating in decisions of the Board about a claim in which that director's sponsoring local authority was interested; and (iv) that the policy forms were typical of those used by commercial insurers and envisaged a relationship between the insured local authority and LAML which in his view was 'inconsistent with *Teckal*.'

29 The Court of Appeal agreed that the *Teckal* principle applied to the Regulations. They also agreed that the control test was not satisfied. Their reasons were as follows:

(1) Pill LJ's reasons appear at paragraphs 126–33 of the Judgment, in particular paragraphs 129–30. He thought that taking an 'overall view' of the arrangements between LAML and its Participating Members, the control exercised by the latter was not equivalent to that which they would have exercised over their own departments: see para. 127. In particular, he drew this conclusion from (i) the directors' power of management and the fact that their duties were owed to the company; (ii) the Board's power under Article 11(b) to terminate the membership of a Participating Member; and (iii) its power to 'establish, collect, manage and redistribute both capital contributions and premiums.'[6]

(2) Moore-Bick LJ's reasons appear at paragraphs 228–37, in particular paragraph 236. He did not agree with Burnton LJ's view that management role of Charles Taylor was inconsistent with the control test. But he agreed that the test was not satisfied, because LAML could not be regarded as 'effectively a department of each of the participating local authorities': para. 237. This was because (i) the Board managed the business of the company and in particular made decisions on capital contributions, reserves, membership and terms of cover; (ii) the directors owed their duties to the company; (iii) Rule 22 made the Board responsible for deciding on claims in the absence of any director sponsored by the insured authority making the claim; and (iv) there was an 'air of unreality' about assimilating insurance through a mutual such as LAML to insurance through a public authorities own departments, because insurance by definition involved a transfer of risk, which was impossible if it was effected through a department.

(3) Hughes LJ agreed with both judgments: para. 255.

30 It is submitted, with respect, that these reasons miss the wood for the trees. They disclose an excessive concentration on the constitutional mechanics of LAML's operation, and an insufficient attention to the constitutional reality, the company's purpose, or the underlying

---

6 This appears be a reference to Article 12 (which empowers the Board to apply receipts of premium to general reserves, regulatory solvency margins, the minimum guarantee fund or general and operating expenses), and Rule 11 (which empowers the Board to determine the application money received by way of premium, supplementary calls and capital contributions).

principle of law. They also suffer from the inability of the Court to take account of the important decision of the European Court of Justice in *Commission v. Germany*, which was issued too late to contribute to their reasoning.

31 The main point, which is made in all of the Judgments below, is that the powers of management were vested in the directors, who owed their duties to LAML. This is not of course disputed. But it is only part of the picture. The following points are made:

(1) The control test does not require total control but only 'decisive influence', and it is not concerned with routine matters of day-to-day management but only with what the European Court described in *Parking Brixen* as 'strategic objectives and significant decisions'. Moreover, the European Court has regard not just to the constitutional possibilities, but to the practical realities: see *Carbotermo* at para. 67(e), and Advocate-General Stix-Hackl in *Parking Brixen* at paragraph AG40.

(2) The Board of LAML was subject to directions by the Participating Members by special resolution, a fact which is brushed aside for no apparent reason in the Judgments below. The power to direct the Board by special resolution is important, and exists precisely to deal with disagreements between the Participating Membership and the Board about 'strategic objectives and significant decisions'. It has been pointed out above that in *Carbotermo*, it was precisely the absence of a right in the shareholders to give such a direction that supplied the main reason why the control test was not satisfied.[7] In a consortium like LAML where voting rights at general meetings are more evenly spread among the membership, the right of direction is exercisable only collectively with other members. But that is common to most consortium companies, and has never been treated by the European Court as being inconsistent with the control test.

(3) The management discretions of the Board may be circumscribed by the Rules, and most of the more significant ones in fact are. The original Rules are annexed to the Articles and were decided by the ten local authorities subscribing to Memorandum and Articles before the company came into existence. Thereafter, alterations to the Rules are determined under Article 76 by ordinary resolution of the Participating Members. Although this

---

7 The statutes 'did not reserve for the Comune of Busto Arsizio any control or specific voting powers for restricting the freedom of action conferred on those Boards of Directors' (paragraph 38).

is subject to the Board's approval of any change, unless a proposed change is in some way improper it is hardly conceivable that the majority of Member Directors would withhold their approval where the Majority of Participating Members wanted the change.

(4) It is not disputed that there remains a significant degree of management discretion vested in the Board. But, as the European Court pointed out in *Coditel,* this is inherent in the whole concept of a consortium company. A distinct juridical entity created and owned by a group of local authorities to serve their common purposes cannot operate without conferring substantial discretions on the management of that entity, subject in the generality of cases to the right of the authorities to direct the management collectively. At paragraph 131 of his Judgment in the Court of Appeal Pill LJ recognised this, but failed to appreciate its significance. He found it

> difficult to see how LAML can operate effectively unless its Board has considerable freedom to manage its insurance business. The nature of the business, and the possibility of different interests of different authorities and affiliates, are antithetic to the necessary local authority control.

It is respectfully submitted that this cannot be correct. Contracts with such bodies have repeatedly been held by the European Court to be capable of falling outside the EU procurement regime. It is, for example, clear from the report of the European Court's decision in *Coditel* that Brutélé, the consortium contractor in that case, was managed by a governing council with very extensive discretions, but that it nevertheless satisfied the control test.

(5) More generally, the reasoning of the courts below on this question assumes a natural conflict of interest between the company and its Participating Members which is characteristic of the relations between a commercial insurer and its policy-holders. But it is not realistic to ignore the mutual character of the company, the fact that its insureds are also its proprietors, the comparatively small size of its membership, both actual and potential, the main objects recorded in the Memorandum, the circumstances and the purpose of its creation by the subscribing local authorities, and the critical role of those authorities in nominating Member Directors to the Board and approving the Rules. While the Board undoubtedly owes its duties to the company, those duties are to further the purposes of the company. The purposes of this company are to serve the insurance needs of the general body of its Participating

Membership. This is not a situation which can readily be compared to the position of the Board of a commercial insurer trading at arms' length with its insureds and primarily concerned to maximise its profits for the benefit of a separate body of proprietors.

32 Turning to what may fairly be called the subsidiary points:

(1) It is difficult to understand why Burnton LJ (alone of the judges below) should have thought that the mere fact of the employment of Charles Taylor & Co. Ltd. to manage the day-to-day business of LAML amounted to a substantial private involvement in its affairs comparable to that which was said to be inconsistent with the control test in *Stadt Halle* and *Carbotermo*. In *Stadt Halle* the relevant private involvement consisted in a 25% shareholding interest in the contractor belonging to a commercial company. That raises a different issue. In *Carbotermo*, there was no private involvement at all, although the statutes of the company provided for the possibility of a private shareholding.[8] None of this has any bearing on the position of Charles Taylor & Co. Ltd. On the face of it, their function was simply to manage the company in accordance with the policy of the Board and the Rules determined by the Members, and was no more significant than the hiring of an individual employee would have been. It is simply one of the many services which a consortium company is likely to have to buy in order to serve its purposes and those of its incorporators.

(2) Any exercise of the powers of the Board to decide upon applications for membership (Rule 4) and to expel a Member on the ground that it has become 'undesirable' (Article 11) is preventable or reversible by the Participating Membership by special resolution, like any other decision of the Board. It may fairly be added that a discretion whether to admit a new member cannot in principle affect the degree of control exercisable over the company by the existing members, and that expulsion is an extreme remedy whose inclusion in the Articles among the powers of the Board does not throw any substantial light on the character of the arrangements in normal circumstances.

---

8 Burnton LJ pointed out that the interposition in *Carbotermo* of a wholly owned holding company between the local authority and the contractor was held to have attenuated the local authority's control. This seems a little unrealistic, but it is in any event a different state of affairs to the employment by the consortium company of a manager.

(3) The exclusion of a Member Director from the consideration by the Board of a claim by his own sponsoring authority was relied upon by Burnton LJ and Moore-Bick LJ, but adds nothing to the ordinary requirement that a director should not participate in a decision on which he has a conflict of interest: cf. Article 34. It does no more than ensure that claims are determined objectively, in the common interests of the general body of Participating Members.

(4) The use by LAML of policy forms including terms in common use by commercial insurers, does not mean that LAML was a commercial insurer or that it was not controlled by its Participating Membership. All that it shows is that the insurance which LAML provided to its Participating Members was a product the main features of which were also obtainable commercially in the market. But that is true of virtually every case in which public authorities procure goods and services in-house, whether they do so individually or collectively.

33 All three members of the Court of Appeal concluded that the arrangements for the collective provision of insurance through LAML failed to satisfy the control test because the control exercised by the Participating Members was not comparable to that which they might have exercised over their own internal departments. It is submitted that the Court of Appeal are taking the analogy with internal departments too literally. The question is not whether each public authority in a consortium was in a position to treat the consortium company like a department of itself (see Moore-Bick LJ at paragraph 237). It is whether the participating authorities collectively are in a position to exercise a degree of control over it which is similar to that which any one of them could exercise over its own departments. The answer to this question in the present case is that individually they could not, but collectively they could. It has been submitted above that the reason why the control test does not require an individual authority to be in a position to control the contractor in the same way as its own internal departments, is that the test as it has been developed by the European Court of Justice is simply a way of determining whether the contractor is sufficiently identified with the public purposes of the participating authorities. If all the other participants in a consortium are also public authorities, then the fact that the fact that they have to share control and exercise it collectively is irrelevant.

34 The extreme example of the over-literal use of the analogy with internal departments is the observation of Moore-Bick LJ that the provision of insurance through LAML was not comparable to its provision 'in-house' because it would have been impossible for the authorities to insure themselves 'in-house'. This misses the point, namely that the analogy with the control exercised by public authorities over their

internal departments is no more than a way of illustrating the principle that a public authority is entitled to perform its functions by the use of its own resources, and to do so collectively if it chooses: see, for example, *Stadt Halle* (paragraph 48), and *Coditel* (paragraph 48). In remarking that a local authority could not have insured itself through an internal department, Moore-Bick LJ is going well beyond the use of an authority's internal departments as a paradigm of control or an illustration of the provision of goods and services from an authority's own resources. He is treating it as a condition for the application of the *Teckal* principle that the relevant goods or services should have been capable of being provided by a department of the public authority in question. There is no basis for this suggestion in the authorities, nor is it warranted by any principle underlying the authorities. Some transactions (like the waste treatment project in *Commission v. Germany*) are only feasible through collective action between local authorities.[9]

35 The decision and reasoning of the Court of Appeal make cooperative arrangements between local authorities difficult or impossible to achieve lawfully for no purpose which can plausibly be related to any recognised legal policy. It is characteristic of such arrangements, not just in the realm of insurance but in many other fields of procurement, that they will involve a significant dilution of the control exercisable by each individual authority. Depending on the nature of the goods or services procured, some degree of discretionary management is also likely to be required. If arrangements on these lines are not permitted, local authorities will have to outsource the provision of these goods and services to third party market operators, which would amount to the enforced privatisation of services provided in the public interest, by way of the public procurement rules. It is submitted that since this result is no part of the purpose of these rules, it is unlikely to be their effect.

Reference

36 A reference has been sought by the Respondents. It is submitted that there is no justification for one. In the first place, the problem with the judgments of the courts below lies not so much in their analysis of EU

---

9 Burnton LJ's analogy with a captive insurer was dismissed by Moore-Bick LJ (para. 237), but it is submitted that there is much to be said for it. If a public authority set up a wholly owned and controlled entity, managed by its employees, to serve as a captive insurer, effectively fronting the risk and reinsuring it into the market, it is plain that the control test would be satisfied. The captive would be as much under the authority's control as an internal department, notwithstanding that an internal department could not have insured its own authority. It would make no difference to the application of the control test if the public authority sufficiently capitalised the captive so that it could reinsure only part of the risk into the market; or if similar arrangements were made by a consortium of public authorities collectively exercising the same control over the captive.

law, but in its application to this particular case. Secondly, the relevant law should not itself be controversial. The European Court of Justice has pronounced on these same questions at least nine times in the last five years.[10] Much of the reasoning in these cases has consisted in repetition, generally in the same language, of general principles stated in the preceding cases. There must come a point when the application of general principle to particular cases is a matter for national courts. It is submitted that in this field, that point has been reached. The present case is *acte clair*.

Conclusion

37 In the Appellant's submission the appeal should be allowed and the order of Burnton LJ set aside, for the following among other:

Reasons

(1) BECAUSE the Participating Members of LAML collectively enjoy decisive influence over its strategic objectives and significant decisions;

(2) BECAUSE LAML carries out all of its activities as an insurer with its Participating Members;

(3) BECAUSE LAML is sufficiently closely identified with the public purposes and functions of its Participating Members to warrant treating it as if it were a department of any Participating Member which contracts with it.

Good practice suggestion

Summarising at the conclusion is often a wasted opportunity where advocates tend to say 'for the above reasons the appeal/application should be allowed' or some such. Make the summary or conclusion stand out, either visually or by the choice of words used. End on an upbeat. Remind the judge of the key to your case, using different words to those used in the substantive argument. Make it simple. And remember that some judges may start at your last paragraph if they are pressed for time. Make it informative.

---

10 Eight of these cases are cited above. In addition, the same questions were considered in a rather special context in C-382/05 *Commission v Italy* [2007] ECR I-6657.

Example P

Supreme Court – Case of the Crown as Respondent by Lord Pannick QC with Louis Mably and James Segan, December 2010 – 38pp.

In R v Chaytor, Morley and Devine the court was concerned with criminal proceedings against members of Parliament for allegations of false accounting contrary to the Theft Act 1968 s.17(1)(b) for allegedly fraudulently submitting claims for the payment of expenses to compensate them for expenditure in carrying out their parliamentary duties. The Supreme Court was asked to determine whether the Bill of Rights 1688, Article 9 ECHR, or the exclusive cognisance of the House of Commons posed any bar to the jurisdiction of the Crown Court to try Members of Parliament on such charges.

In this submission the writer is inviting the court to determine the scope of parliamentary privilege. As a matter of content, it exemplifies an answer the question 'into how much detail should an advocate go when responding to an appeal in which his case has succeeded at first instance and also in the Court of Appeal?' Here counsel recognise that wide public interest in the outcome of the case renders it necessary to provide a detailed history and analysis of the law irrespective of previous success. The argument is built into the narrative.

The appeal failed.

The case is reported at [2010] UKSC 52 Lord Rodger JSC, Lady Hale JSC, Lord Brown JSC, Lord Mance JSC, Lord Collins JSC, Lord Kerr JSC, Lord Clarke JSC); [2010] 3 WLR 1707; [2011] 1 All ER 805; [2011] 1 Cr App R 22; [2011] 1 AC 684; *The Times*, December 6, 2010; Lawtel AC0126580; and in the Court of Appeal at [2010] EWCA Crim 1910 CA (Crim Div) (Lord Judge LCJ, Lord Neuberger of Abbotsbury MR, Sir Anthony May (President QB); [2010] 2 Cr App R 34; *The Times*, August 23, 2010; Lawtel – AC0125731.

RESPONDENT (CROWN)'S CASE

WRITTEN SUBMISSIONS FOR THE CROWN

ON PARLIAMENTARY PRIVILEGE

LISTED FOR 18–19 OCTOBER 2010

Introduction

1 The Crown submits that the Court of Appeal correctly decided that parliamentary privilege does not prevent the prosecution of the Defendants (the Appellants) on charges of false accounting, contrary to section 17(1)(b) of the Theft Act 1968.

2 Each of the Defendants has been committed for trial in the Crown Court. The prosecution alleges that the Defendants made fraudulent expenses claims to the relevant authorities in Parliament. The expenses claims were made by the Defendants as members of the House of Commons. (None of the Defendants stood as a candidate in the 2010 General Election).

3 Elliot Morley is charged with two counts of alleged false accounting:

(1) Count 1: Between 1 April 2004 and 28 February 2006, Mr Morley made use of monthly (save in February, March, April and July 2005) expenses claim forms which each claimed £800 for mortgage interest payments in respect of his house at 9 West Street, Winterton, when in truth the interest element of the payment was far lower, and the remainder of the £800 was capital repayment (which he was not entitled to claim under the relevant rules).

(2) Count 2: Between 1 March 2006 and 30 November 2007, Mr Morley presented a further twenty one monthly expenses claim forms which each claimed £800 for mortgage interest payments in respect of the same house, when in truth he no longer had any mortgage in respect of that property, the mortgage having been paid off in February 2006.

4 David Chaytor is charged with three counts of alleged false accounting:

(1) Count 1: On or about 19 May 2006, Mr Chaytor made use of (a) an expenses claim form, and (b) two purported invoices, for £975 each, for IT services allegedly supplied by Paul France in

February and March 2006, when in fact such services had never been supplied.

(2) Count 2: Between 1 November 2005 and 30 September 2006, Mr Chaytor made use of (a) expenses claim forms in respect of monthly rent of £1,175 per month, which he claimed to be paying in rent to a "Sarah Elizabeth Rastrick", the alleged owner of 152 Hide Tower, Regency Street, London, and (b) a purported tenancy agreement between himself and "Sarah Elizabeth Rastrick", when in fact he was the owner of the premises and was not paying any such rent. Ms Rastrick is Mr Chaytor's daughter and the tenancy agreement, says the prosecution, was a sham.

(3) Count 3: Between 1 September 2007 and 31 January 2008, Mr Chaytor made use of (a) expenses claim forms in respect of £775 per month rent, plus one month's deposit, in respect of the rental of Delph Cottage, 1 Castle Street, Summerseat, and (b) a purported tenancy agreement in respect of that property. The prosecution says that he was not in fact paying any rent. In any event, the landlord was in fact Mr Chaytor's mother and the rules preclude a claim for the cost of leasing property from a family member.

5 James Devine is charged with two counts of alleged false accounting:

(1) Count 1: Between 1 July 2008 and 31 April 2009, Mr Devine made use of (a) five expenses claim forms, and (b) five purported invoices, which appeared to show that he had incurred a liability of £3,240 for cleaning and maintenance services when in fact such services had not been supplied.

(2) Count 2: In March 2009, Mr Devine made use of (a) two expenses claim forms, and (b) two invoices, which appeared to show that he had incurred expenditure of £5,505 in respect of stationery when in fact such stationery was not supplied.

6 Each of the Defendants contends that a criminal trial would be unlawful for two linked reasons:

(1) They rely on Article 9 of the Bill of Rights 1689 which states:

> "Freedom of speech – that the freedom of speech and debates or proceedings in Parliament ought not to be impeached or questioned in any court or place out of Parliament".

(2) They rely on the constitutional principle (of which Article 9 is one element) of the separation of powers between the courts and Parliament, and the exclusive jurisdiction of Parliament to regulate its own affairs.

7 The Crown Court ordered Preparatory Hearings under section 29 of the Criminal Procedure and Investigations Act 1996 to consider the issues identified in paragraph 6 above.

8 Mr Justice Saunders held in the Crown Court, and the Court of Appeal (Lord Judge CJ, Lord Neuberger MR and Sir Anthony May, the President of the Queen's Bench Division) agreed, and the Crown contends, that parliamentary privilege does not prevent a criminal prosecution in the present context:

(1) The criminal proceedings do not involve a challenge to the content of the scheme adopted by the House of Commons for expenses and allowances, or indeed to any decision made by Parliament in respect of expenses and allowances.

(2) Nor do the criminal proceedings impugn the conduct of a Member of Parliament in speaking in Parliament, or contributing to the work of a Committee.

(3) The case is concerned rather with impugning administrative acts by the Defendants in submitting a claim form for expenses. The claiming of such expenses and allowances by submitting a form is not of itself the performance of a core parliamentary function.

(4) There is no authority which suggests that an alleged criminal act committed by an MP is covered by privilege because it is associated with the performance of parliamentary functions, and any such conclusion would conflict with the need (recognised by high judicial authority) to restrict the scope of parliamentary privilege to the essential functions of MPs for good reasons of public policy.

9 Since the occurrence of the alleged acts which form the basis of these prosecutions, Parliament has enacted the Parliamentary Standards Act 2009 which confers on an independent body (IPSA) the function of deciding on the expenses and allowances for MPs (though not for Peers). The submissions set out below do not address the new scheme in relation to expenses.

The role of the court

10 It is for the Court to determine the proper scope of parliamentary privilege. In *Pepper v Hart* [1993] AC 593, 624D, Lord Browne-Wilkinson (for the Appellate Committee of the House of Lords) noted:

> "The Attorney-General, while submitting that such use of parliamentary material would breach Article 9, accepted that it was for the courts to determine the legal meaning and effect of Article 9".

11 But in determining the proper scope of parliamentary privilege, the courts will consider very carefully the position adopted by Parliament on this subject. As Lord Browne-Wilkinson stated for the Judicial Committee of the Privy Council in *Prebble v Television New Zealand Limited* [1995] 1 AC 321, 332D,

> "The courts and Parliament are both astute to recognise their respective constitutional roles".

No general immunity for MPs and Peers

12 MPs are not immune from proceedings, civil or criminal, by reason of their status. See *Bradlaugh v Gossett* (1884) 12 QBD 271, 283 per Stephen J:

> "I know of no authority for the proposition that an ordinary crime committed in the House of Commons would be withdrawn from the ordinary course of criminal justice".

As the Court of Appeal stated in its Judgment at paragraph 31:

> "This statement of principle has never been challenged in any subsequent authority. Equally it has never been suggested that Stephen J was limiting his observations to crimes committed within the House by non-members, or that his observations in relation to members of the House were limited to offences where unlawful force had been used".

13 So an MP would enjoy no immunity if charged with assault of another MP in his office as revenge for the latter's speech or vote, or driving dangerously to get to Parliament in time to speak or vote, even though such activities may be said to be connected to Parliamentary functions. The Court of Appeal was correctly concerned in the present case to identify whether the acts alleged against the Defendants were "ordinary crimes" (and so not protected by privilege) or were extraordinary in the sense that they were so closely connected to the discharge of core Parliamentary functions that privilege applies. The Defendants' criticism of the approach of the Court of Appeal (at paragraphs 13–19 of their Written Submissions) is therefore misguided.

14 The Joint Committee on Parliamentary Privilege (chaired by Lord Nicholls of Birkenhead) referred in its report (Session 1998–1999, HL Paper 43-I, HC 214-I) at paragraph 18 to the statement by the House of Commons Committee of Privileges in 1831 that it was now "established generally that privilege is not claimable for any indictable offence".

Parliamentary privilege for the benefit of Parliament

15 Parliamentary privilege exists for the benefit of Parliament as a whole, and not for the benefit of individual MPs and Peers. See Lord Browne-

Wilkinson for the Appellate Committee of the House of Lords in *Hamilton v Al Fayed* [2001] 1 AC 395, 408C–D:

> "All parliamentary privilege exists for the better discharge of the function of Parliament as a whole and belongs to Parliament as a whole".

16 As noted by the Court of Appeal at paragraphs 49–50 and 70–73 of its Judgment and by Mr Justice Saunders at paragraph 21 of his Judgment, Parliament has failed positively to assert any privilege in the context of allegedly dishonest expenses claims. Moreover, Parliament, through its relevant Committees, has expressly stated that it does not wish to assert privilege in respect of these matters:

(1) See House of Commons Members Estimate Committee Review of Past ACA Payments (First Report of Session 2009–10) at p.1, paragraphs 1–2 on the terms of reference for Sir Thomas Legg's review, and at p.5 in paragraph 8 and p.14 in paragraph 43 for the report of Sir Thomas Legg.

(2) This is consistent with the approach adopted in February 2003 by the then Parliamentary Commissioner for Standards, Sir Philip Mawer, in 2003 and adopted by the House of Commons Committee on Standards and Privileges. Sir Philip stated (in paragraph 46 of the Appendix to the Third Report of the House of Commons Committee on Standards and Privileges, 2003):

> "The decision whether Mr Trend or any other Member who may be shown to have wrongly claimed parliamentary allowances should face a criminal prosecution is one for the police and the prosecuting authorities, not for me. ... However, the point that needs to be made here is that claiming an allowance is not a proceeding in Parliament and the provisions of parliamentary privilege do not apply. Members of Parliament are no less subject to the criminal law in this respect than anyone else. They must have its provisions in mind at all times like anyone else, and decisions about whether it should be invoked against them must be taken applying the same tests as would be applied to any other citizen".

The House of Commons Committee did not dissent from that view.

(3) Indeed both Houses of Parliament have stated as a general principle that their disciplinary jurisdiction is postponed pending the exhaustion of the criminal jurisdiction of the courts:

(a) See the Eighth Report of the House of Commons Committee on Standards and Privileges, Session 2007–08, at pp.3 and 4–5.

(b) See also paragraphs 1–3 of the Report of the House of Lords' Committee for Privileges into the Conduct of Lord Clarke of Hampstead (4th Report of Session 2009–10).

(4) All of this is also consistent with the view expressed by the Clerk of the House of Commons that parliamentary privilege does not apply in the present context. See the Memorandum from the Clerk of the House of Commons dated 9 September 2009:

> "Although I accept that the ACA scheme arises from Resolutions of the House, the proposition that all actions or claims under it are proceedings, seems to me to be unsustainable".

Article 9 and the broader principle of separation of powers

17 Although the Defendants rely separately on Article 9 and on the broader constitutional principle of parliamentary privilege of which it is part, much of the legal argument is relevant to both aspects of the case. Nevertheless, it may assist the Court for these Written Submissions to consider first Article 9 and then the broader principle.

Article 9 of the Bill of Rights

18 The central question in relation to Article 9 of the Bill of Rights is whether the criminal prosecutions of the Defendants impugn or question "proceedings in Parliament".

19 The Crown submits that only core parliamentary activities justify the protection of privilege under Article 9:

(1) See *Attorney-General of Ceylon v de Livera* [1963] AC 103, 120 (Viscount Radcliffe for the Judicial Committee of the Privy Council):

> "... there is no doubt that the proper meaning of the words 'proceedings in Parliament' is influenced by the context in which they appear in article 9 of the Bill of Rights ... [G]iven the proper anxiety of the House to confine its own or its members' privileges to the minimum infringement of the liberties of others, it is important to see that those privileges do not cover activities that are not squarely within a member's true function".

Viscount Radcliffe referred at p.121 to the

> "reluctance to treat a member's privilege as going beyond anything that is essential ...".

(2) The judgment of Viscount Radcliffe was approved in *Buchanan v Jennings* [2004] UKPC 36, [2005] 1 AC 115, 123F–124A, paragraph 9, where Lord Bingham of Cornhill (for the Judicial Committee of the Privy Council) also referred with approval to the observations of the Joint Committee on Parliamentary Privilege (chaired by Lord Nicholls of Birkenhead) in its report (Session 1998–1999, HL Paper 43-I, HC 214-I) at p.1 (executive summary):

> "This legal immunity is comprehensive and absolute. Article 9 should therefore be confined to activities justifying such a high degree of protection, and its boundaries should be clear".

At paragraph 110 of its Report, the Joint Committee added:

> "Article 9 provides an altogether exceptional degree of protection, as discussed above [that is paragraph 38, where the Committee emphasised that 'the immunity is also absolute; it is not excluded by the presence of malice or fraudulent purpose']. In principle, this exceptional protection should remain confined to the core activities of Parliament, unless a pressing need is shown for an extension".

See also paragraphs 241–242 in relation to the right of each House to administer its internal affairs within its precincts:

> "241 Here, as elsewhere, the purpose of Parliamentary privilege is to ensure that Parliament can discharge its functions as a legislative and deliberate assembly without let or hindrance. This heading of privilege best serves Parliament if not carried to extreme lengths.
> 242 One point is clear: the right is intended to protect each *House* in respect of the conduct of *its* internal affairs. This principle does not embrace and protect activities of *individuals*, whether members or non-members, simply because they take place within the precincts of Parliament. ...".

See also the Report at paragraph 247:

> "the dividing line between privileged and non-privileged activities of each House is not easy to define".

The Joint Committee suggested, at paragraph 247, that

> "the privileged areas must be *so closely and directly connected with proceedings in Parliament that intervention by the courts would be inconsistent with Parliament's sovereignty as a legislative and deliberative assembly*" [emphasis added].

The Joint Committee added, at paragraph 248 that

> "The boundary is not tidy",

and that the resolutions and orders governing members' salaries

> "are proceedings in Parliament, but their implementation is not".

20 There are strong reasons why parliamentary privilege should be confined to core parliamentary activities:

(1) When the court decides on the scope of parliamentary privilege, a number of public interests are relevant.

(2) There are the interests to which the Defendants have drawn attention, in particular the need to ensure that the functions of Parliament are not impeded.

(3) But there is also the public policy of ensuring that, where immunity is not necessary to enable Parliament to perform its functions, a person does not – by reason of his status as an MP – enjoy a special protection against prosecution. See the general principle to which Lord Bingham of Cornhill drew attention (for the Judicial Committee of the Privy Council) in *Sharma v Browne-Antoine* [2006] UKPC 57, [2007] 1 WLR 780, 786H–787A:

> "The rule of law requires that, subject to any immunity or exemption provided by law, the criminal law of the land should apply to all alike. A person is not to be singled out for adverse treatment because he or she holds a high and dignified office of state, but nor can the holding of such an office excuse conduct which would lead to the prosecution of one not holding such an office. The maintenance of public confidence in the administration of justice requires that it be, and be seen to be, even-handed".

See the Judgment of the Court of Appeal at paragraph 42.

(4) Also of importance is that for the courts to recognise too broad a scope for parliamentary privilege would damage the reputation of Parliament. See *Wellesley v The Duke of Beaufort* (1831) 2 Russell & Mylne 639, 659, where Lord Chancellor Brougham explained

> "... how incumbent it is upon the Courts of law to defend their high and sacred duty of guarding the lives, the liberties, and the properties of the subject, and protecting the

> respectability and the very existence of the Houses of Parliament themselves, against wild and extravagant, and groundless, and inconsistent notions of privilege".

The Crown does not suggest that the Defendants are making "wild and extravagant" claims to privilege. But the Crown does respectfully suggest that this Court should have regard, in defining the scope of privilege, to the need to ensure that privilege is confined in a reasonable and proportionate manner so as to avoid damaging the reputation of Parliament. No doubt Parliament has this well in mind when not asserting privilege in relation to allegations of dishonest claims for expenses and in relation to crime generally (see paragraph 16 above).

(5) Another important public interest is to ensure the protection of the constitutional principle of the separation of powers under which it is the criminal courts that are established specifically to consider allegations that persons, including MPs, have committed criminal offences, and to ensure that such allegations are fairly tried by a proper procedure before independent and impartial judges. Allegations of serious crime should normally be considered in the courts of law, and not in a Parliament of politicians. To leave Parliament to consider such allegations would conflict with the separation of powers and should be restricted to cases which have a very close connection with the core functions of Parliament. No doubt Parliament also has this well in mind when not asserting privilege in relation to allegations of dishonest claims for expenses and in relation to crime generally (see paragraph 16 above).

(6) The separation of powers was a principle to which Mr Justice Buckley referred in *R v Greenaway* (1992), reported in (1998) *Public Law* 356, when ruling (in the Central Criminal Court) that parliamentary privilege under Article 9 does not prevent the prosecution of an MP for allegedly accepting a bribe to influence him in his conduct as a member of the House of Commons. Mr Justice Buckley stated (at p.363):

> "That a Member of Parliament against whom there is a prima facie case of corruption should be immune from prosecution in the courts of law is to my mind an unacceptable proposition at the present time. I do not believe it to be the law. The Committee of Privileges is not well equipped to conduct an enquiry into such a case, nor is it an appropriate or experienced body to pass sentence. Unless it is to be assumed that it would be prejudiced in his favour, I cannot see that it would be in the Member's own interest for the

> matter to be dealt with by the Committee. The courts and legislature have over the years built up a formidable body of law and codes of practice to achieve fair treatment of suspects and persons ultimately charged and brought to trial. Again, unless it is to be assumed that his peers would lean in his favour, why should a Member be deprived of a jury and an experienced judge to consider his guilt or innocence and, if appropriate, sentence ? Why should the public be similarly deprived ?"

Mr Justice Buckley also regarded the principle of equality (see (3) above) as relevant: see p.361.

21 The Crown's contention that Article 9 should be confined to core parliamentary activities is also supported by the purpose of Article 9:

(1) Lord Browne-Wilkinson stated for the Appellate Committee of the House of Lords in *Pepper v Hart* [1993] AC 593, 638D–E that

> "Article 9 is a provision of the highest constitutional importance and should not be narrowly construed".

However, it is essential to set this statement in the context of the argument which Lord Browne-Wilkinson was considering and rejecting, and the purpose of Article 9 which he identified, at p.638C–G:

> "... The submission was that the use of Hansard for the purpose of construing an Act would constitute a 'questioning' of the freedom of speech or debate. The process, it is said, would involve an investigation of what the Minister meant by the words he used and would inhibit the Minister in what he says by attaching legislative effect to his words. This, it was submitted, constituted 'questioning' the freedom of speech or debate.
>
> Article 9 is a provision of the highest constitutional importance and should not be narrowly construed. It ensures the ability of democratically elected Members of Parliament to discuss what they will (freedom of debate) and to say what they will (freedom of speech). But even given a generous approach to this construction, I find it impossible to attach the breadth of meaning to the word 'question' which the Attorney-General urges. ...
>
> In my judgment, the plain meaning of article 9, viewed against the historical background in which it was enacted,

was to ensure that Members of Parliament were not subjected to any penalty, civil or criminal for what they said and were able, contrary to the previous assertions of the Stuart monarchy, to discuss what they, as opposed to the monarch, chose to have discussed".

(2) The passage, read as a whole, therefore shows that Lord Browne-Wilkinson was considering Article 9 in the context of its core purpose, that is, the protection of the freedom of speech and debate in Parliament. It is readily comprehensible that the words "impeached or questioned" should not be "narrowly construed" in such a context. However, Lord Browne-Wilkinson was not considering in *Pepper v Hart* the question of which statements or acts would constitute "proceedings in Parliament", since it was clear, and not in dispute, that a statement by a Minister in Parliament (the subject of *Pepper v Hart*) was such a proceeding.

(3) Lord Browne-Wilkinson's speech, therefore, does not offer any support for the proposition that the words "proceedings in Parliament" ought in themselves to be widely construed so as to protect individual acts of MPs which bear little or no relationship to the freedom of speech of Parliament or its decision-making process. Otherwise, what Lord Browne-Wilkinson said would be inconsistent with *Buchanan v Jennings*. And it would also be inconsistent with his judgment in *Prebble v Television New Zealand Limited* [1995] 1 AC 321, 334A–C which again emphasised that Article 9 was designed to protect free speech in Parliament.

22 The Crown recognises that decisions made by the House of Commons, or by the Speaker on behalf of the House of Commons, or by a Committee of the House of Commons, as to parliamentary issues may be covered by Article 9 or by the broader concept of parliamentary privilege. The Crown does not dispute the judgment of Mr Justice Kerr in *Re McGuinness's Application* [1997] NI 359, 365–366 that:

> "In extending the restrictions on facilities and services the Speaker was thus acting on behalf of the House. ... [H]er decision to introduce these restrictions was a proceeding in Parliament".

The Crown considers that the same must be true in relation to expenses: the Resolutions and Committee decisions which constitute and govern the expenses systems of the House of Commons are "proceedings in Parliament" for the purposes of Article 9. If an MP (or a third party) were to challenge the content of the Resolutions by way of judicial review, the court would refuse jurisdiction.

23 Parliamentary privilege applies not just to decisions made by the House of Commons or the House of Lords, or by a Committee or by the Speaker. It also applies to some individual acts of an MP, for example speaking in Parliament or contributing to the work of a Committee. But that is because the MP is thereby performing the essential functions of an MP and so directly contributing to the ability of the House to perform its functions.

24 However, the submission of an expenses form – which is the act in issue in the criminal proceedings – is not the performance of any essential parliamentary function of an MP, having regard to the need to confine privilege (for the reasons set out in paragraphs 12–21 above):

(1) The Crown accepts that submitting an expenses form is linked to the performance of core parliamentary functions in that the terms of the expenses schemes have been determined by Parliament, the schemes require the submission of a claim form, Parliament has accepted that the payment of expenses and allowances will assist the MP to perform his core parliamentary functions, and the expenses claim arises out of the performance of parliamentary functions in the past.

(2) But to claim expenses is not of itself to perform a core parliamentary function. It is an administrative act carried out to obtain funds which may better equip the MP then to carry out his or her parliamentary functions.

(3) Moreover, to claim expenses falls well outside the scope of the freedom of speech justification for Article 9 summarised by Lord Browne-Wilkinson for the Appellate Committee in *Pepper v Hart* (see paragraph 21 above).

(4) The submission of the claim form for expenses is an act primarily concerned with the claiming of a sum of money for the personal benefit of the MP himself. Parliamentary privilege exists for the benefit of Parliament, not for the benefit of individual MPs: see paragraph 15 above.

(5) Parliament has failed to assert privilege in relation to dishonest expenses claims, and has recognised that the criminal process may properly be applied in respect of allegations of dishonesty in this context: see paragraph 16 above.

25 Therefore the submission of a form claiming expenses is not covered by parliamentary privilege. See paragraph 76 of the Judgment of the Court of Appeal. If acts done by a Member of Parliament benefit from parliamentary privilege – even though they are not the performance of

core Parliamentary functions, far less covered by the free speech justification for Article 9 – then an MP would be able to claim privilege for driving dangerously around Parliament Square in order to arrive in time to speak or vote in Parliament, or dishonestly using someone else's chequebook to repay sums which Sir Thomas Legg ordered to be paid. If (as the Defendants contend) the expenses scheme is part of parliamentary proceedings, and so privilege applies, what if an MP is in dispute with the Fees Office, who refuse a claim for £100 which he regards as properly made, and so he assaults the member of staff in the Fees Office by pushing him aside so he can help himself to the sum from the Petty Cash box. Is the MP immune from prosecution ? What if he racially abuses and threatens a member of the Fees Office who refuses to approve his claim ? As the Court of Appeal stated at paragraph 77 of its Judgment, "it would be an insult to Parliament to dignify" criminal conduct "with some adjective or epithet which implied" that it is not "an ordinary crime" subject to the criminal law jurisdiction of the courts (see Stephen J at paragraph 12 above) "or excuse it on the basis of parliamentary privilege".

26 The Defendants have contended that parliamentary privilege does apply to decisions taken by officials of Parliament in the administration of the Resolutions.

27 At paragraph 19(ii) of his Judgment, Mr Justice Saunders doubted whether the Crown was correct to concede before him that parliamentary privilege would apply to decisions by the Fees Office on expenses' claims. In the light of those observations, the Crown reconsidered its position and withdrew the concession in the Court of Appeal. (Of course no such concession could bind the Court in any event).

28 The Joint Committee on Parliamentary Privilege (chaired by Lord Nicholls of Birkenhead) stated in its report (Session 1998–1999, HL Paper 43-I, HC 214-I) at paragraph 247 that

> "the dividing line between privileged and non-privileged activities of each House is not easy to define".

The Joint Committee suggested, at paragraph 247, that

> "the privileged areas must be so closely and directly connected with proceedings in Parliament that intervention by the courts would be inconsistent with parliament's sovereignty as a legislative and deliberative assembly".

The Joint Committee added, at paragraph 248 that

> "The boundary is not tidy",

and that the resolutions and orders governing members' salaries

> "are proceedings in Parliament, but their implementation is not".

29 The Crown submits as follows:

(1) Implementation of the Resolutions by the Fees Office is an administrative act outside the core functions of Parliament and so not covered by parliamentary privilege. If (before the creation of IPSA) a member of staff responsible for paying MPs' salaries helped themselves to some of the funds, it could not sensibly be suggested that they would enjoy an immunity from criminal prosecution. On 31 August 2010, a former House of Commons official, Andrew Gibson, pleaded guilty at Southwark Crown Court to charges of fraud in that he was involved in the submission of expenses claims forms that contained forged signatures of former MPs. There was no suggestion that parliamentary privilege applied and he could only be tried by the House of Commons.

(2) In any event, it is not necessary to the Crown's case on this appeal that the Court should determine whether parliamentary privilege applies to the decisions of the Fees Office. Whatever the true analysis of the status of a decision of the Fees Office, it is to be contrasted with the act which is in issue in the present proceedings which is the act of an individual MP to submit a claim form. If a decision of the Fees Office enjoys parliamentary privilege, it is because it is a decision made on behalf of the House. See the Judgment of the Court of Appeal at paragraph 78.

30 The Defendants emphasise (paragraphs 19, 42–43 and 62 of their Written Submissions) that the Joint Committee on Parliamentary Privilege recognised at paragraphs 119–124 of its Report that the Scheme for the Registration of Members' Interests is, or should be, covered by privilege. The Crown observes:

(1) The Register of Interests is very closely connected with the free speech rationale of Article 9: the purpose of the Register is to enable people to know whether an MP has a conflict of interest when speaking in Parliament or otherwise contributing to the work of Parliament.

(2) The Committee did not consider the width of the privilege and whether it would apply to criminal conduct. Indeed, it is not easy to envisage criminal conduct in relation to the Register.

31 The Defendants rely (paragraphs 24–25 of their Written Submissions) on the fact that the Members Estimate Committee of the House of Commons took the view that because parliamentary privilege applies, MPs could not appeal to the courts against the decisions of Sir Thomas Legg on repayments of expenses and so should have an opportunity to appeal to Sir Paul Kennedy. But the reason why the Members Estimate Committee so concluded was because

(1) The Committee had agreed to recommend to the House of Commons that any overpayments identified by Sir Thomas Legg should be repaid by MPs. So there would be a decision of the House of Commons itself on this matter.

(2) No court would interfere with a decision of the House of Commons, approving the decision of a Committee of the House, requiring MPs to repay sums of money wrongly paid as expenses. Such a matter is plainly covered by parliamentary privilege.

32 The Defendants rely (paragraph 57 of their Written Submissions) on the fact that the Clerk to the House of Commons Members Estimate Committee regarded decisions on whether to pay Members a resettlement grant at the end of their tenure as parliamentary proceedings covered by privilege. But, as the letter from the Clerk to the Committee explained, parliamentary privilege applies because the relevant decision (to suspend the payment of the resettlement grant) was taken by the Committee and implemented by the Speaker on behalf of the House.

33 The Defendants rely on section 13 of the Defamation Act 1996. The Crown observes:

(1) This is not a statutory definition of parliamentary privilege for general purposes. It is confined to defamation proceedings.

(2) Since the purpose of section 13 is to allow a person to waive privilege in so far as his conduct is in issue in defamation proceedings, and so assists him to seek to clear his own name, it is not surprising that Parliament adopted a broad approach in section 13(5) to the scope of proceedings in Parliament.

(3) Section 13(5) has to be read in the context of section 13(4), which refers to

> "... any enactment or rule of law *so far as* it protects a person ... from legal liability for words spoken or things done in the course of, or for the purposes of or incidental to, any proceedings in Parliament" [emphasis added].

See the Judgment of the Court of Appeal at paragraph 17.

(4) In any event, Parliament cannot have intended that any document sent by a person to a Parliamentary Committee is covered by privilege, even if, for example, it contains a threat to kill.

34 The Defendants also rely (paragraphs 45–49 of their Written Submissions) on the test suggested by the Joint Committee on Parliamentary Privilege at paragraph 129 of its Report (as well as earlier suggested definitions). But this was a proposal for a definition "on the following lines", formulated in order to encourage discussion and debate which would then have focused on more specific circumstances. The proposal was never enacted, and indeed never subjected to scrutiny through the Parliamentary process as to the content of the drafting. It was not addressing the issues in the present case. Moreover, the Joint Committee was itself concerned to ensure that parliamentary privilege was confined in its scope (see paragraph 19(2) above). It would be very surprising if the Joint Committee were to have intended privilege to apply in the circumstances of this case.

35 The Defendants suggest (paragraph 61 of their Written Submissions) that parliamentary privilege would apply if the circumstances were different, involving an oral statement on the floor of the House of Commons, or oral or written statements to a Committee of the House. The difficulty with that submission, as the Court of Appeal noted at paragraphs 74–75 of its Judgment, is that this is not the means by which claims for expenses are made:

> "A claim for expenses is not submitted to any other member of the House, nor even to the Speaker ... or to his ... office: it is submitted to an official in the Fees Office, and although that official is appointed by, and is an agent of, the House, he is not officiating in connection with the business carried on within the Chamber or within a committee. he is merely carrying out an administrative task, albeit one mandated by the relevant House, and one subject to the detailed rules approved by that House".

Were the circumstances different, then different questions would arise as to the application of Article 9.

36 The Crown's argument, drawing a distinction between the conduct of the House of Commons and the impugned conduct of an MP or Peer which is not the performance of a core parliamentary function, is supported by the judgment of Lord Woolf MR for the Court of Appeal in *R v Parliamentary Commissioner for Standards ex parte Al Fayed* [1998] 1 WLR 669. The Court of Appeal held that decisions by the Parliamentary Commissioner for Standards in relation to allegations that an MP had

acted in a corrupt manner were not subject to judicial review because the Parliamentary Commissioner is concerned with the workings of Parliament. Lord Woolf MR said at pp.672H–673C:

> "[counsel] rightly says that parliamentary privilege would not prevent the courts investigating issues such as whether or not a Member of Parliament has committed a criminal offence, or whether a Member of Parliament has made a statement outside the House of Parliament which it is alleged is defamatory. He submits that, consistent with this, the sort of complaint which the applicant makes in this case is not in relation to an activity in respect of which the member of Parliament would necessarily have any form of parliamentary immunity.
>
> As to those arguments of [counsel], it seems to me that we are not concerned here with what the Member of Parliament was doing, but the nature of the role of the Parliamentary Commissioner for Standards. He was conducting his activities under the supervision of the relevant committee, because the activity which is complained of could have an effect on the workings of Parliament. It is therefore directly related to what happens in Parliament".

Lord Woolf MR was accepting that there is a distinction between an attempt to challenge a decision made by the House authorities (which included the Parliamentary Commissioner) – matters which are covered by privilege – and the conduct of an individual MP (alleged corruption in the performance of his functions as an MP) – which was not covered by privilege.

37 For all these reasons, Article 9 of the Bill of Rights does not assist the Defendants in the circumstances of these prosecutions.

Separation of Powers and the Exclusive Jurisdiction of Parliament to Regulate its own Affairs

38 Article 9 is part of a wider principle of separation of powers, one aspect of which is the exclusive jurisdiction of Parliament to regulate its own affairs. See Lord Browne-Wilkinson for the Judicial Committee of the Privy Council in *Prebble v Television New Zealand Limited* [1995] 1 AC 321, 332C–D:

> "In addition to Article 9 itself, there is a long line of authority which supports a wider principle, of which Article 9 is merely one manifestation, viz. that the courts and Parliament are both astute to recognise their respective constitutional roles. So far as the courts are concerned they will not allow any challenge to be made to what is said or done within the walls of Parliament in performance of its legislative functions and protection of its established privileges ...".

The case concerned statements made in the Houses of Parliament during Parliamentary debates.

39 The cases which identify and protect the general principle of parliamentary privilege are concerned with

(1) Decisions of Parliament, such as *Bradlaugh v Gossett* (1884) 12 QBD 271 where a resolution of the House of Commons which prevented an MP from taking the oath, and hence contributing to parliamentary debate, was held to be beyond the jurisdiction of the Courts, even if it contravened the Parliamentary Oaths Act 1866; and *Burdett v Abbot* (1811) 14 East 1, 104 ER 501 (a decision by Parliament to arrest an MP); and decisions by the Speaker on behalf of Parliament, such as *Re McGuinness's Application* [1997] NI 359.

(2) Contributions by MPs and Peers to debates in Parliament (which are also covered by the free speech rationale and indeed the language of Article 9).

40 As with Article 9, so with the general concept of parliamentary privilege it is important to ensure that only core parliamentary activities are protected for all the reasons, supported by all the authorities, referred to in paragraphs 12–36 above.

41 Parliamentary privilege is not breached by the prosecution in the present case:

(1) The court is not being asked to entertain a challenge to any decision by Parliament (or the Speaker) or to the performance of the core functions of an MP such as speaking in Parliament or contributing to the work of a Parliamentary Committee. What is challenged in the present case is the administrative act of the individual MPs in claiming expenses.

(2) The Defendants emphasise that Parliament itself could exercise a jurisdiction over them in relation to the alleged wrongdoing. They rely on the statement by Lord Coleridge CJ in *Bradlaugh v Gossett* (1884) 12 QBD 271, at 275:

> "The jurisdiction of the Houses over their own members, their right to impose discipline within their walls, is absolute and exclusive".

This proves too much. If an MP were to steal from the office of a colleague, or assault him, in the Palace of Westminster, Parliament could exercise a disciplinary jurisdiction. But the Defendants themselves accept (at paragraph 5 of their Written Submissions) that this does not prevent a criminal prosecution in such a case. To define parliamentary privilege by reference to the scope of that disciplinary jurisdiction would plainly conflict with, and substantially undermine, the principles set out in paragraphs 12–14 and 20 above – that MPs are subject to the jurisdiction of the criminal courts and that equality before the law is of fundamental importance.

(3) For the Defendants to contend that parliamentary privilege is breached by their prosecution, "as a matter of comity or mutual respect as between the ordinary courts and Parliament" (Defendants' Written Submissions at paragraph 81), is especially difficult when Parliament has declined to assert immunity and has been content for the criminal process to take its course, and when both Houses of Parliament have adopted the general principle that their disciplinary jurisdiction is secondary to the criminal jurisdiction of the courts in that the disciplinary jurisdiction will not be exercised unless and until criminal proceedings have been exhausted (see paragraph 16 above).

(4) Moreover, to rely on the constitutional principle of separation of powers to preclude criminal prosecutions in the present circumstances would be to ignore the fact that an important aspect of the separation of powers is that the criminal courts are established to consider allegations that persons, including MPs, have committed criminal offences, and to ensure that such allegations are fairly tried by a proper procedure before independent and impartial judges. See paragraph 20(5) and (6) above.

42 The Defendants rely (paragraphs 89–92 of their Written Submissions) on the decision of Mr Justice Morland in the Crown Court in the *Huckfield* case, concerning a prosecution of a former MEP for allegedly making dishonest expenses claims to the European Parliament. In *R v Manchester Crown Court ex parte DPP* [1993] 1 WLR 693, the Divisional Court (Leggatt LJ and Pill J) overruled the decision of Mr Justice Morland that the prosecution would infringe the sovereignty of the European Parliament because the court would need to interpret the rules of the European Parliament relating to the payment of expenses. Leggatt LJ noted at p.705G that

> "the validity of the rules of the Parliament and of its political groups about expenses is not challenged. What is alleged is that Community funds were dishonestly appropriated without the Parliament or the relevant political group being aware of the dishonesty".

He added at p.706A–B that

> "the fact that national proceedings may give rise to the need to interpret them [the Parliament's rules] cannot deprive the national court of jurisdiction".

Leggatt LJ concluded at p.708C–D that the prosecution did not call into question the rules adopted by the European Parliament:

> "What is called in question is the honesty of the defendants in claiming expenses as provided by the rules".

On appeal, the Appellate Committee of the House of Lords held that, because of section 29(3) of the Supreme Court Act 1981, the Divisional Court did not have jurisdiction to overturn the decision of the trial judge, Mr Justice Morland: *R v Manchester Crown Court ex parte DPP* [1993] 1 WLR 1524. The House of Lords did not address the merits of the sovereignty arguments. Lord Browne-Wilkinson commented at pp.1530H–1531A that if the question were to arise in another case whether the jurisdiction of the criminal courts to entertain such a prosecution is excluded by the alleged "sovereignty" of the European Parliament, the decision of the Divisional Court (having been made without jurisdiction) would not be binding.

43 For these reasons, the general principle of parliamentary privilege (based on the separation of powers and the exclusive jurisdiction of Parliament to regulate its own affairs) does not prevent the hearing of these criminal charges.

Issues which may arise during the criminal trials

44 The Defendants have suggested at paragraph 68 of their Written Submissions that if the criminal trials are to continue, they will wish to investigate "why they have been singled out for criminal investigation and prosecution", and they will wish to consider matters such as "the cultural attitudes towards the schemes within the House, the systemic quirks and potential weaknesses inherent within the schemes ...".

45 The Crown's case is that the reason why these Defendants have been prosecuted is because of the evidence that their expenses claims were fraudulent. "Cultural attitudes" and "systemic quirks" have no relevance to allegations that, for example,

(1) Mr Morley claimed for mortgage interest payments in respect of a house, even though the mortgage had earlier been paid off.

(2) Mr Chaytor claimed expenses for rent which he claimed to be paying to a "Sarah Elizabeth Rastrick", the alleged owner of the property, when he was in fact the owner of the premises and

was not paying any such rent, Ms Rastrick is Mr Chaytor's daughter and the tenancy agreement on which Mr Chaytor relied was a sham.

(3) Mr Devine claimed expenses for invoices which appeared to show that he had incurred expenditure of £5,505 in respect of stationery when in fact such stationery was not supplied.

46 In any event, the submissions by the Defendants as to issues which may arise in the criminal trials are premature. Such submissions beg a number of questions:

(1) Is the specific line of inquiry which the Defendant wishes to pursue a relevant one ?

(2) If so, is the Crown willing to make an admission or can the Defendant obtain the information from another source or is Parliament willing to provide information if requested by the trial Judge ?

(3) If not, does parliamentary privilege prevent such a line of inquiry from being pursued ?

(4) If so, will a fair trial still be possible ?

47 Such issues are speculative and theoretical at present. They will be matters for consideration and determination by Mr Justice Saunders as the trial judge at an appropriate time. Mr Justice Saunders is, of course, well aware of his continuing duty to ensure that parliamentary privilege is not breached.

48 The Crown emphasises that parliamentary privilege does not prevent evidence being adduced in the criminal trials as to matters of fact, including the fact that expenses and allowances were paid by the Fees Office in particular cases. To refer to proceedings in Parliament as a matter of record is not to impugn them. See, for example, *Buchanan v Jennings* [2005] 1 AC 115 (Judicial Committee of the Privy Council in relation to reliance on what was said in Parliament in order to interpret a statement made outside Parliament) and *Pepper v Hart* [1993] AC 593, 638H–639C and 639E–F (House of Lords on referring to Hansard in judicial review proceedings). Indeed the Judicial Committee of the Privy Council in *Prebble v Television New Zealand Ltd* [1995] 1 AC 321, 337D criticised an earlier case for failing to distinguish between the right to prove the occurrence of events in Parliament and the prohibition on questioning their propriety.

Conclusion

49 The Crown therefore invites the Court to reject the Defendants' contentions that the hearing of the criminal charges would breach parliamentary privilege.

Good practice suggestions

Key dates

If you are not putting in a formal chronology make sure that you refer in the body of the skeleton to the relevant key dates. Again, be highly discriminating about what it is necessary to refer to.

Citation

The amount and extent of citation of authorities depends on the intellectual density of your argument, particularly where issues of law are more extensive than factual issues. Be reasonably sparing in citing any. Only refer to key parts. Do not disrupt the flow of text. Most judges will look at the authorities themselves, and prefer to do so. Therefore use dicta within your skeleton only if you have a particularly riveting passage, and then just the bit that works.

A good rule of thumb is to cite at length only when to do so makes the point better than you can. In a really difficult question you can set out the whole of the relevant passage but it must be very much on point to retain the judge's interest.

Even where fairly extensive legal argument may be required try to use your best authority or one where your position is most persuasively put in order to make your propositions of law seem self-evidently right. There is nothing worse than a collection of bits of citation.

It may be a useful discipline for juniors to have authority for everything they propose, but such an approach matures over time. As an advocate the more senior or experienced or respected you become, the easier it will be both to decide what to omit by way of supporting authority, and what the court will accept from you without citation.

10 Conclusion: Fifteen Key Points to Writing a Successful Skeleton

Here is a simple truth. Preparing a skeleton argument is not a chore to be put up with. It is not a mechanical process devoid of thought and proper attention. It is not a waste of time simply because argument will have to be prepared again for the hearing itself. It is an opportunity to sway the mind of the tribunal in favour of the client and against that of an opponent before the advocate opens his mouth.

It is an extraordinary opportunity, and one not to be thrown away. Counsel can grab the judge's attention; can earn his gratitude for showing him the way into the case; can capture his interest; and can create a momentum with written argument that makes his case appear right and obvious and irresistible. If an advocate applies himself properly to the task, he can get more than half way to winning before he arrives at court.

This is what the most successful advocates have learned and understand. It means they have a reasonable chance – nearly one in two – of succeeding on appeal without being called upon to argue their case orally. It means that a trial judge will lean in their favour, either consciously or subconsciously, from the outset of the proceedings. It gives counsel who are skilled in expressing themselves in writing an edge in interim applications. And they do it by the skilful preparation of, and application of thought to, their skeletons.

There are key points to be found in all successful skeleton arguments, irrespective of their intended use or the style of the writer. Here are 15 of the most effective:

1. Engage the judge by giving him a way into the case.

2. Persuade him you have an overview that makes sense.

3. Make him feel confident that you have given considerable thought to the document, that he can use it and come back to it.

4. Ensure that it is completely accurate and reliable as to the facts.

5. Make it as short as the subject matter permits.

6. Always start with what the hearing is for.

7. Describe briefly in the first paragraph what the dispute is about, and roughly what your client says.

8. Say something reasonably interesting about the case within the first two paragraphs.

9. Tell a good, easy-to-follow story using non-contentious facts or propositions in such a way as to make your client's case appear irresistible.

10. Try and keep the language low key.

11. Get to the heart of the matter very quickly.

12. Take every live point and tell the Judge everything he needs to know, but no more.

13. Do not bore the reader.

14. Try to give the impression there is no sensible view to reach other than your own.

15. Your overall perceived intention should be to 'help' rather than persuade, so that judge forgets you are trying to win the case. Be seen more as a judicial assistant than a partisan figure.

Part 4
Written Advocacy Outside the Courts

11 Inter-partes Correspondence: The 'Dear Judge' Letter

Less than ten percent of all claims or disputes result in proceedings being issued. And less than two per cent of issued claims go to trial. So, in over ninety eight per cent of claims, either liability is conceded and the case settles, or the claim is withdrawn. Invariably the defendant or the claimant, respectively, is persuaded of the merits or demerits of the claim in the course of inter-partes correspondence. This provides a tremendous opportunity to develop and practice written advocacy skills: every litigation solicitor should have a firm grasp of the tactics of adversarial writing, and the use of language to persuade. English is particularly well suited to be a language of debate, with its diversity of meaning, nuances, subtleties and tone, and the quaintness of professional jargon. By the same token lawyers have a responsibility to ensure that the language they use is sufficiently precise to avoid any misunderstanding with clients of either side for whom English is not their first language, and foreign lawyers in cross-border claims.

Practitioners rarely have time to really polish and hone their correspondence, but a well-phrased and well-timed letter can have a devastating effect on the confidence of the other side. It may also have a significant impact on the judicial reader who will come upon it months, or perhaps even years after it has been written, and who will evaluate its importance in the context of the dispute as a whole. That evaluation may have a significant bearing on the outcome of the claim, either substantively or on the question of costs. As a consequence every letter that you write to the other side should be composed with one eye on how it will read to a judge.

This can be done on two levels: at its highest you can send a positive, subliminal message to the judge. Whatever you may be writing to your opponent you are actually saying, 'Dear Judge, look how I am bending over backwards to explain to the other side the merits of my client's case as clearly as possible; look how correct his case is; and look how reasonable he is being in pursuit of his claim' Or conversely you could say, 'Dear Judge, look what the other side are doing: obfuscating a case which is devoid of merit; making us deal with unmeritorious points, and generally acting unreasonably in driving up costs.' This may well impact on the trial judge's view of the merits. It may help him in his quest to do substantive justice.

And it may make him less inclined to favour a party of whose conduct he disapproves. At a lower level you are flagging up issues for consideration later when costs come to be considered under CPR Part 44.

The moral is simple. Write your letter. Make it as forceful or vituperative as you like, but never send it without asking yourself, 'What is the Court going to make of this when the time comes?' It is not a mechanical exercise and may provide very concrete benefits to your client.

Once this activity was conducted only by the astute litigator. Now it should be a feature of universal litigation practice in view of Part 44 and the rules affecting costs practice in specialist and other jurisdictions: the Court is concerned with conduct, with proportionality, and with the parties being seen to act reasonably towards one another and to the Court.

When writing adversarial correspondence these simple tips should be of assistance:

1. *Courtesy*
   Observe the usual professional courtesies, particularly in titles, mode of address and references to the respective clients and their witnesses. Judges are easily irritated by a failure to do so.

2. *Do not use emotive language*
   Be business-like. Litigation is not a drama. Overly emotive language may well offend the opposite party and diminish the chance of settlement.

3. *Adverbs*
   Do not argue by adverb: 'clearly', 'obviously', 'undeniably', 'patently', 'undoubtedly,' or use them in a different form e.g. 'it is plain that.' This is precisely the same point as the guidance offered for skeleton arguments. Base your assertions on the facts, with substantive argument by reference to the evidence.

4. *Do not assert your opinion*
   If you have that of counsel, or of an expert, so be it. Otherwise, confine yourself to the facts, or the law. Let these speak.

5. *Argue rationally and logically*
   If what you assert does not make sense, or offends common sense or natural justice, it is unlikely to persuade.

6. *Be costs conscious always*
   This should condition your whole approach to litigation practice.

7. *Avoid trench warfare*
   Your client has enough on his plate with his own dispute. He does not need the costs and aggravation of you opening up a second front by complaining that the opposing party's lawyers have not complied with this or that particular direction, unless it is vital to his case. You will create an entirely secondary dispute, the costs of which will make the claim that much harder to settle.

8. *Always, always, always check grammar and spelling*
   Not only are mistakes an irritant and unprofessional, they serve as a great distraction to the reader. Poor spelling may not matter to our present educators, but to your opponent and certainly to a judge it will demean your firm, and your competence will be questioned.

12 Pre-action Protocol Letters of Claim and Reply

In Chapter 10 of his final report on Access to Justice (1996), Lord Woolf said that what was needed was a system which would enable parties to a dispute to embark on meaningful negotiations as soon as the possibility of litigation was identified and to ensure that as early as possible they had the relevant information to define their claim and make realistic offers to settle. Pre-action protocols, he said, "are intended to build on and increase the benefits of early but well informed settlements which genuinely satisfy both parties to disputes".[1]

One of the principal themes of the Civil Procedure Rules 1998 (CPR) was to introduce a "cards on the table" approach, enforced by a penalty costs regime. This had been developing in litigation procedure in the 1990s, especially with the introduction of exchange of witness statements and experts' reports. The whole thrust of civil and family litigation is that courts now expect co-operation between the parties and their legal representatives from an early stage, in disclosing their case in outline in letters of claim and response, and by exchanging information, including key documents.[2]

The structure and timetable for the pre-action provision of information are now contained in the current 11 Pre-action Protocols that inform practitioners of what their case outline should consist, and the policy of the Court contained in the Practice Direction on Pre-action Conduct (PDPAC[3]) which provides broader guidelines. But just because templates are offered the possibility of effective written advocacy is not shut out – rather the contrary. The astute practitioner will enhance the information he is required to provide by making his case persuasive from the very outset. If he is acting for a claimant he will wish to overwhelm. If he acts for a defendant his reply will try to disappoint the claimant, at least to the extent of deflating his expectation. The earlier this is done, the greater the potential for cost saving in the long run.

And it is entirely proper to do this, since it accords with the policy of the CPR and FDR:

---

1 White Book Vol.1. C1A-001.

2 C1A-002.

3 C1-001.

- to focus the attention of litigants on the desirability of resolving disputes without litigation;
- to enable them to obtain information they reasonably need in order to enter an appropriate settlement;
- to make an appropriate offer (of a kind which can have costs consequences if litigation ensues);
- if pre-action settlement is not achievable, to lay the ground for expeditious conduct of proceedings;
- to define and narrow the issues in dispute before proceedings are issued so that the case can be allocated to a track, a timetable set for the disclosure of evidence and the trial at an early case management stage
- to demonstrate willingness to use ADR, and in particular negotiation, mediation or some other intervention by a third party neutral as necessary.

Even where protocols do not currently apply it is still a PDPAC requirement for the claimant to send a detailed letter of claim to the prospective defendant and to wait a reasonable period for the defendant to respond before issuing proceedings, subject to the need for urgent interim relief, or to preserve a limitation position. This is entirely consistent with the expectation of the overriding objective at CPR r.1.1 (2) and its practical application which make it clear that the approach to all disputes should be:

- The claimant to write a reasonably detailed and self-contained letter of claim, enclosing copies of essential documents and asking for those in the defendant's possession.
- The claimant to set a reasonable timetable in the letter for the defendant to admit or deny liability, (one month is suggested for many claims).
- The defendant to acknowledge the letter within 21 days and reply within the suggested timescale if possible or as a minimum explain steps that are being taken to look into the matter and when a full reply is likely to be possible.
- The defendant's reply should accept the claim and make proposals for settlement, or if disputing the claim explain why and enclose essential documents.
- Both parties should reply to the other's reasonable requests for further information.

- Both parties should show a willingness to consider a settlement, including mediation or other form of ADR.

The specimen letters of claim and templates for letters of claim and response in the personal injury, clinical disputes and judicial review protocols can be adapted for other types of disputes.

Failing to send a letter of claim at all is unreasonable conduct, which will invariably attract a penalty costs sanction.[4]

At the time of writing, pre-action protocols are in force for claims involving personal injury, clinical disputes, construction and engineering disputes, defamation, professional negligence, judicial review, disease and illness, housing disrepair, possession claims based on rent arrears, possession claims based on mortgage arrears, and low value personal injury claims in road traffic accidents. The personal injury and RTA protocols are primarily designed for those road traffic accidents, tripping and slipping and accident at work cases which include an element of personal injury with a value of less than £15,000 that are likely to be allocated to the fast track. However, the "cards on the table" approach advocated by each protocol is equally appropriate to some higher value claims, particularly in respect of letters before action, exchanging information and documents and agreeing experts.

Each of the protocols provides for early notification. The claimant's solicitor may wish to put the defendant and/or his insurer on notice of a claim as soon as he knows it is likely to be made, but before he is able to send a detailed letter of claim, particularly for instance, when the defendant has no or limited knowledge of the incident giving rise to the claim or where the claimant is incurring significant expenditure as a result, for example, of the accident which he hopes the defendant might pay for, in whole or in part. The personal injury, clinical negligence and judicial review protocols provide specimen letters of claim at Annex A to C2–018 of volume 1 of the White Book.

Letters of claim and response under the protocols are not intended to have the same status as a statement of case in proceedings since matters may come to light as a result of investigation after the letter of claim has been sent, or after the defendant has responded, particularly if disclosure of documents takes place outside the recommended three-month period. These circumstances could mean that the "pleaded" case of one or both parties is presented slightly differently than in the letter of claim and response. It would not be consistent with the spirit of the protocol for a party to "take a

---

4 *Phoenix Finance Ltd v Federation International de L' Automobile* [2002] EWHC 1028 (Ch), 146 SJLB 145; *Taylor v D Coach Hire* (2003) CL November 3; *Northfield v DSM (Southern) Ltd* [2000] CLY 461; *Linton v Williams Haulage Ltd* [2001] CLY 516.

point" on this in the proceedings, provided that there was no obvious intention by the party who changed their position to mislead the other party.

Under the protocol letter of claim for personal injury the claimant has to set out a clear summary of the facts on which the claim is based together with an indication of the nature of any injuries suffered and of any financial loss incurred. In cases of road traffic accidents, the letter should provide the name and address of the hospital where treatment has been obtained and the claimant's hospital reference number. The letter should ask for details of the insurer and that a copy should be sent by the proposed defendant to the insurer where appropriate.

Sufficient information should be given in order to enable the defendant's insurer/solicitor to commence investigations and at least put a broad valuation on the "risk". If the defendant denies liability, he should enclose with the letter of reply, documents in his possession which are material to the issues between the parties, and which would be likely to be ordered to be disclosed by the court, either on an application for pre-action disclosure, or on disclosure during proceedings. Where the defendant admits primary liability, but alleges contributory negligence by the claimant, the defendant should give reasons supporting those allegations[5]. Where the defendant admits liability in whole or in part, before proceedings are issued, any medical report obtained by agreement under this protocol should be disclosed to the other party. The claimant should delay issuing proceedings for 21 days from disclosure of the report, to enable the parties to consider whether the claim is capable of settlement.

The C2–018 Annex A Letter of Claim set out below (and modified for use in clinical negligence and judicial review claims) is fairly skeletal, and therefore provides considerable scope for enhancement by the solicitor who wants to persuade insurers from the outset that there is little prospect of contesting liability or raising contributory negligence.

---

5 Para 3-10, Personal Injury Pre-action Protocol.

PRE-ACTION PROTOCOL LETTER OF CLAIM

Dear Sirs

Re: Claimant's full name

Claimant's full address
Claimant's Clock or Works Number
Claimant's Employer (name and address)

We are instructed by the above named to claim damages in connection with an accident at work/road traffic accident/tripping accident on day of (year) at (place of accident which must be sufficiently detailed to establish location).

Please confirm the identity of your insurers. Please note that the insurers will need to see this letter as soon as possible and it may affect your insurance cover and/or the conduct of any subsequent legal proceedings if you do not send this letter to them.

The circumstances of the accident are: (brief outline)

The reason why we are alleging fault is: (simple explanation, e.g. defective machine, broken ground)

A description of our clients' injuries is as follows: (brief outline)

(In cases of road traffic accidents) Our client (state hospital reference number) received treatment for the injuries at (name and address of hospital).

He is employed as (occupation) and has had the following time off work (dates of absence). His approximate weekly income is (insert if known).

If you are our client's employers, please provide us with the usual earnings details which will enable us to calculate his financial loss.

We are obtaining a police report and will let you have a copy of the same upon your undertaking to meet half the fee.

We have also sent a letter of claim to (name and address) and a copy of that letter is attached. We understand their insurers are (name, address and claims number if known).

At this stage of our enquiries we would expect the documents contained in parts (insert appropriate parts of standard disclosure list) to be relevant to this action.

A copy of this letter is attached for you to send to your insurers. Finally we expect an acknowledgment of this letter within 21 days by yourselves or your insurers.

Yours faithfully

The clinical negligence letter of claim should, in more complex cases, include a chronology of the relevant events particularly if the patient has been treated by a number of different healthcare providers, and refer to any relevant documents, including health records. Sufficient information must be given to enable the healthcare provider defendant to commence investigations and to put an initial valuation on the claim. By Part C3–023 Annex C1 the template for the clinical negligence letter of claim lists its essential contents as:

1. Client's name, address, date of birth, etc.;

2. Dates of allegedly negligent treatment;

3. Events giving rise to the claim;

    - An outline of what happened, including details of other relevant treatments to the client by other healthcare providers

4. Allegation of negligence and causal link with injuries;

    - An outline of the allegations or a more detailed list in a complex case an outline of the causal link between the allegations and the injuries complained of

5. The Client's injuries, condition and future prognosis;

6. Request for clinical records (if not previously provided);

    - Use the Law Society form if appropriate or adapt
    - Specify the records required
    - If other records are held by other providers and may be relevant, say so
    - State what investigations have been carried out to date, e.g. information from client and witnesses, any complaint and the outcome, if any clinical records have been seen or expert's advice obtained

7. The likely value of the claim.

    - An outline of the main heads of damage, or in straightforward cases the details of loss

Optional information which may be provided includes what investigations have been carried out, suggestions for obtaining expert evidence, suggestions for meetings, negotiations, discussion or mediation and an offer to settle made without supporting evidence.

Possible enclosures include a chronology, clinical records request form and client's authorisation, expert's report, schedule of loss and supporting evidence.

For Disease and Illness Claims the protocol provides for a template letter of claim at Annex B C9-014 of the White Book:

PRE-ACTION PROTOCOL LETTER OF CLAIM

To: Defendant

Dear Sirs

Re: Claimant's full name
Claimant's full address
Claimant's National Insurance Number
Claimant's Date of Birth
Claimant's Clock or Works Number
Claimant's Employer (name and address)

We are instructed by the above named to claim damages in connection with a claim for:
(specify occupational disease)

We are writing this letter in accordance with the pre-action protocol for disease and illness claims.

Please confirm the identity of your insurers. Please note that your insurers will need to see this letter as soon as possible and it may affect your insurance cover if you do not send this to them.

The Claimant was employed by you *(if the claim arises out of public or occupiers' liability give appropriate details)* as job description from date to date. During the relevant period of his employment he worked:
(description of precisely where the Claimant worked and what he did to include a description of any machines used and details of any exposure to noise or substances)

The circumstances leading to the development of this condition are as follows:
(give chronology of events) (and in appropriate cases attach a work history from HM Revenue and Customs)

The reason why we are alleging fault is:
(details should be given of contemporary and comparable employees who have suffered from similar problems if known; any protective equipment provided; complaints; the supervisors concerned, if known)

Our client's employment history is attached.

(We have also made a claim against: *(insert details)*
Their insurers' details are: *(insert if known)*)

We have the following documents in support of our client's claim and will disclose these in confidence to your nominated insurance manager or solicitor when we receive their acknowledgement letter. *(e.g. occupational health notes; GP notes)*

We have obtained a medical report from *(name)* and will disclose this when we receive your acknowledgement of this letter.
(this is optional at this stage)

From the information we presently have:

(i) the Claimant first became aware of symptoms on *(insert approximate date)*

(ii) the Claimant first received medical advice about those symptoms on *(insert date) (give details of advice given if appropriate)*

(iii) the Claimant first believed that those symptoms might be due to exposure leading to this claim on *(insert approximate date)*

A description of our client's condition is as follows:
(this should be sufficiently detailed to allow the Defendant to put a broad value on the claim)

(For appropriate cases) Our client is still suffering from the effect of his/her condition. We invite you to participate with us in addressing his/her immediate needs by use of rehabilitation.

He has had the following time off work:
(insert dates)

He is presently employed as a *(job description)* and his average net weekly income is *(£)*

(If you are our client's employers, please provide us with the usual earnings details, which will enable us to calculate his financial loss.)

(Please note that we have entered into a conditional fee agreement with our client dated in relation to this claim which provides for a success fee within the meaning of section 58(2) of the Courts and Legal Services Act 1990. Our client has taken out an insurance policy dated with *(name and address of insurance company)* to which section 29 of the Access to Justice Act 1999 applies in respect of this claim. The policy number is *(insert)*, the policy is dated *(insert)* and the level of cover is *(insert)*. The premiums payable under the insurance policy *(are not) (are)* staged *(and the points at which the increase premiums are payable are as follows:)*)

A copy of this letter is attached for you to send to your insurers. Finally we expect an acknowledgement of this letter within 21 days by yourselves or your insurers.

Yours faithfully

The Construction and Engineering Protocol applies to all construction and engineering disputes and must be read in conjunction with CPR Part 60 (Technology and Construction Court claims). It includes professional negligence disputes against building professionals. A feature of the pre-action correspondence is that the claimant is required to include the remedy sought and details of how it has been calculated. The letter of claim must state the principal contractual terms and statutory provisions relied on and the nature of the relief claimed: if damages are claimed, a breakdown showing how the damages have been quantified; if a sum is claimed pursuant to a contract, how it has been calculated; and if an extension of time is claimed, the period claimed.

The Defamation Protocol should be read with CPR Part 53 (Defamation Claims). The letter of claim should identify specifically the publication, words, inaccuracies or unsupportable comments to which the claimant objects, together with any special facts with regard to the interpretation or meaning of the words or in relation to the damage caused. Where possible, a copy or transcript of the words complained of should be enclosed. The defendant is required to respond to the letter of claim as soon as possible, preferably within 14 days and must either admit liability and offer a remedy, or deny the claim and give reasons.

The Professional Negligence Pre-action Protocol[6] requires that the letters of claim and response should be detailed and "open", i.e. not without prejudice; the letter of claim should include a chronology and enclose key documents, should particularise the allegations of negligence and explain how they have caused the loss, which should be calculated (and supporting documents should be enclosed) and should identify any experts appointed. The defendant may send a separate letter of settlement on a without prejudice basis with the letter of response.

The letter of claim should state:

(a) The identity of any other parties involved in the dispute or a related dispute.

(b) A clear chronological summary (including key dates) of the facts on which the claim is based. Key documents should be identified, copied and enclosed.

(c) The allegations against the professional. What has he done wrong? What has he failed to do?

(d) An explanation of how the alleged error has caused the loss claimed.

---

6 C7A–001; see also Guidance Note C3.1.

(e) An estimate of the financial loss suffered by the claimant and how it is calculated. Supporting documents should be identified, copied and enclosed. If details of the financial loss cannot be supplied, the claimant should explain why and should state when he will be in a position to provide the details. This information should be sent to the professional as soon as reasonably possible. If the claimant is seeking some form of non-financial redress, this should be made clear.

(f) Confirmation whether or not an expert has been appointed. If so, providing the identity and discipline of the expert, together with the date upon which the expert was appointed.

(g) A request that a copy of the letter of claim be forwarded immediately to the professional's insurers, if any.

The letters of response and settlement can be contained within a single letter. It should contain a reasoned answer to the claimant's allegations:

(a) If the claim is admitted the professional should say so in clear terms;

(b) If only part of the claim is admitted the professional should make clear which parts of the claim are admitted and which are denied;

(c) If the claim is denied in whole or in part, the letter of response should include specific comments on the allegations against the professional and, if the claimant's version of events is disputed, the professional should provide his version of events;

(d) If the professional is unable to admit or deny the claim, the professional should identify any further information which is required;

(e) If the professional disputes the estimate of the claimant's financial loss, the letter of response should set out the professional's estimate. If an estimate cannot be provided, the professional should explain why and should state when he will be in a position to provide an estimate. This information should be sent to the claimant as soon as reasonably possible;

(f) Where additional documents are relied upon, copies should be provided.

A separate letter of settlement will normally be a without prejudice letter and should be sent if the professional intends to make proposals for early settlement. It should set out the professional's views to date on the claim identifying those issues which the professional believes are likely to remain in dispute and those that are not and make a settlement proposal or identify any further information that is required before the professional can formulate proposals.

The Judicial Review Pre-action Protocol letter before claim should contain the date and details of the decision, act or omission being challenged and a clear summary of the facts on which the claim is based. It should also contain the details of any relevant information that the claimant is seeking and an explanation of why this is considered relevant. C8–002 Annex A provides a standard template.

The Housing Disrepair protocol[7] requires an early notification letter to be sent to the landlord giving:

(i) the tenant's name, the address of the property, tenant's address if different, tenant's telephone number and when access is available;

(ii) details of the defects, including any defects outstanding, in the form of a schedule, if appropriate;

(iii) details of any notification previously given to the landlord of the need for repair or information as to why the tenant believes that the landlord has knowledge of the need for repair;

(iv) the identity of a proposed expert and proposed letter of instruction;

(v) the tenant's disclosure of such relevant documents as are readily available.

This is to be followed by a letter of claim which should provide any information not already given together with the effect of the defects on the tenant and details of any special damages.

The landlord should normally reply within 20 working days of the date of receipt of the letter of Claim and this should include:

(i) whether liability is admitted and if so, in respect of which defects. If liability is disputed in respect of some or all of the defects, the reasons for this;

(ii) any point which the landlord wishes to make regarding lack of notice of the repair or regarding any difficulty in gaining access;

(iii) a full schedule of intended works including anticipated start and completion dates and a timetable for the works;

---

7 C10A–001.

(iv) any offer of compensation;

(v) any offer in respect of costs;

(vi) all relevant records or documents including:

  (a) copy of tenancy agreement including tenancy conditions

  (b) documents or computerised records relating to notice given, disrepair reported, inspection reports or requirements to the property

(vii) a response to any proposals of the tenant for instructing an expert including:

  (a) whether or not the proposed single joint expert is agreed

  (b) whether the letter of instruction is agreed

  (c) if the single joint expert is agreed but with separate instructions, a copy of the letter of instruction

  (d) if the appointment of a single joint expert is not agreed, whether the landlord agrees to a joint inspection.

Templates for early notification letters and letters of claim and response may be found at Annex A C10-006 and 007.

Templates for letters in the hands of experienced advocates should be like bare clay to a sculptor, ready to absorb his creativity. In producing this correspondence you have a choice. You can make it an information giving exercise, or, by applying your mind, you may turn what is a requirement into an important opportunity to create an instrument of persuasion.

13 Part 36 Offers

The formal regime for offers to settle civil claims, whether or not upon the basis of payments being made or accepted, is set out in CPR Part 36. The form and content of Part 36 offers are set out in CPR Part 36.2(2). Such an offer *must*:

(a) be in writing;

(b) state on its face that it is intended to have the consequences of Section I of Part 36;

(c) specify a period of not less than 21 days within which the defendant will be liable for the claimant's costs in accordance with rule 36.10 if the offer is accepted;

(d) state whether it relates to the whole of the claim or to part of it or to an issue that arises in it and if so to which part or issue; and

(e) state whether it takes into account any counterclaim.

(Rule 36.7 makes provision for when a Part 36 offer is made.)

In appropriate cases, a Part 36 offer must contain such further information as is required by rule 36.5 (Personal injury claims for future pecuniary loss), rule 36.6 (Offer to settle a claim for provisional damages), and rule 36.15 (Deduction of benefits).

The offer must be clear, and must comply with these provisions to be effective. If the offer is insufficiently clear the recipient can apply for clarification under r.36.8

Rules 36.10 and 44.3 enable the Court to take into account an offer to settle made by any party before the commencement of proceedings.

Both of these provisions create scope for effective written advocacy by the practitioner who is tactically astute, irrespective of which side he represents. The trick is to measure to a nicety the minimum amount the opposing party is likely to accept or want in satisfaction of his claim. From the claimant's point of view it is what he will settle for to avoid the risk and costs consequences of proceeding further; for the defendant, it is that sum which will adequately pressurise the claimant to walk away or otherwise risk a Pyrrhic victory.

Where advocacy comes in is to persuade the other side that the sum offered is, on the one hand (i.e. acting for the claimant), the right amount to pay, and on the other (acting for the defendant), the best amount achievable with the minimum of risk and inconvenience. To be successful at doing so the practitioner who devises and settles a Part 36 offer must have certain qualities. He should:

- be confident in, and realistic about, his own case;
- be able to hold his nerve;
- be able to assess and explain the risk in the litigation, and to convey that risk to other side; and
- be analytical and unemotional.

When you convey your Part 36 offer to the other side to make it effective:

(a) Use language that is flat, fact based and business like.

(b) Convince your opponent that the offer will not change.

(c) Justify the figure offered by reference to either:

  (i) the perceived litigation risk or

  (ii) some factual or legal impairment that you think will damage or undermine the other side's case or

  (iii) some particular fact in your own case.

(d) Wherever possible offer the figure as a reasoned mathematical calculation.

(e) Do not just provide a figure with no explanation or justification.

(f) Always break down the claim into its component parts to attribute value, or lack of it.

(g) Do not criticise the claimant or defendant on a personal level, or his lawyers.

(h) Take into account interest and deal with it – both as to liability and quantum.

(i) Prepare to be questioned about your assessment of risk.

(j) Do not try to bluff or exaggerate – if you have a weak case grasp the nettle – nuisance value is also a useful negotiating tool.

(k) Deal with the adverse costs consequences of a refusal in real terms i.e. with reasonably accurate costs projections being given. This information will appear in the allocation questionnaire anyway so there is little point in being coy about it.

Remember that you have two aims that must be balanced, and in that sense Part 36 offers operate as both shield and sword. First, you wish to cause your opponent to despair about his case, or an aspect of it. Second, you must identify the minimum amount of money on the table which will enable your client either to accept a payment with good grace, or to buy off the other side as cheaply as possible, and in either case you must be able to persuade him that this is the right sum.

14 Introduction to Worked Examples

I am grateful to those firms of solicitors and their lay clients who have granted permission for me to reproduce, in anonymised form, letters before action and replies, drawn from real claims. They are detailed, fact orientated, unemotional and businesslike. Both claims and defences are particularised, and in three cases authority supports the material contentions.

They are not produced here as models or precedents, but to demonstrate the adversarial nature of correspondence. All seek to persuade the recipient that their client's position is both correct and reasonable and, as important if not more so, (a) to dissuade the other side from taking further steps towards or within the litigation and (b) to recognise the adverse costs implications of doing so. The detail makes these examples lengthy. But the facts are used either to justify threatening proceedings or to stop a potential claim in its tracks. Such advocacy within correspondence is a key part of negotiation, and, should it subsequently have to make an award of costs, an important feature of the Court's consideration under CPR Part 44 of the parties' behaviour.

As in Part 3, 'Good practice suggestions' are provided at the end of each example, for use by experienced practitioners as much as a checklist of what they ordinarily do as an encouragement to develop an effective adversarial style of writing.

Example Q

Letter of claim combined with claimant's pre-action Part 36 offer under the Professional Negligence Pre-Action Protocol and CPR rules 3.1(4) and 5, and 44.3(5)(a). This was a claim brought against solicitors for breach of retainer arising from the sale of a property by the claimant, in which it was advised wrongly that it could, without risk, rescind a contract of sale with a purchaser and retain the deposit, and then exchange contracts for sale with a second purchaser.

The detailed history of the complaint is set out. Core documents are sent in a bundle attaching to the letter, thus providing pre-action disclosure at the earliest opportunity. A list of dramatis personae is included. Liability and causation are addressed separately and in depth with a view to snuffing out the possibility of a defence. As much detail of the heads of damage available is provided, together with supporting documents, to lay the ground for an early Part 36 offer, the quantum of which can be justified on the claimant's case.

The language used is non-emotive, fact-drive and therefore rather understated.

The claim settled before the issue of proceedings.

PRE-ACTION PROTOCOL LETTER OF CLAIM

Dear Sirs

ABC Limited trading as Fleet Street Homes Re: 1 Kings Road, London, W27

We refer to our letter of 5 April, 2011.

We act for the above-named company which has instructed us to bring a claim for damages for breach of professional retainer against your firm. This letter is written in accordance with the Professional Negligence Pre-Action Protocol and CPR Parts 3.1(4) and 5, and 44.3(5)(a). We respectfully suggest that you pass it without delay to your professional indemnity insurers.

We further invite you to note our client's offer of settlement in connection with this matter. To that end this letter should also be treated as, and have the consequences of, an offer made in accordance with CPR Part 36.10(1).

In order to assist your early investigation of our client's claim we append herewith a paginated bundle of documents to which reference is made thus '[1]' in the body of this letter. For your ease of reference we have also numbered the substantive paragraphs of this letter.

Background

1. In early May 2009 your firm was instructed to examine information concerning a property at auction and on 13th or 14th May 2009 after the auction your firm by Mr Z was instructed by Mr B, the managing director of our client, who is also an architect in private professional practice, to convey the purchase by our client of property at 1 Kings Road, London, W27 which was acquired at the FPD Savills' auction on 13 May, 2009. The purchase price was provided by Mr and Mrs B and a group of private investors, with the balance by way of bridging finance. Mr Z was also instructed to convey the mortgage. By a letter dated 19 May 2009 [1–2] Mr Z was given instructions about the investment arrangements. By a letter dated 27 May 2009 [3–4] Mr Z advised our client that a trust fund should be created into which the various investors place monies for the company to purchase property and carry out development. He also prepared an outline document and timetable [5–8] entitled 'Notes Regarding Legal Documentation for Fleet Street Purchase and Development of 1 Kings Road, London W.27.' It will be seen from this that Mr Z advised the settling of a trust deed and a second legal charge which would be registered against the property to protect the interests of the investors.

2. We are instructed that Mr Z was made aware that this project was intended by the company and its investors to be the first of a series of property development ventures specialising in 'backland' or 'small brownfield' sites using bridging finance.

3. The declaration of trust was settled by Mr Z and executed [9–15] on 16 September 2009. Although he settled a second charge we are instructed that it was never registered; fortunately we have been unable to ascertain any loss flowing from such failure.

4. In December, 2009 a buyer, OP Properties Ltd afterwards COD Properties Limited, was found for the property and on 20 December the sale was agreed in the sum of £500,000. We are instructed that the seller agreed to sell to OP Properties as apparently it did not require finance and could complete quickly. We append a copy of Mr Z's attendance note record [16] of that date.

5. On or about 8 January 2010 your firm by Mr Z was retained by our client to conduct the conveyance of the sale and redeem the mortgage on the property. We append a copy of the estate agent's letter of 7 January and memorandum [17,18] and three letters dated 9 January 2010 from Mr Z to our client [19], the mortgagee [20] and the agent [21], and his letter dated 13 January 2010 [22] to the buyer's solicitor. We regret that we have been unable to find any client care letter passing from Mr Z to our client in respect of this instruction in compliance with Practice Rule 15 (13.02.7 of the Guide to Professional Conduct of

Solicitors, 8th Edition) and the OSS Client Care Guide for Solicitors. If one exists no doubt you will forward it to us in due course.

6. Our client's claim derives from the negligent conduct by Mr Z of this piece of conveyancing, and in particular the advice, or lack of it, provided by him to our client in May, 2010 which, we are instructed, has caused our client recoverable loss. To that end we consider it may be of assistance to you in your investigation to set out the dramatis personae involved in the subject matter of our client's complaint:

Dramatis Personae

BEE Mortgagee's solicitors Fleet Street Homes Trading name of seller
B, Seller's director
Z, Seller's conveyancer
COD Properties Ltd Buyer
HD Seller's agent
Hoxtons Seller's estate agents
L Mortgage Corporation Ltd Mortgagee
KH Third party buyer
KD Buyer's conveyancer
KS Buyer's conveyancing solicitors
ABC Ltd Seller
MG Seller's counsel
PA Buyer's conveyancing assistant
OP Properties Ltd Buyer's former name
RHY Third party buyer's solicitors
RI Seller's litigator
Ss Buyer's litigation solicitors

The Claim

7. On 10 March, 2010 contracts for the sale of the property were exchanged in accordance with Law Society Formula B with completion on 22 April, 2010 (Mr Z's attendance note of 7 March [23] and letter of 11 March [24] refers). However, notwithstanding the fact that the seller was ready willing and able to complete on that date, the buyer was not. We are instructed that Mr B of our client sought specific advice from Mr Z by telephone as to what the seller's options were, and that Mr Z rang him back after he himself had sought advice from a colleague, to say that the seller should either wait and see what transpired or serve a notice to complete under the terms of the contract. Having explained to Mr B what such a notice was, Mr Z was instructed to serve one upon COD Properties' solicitors, KS.

8. We should make the point at this stage that in our view, and that of counsel, the attendance records kept by Mr Z are entirely unsatisfactory

in respect of this transaction. The attendance notes are incomplete, and in any event appear to be simply lists of telephone messages. This is best illustrated from the fact that over the period 22, 23, 24 April, 2010 Mr Z's lists of messages [25, 26, 27] does not record the fact that the buyer had failed to complete, or any conversation prior to 24 April which states that Mr B was so informed. Since a Notice to Complete under condition 6.8 of the Standard Commercial Property Conditions of Sale (1st Edition) was served on 23 April [28] this strongly suggests that the telephone conversations between Mr B and Mr Z outlined above went unrecorded. Certainly it appears that any advice provided to Mr B was not reduced to writing and sent by letter which is a feature of Mr Z's conduct throughout.

9. On 28 April, 2010 your firm recorded a telephone message note [29] from AP say that the buyer was not ready to complete because it was awaiting a report from its bank's surveyor. On 1 May the List of Messages [30] shows that Mr K telephoned to say that the buyer's mortgagees had down-valued the site and confirmed that the buyer needed finance. On 6 May the List of Messages [31] indicates that Mr B instructed Mr Z that unless the buyer completed by Friday 9th May, 2010 the property would be put back on the market.

10. We are instructed that Mr Z was so instructed as a result of advice which Mr B sought from Mr Z, namely what was the position of the seller if the buyer failed to comply with the notice to complete. Mr Z advised Mr B that if COD Properties did not complete the seller could rescind the contract at any time and forfeit the buyer's deposit. We understand that this advice was repeated orally by Mr Z on either three or four occasions between 6 May and 23 May 2010. Although it was not reduced to writing by Mr Z support for the assertion that this is the advice which was given is to be found in paragraph 30 of the witness statement prepared for Mr B by Mr R of your firm in the ensuing litigation, both in its draft form prepared 29th October 2009 [32–40] and in its final form signed under a statement of truth dated 21 November, 2009 [41–49]. We flag up at this stage that the advice given was not qualified in any way.

11. On 8 May the buyer sought, and on 9 May the seller agreed that there would be an extension of time for the expiry of the notice to complete until 4.00 p.m. on Friday, 16 May, 2009 upon payment of a further sum of £10,000 by way of deposit (the letter of 9 May, 2009 from KS refers [50].) In fact this sum was not sent.

12. We are instructed that Mr B sought specific advice from Mr Z should the buyer fail to complete by close of business on 16 May. Mr Z explained that the seller could bring an action for specific performance but an action against a company with limited funds would result in a

judgment being fruitless. Mr B asked Mr Z to explain the meaning of rescission, a word with which he was not familiar, and was informed that it was the cancelling of the contract for the failure of the other side to meet its obligations; and that the seller could keep the deposit and sue for damages. Mr B informed Mr Z that the seller's expenses on the sale were between £30,000 and £35,000 and asked whether he was sure that the entire deposit of £50,000 could be kept, since if that were so the seller would not sue for any additional damages. Mr B was aware that during the day on 16 May a revised completion statement was sent to KS, and that an agreement had been reached on estate agents' fees by him directly with Mr H.

13. We are instructed that Mr B gave no instructions to Mr Z between 16 May and 20 May, 2009. This would appear to be born out by the absence of any listed telephone records or any notes in writing that we have seen.

14. On Monday 19 May the seller placed the property back on the market at the same price as previously agreed with COD Properties. Mr B telephoned a number of agents on 19 and Tuesday 20 May and the seller received offers to purchase almost immediately. On 21 May the seller held a confirmed offer to purchase from a Mr KH for £500,000.

15. It transpires from Mr Z's List of Messages dated 20 and 21 May, 2009 [51, 52] that Mr Z was continuing to make arrangements with Mr K for the completion of the sale to COD Properties. To that end Mr Z indicated to Mr K on 20 May [51] what monies he expected to receive from KS and informed Mr B that completion could take place on 21 May.

16. At 13.40 on 21 May KS sent a fax [53] to your firm indicating that it had transferred £528,750.88 to be held to order with a view to completing the transaction. At or about 2.00 p.m. Mr B orally instructed Mr Z to rescind the contract with COD Properties, who thereupon left a message to that effect with KS [52] and sent by fax timed at 14.17 that day a letter of rescission [54] and arranged for the return of the monies which were in any event £83.22 short of one day's interest. Later that day Mr B advised Mr Z [52] that the seller wished to exchange contracts with Mr KH within 24 hours and complete with him within two weeks, and that terms would be agreed the following day. The attempt to return the monies to KS was too late for the transaction to be effected on 21 May. We are instructed that Mr B was aware that the COD monies had not yet been returned overnight and sought an assurance from Mr Z that the seller could properly rescind. Mr Z informed him that since insufficient monies had been provided by KS the position on rescission was unaffected.

17. On 22 May, 2009 KS faxed a letter to your firm [55] denying that the seller was entitled either to rescind the contract with COD Properties or to forfeit the deposit. By a faxed reply sent 09.35 on 23 May [56] your firm took issue with the factual basis upon which the letter from KS was advanced and asserted "The completion notice expired over a week ago and accordingly our client was entitled to rescind the contract at any time". On the same day Messrs Ss, litigation solicitors for COD, wrote a letter before action to your firm [57–58] threatening an action for specific performance unless by 9.30 a.m. on 27 May you confirmed that the seller would complete at the earliest possible date after funds had been retrieved.

18. On 23 May Mr Z had three conversations with Mr B, as appears by his List of Messages for that day [59]. We are advised that Mr Z reiterated to Mr B that there had been no completion and that the seller was entitled to rescind. We are advised that Mr B, in reliance upon that advice instructed Mr Z to exchange contracts with Mr KH's solicitors, which he did on that date, with completion to take place on 20 June, 2009. At the time of writing this letter we have not received from your firm our client's conveyancing file relating to the sale to Mr KH despite our original request.

19. On 2 June Ss wrote to your firm [60] indicating that counsel was currently settling proceedings for issue against the seller and that they had registered a caution against dealings against the property which they would lift against an undertaking by the seller not to dispose of any interest prior to the determination of their client's claim. It will be our client's contention that no prior warning of the possibility of this happening was given by Mr Z to Mr B, who had anticipated that funds from Mr KH might be used by the company to fight the anticipated litigation.

Ensuing Litigation

20. On 4 June, 2009 COD Properties issued proceedings in the High Court against ABC seeking specific performance, or the return of the deposit and damages.

21. On 9 June your firm's files were transferred from the conveyancing department to the litigation department. Mr Z prepared a memorandum [61–62] for RI who on 11 June delivered papers and sought the advice of MG of counsel. By paragraph 7 of the Instructions to Counsel [63–68] your firm wrote "The Defendant ... now finds itself acutely embarrassed by the proceedings and, potentially exposed to a claim for breach of contract from the third party. There are also possible professional implications for Instructing Solicitors..."

22. Your firm, together with MX of counsel, very properly indicated to Mr B the existence of a conflict of interest. Indeed it appears that on 19 June, [69] RI was concerned that your firm were negligent in permitting ABC to exchange contracts with Mr KH. Entirely without prejudice to such conflict your firm were retained in the conduct of the litigation and on 18 June Mr B signed a client care letter, which he had been sent by yourselves.

23. Between 20 June and 25 November, 2009 your firm and counsel advised our client that the COD action could be defended successfully on the basis that there had been no action on the part of Mr Z after the expiry of the notice to complete on 16 May, 2009 which could be construed by the court as an unequivocal promise or representation not to rescind the contract. This advice was reduced to writing in a letter dated 24 November, 2009 [70–73]

24. On 24 November Messrs. Ss served on your firm draft Amended Particulars of Claim [74–89] and three supplementary witness statements [90–103] all of which went to the effect of the conduct of Mr Z on 20 May, 2009, and which it was now said could be properly construed as an unequivocal promise or representation not to rescind the contract. We are instructed that Mr B had not previously been made aware of the List of Messages of 20 May [51] or the significance of its contents. In view of the paucity of the record Mr Z was unable to gainsay the new contention of the claimant, and on 25 November in a pre-settlement meeting Mr G advised Mr B that the company's position was no longer tenable.

25. On 25 November the parties agreed a settlement by way of Tomlin Order [104–107] sealed 10th December, under the terms of which our client was to repay the sum of £45,000 inclusive of interest with no order as to costs, whereupon the claimant would release its caution against the property. We have no complaint about the terms of the compromise which, on any objective view, were beneficial to the company.

26. On 19 December, 2009 the sale of the property to Mr KH completed.

Breaches of Retainer

27. Our client has had the benefit of the advice of senior professional negligence counsel who takes the view, which we share, that the conduct by Mr Z of your firm's retainer of the sale of the property departed from that standard of care to be expected of a reasonably competent and careful conveyancer in the circumstances. It is our client's contention that on more than one occasion between 22 April and 23 May 2009, when advising Mr B of the legal effect of the failure

by COD Properties to complete the purchase of the property in compliance either with the provisions of the Standard Commercial Property Conditions contained in the contract, or the Notice to Complete of 23 April, 2009 as extended, Mr Z failed:

(i) to qualify his statement that the seller could rescind at any time;

(ii) to advise Mr B of the effect in law on the contract and or notice to complete of the doctrines of affirmation, waiver of time limits and estoppel;

(iii) to have regard to the line of authority on implied extensions of notices to complete, namely *Webb v Hughes* (1870) LR 10 Eq 281; *Luck v White* (1973) 26 P&CR 89; and Buckland v Farmer & Moody [1978] 3 All ER 929 which required reasonable notice to be given to a defaulting buyer that the seller would rescind;

(iv) to have regard to his conduct in continuing to deal with Messrs KS after 16 May 2009, namely whether such conduct might affirm the contract, or waive the time limit contained in the extended Notice to Complete, or give rise to an estoppel, or otherwise impair the ability of the seller to rescind and or to seek express instructions about such conduct in the light of full and adequate advice;

(v) to consider and advise the seller adequately upon the legal effect and or consequences of the letter from KS dated 22 May 2009 [55] or the letter before action from Messrs Ss dated 23 May 2009 [57–58] and seek express instructions from the seller only in the light of that advice having been given and received;

(vi) in view of the foregoing, to warn the seller against exchanging contracts with Mr KH and or explain adequately the legal consequences of doing so;

(vii) to advise that COD Properties Ltd could register a caution against dealings against the property and so prevent or suspend the sale to Mr KH.

28. The foregoing breaches are not intended to be exhaustive and it may well be that a closer inspection of the documents we have received, together with a perusal of those we have yet to receive from your firm, will uncover more causes of action or particulars thereof.

Causation

29. We are instructed by our client that had Mr B been properly and adequately advised by your firm it would not have exchanged contracts with Mr KH, but would have completed the sale to COD Properties Ltd on 21 May, 2009 utilising the monies available of £528,750.88 subject to an undertaking being given for, or the early receipt of, the missing interest of £83.22.

30. It follows that had that been the case (i) the litigation which ensued would not have come about; (ii) our client would have had the use of the sale proceeds on 21 May, 2009 rather than 19 December; and (iii) our client would also have discharged the encumbrances and its obligations in respect of the property seven months before it could do so.

Heads of Recoverable Loss

31. Our client's claim is based on the consequences which flowed from your firm's failure properly to advise. Some of the heads of claim represent losses which continue, or which continue to attract interest for the loss of use of money. That being the case this calculation is to be regarded as confined to the date of this letter, and you will understand that if proceedings are issued the sum claimed will be greater.

    (i) Litigation costs

    Our client incurred fees and disbursements in respect of litigation, which would have proven unnecessary to expend:

    (a) Fees and disbursements charged by your firm and taken from the proceeds of sale: £19,802.25 [108–110].

    (b) Litigation costs of Mr KH: £2,784.75 [109–111].

    (ii) Costs associated with retaining the Property until 19 December 2009 rather than completing 21 May 2009

    (c) Additional insurance premium: £50.35[112].

    (d) Additional Community Charge Business Rates: £966.00 [113].

    (e) Emergency repairs to dangerous wall, September 2009: £520.00 [114].

(iii) Extended bridging finance beyond June 2009. It was within Mr Z's knowledge that our client's existing facility was only for 12 months from 7th June 2008

(f) Facility and exit fees: £10,300.00 [115–116]

(g) Additional interest on bridging finance: £19,467.00 [117–124]

(iv) Costs associated with Mr KH's purchase, which would not have occurred

(h) Conveyancing costs of KH purchase: £2,570.00 [109] (N.B. The aborted conveyancing costs of the COD transaction have not been claimed, as these fall outside the ambit of the negligence).

(i) Additional interest incurred by Mr KH from 23 May to 19 December 2009: £16,746.58 [111]

(v) Loss of profit

(j) We refer to paragraph 2 of this letter. Had the property been sold on 21 May 2009 our client would have discharged its borrowing of £206,000 and had available around £300,000 (to include bank balances, interest and additional funds) to inject into a new project. Our client's primary case is that it would have been able to do so quite easily in May or June, 2009. Mr B is able to produce a portfolio of development opportunities in which he was interested at the time and he had two employees who were engaged in looking for the appropriate deals. On 22 April, 2009 Mr B alerted Mr Z to the next potential project, a tenanted property in Vauxhall costing £300 – £350,000 [125–126].

(k) The transaction involving the property, the subject matter of these proceedings, was to have generated a profit of some £90,000 had completion been effected in accordance with the contract. Our client anticipates that it could reasonably have generated £100,000 profit on the next development opportunity over the course of the twelve months between late May/early June 2009 and June, 2010. Therefore should this matter be litigated we are instructed to advance a claim in respect of loss of profit of £66,000 which our client believes to be both reasonable and conservative.

(vi) Interest as damages

(l) Our client has been deprived of the benefit of the use of the monies which it should have received on 21 May, 2009 namely £528,834.10. After deducting the bridging finance of £206,000 which would have been paid on the redemption of the mortgage subtracting your fees, the bridging finance exit fees, VAT and adding the deposit and VAT on agent's fees, it has lost the use of £281,182.17 for seven months less two days. At 8% per annum simple we calculate the value of that loss to be £13,126.97.

(m) Should our client not be able to prove to the court its case on loss of profit, its secondary position will be to advance in the alternative the claim for interest at £13,126.97 to 19 December 2009 and thereafter continuing at the rate of £61.62 daily.

Interest as interest

32. Our client contends that each of the sums referred to at paragraph 31(a)–(i) above should not have been incurred, and that having been incurred our client has lost the benefit of the use of that money which, together amounts to £73,206.93. Although these sums attract interest each from the date which they were discharged, for the purpose of this letter only our client will advance its claim for interest on that sum at 8% per annum from 1 January, 2010 to the date of this letter, namely £1,813.12 and continuing at the rate of £16.04 daily.

Mitigation and Credit

33. Our client will give credit for the sum of £5,000 plus interest of £366.66 retained from the COD deposit, which was forfeited on 21 May 2009, and which did not pass back under the terms of the Tomlin Order. That apart it is difficult to see how our client could reasonably have mitigated any of the foregoing heads of damage particularly in view of the contents of paragraph 23 above.

Settlement

34. Both counsel and this firm have advised our client that as presently instructed your firm does not appear to have any proper defence to this claim. However it is not the wish of our client to pursue the matter to litigation if there is any reasonable prospect of settlement, although you should please be assured that proceedings will be prosecuted if necessary. To that end we have been instructed that the issue of proceedings on behalf of our client is to be regarded as a last resort, and

we are happy to meet with your insurers and or yourselves, once you have had a chance to investigate this claim, to attempt to reach a satisfactory compromise without incurring unnecessary expense. Our client is prepared to take a pragmatic view and to offer a discount against his recoverable losses in order to secure an early payment and avoid the costs of preparing this matter for proceedings to be issued and thereafter pursued.

35. We have advised our client that its primary claim is conservatively worth something in excess of £145,000.00. We believe of that sum some £90,000 is beyond argument, subject to proof of quantum. We are prepared to attribute a 55% litigation risk to the balance of £55,000, in your favour. We have therefore advised our client, and it has instructed us to say that for the purposes of CPR Part 36(10)1 we will accept the sum of £120,000 in full and final settlement of its claim herein, inclusive of interest, but exclusive of our client's costs which it requires you to pay, to be assessed if not agreed. This letter is therefore intended to have the consequences of CPR Part 36 and our client's offer is open for acceptance for 21 days from the date of this letter.

36. In view of the requirements of the timetable contained in the Professional Negligence Pre-Action Protocol this offer will remain open for 3 calendar months from the date of this letter. This offer is therefore worth an additional saving in interest of a minimum of £2,400 a fact that we shall bring to the attention of the court if required at the appropriate time.

We look forward to the favour of your early reply.

Yours faithfully

Good practice suggestions

Do not worry about length, particularly if the facts are detailed or the matter is complex.

Stand back and ask yourself, 'Does this work? How would I feel as the recipient of this letter? If possible ask his opinion of a colleague who has no knowledge of the matter.

Keep in mind adversarial writing is intended to persuade – in this example to overwhelm by detail – but it is not combative for its own sake. Never make an idle threat since to do so is both self defeating and likely to be a breach of professional conduct. Use the facts.

Example R

Post-issue letter of claim suggesting moratorium for investigations under the Professional Negligence Pre-Action Protocol. This was a claim brought against Surveyor Planning Consultants for breach of retainer arising from the proposed development of a property by the claimant, in which the size of the proposed development was misstated on the drawings, leading to building works being made the subject of a stop order when it became apparent to the local authority that the building was disproportionate to the site and planning permission was withdrawn.

Proceedings were issued to protect the claimant's position on limitation. The detailed history of the complaint is set out. Core documents are sent in a bundle attaching to the letter, thus providing pre-action disclosure. The claimant was unable to determine the full extent of his financial loss and unable to make a pre-action Part 36 offer.

The recipient accepted an offer of moratorium in order to conduct its own investigation.

POST-ISSUE LETTER OF CLAIM

Dear Sirs

Our Client: A Re: 1 High Road, Easton, London W15 XL5

Letter of Claim pursuant to the Professional Negligence Pre-Action Protocol

Further to our previous correspondence we act for Mr A and wish to draw to your attention the following detailed claim which we are instructed to bring against you. You will recollect that on 16th September, 2010 we effected service upon you of a Claim Form in claim no. 0CL0000 issued out of the Central London County Court. This was undertaken to preserve Mr A's claim within the primary limitation period.

We are content to suspend the further operation of proceedings to enable you to undertake such further investigation under the Professional Negligence Pre-Action Protocol as you may feel necessary to be able properly to respond to this claim. Should you not wish us to suspend the operation of time we shall serve upon you Particulars of Claim which are in the process of being settled by counsel. We should also indicate at the outset that, notwithstanding the strength of Mr A's position, for the sake of avoiding unnecessary costs he will be prepared to entertain either a negotiated or mediated settlement at your early convenience.

We include for your perusal and consideration by way of early disclosure a bundle of relevant documents, marked [*] in the text of this letter.

The facts

1. At all material times Mr A was the owner of property at 1 High Road, London W.15 and land neighbouring it which he wished to develop by constructing a new four-bedroom/eight room house on what was a corner plot adjacent to Station Road.

2. On 31st May 2005 Z Property Services ('Z') were retained by Mr A [*] and appointed to prepare initial drawings and carry out initial planning research with Easton Borough Council Planning Services ('LA') (the relevant Local Planning Authority) in respect of the site, namely part of the garden of No. 1 High Road. The site survey and drawings were in fact prepared by XYZ Design and Detailing Services who were engaged to do so by LA. Consequent upon the preparation of drawings Z were instructed by Mr A [*] towards the end of July, 2005, to apply for planning permission in accordance with them.

3. On 5th August 2005 Z sought planning permission [*] from Easton for a development of a four-bed roomed detached house. The application described the house as having a floor space of 190m2 on a site of 345m2 and was accompanied by drawing no.98/00/2A [*]. On 7th January 2006 permission was granted [*] in terms of the application.

4. W Limited were appointed as contractors and AAD Limited as supervising architects. Work commenced in the summer of 2006 and the house was constructed to plate level in accordance with the approved designs. The site boundaries were defined and went unaltered.

5. In or about January 2007 Easton apparently received complaints from nearby residents concerning the position of the house on the plot and caused a building inspector to attend the site. Subsequent site visits concluded that the original site area had been incorrectly surveyed and the site was substantially smaller (329m2) than noted in the planning application, although the house was being built to the dimensions originally approved.

6. Accordingly on 28th March 2007 Easton served a stop notice on Mr A [*] requiring the development to cease. In order to deal with this Z met with Easton at the end of April, 2007 and by a letter dated 15th May [*] advised Mr A as to the ways in which the problem might be resolved. In accordance with such advice he first made a revised planning application for permission to Easton for a house considerably reduced in size (floor space 177m2). This scheme was approved on 3rd August, 2007. Mr A then sought to amend this permission to cover the house as built. A further application was duly made by Z on 18th December 2007 for a larger house (floor space 184m2) on the same site. This application

was refused on 8th March 2008, and Easton served an enforcement notice for the demolition of the partially as-built house [*].

7. Mr A appealed the enforcement notice, thereby making a deemed application for the as-built house, and the refusal of his December application, and sought a Certificate of Law Development. On 14th May 2008 in determining the appeal the Inspector decided that a Certificate of Lawful Development be refused but that the deemed planning permission for the as-built house be allowed subject to conditions; the Inspector also awarded Mr A his costs of the appeal. In June, 2008 Mr A transferred his interest in the property to his son.

The Claim

8. Counsel has advised that no reasonably competent and careful planning consultant in the position of Z would have prepared and submitted a planning application to Easton based on a site size of 345m2, and that Z was accordingly negligent and in breach of the implied term giving rise to a duty of care in its retainer by Mr A. But for such negligence and breach of retainer Mr A would, on the balance of probability, have obtained appropriate planning consent for a building scheme which would have proceeded to completion uninterrupted by a stop notice, and he would have completed the development of the property during the course of 2007. As it was, Mr A had to incur additional financing costs, insure, secure and otherwise deal with an incomplete and inactive building site, obtain additional professional advice and make further planning applications.

Heads of damage

9.1 Mr A was financing the costs of the development from bank borrowings. He seeks (i) the cost of arranging additional finance [*]; and (ii) the additional interest payments on the account (Lloyds TSB 123456) from April, 2006 to May 2008 inclusive, namely 25 months [*]

9.2 Mr A incurred the cost of an additional site survey on 23rd August 2007 at a cost of £822.50 [*].

9.2 Mr A paid additional property insurance premiums for 2007 and 2008 [£1645] [*] which he would not have incurred if he had completed and sold the property in 2007.

9.3 Mr A was obliged to secure and maintain the site between 28th March 2007 and May, 2008 by the use of hired block work and fencing at a cost of [£1,050] [*]

9.4 In making the revised planning applications and conducting the planning appeals Mr A expended legal costs and disbursements in the sum of £21,667 plus VAT; the amount not recovered from Easton amounted to £6,286 plus VAT. [*]

9.5 In addition Mr A seeks interest on all such sums from 1st June 2007 until payment at the judgment rate of 8%.

10. The following are not to be taken as an exhaustive list, although it is not anticipated that any further major claims arise. It is hoped that the appended documents are sufficient to provide you at this early stage, with sufficient information by which Mr A expects to substantiate his claim against Z in respect of both liability and quantum.

We therefore await your early acknowledgement of receipt of this letter and its enclosures and invite you, in the first instance, to indicate whether you wish to suspend the operation of time for the purpose of taking advantage of the three month window available under the Professional Negligence Pre-Action Protocol at the end of which we will be happy to explore settlement options including the use of ADR/mediation. Failing that indication we will be obliged to instruct Counsel to finalise Particulars of Claim to be served upon you in due course which we would wish to avoid if there was a reasonable prospect of early settlement in this matter.

Yours faithfully

Good practice suggestions

Be consistent with your cards-on-the-table approach. If you are missing information but pressed for time, for example owing to the approach of limitation, provide as much as you can while you protect your client's position.

If you have a difficulty tell the other side what it is, but tell them also how you intend to meet it. It is not a weakness but an opportunity: remember, 'Dear Judge, look how reasonable I am being. I want to cash in my brownie points as costs in the future…'

Example S

Letter in reply to a Pre-action Protocol claim of solicitor's negligence. No Part 36 offer is made and no settlement proposals are offered. The letter is designed to be a complete answer to the claim and sets out a detailed analysis of the issues of liability, causation, contributory negligence, failure to mitigate and quantum of damage with strong support from legal authority. The language is polite but firm and business-like.

Again, the key to success is in the detail, which is intended to overwhelm the claimant's solicitor and force the claimant to look again at the strength of the case, certainly to see whether it is cost effective to proceed any further.

No proceedings were issued.

LETTER IN REPLY TO A PRE-ACTION PROTOCOL

Dear Sirs,

AB 1 Zoo Road, St. Johns Wood, London N.W.8.

We write further to our letters of 28 June, 31 July and 5 September 2009.

Having considered our original files, examined the material which you have kindly supplied and consulted experienced specialist counsel we are now in a position to deal substantively with your letter of 26 June 2009 in which you raised a detailed claim against this firm in accordance with the professional negligence pre-action protocol.

As you rightly say, this firm was retained by your client to convey the purchase by her on 1st September 2004 of a long lease of a flat at 1 Zoo Road, St John's Wood. London N.W.8 for £73,500. To the knowledge of your client the property was then tenanted by a Mr Z who had entered into occupation in October 2000 and signed a standard form document entitled Residential Assured Shorthold Tenancy Agreement and a statutory notice under s.20 Housing Act 1988, both dated 10th October 2000, for a tenancy commencing on 13th October 2000. Mr Z held over on a monthly basis after the expiry of his fixed term. So far as this firm was instructed the property was being purchased as an investment by your client and was not intended for occupation by her.

In February 2004 Mrs B instructed this firm upon the sale of the property with vacant possession to a buyer who was prepared to pay £150,000. In March 2004 it became apparent that there might be difficulties in securing vacant possession because of the status of Mr Z and JS of counsel was instructed to advise upon the position and settle the appropriate Housing Act notice to quit for service upon Mr Z. Counsel advised that certain defects appeared upon the face of the Assured Shorthold Tenancy Agreement and section 20 Notice which raised the possibility that Mr Z was not an assured shorthold tenant but an assured tenant, in respect of whom Mrs B would require an appropriate Housing Act case in order to obtain a possession order. On 8th May 2004 the buyer rescinded the contract as he was entitled to do under its terms.

We have considered with our Counsel the matters raised by the Advice dated 21st March 2009. The principal difficulty is that the section 20 notice appears to have been unsigned by either the landlord or landlord's agent, however it may well be that the copy actually served on Mr Z was signed, since his signature indicating its receipt appears on the Claimant's retained copy. Notwithstanding that, the conclusion to which Counsel has come is that, applying *Mannai v Eagle Star*[1], *York and Ross v Casey*[2] and the conjoined appeals in *Ravenseft Properties Ltd v Hall; Chubb v White; Freeman v Kasseer*[3] it is sufficiently arguable that the section 20 notice was valid and the status of Mr Z is that he was and is an assured shorthold tenant. We will advance that contention notwithstanding the factual analysis of Ms X, the Casework Support Officer of Shelter Legal Services in her letter to you of 11th October 2008, by which she considered it inappropriate for your client to proceed against Mr Z by way of accelerated possession proceedings.

We refer to the numbered paragraphs in your letter. We agree the outline of facts contained in paragraphs 1–8. However, we do not accept that the omissions set out in paragraph 8 amount of themselves to any act of negligence nor, in the circumstances are they a breach of retainer since a reasonably careful and competent conveyancer would not have sent a copy of the tenancy agreement to his client prior to exchange of contracts, nor would he reasonably have "highlighted the position under s.20 of the 1988 Act" to his lay client if he was himself satisfied that Mr Z was an assured shorthold tenant.

As to your analysis at paragraph 9 we do not accept that the advice of Mr T was incorrect. We are advised that as a matter of construction, in view of the insertion by the parties of a clause 6.2 and subsequently their signatures, they would be taken by the Court implicitly to have agreed clause 6.1.

It seems to us that the highest at which you can put your client's case is that Mr T failed to advise that the position of Mr Z was less certain than he

1 [1997] AC 749, [1997] 1 EGLR 57.

2 (1999) 31 HLR 209.

3 [2001] EWCA Civ 2034, [2002] HLR 624.

believed. We reiterate our view that this failure was not a departure from the reasonable conduct by this firm of its retainer, and accordingly we are not in a position to make any admission of liability.

However, even were it the case that Mr T departed from the requisite standard of care, we take issue with the causation of each aspect of the claim for damages you have raised on behalf of your client. You contend on her behalf that had she been properly advised of the potential difficulty in removing Mr Z, Mrs B either would not have purchased the property or would have attempted to negotiate a substantial reduction in the purchase price. You claim on her behalf to recover (this being a non-exhaustive list) a) the difference in value between the property "as it is now" and the value that it would have if Mr Z was either not in occupation or capable of being evicted; b) all of the legal costs she has occurred in attempting to evict Mr Z since the beginning of 2005 and c) damages for distress and inconvenience. With respect, we suggest that each of these claims is misconceived in law.

It appears to us that that even if, which is not accepted, Mr T was in breach of duty to your client, if Mr Z is an assured shorthold tenant, the only loss caused to Mrs B which falls within the scope of the duty owed[4] is the additional cost of removing him occasioned by the difficulty in clarifying the position.

If, on the other hand, Mr Z is in law an assured tenant, either because our analysis is wrong or on the basis of your client's serving upon him a notice under section 8 Housing Act 1988 as amended, the discontinuance of her possession proceedings, or by other concession made by you (as to which we refer below in connection with the failure of your client to mitigate her position and or contributory negligence), the loss falling within the scope of the duty owed by this firm will extend to your client having an assured tenant in occupation rather than an assured shorthold tenant. The law would, we suggest, limit the loss occasioned by the breach of duty complained of to the following:

(i) If Mr Z is in law an assured tenant rather than an assured shorthold tenant then the normal measure of damage representing the true loss to a claimant is the difference in the value of the property[5] she was purchasing having regard to that fact, at the date of purchase[6]. This follows the established principle that unless there is an exceptional distinguishing feature a claimant will be awarded such damages at the date of the breach as will put her back into the position she would have

4 As to which see *South Australia Asset Management Ltd v York Montague* [1997] AC 191 on the scope of the duty argument.

5 See *Ford v White* [1964] 1 WLR 885; *Hayes v Dodd* [1990] 2 All ER 815; *Watts v Morrow* [1991] 1 WLR 1421.

6 See *Wapshott v Davies Donovan & Co* [1996] PNLR 361.

been but for the breach. Since Mrs B contends that she would not have permitted contracts to be exchanged on her own case the relevant date is 29th August 2004.

(ii) If you contend that she would not have purchased at all, in our view she must prove what else she would have done with the purchase price, and give credit for both the rental income and the value of the property at trial. On that basis any provable loss has been extinguished by the substantial increase in the value of the property even in occupation by an assured tenant.

(iii) If, as is more likely, your client would have negotiated a better price the maximum measure of her loss is the difference in value on that date between the property as purchased with a perceived assured shorthold tenant and the property with an assured tenant in occupation, since that is what the law apprehends she might have negotiated. We have obtained an expert valuation report and have been advised that this figure is unlikely to exceed 10% of the market value, namely £7,350. This together with interest, we submit, is the maximum value of your client's claim subject to our defence on liability, causation, contributory negligence and failure to mitigate. Taking such matters into account we suggest that the true value of your client's claim is either nothing or very little.

(iv) The costs claimed by your client are not recoverable in law for a number of reasons:

(a) The flat was being purchased with a tenant in situe. By virtue of section 1 Protection from Eviction Act 1977 Mr Z as a residential occupier could only be removed by the grant and execution of a possession order, whether he was an assured or assured shorthold tenant or even a squatter. Thus legal costs would be incurred in removing him in any event, and that being so this head of loss falls outside the scope of the breach of duty complained of.

(b) The costs occasioned by an application under Case 8 were in any event outside the scope of the breach of duty complained of since this firm did not warrant that Mr Z would pay his rent, and the possession proceedings were brought against him on that basis.

(c) The valuation exercise which distinguishes between the discount from the market value to be applied to an assured tenant and that to be applied to an assured shorthold tenant must be taken to factor in the additional cost of removing the assured tenant.

Thus this element of the claim is already absorbed into the diminution in value.

(d) The costs which your client seeks are in respect of possession proceedings which failed. If the proceedings failed such costs cannot be visited against this firm since it is self-evident that such an attempt at mitigating the Claimant's position, if that is how it could be deemed, should not be regarded as reasonable.

(v) In the absence of physical distress and inconvenience flowing from the breach, the law does not extend so to make recompense for distress not affecting health[7]. Mrs B purchased the property as an investment from which to derive a rental income. Even if she was inconvenienced after May 2001 when her sale fell through against any award of damage she would have to give credit for the rent stream after that date, and possibly the increase in the capital value of the property. This would extinguish the maximum value of her claim.

Counsel has also considered in cases such as this the more traditional measure of damage in dealing with "defective title" claims is the cost of remedying the defect. In this case that would be the cost of removing Mr Z. This measure is mutually exclusive to the diminution in value measure: if Mr Z were removed there would be no residual, consequential or separate damage recoverable in law. However, in considering this approach, we are led inexorably to the conduct of your firm as a novus actus in abandoning the contention that Mr Z was in law an assured shorthold tenant.

It is our view, and we have been so advised, that the principal cause of your client's present situation is the failure of your firm, having sought to mitigate the position, to argue that Mr Z was in law an assured shorthold tenant, which it remains our view he was. In conceding by paragraph 3 of the Particulars of Claim for Possession dated 15th November 2005 that Mr Z was an assured tenant (with a statement of truth signed by a member of your firm) and then discontinuing the proceedings, you have presented Mr Z with the opportunity of running issue estoppel on his status and attracting an unassailable Henderson v Henderson abuse of process defence to any further attempt to remove him on Schedule 2 Housing Act 1988 grounds.

We believe that this goes to both causation and substantial contributory negligence, however were we wrong in that regard it is undoubtedly a significant failure to mitigate. In that regard your client should be looking for her principal loss not to this firm but to your own.

---

7 *Hayes v Dodd* [1990] 2 All ER 815; *Watts v Morrow* [1991] 1 WLR 1421; *Johnson v Gore-Wood* [2001] 2 WLR 72; *Channon v Lindley Johnstone* [2002] PNLR 884.

It follows from the foregoing that we believe we have a complete answer to the matters that you have raised and we have no proposals to offer. We invite a careful analysis of the contents of this letter and those authorities which we have cited in support of our position which we hope will persuade your client that there is nothing to achieve by continuing to prosecute this claim.

Yours faithfully

Good practice suggestions

Meet letters of claim with a detailed rebuttal. Some claims, if inadequately formulated, are balloon-like, floated to see what response will be given. These should be burst, together with the claimant's expectation, by the reply giving a careful analysis of duty, causation and quantum: don't automatically reach just for a denial of breach, which is the typical gut reaction of the defendant.

Always be polite and business-like, no matter how preposterous the claim or the form in which it is advanced.

Be sympathetic where possible. If there is no legal liability, an apology costs nothing and may be all that the claimant (though not necessarily his lawyer) seeks.

Example T

Extract of a letter in reply to a threat of injunction in commercial proceedings. The claim concerned a dispute between a franchisor and its regional licensees. The correspondence was outside the pre-action protocol regime but illustrates the use of argument and persuasion to ward off precipitate court action.

The language is formal and legalistic, but the writer succinctly undermines his opponent's position by referring to the parties different positions under the contract in question, and showing how this is likely to impact on the remedies available to the Court.

The threatened injunction was not proceeded with. The parties negotiated an overall settlement.

REPLY TO A THREAT OF INJUNCTION

...

It has become perfectly apparent to our client that by the conduct of Mr C, amply illustrated above, your clients have evinced an intention no longer to be bound by the terms of their respective Agreements.

Accordingly our client intends to accept your clients' repudiatory breaches and to terminate immediately the Agreements under clauses 24.1.2, 24.1.3 and 24.1.4 thereof. By way of courtesy we append for your information copies of the termination notices we have today served upon the registered offices of Z (Scotland) Ltd, Z (Northern Ireland) Ltd and upon Mr C as principal under both Agreements.

We have given careful thought to your threat of injunction proceedings. It appears to us that commercial relations between our respective clients have broken down completely, on our instructions by Mr C's disruptive behaviour, which does not attract the support of either his co-regional licensees or, more importantly, the franchisees themselves. Our client holds both the intellectual property rights (as defined) and the know-how and goodwill in the franchise: see clauses 4.1, 4.3, 4.5, 4.7, 4.12 of the Regional Licence Agreement and the definition and clauses 10.1, 10.3, 10.4 and 10.5 of the Standard Franchise Agreement. On that basis even if, which we deny, your clients may claim to have an action in damages against our client, which we would in any event defend and set-off, it would not be appropriate for the Court to grant an injunction to force our client either to continue its licence to yours, or to have our client engage in business with yours when no business confidence remains.

Our client, on the other hand, has a legitimate commercial interest in the protection of both its intellectual property and its entire franchise network, by injunction if necessary. We remind your clients' of their post-termination obligations set out in clause 25.1 of the Agreements and the sub-clauses set out below. In particular your client is proscribed from making or receiving telephone calls in connection with the franchise (clause 25.1.2). To that end your clients should henceforth make no attempt to contact the franchisees. Our client will shortly direct what its requirements are in effecting the transfer of business telephone line subscriptions. Your clients will deliver up to ours all copies in their possession of the operating manual. Your clients will change their corporate name to cease to use the word "Z....s" which forms part of our client's intellectual property rights.

In accordance with clauses 25.1.10, 26.1 and 26.1.1 of the Agreements our client requires Mr C as director of Z (Scotland) Ltd, Z (Northern Ireland) Ltd, and as principal, to execute an assignment of each of the Standard Franchise Agreements in favour of our client in a form to be settled and supplied by us within the next seven days.

We feel sure, having absorbed the contents of this lengthy letter and taken instructions, it will be apparent that your clients' best interest will be served by complying with their obligations and so avoiding litigation which would certainly follow should they decline to do so. We, like you, consider that commercial disputes are best resolved in the market place and not by having resort to the Courts. Financial claims apart, the issues between our clients boil down to whether it is appropriate in the circumstances for your clients to continue to act as our client's regional licensees. We consider it most unlikely that a Court would agree that they should against our client's wishes. Whilst we hope that it will be entirely unnecessary for the Court to examine this question, your clients should be aware of the resolve of our client. Accordingly would you confirm by return whether your clients will be complying with their post-termination covenants, and, as necessary, whether you have instructions to accept service of proceedings.

Yours faithfully

Good practice suggestions

Be quick to deal accurately with any misapprehensions of the law by the other side. Taking the wind out of the opposing lawyer's sails is the most effective way to stop a claim. At the very least it will make him re-think his position, and may damage the confidence in him of his lay client.

The same technique should be adopted with mistakes of fact. Disclose at the earliest opportunity any core document that will demonstrate objectively that the claimant's view of a fact is either wrong, or, if not, at least any court will think it wrong.

Example U

Part 36 offer – County Court, claim and counterclaim for trespass and nuisance – The claim concerned an interference with neighbouring property by excessive drainage from higher land to lower.

The offer is the subject of considerable detail and deals with each cause of action separately.

WITHOUT PREJUDICE PART 36 OFFER

Dear Sirs,

Re: X v Z

We write further to your letters of 6 April 2010.

This letter constitutes and is intended to have the consequences of a part 36 offer and will remain open for acceptance for 21 days from the date it is made. After that period of 21 days the Defendant may only accept it if the parties agree the liability for costs.

As you are aware there are a number of issues between the parties and by this letter the Claimant puts forward his proposal for the settlement of each of them. In order to reduce the number of issues between the parties in the litigation the Claimant's offers in respect of the various issues identified below are independent of each other. That is to say the Defendant may accept all or any of the offers in respect of the various issues and the acceptance of any offer will be without prejudice to the rights and claims of the parties in any remaining issues.

The Outlet Pipes

Our client's proposals regarding the pipes located at points A, B and C on the plan annexed to the Defendant's Defence and Counterclaim ("the Plan") are as follows:

(1) the Claimant will grant the Defendant and his successors in title an easement to discharge water into the pond via a pipe located at points A, B and C on the Plan provided that:

  (a) the pipes shall not have a greater diameter than the pipes presently installed;

  (b) the burden of the easement shall not be increased.

(2) it shall be a condition of the said easement that the Defendant and his successors in title install and regularly maintain a silt trap on the pipe located at point C on the Plan;

(3) the Defendant will acknowledge that there are no pipes discharging water from his land into the pond other than those located at points A, B and C on the Plan and that he has no right of drainage into the pond other than under the easement to be granted;

(4) this proposal is made without prejudice to and does not compromise the Claimant's claim that the installation of the pipe at point C on the Plan has caused damage to the Claimant's land and the pond in particular which must be made good;

(5) The parties shall return their own costs on this issue.

Damages for Trespass

Our client's proposals in relation to his claim for damages for trespass are as follows:

(1) the Defendant shall pay the claimant the sum of £100 in respect of the acts of trespass referred to in paragraphs 2 and 4 of the Claimant's Particulars of Claim;

(2) the Defendant shall undertake not to enter the Claimant's land without permission provided that the Defendant may when reasonably necessary enter the Claimant's land to repair and maintain the outlet pipes at points A, B and C on the Plan;

(3) this proposal is made without prejudice to and does not compromise the Claimant's additional claim that the acts of trespass committed by the Defendant have caused damage to the Claimant's land which must be compensated or made good

(4) the Defendant shall pay half of the Claimant's costs on this issue.

Damage to Claimant's Land – Silting of Pond

As a result of the Defendant's works a considerable amount of silt has entered the pond which must be removed. As well as forming part of the Claimant's claim for damages an order that the Defendant remedy this damage is included at paragraph 3 of the prayer. Our client has obtained a quotation for the removal of the silt for £14,800 plus VAT (a copy of which is served with our second letter sent today). Our client's proposals in relation to the removal of the silt which has entered the pond as a result of the Defendant's conduct are that:

(1) the Defendant pay £4,000 towards the costs of de-silting the pond;

(2) the Defendant shall pay half of the Claimant's costs on this issue.

Damage to the Claimant's Land – the Sill

Our client's proposals in relation to the damage to the sill at the northern end of the pond are as follows:

(1) your client will pay for the necessary work to re-instate the sill to its condition prior to December 2008 in accordance with the specification served;

(2) the work will be contracted by submitting a specification to tender to no less than three contractors having no connection with either party and the Claimant shall accept the lowest tender

(3) the Defendant shall pay the Claimant's costs on this issue.

The Boundary

There has already been correspondence regarding the terms on which the parties are prepared to settled this issue. Our client's proposals regarding the location of the boundary between the Old Hall and New Farm are as follows:

(1) the parties agree that the boundary runs along the top of the bank of the pond at its present location;

(2) the parties will hold a site meeting for the purpose of agreeing the top of the bank and therefore where the boundary runs;

(3) in the event the parties are unable to agree on the location of the top of the bank at the site meeting the parties are to jointly instruct a surveyor at their joint expense (to be nominated by the President of the Royal Institution of Chartered Surveyors in the event the parties are unable to agree upon whom to instruct) to decide where the top of the bank is and the joint surveyor's decision will be binding on both parties;

(4) there be no order as to costs on this issue.

We look forward to hearing from you in due course etc.

Yours faithfully

Good practice suggestions

It is essential to build up a case that is going to justify your negotiating position. You may have to defend yourself to a costs judge months or even years later.

Your offer should be reasoned. You should be able to break it down if asked.

Never bluff. The risk of being found out, and your house of cards falling down with adverse costs consequences, is too great.

15 Conclusion

Written advocacy is no less important than skilled oratory for being in writing. On the contrary, its relative permanence as a medium enables you to craft and perfect it, and in particular to identify and revise those flaws that may slip out under the pressure of scrutinised speech.

If you practice in contentious business your approach to the composition of persuasive writing in dealing with an opponent should be no different whether it is in correspondence or the preparation of written submissions for the court. Nor should it matter at what stage the case has reached. Be firm; be polite; be justified in your assertions of fact and law; and be seen to be reasonable. Measure your position to a nicety and always ask yourself how best you are serving your client's case by what you are doing. Write with one eye on the judge at your shoulder, and you should protect your client's position on costs even if you cannot persuade the other side of the merits of your case.

Select Bibliography

Books

Aldisert, Judge Ruggero J. *Winning on Appeal: Better Briefs and Oral Argument* (1999)

Bentele, Ursula and Cary, Eve *Appellate Advocacy: Principles and Practice* (4th edn 2004)

Blake, Gary and Bly, Robert W. *The Elements of Technical Writing* (1993)

Garner, Bryn A. *Legal Writing in Plain English: A Text With Exercises* (Chicago 2001)

Garner, Bryn A. *The Winning Brief: 100 Tips for Persuasive Briefing in Trial and Appellate Courts* (2nd edn. OUP 2004)

Goodman, Andrew *How Judges Decide Cases: Reading, Writing and Analysing Judgments* (xpl 2005)

Hooper QC, Toby ed. *Inner Temple Advocacy Handbook* (7th edn 2004–5; 8th edn 2007)

Orwell George, *Politics and the English Language: Four Collected Essays* (New York 1968)

Rutledge, Wiley B. *Advocacy and the King's English in The Appellate Brief* (1942)

The Chicago Manual of Style (16th edn Chicago 2010)

The Economist Style Book 2010

Wiener, Frederick Bernays *Briefing and Arguing Federal Appeals* (2001 Lawbook Exchange, N.Jersey)

Wydick, Richard C. *Plain English For Lawyers* (5th edn 2005)

Articles

Appellate Advocacy: Some Reflections from the Bench (1993) 61 Ford L. Rev 829

Hamilton, Hon. Clyde H. Effective Appellate Brief Writing (1999) 50 SCL Review 581

Hunt, The Hon. Mr Justice James The Anatomy Lesson Counsel Feb 2002 18

McElhaney, James W. Writing to the Ear Dec 1995 ABAJ 71

Michel, Hon. Paul R. Effective Appellate Advocacy Litigation Summer 1998 19

Pannill, William Appeals: The Classic Guide Litigation (Winter 1999) vol 25. no 2 p.6.

Porto, Brian L The Art of Appellate Brief Writing 2003 29 Vermont Bar Journal and Law Digest 30

Lectures

Davis, John W. The Argument of an Appeal (address to the Association of the Bar of the City of New York 22.10.1940) 26 ABAJ 895

Lightman, The Hon. Mr Justice 'Advocacy – A Dying Art?' (address to the Chancery Bar Association Conference, 26th January 2004)

Index

References are to page number